DATE DUE

ANNALS OF COMMUNISM

Each volume in the series Annals of Communism will publish selected and previously inaccessible documents from former Soviet state and party archives in the framework of a narrative text that focuses on a particular topic in the history of Soviet and international communism. Separate English and Russian editions will be prepared. Russian and American scholars work together to prepare the documents for each volume. Documents are chosen not for their support of any single interpretation but for their particular historical importance or their general value in deepening understanding and facilitating discussion. The volumes are designed to be useful to students, scholars, and interested general readers.

The Soviet World of

American Communism

Harvey Klehr, John Earl Haynes,
and Kyrill M. Anderson

Yale University Press

New Haven and London

This volume has been prepared with the active support of the Russian Center for the Preservation and Study of Documents of Recent History (RTsKhIDNI) of the State Archival Service of Russia in the framework of an agreement concluded between RTsKhIDNI and Yale University Press.

Copyright © 1998 by Yale University.
All rights reserved.

Documents that are held by RTsKhIDNI are used by permission.

Designed by James J. Johnson and set in Sabon and Melior Roman types by The Composing Room of Michigan, Inc.

Printed in the United States of America by Vail-Ballou Press, Binghamton, New York.

Library of Congress Cataloging-in-Publication Data

Klehr, Harvey.
    The Soviet world of American communism / Harvey Klehr, John Earl
Haynes, and Kyrill M. Anderson.
        p.   cm. — (Annals of communism)
    Includes bibliographical references (p.   ) and index.
    ISBN 0–300–07150–7 (alk. paper)

    1. Communist Party of the United States of America—History—
Sources.   2. Communism—United States—History—Sources.
3. Communist International—History—Sources.   4. Communism—
History—Sources.   I. Haynes, John Earl.   II. Anderson, K. M.
(Kirill Mikhaĭlovich)   III. Rossiĭskiĭ t͡sentr khraneniia i
izucheniia dokumentov noveĭsheĭ istorii.   IV. Title.   V. Series.
JK2391.C5K563   1998
324.273'75'09041—dc21   97–18123

A catalogue record for this book is available from the British Library.

The paper in this book meets the guidelines for permanence and durability of the Committee on Production Guidelines for Book Longevity of the Council on Library Resources.

10   9   8   7   6   5   4   3   2   1

Publication of this volume was made possible in part by a generous gift to Yale University Press from the Daniel and Joanna S. Rose Fund, Inc. We are grateful for their vision and support.

Yale University Press gratefully acknowledges the financial support given for this publication by the Foundation for Cultural Initiative (Moscow), the Historical Research Foundation, the John M. Olin Foundation, the Lynde and Harry Bradley Foundation, the Open Society Fund (New York), and the Smith-Richardson Foundation.

Contents

Documents Reproduced in Facsimile

Preface

From 1919 until 1943 the Communist International (or Comintern), head-quartered in Moscow, supervised the activities of Communist parties through-out the world. After Stalin disbanded the Comintern in 1943, its records were stored in an archive that, after various changes in name and affiliation, became the Russian Center for the Preservation and Study of Documents of Recent History (RTsKhIDNI) in late 1991. This archive holds the bulk of the records of the central bodies of the Communist Party of the Soviet Union (CPSU) from the early 1920s to Stalin's death in 1953.

In addition, the archive contains extensive records for foreign Communist parties, including the Communist Party of the United States of America (CPUSA). Throughout the 1920s and 1930s American Communist officials traveled to Moscow to report on their activities to the Comintern. These reports often took the form of testimony before a Comintern committee, some-times an especially designated American Commission, sometimes the Anglo-American Secretariat, a standing Comintern committee that supervised the Communist parties of the United States, Great Britain, Canada, and several other English-speaking nations. The testimony would often be interrupted by questions from members of the committee, and the minutes of these various meetings total thousands of pages.

In addition to CPUSA officials, the Anglo-American Secretariat also ques-tioned American students attending the International Lenin School, a training institution for Communist cadre. The American Communist party also sta-tioned an official representative to the Executive Committee of the Comintern in Moscow to keep the Comintern up to date about CPUSA activities. This representative sent regular communications back to the CPUSA that laid out the current policy directives and relayed the orders of the Comintern. In addition to the official representative, at any time a half-dozen to a dozen other CPUSA functionaries could be found in Moscow serving one- or two-year stints in various Comintern offices. Their paperwork has also been preserved in the RTsKhIDNI archives.

The Comintern, for its part, retained at least one and often more representatives in the United States. The representative supervised the activities of the CPUSA and sent reports back to Moscow about them. These cables and letters, along with transcripts or summaries of the deliberations of the CPUSA's ruling bodies, the Political Bureau and the Central Committee, were deposited in the archives.

After the Comintern was disbanded, its jobs were divided among various agencies of the Soviet government and the Communist Party of the Soviet Union. Several of the documents in this volume from the post–World War II period come from the Department of Foreign Policy of the Central Committee of the CPSU, one of the agencies that absorbed the functions of the Comintern. Those records, too, are held by the RTsKhIDNI.

Documents in the RTsKhIDNI are organized into a series of collections and stored in folders. Each folder has a short description of its contents printed in well-organized and detailed finding aids prepared by archivists. In this volume, a three-part numerical citation is given to each document. The first part is the number of the collection (*fond* in Russian), the second part provides the number of the subseries or description (*opis*) of that collection, and the third part gives the number of the file or folder (*delo*) in which the document is found. Thus, a document cited "RTsKhIDNI 495–37–65" refers to *fond* 495 (the Communist International, or Comintern), *opis* 37 (the American Commission of the Executive Committee of the Communist International), *delo* 65.

After the failure of the Communist coup directed against Mikhail Gorbachev in 1991, the Russian government seized the property of the Communist Party of the Soviet Union, including this archive. Its voluminous records, long closed to all but a few ideologically loyal Communists, were then made available to scholars.

When we examined the records of the Comintern in 1992, 1993, and 1994, virtually all of its collections were open for research. Since then, however, the Russian government has restored some of the powers of the Russian security agencies over archival material. When John Haynes returned to the RTsKhIDNI in 1995 and 1996, several of the Comintern collections used in earlier research had been closed. Further, when the CPSU Department of

Foreign Policy records were examined in 1995, the finding aid to the records bore stamps indicating that the records had been examined by Russian security authorities. Although most of the files regarding contacts between the CPSU Department of Foreign Policy and the CPUSA were open to research, some had been closed for security reasons.

In addition to the records of the Comintern's various agencies, the RTsKhIDNI holds a separate collection of records of the CPUSA containing more than 4,300 files that span the years 1919 to 1944. Each file holds between ten and a hundred pages of documents; some contain several hundred pages. These include the records of the national headquarters of the CPUSA: incoming mail, carbons of outgoing correspondence, reports from regional and local organizers, and internal memoranda produced by officials and offices of the national headquarters. In addition to CPUSA records produced in America, these files also contain some documents written in Moscow by CPUSA representatives to the Comintern. Most of the material in these records is in English, although in many files key documents are accompanied by Russian translations. In a few cases, the English original is missing, and only the Russian translation remains. The existence of these Russian translations indicates that the files were sent to Moscow for Comintern review as well as for safekeeping. In addition to the Russian translations, the records of the CPUSA's myriad foreign-language bureaus contain material in various languages (Finnish, Yiddish, German, Hungarian).

The CPUSA collection is not complete. Records are spotty for the period 1919–1922, when the party was first being organized. At that time there were several competing Communist parties, and government officials were liable to arrest Communist organizers and seize their papers. The records from 1922 up to 1936 appear to be largely intact. After 1936 the records thin out once more. Because these records would be retained in the United States for several years after their creation for CPUSA use, the reduced volume after 1936 probably reflects the start of World War II and the increased difficulty of sending them safely to the USSR. Before 1940, originals tended to be sent to the Soviet Union. From 1940 on, however, a significant portion of the documents are prints made from microfilm. This suggests that the originals were kept in the United States and the film sent to Moscow to reduce the problem of bulk shipment during wartime. Supporting this theory is a Comintern cover memo attached to copies of CPUSA memoranda regarding party membership and Young Communist League activities in 1942. It notes that the attached material is difficult to read because the film had obviously been wet when it was mailed.

The CPUSA collection in the Comintern archives ends with material from 1944. We do not know whether the CPUSA stopped routinely sending records to Moscow after that date or whether the 1944 cutoff reflects the bureaucratic fact of the Comintern's dissolution, after which CPUSA records were placed in a repository that remains closed.

Acknowledgments

As we noted in *The Secret World of American Communism,* the first volume in our study of the Communist Party of the United States of America, this research project has been the most complicated and challenging any of us has ever undertaken, and it would not have been possible without the cooperation, assistance, expertise, and goodwill of many people and institutions.

Harvey Klehr made two trips to Moscow to work in the Russian Center for the Preservation and Study of Documents of Recent History (RTsKhIDNI) and John Haynes made four. We greatly appreciate the help and assistance of the directors and staff of the archive. Russian archivists face daunting problems, not the least of which is dealing with American academics used to different rules and a different pace of research. We are grateful for all the assistance we were given and the many ways the archive staff made our task easier. We particularly wish to acknowledge the aid of our Russian co-author, Kyrill M. Anderson, archive director; Oleg Vladimirovich Naumov, associate director; and Svetlana Markovna Rosenthal, who had the unenviable task of dealing with our requests to copy documents.

Two Russian scholars, Mark Isaakovich Lapitsky and Inna Mkrtychevna Tatarovskaya, spent many months reading files for us to make our visits more productive. We owe them a debt of gratitude not only for their scholarly work but also for their friendship and hospitality. We greatly benefited from the advice and research guidance on obscure areas of Comintern history of Fridrikh Igorevich Firsov, for many years the leading Comintern historian at the RTsKhIDNI. Nikolai Petrovich Yakovlev, Yale University Press's representative in Moscow, helped us in many ways. Todd Weinberg arranged housing for us in Moscow.

Our Russian translators were indispensable. Nikolai N. Silin arranged Harvey Klehr's first visit to the archives and worked tirelessly and selflessly to ensure that the visit was a success. On subsequent visits, Datia Lotareva translated for John Haynes and provided practical advice on understanding Russian documents. Svetlana Savranskaya worked as a translator in both Moscow and Atlanta. She is a treasure. Moshe Haspel has assisted with both translation and making sure we were able to function in Moscow. Laura Kennedy did some of the initial translations from the Russian, and Emory University undergraduate Ian Jefferson was also helpful. Most of the final translations for this volume were prepared by Laura Wolfson; others were the work of Tim Sergay. Richard Miller helped edit the translations. Their skill and ingenuity are much appreciated.

Dan Leab read the entire manuscript and made numerous suggestions about style, tone, and organization. Herb Romerstein was extraordinarily generous in making available his own collection of materials from the RTsKhIDNI, as well as his encyclopedic knowledge of American communism. Michael Dobbs, the *Washington Post* Moscow correspondent, generously provided copies of documents regarding Soviet funding of the CPUSA in the 1980s. Alan Cullison, an Associated Press reporter in Moscow, located Lovett Fort-Whiteman's KGB file in post-Soviet Kazakhstan and graciously made it available to us. David Hornstein reviewed our list of Cominternists with connections to the United States. The late Thomas Sgovio provided us with the documentation of his own harrowing experience in the Gulag and allowed us to reprint it. Verne Pedersen, who had just finished his own doctoral dissertation on communism, accompanied us to Moscow in the summer of 1993; he was a great help, and we could not have covered as much ground as we did without his research assistance. Tom Remington of Emory University has frequently enabled us to draw on his talents and Russian expertise.

The administrative staff in the Political Science Department at Emory University—Karen Salsbury, Esther Nerenbaum, Denise Brubaker and Jennifer Combs—have endured, patiently and with good cheer, a variety of organizational emergencies.

Our debt to the people at Yale University Press is substantial. John Ryden, the director, has encouraged this project and our work on it from the beginning. Susan Laity was a superb manuscript editor. We are also grateful to designer Jim Johnson. Our greatest debt, however, is to our editor and the orchestrator of the Annals of Communism series, Jonathan Brent. His enthusiasm, support, and prodding have made not only this book but the whole series possible. Through all the vicissitudes of the project, Jonathan has retained his sense of humor, for which we are grateful.

Several foundations and institutions have made this project financially possible. Without the generous support of the Lynde and Harry Bradley Foundation, the John M. Olin Foundation, and the Smith-Richardson Foundation, none of our research would have been feasible. We are deeply grateful for their confidence.

Finally, we would like to thank our families and friends. Finishing this book without his wife, Elizabeth, reminded Harvey Klehr how much he owed her and how deeply he misses her. His sons, Benjamin, Gabriel, and Joshua, are a joy and a blessing. He particularly wishes to thank Leonard and Susan Klehr, Kenneth and Robin Avia, and John and Carolyn Neely for their support. One of the benefits of tragedy is to discover how many friends one has: thanks to Alan and Ann Abramowitz, Merle Black and Debra Larson, Karl and Debra Saxe, Ira and Janet Schwartz, Mel Konner, Tom and Nancy Remington, Gene and Mary Jane Brisbane, Marcia and Mark Swanson, Rabbi Louis Feldstein, Linda Hilsenrad, and Marcie Steinberg. John Haynes deeply appreciates the patience and understanding his wife, Janette, daughter Amanda, and son Bill have shown about his absences in Moscow.

A Note on the Documents

The reproduction of the documents included in this volume is intended to preserve their original character. Grammatical, spelling, and stylistic errors in the original documents have been retained. Orthographic and typographical errors that were corrected by the author of the document (words or letters crossed out—for example, "comm~m~unicates" and clerical notations that are irrelevant to the content of the documents and that were added when the documents were placed in the archive have not been reproduced. Handwritten comments added to the documents are included and appear in *italic* type. Our interpolations, as well as illegible or indecipherable words, are enclosed in brackets. Single underlining indicates that a word or phrase was underlined using a typewriter; double underlining indicates that the underlining was done by hand. The headnote accompanying each document provides information about the language of the original document, the archival citation, and any exceptions to the guidelines presented here.

Glossary of Individuals and Organizations

Individuals, organizations, and acronyms are identified when they first appear in the text. Listed here are individuals and organizations mentioned in more than one chapter.

American Federation of Labor (AFL): National federation of the chief trade unions in the United States, dominated in the 1930s by unions organized by craft rather than on an industrial basis.

American Negro Labor Congress (ANLC): The African-American auxiliary of the CPUSA in the 1920s, it was founded in 1925 and disbanded in 1930.

Amter, Israel (1881–1954): A founding member and leading figure in the American Communist party in the 1920s. In early 1930s Amter directed party work among the unemployed; in the later 1930s he became the leader of the New York Communist party.

Anglo-American Secretariat: Section of the Comintern that supervised Communist parties in America, Canada, Britain, and certain other English-speaking territories.

AUCP(b): All-Union Communist Party (Bolshevik). See RCP(b).

Baker, Rudy (1898–?): CPUSA official who headed the Pan-Pacific Trade Union Secretariat operations in Shanghai and San Francisco in the early 1930s and directed the CPUSA's secret apparatus from the late 1930s through World War II. He returned to his native Yugoslavia in the late 1940s.

Bedacht, Max (1883–1972): A founding member and contender for national leadership of the American Communist party in the 1920s. In the 1930s he headed the International Workers Order, a party-aligned federation of immigrant and ethnic associations. In the early 1930s he was liaison with the Soviet intelligence agencies.

Bolsheviks: Members of a revolutionary Russian political party led by Lenin; they advocated Marxism-Leninism and took power in Russia in 1917; founders of Soviet communism.

Borodin, Michael (1884–1951): Early Comintern operative in the United States, Mexico, Spain, and China. He was arrested in 1949 and died in the Gulag.

Browder, Earl (1891–1973): Early Communist party organizer and first head of the Comintern's Pan-Pacific Trade Union Secretariat. Led the CPUSA in the 1930s, its period of greatest growth, but was driven from the leadership in 1945 and expelled in

1946 when his policies lost favor in Moscow. His attempts to win reinstatement in the late 1940s were rebuffed.

Bukharin, Nikolai (1888–1938): Prominent Bolshevik leader defeated by Stalin in the struggle to succeed Lenin. He was accused of right-wing deviation from Marxism-Leninism and was later executed.

Bukharinist (Bukharinite): Follower of Nikolai Bukharin. Jay Lovestone and his followers in the CPUSA were accused of holding Bukharinist views.

Cannon, James (1890–1974): A founding member and leading figure in the CPUSA in the 1920s, he aligned himself with Leon Trotsky and was expelled from the party in 1928. Was the leader of American Trotskyists from the 1930s into the 1950s.

Central Committee (CC): Consisted of the CPUSA's national leaders along with leaders and representatives of its regional bodies and its auxiliary organizations.

Central Control Commission (CCC): CPUSA body charged with supervising internal discipline and security.

Childs, Jack (1907–1980): A mid-level CPUSA operative who worked in a variety of party positions. In 1952 the FBI recruited Jack and his brother, Morris, as informants. Became courier for Soviet subsidies to the CPUSA.

Childs, Morris (1902–1991): Headed the Communist party in Illinois and became editor of the *Daily Worker* after World War II. Pushed out of the party's leadership in 1947, Childs was then sidelined by a heart attack. In 1952 the FBI recruited Morris and his brother, Jack, as informants. Reentered active party work, playing a leading role as a courier of Soviet subsidies to the CPUSA.

Comintern: Abbreviation for the Communist International. Founded by Lenin in 1919 as the international headquarters of and directing body for all Communist parties. Officially disbanded in 1943.

Communist Labor Party: American Communist party founded by John Reed and Benjamin Gitlow in 1919 in emulation of the Bolshevik party. Later merged with the rival Communist Party of America.

Communist Party of America: American Communist party founded by Charles Ruthenberg and Louis Fraina in 1919 in emulation of the Bolshevik party. Later merged with the rival Communist Labor Party.

Comparty: Comintern abbreviation for Communist party.

Congress of Industrial Organizations (CIO): Begun as the Committee for Industrial Organization in 1935, the CIO was a group of American Federation of Labor unions led by John L. Lewis that sought to organize mass-production workers by industry rather than by craft. Rejected by the AFL leadership, it reorganized as a rival trade union federation, the Congress of Industrial Organizations. The CIO and AFL merged to form the AFL-CIO in 1955.

CPSU: Communist Party of the Soviet Union.

CPUSA: Communist Party of the United States of America. The name of the American Communist party from 1929 until the present. Its predecessor organizations, formed in 1919, were the Communist Party of America and the Communist Labor Party. During the 1920s the CPUSA used the titles United Communist Party, Workers

(Communist) Party, and Workers Party. For a period in 1944 and 1945 it used the title Communist Political Association.

Daily Worker: Flagship newspaper of the CPUSA.

Darcy, Sam (1905–): Head of the California Communist party in the early 1930s, CPUSA representative to Moscow in the mid-1930s, and a senior figure in the national leadership. He was expelled in 1944 for opposing Earl Browder's reorganization of the party.

Dennis, Eugene (1905–1961): CPUSA organizer and Comintern agent, Dennis headed the Wisconsin Communist party in the mid-1930s, served as CPUSA representative in Moscow, and became general secretary of the CPUSA after Browder's expulsion in 1945. He led the party until 1959.

Dimitrov, Georgi (1882–1949): A Bulgarian Communist who gained international fame as a defendant in the Reichstag fire trial in Nazi Germany in 1934. After his acquittal, he became head of the Communist International and enunciated the policy of a Popular Front against fascism at the Seventh World Congress of the Communist International in 1935. He remained head of the Comintern until its dissolution in 1943. In 1945 he became head of the Communist regime installed in Bulgaria by the Soviet Red Army.

Dreiser, Theodore (1871–1945): A major American literary figure, he was a strong sympathizer with the CPUSA in the 1930s and joined the party in 1945.

Dubinsky, David (1892–1982): A Socialist and long-time head of the International Ladies Garment Workers Union, Dubinsky was a firm anti-Communist.

Duclos, Jacques (1896–1975): A leading figure in the French Communist Party. The article published under his name in a 1945 issue of *Les Cahiers du communisme,* the French party's theoretical journal, condemned in harsh terms the theoretical basis of Earl Browder's 1944 reorganization of the American party. American Communists interpreted the article as a message from Moscow, deposed Browder, and scuttled his reforms.

ECCI: Executive Committee of the Communist International, based in Moscow.

Eisler, Gerhart (1887–1968): A German Communist, Eisler was the Comintern's representative to the CPUSA in the early and mid-1930s.

Farmer-Labor Party: The name that was often claimed by movements attempting to form a left-of-center, but not revolutionary or Marxist-Leninist, third party. Minnesota's Farmer-Labor Party dominated the state's politics for most of the 1930s, merging with the state Democratic Party in 1944.

FBI: Federal Bureau of Investigation, chief American internal security agency.

Fort-Whiteman, Lovett (1894–1939): A key African-American leader in the American Communist party in the 1920s, he was the national organizer of the American Negro Labor Congress, the African-American auxiliary of the CPUSA in the late 1920s. Pushed out of the leadership in 1930, he was given a job in Moscow. A victim of Stalin's Great Terror, he died in the Gulag.

Foster, William Z. (1881–1961): Trade union organizer and radical who joined the Communist movement in 1921. Foster headed CPUSA trade union operations in the

1920s and early 1930s and was the party's presidential candidate in several elections. He was a contender for party leadership throughout his life, but he never achieved the most powerful post, that of general secretary.

Fraina, Louis (1892–1953): One of the leading figures in the founding of the American Communist movement, he was the first representative from the Communist Party of America to the Communist International. He became a Comintern operative in Mexico. Under suspicion of mismanaging funds, Fraina left the Comintern in the 1920s. He later resurfaced in the United States as a leading Marxist economist using the name Lewis Corey.

Gitlow, Benjamin (1891–1965): One of the chief founders of the Communist Labor Party in 1919. He became general secretary of the CPUSA in 1929 but was expelled the same year on Stalin's orders as a member of the Lovestone faction. He later became a conservative anti-Communist, writing and speaking against the party.

GPU: Gosudarstvennoe politicheskoe upravlenie (State political directorate). Predecessor to the KGB.

Great Terror: The name given to the most intense period of the Stalin-era purges of Soviet society, from about 1935 to 1939.

Green, Gilbert (1906–1997): A Communist youth leader in the 1930s, he headed the Illinois Communist party in the 1940s and was part of the national leadership in the 1950s.

Gulag: Russian acronym referring to the system of forced labor camps to which millions were sent during the Communist era. During the height of the Stalin regime, the death rate among those sent to the camps was high.

Hathaway, Clarence (1894–1963): A Communist labor organizer in the 1920s, he was a member of the national leadership in the 1930s and editor of the *Daily Worker*. Expelled for personal misbehavior (alcoholism) in 1940, he rehabilitated himself through work for a Communist-aligned union and was readmitted to the party and to the leadership in the 1950s.

Hourwich, Nicholas I. (?–?): A leader of the Socialist Party's Russian-language federation, Hourwich played a key role in the founding of the Communist Party of America in 1919. He was the party's representative in Moscow in the early 1920s until he angered Lenin, and the Comintern removed him from the American party and detained him in the Soviet Union. Nothing further is known about him.

ILS: International Lenin School. Comintern school for mid- and upper-level foreign Communists and for Soviet Communists who worked with foreign Communists.

Industrial Workers of the World (IWW): Radical American labor federation that had a revolutionary orientation. The IWW was the leading radical organization in the United States from 1905 to 1919.

International Red Aid (MOPR): Comintern affiliate that provided assistance to Communists and Comintern-supported individuals facing legal or other difficulties.

KGB: Komitet gosudarstvennoi bezopasnosti (Committee for state security). Chief security service (secret political police) of the USSR. The foreign intelligence arm of the KGB was the largest and principal Soviet intelligence agency. The KGB and its foreign intelligence directorate have a complex organizational history. The predecessor organizations to the KGB include, using their Russian acronyms, the Cheka, the GPU, the OGPU, the NKVD, the NKGB, the GUGB, the MGB, and the MVD. In some periods the foreign intelligence apparatus was organizationally separated from the much larger internal security apparatus.

Krumbein, Charles (1889–1947): An active figure in the CPUSA in the early 1920s, Krumbein worked for the Comintern on various covert assignments abroad and served prison terms in both Great Britain and the United States for use of false passports. He became the CPUSA's national treasurer in 1938.

Kuusinen, Aino (1886–1970): A Finnish Communist and the wife of Comintern figure Otto Kuusinen, Aino was sent to the United States in the early 1930s to work with the CPUSA's large Finnish immigrant federation. She later fell victim to Stalin's purges but survived the Gulag.

Kuusinen, Otto (1881–1964): A Finnish Communist, Kuusinen was a leading figure in the Comintern in the 1930s and for a time supervised the Anglo-American Secretariat.

La Follette, Robert (1855–1925): U.S. senator from Wisconsin (1906–1925), La Follette was a national leader of the progressive wing of the Republican Party. In 1924 he ran for president on the Progressive Party ticket.

Lamont, Corliss (1902–1995): A member of a socially prominent New York financial family, a lifelong ally of the CPUSA, and a leader of such pro-Soviet, pro-Communist groups as the National Council of American-Soviet Friendship and the National Emergency Civil Liberties Committee.

Lenin, Vladimir Ilich (1870–1924): Leader of the Bolshevik Revolution in Russia, founder and first leader of the Soviet state, and creator of Marxism-Leninism and the modern Communist movement.

Lewis, John L. (1880–1969): Long-time leader of the United Mine Workers union and founder of the CIO, Lewis was the most prominent labor leader of the 1930s.

Lore, Ludwig (1875–1942): A founding member of the American Communist party (affiliated with the Communist Labor Party), Lore headed its German-language affiliate. He was expelled in 1925 for ideological deviation.

Lovestone, Jay (1898–1990): Early Communist leader who became general secretary of the CPUSA in 1927 after the death of Charles Ruthenberg. On Stalin's orders he was expelled in 1929 as an adherent to the views of Nikolai Bukharin. Lovestone later became a highly effective anti-Communist labor organizer and chief foreign policy adviser to George Meany of the AFL-CIO.

Lovestoneites (Lovestoneists): Followers of CPUSA leader Jay Lovestone, expelled from the CPUSA in 1929 for Bukharinist (right-wing) ideological deviation. Although comprising only about two hundred activists, the Lovestoneites included a number of talented individuals, among them Will Herberg, later a prominent theologian, Bertram Wolfe, writer and historian, and Lovestone himself.

Lozovsky, Solomon (1878–1952): Long-time leader of the Comintern labor arm, the Red International of Labor Unions (Profintern). After the Comintern was disbanded, Lozovsky became head of the International Information Bureau, a section of the Foreign Policy Department of the CPSU. He was later executed in one of Stalin's anti-Semitic purges.

Marty, André (1886–1956): French Communist and Comintern leader who supervised the Anglo-American Secretariat in the mid- and late 1930s. His personal secretariat continued to deal with American matters until the Comintern was disbanded. Expelled from the French party in 1953.

Marty Secretariat: Section of the Comintern that dealt with American matters, under the leadership of French Communist André Marty.

Mikhailov, Boris (?–?): Purported Soviet journalist who was really a Comintern representative to the CPUSA in the late 1920s under the alias "Williams." He later served on the staff of the Anglo-American Secretariat.

Mikhelson-Manuilov, Solomon Vladimirovich (1893–?): A Cominternist and operative of the International Relations Department (OMS), he was OMS station chief in the United States from 1933 to 1938.

Mingulin, I. (?–?): A Russian, he was a prominent figure in the Comintern's top leadership.

Minor, Robert (1884–1952): A member of the CPUSA upper leadership throughout the 1920s, 1930s, and 1940s, Minor was acting general secretary of the party during Browder's prison sentence for passport fraud in 1941–1942.

Molotov, Viacheslav (1890–1986): A prominent figure in the Soviet Communist movement from 1906 until he fell into disfavor for trying to oust Premier Nikita Khrushchev in 1957. Molotov was active in the leadership of the Comintern from 1928 to 1930. He was Soviet foreign minister, 1939–1949 and 1953–1956.

MOPR: Mezhdunarodnaia organizatsiia pomoshchi revoliutsioneram. Russian name for International Red Aid.

Morning Freiheit: The CPUSA's Yiddish-language newspaper.

Nazi-Soviet Pact: Also known as the Hitler-Stalin Pact and the Molotov-Ribbentrop Pact. The August 1939 treaty between Nazi Germany and the USSR provided for Soviet neutrality when Nazi Germany attacked Poland and for the division of Eastern Europe between the two nations.

New Masses: Literary journal that was strongly aligned with the CPUSA.

NKVD: Narodnyi komissariat vnutrennikh del (People's commissariat of internal affairs). Predecessor to the KGB.

Novyi Mir: The CPUSA's Russian-language newspaper.

OGPU: Obedinennoe gosudarstvennoe politicheskoe upravlenie (United political directorate of the state). Predecessor to the KGB.

OMS: Otdel mezhdunarodnykh svyazei (Department of international relations). Department of the Comintern dealing with international communications and clandestine operations.

Orgburo: A section of the Comintern that included the OMS, the Finance Section, and the Administration Section. Its operatives, called Orginstructors, were assigned to various foreign Communist parties to assist them in their operations.

Orginstructor. See Orgburo.

People's Daily World (later *People's Weekly World*): CPUSA newspaper, successor to the *Daily Worker*.

Pepper, John (1886–1938): Alias for Joseph Pogany, a Hungarian Communist who came to the United States in 1922 as a minor Comintern representative. By misrepresenting his Comintern mandate he managed to become the behind-the-scenes leader of the CPUSA for a few years. Recalled to Moscow in disfavor, he later died in the Great Terror.

Peters, J. (1894–1991): Also known as J. Peter. A CPUSA official accused by Whittaker Chambers of heading the party's underground organization in the mid-1930s. He was deported to Hungary in 1949 and remained there until his death.

Piatnitsky, Osip (1882–1939): Comintern official who headed the Comintern's International Relations Department (OMS) in the 1920s and remained one of its ranking officials in the 1930s. In the late 1930s he fell victim to Stalin's Great Terror and died in prison, probably executed, in late 1939.

Political Bureau: The highest executive agency in the CPUSA, consisting of the general secretary and the party's chief officials. Also known as the Politburo, Polburo, and PB. In the early years of the party, this body was called the Central Executive Committee.

Popular Front: Name given to the broad liberal-left alliance based on antifascism and reformist policies that was created and dominated by the Communist party from 1935 to 1939. The alliance was also called the People's Front and the Democratic Front.

Profintern: Russian abbreviation for the Krasnyi internatsional professionalnykh soyuzov (Red International of Labor Unions). Sometimes known by the English acronym of RILU. The Profintern was the Comintern's trade union arm.

Randolph: Pseudonym used by a series of American CPUSA representatives to the Comintern in the 1930s.

RCP(b): Russian Communist Party (Bolshevik). The official title of the Soviet Communist party from 1918 until 1925 when it became the All-Union Communist Party (Bolshevik), or AUCP(b). In 1952 it became the Communist Party of the Soviet Union (CPSU).

Red International of Labor Unions (RILU): The Comintern's trade union arm. See Profintern.

Reed, John (1887–1920): Well-known American journalist and one of the founders of the Communist Labor Party in 1919. He died in Soviet Russia in 1920 and was buried beneath the Kremlin wall with a Red Army honor guard in attendance.

Ross, Nat (1904–): A CPUSA functionary from 1929 until the early 1950s, he was party organizer in the South and in Minnesota during the 1930s. From 1939 to 1943 he was stationed in Moscow as a representative of the CPUSA. He left the party in 1956 and became a successful businessman.

RTsKhIDNI: Rossiiskii tsentr khraneniia i izucheniia dokumentov noveishei istorii (Russian Center for the Preservation and Study of Documents of Recent History). Archive holding records of the Comintern, the CPUSA up to 1944, and the CPSU up to 1953.

Russian Center for the Preservation and Study of Documents of Recent History. See RTsKhIDNI.

Ruthenberg, Charles (1882–1927): One of the founders of the Communist Party of America in 1919 and first general secretary of the party after it merged with the rival Communist Labor Party. He remained head of the American Communist party until his death in 1927. He was buried beneath the Kremlin wall in Moscow with a regiment of the Red Army in attendance.

Sherman: Pseudonym used by American CPUSA representatives to the Comintern in the 1930s, most notably William Schneiderman.

Stachel, Jack (1900–1965): An active CPUSA figure from the mid-1920s to the late 1950s, Stachel played a major role in the party's trade union work in the 1930s and was a member of the national leadership throughout the 1930s and early 1940s.

Stalin, Joseph [Iosif Vissarionovich Djugashvili] (1879–1953): Soviet dictator who ruled the USSR from Lenin's death in 1924 until his own death in 1953.

Toohey, Pat (1904–1978): CPUSA trade union organizer and representative to the Comintern in the late 1930s.

Trade Union Educational League (TUEL): Trade union arm of the American Communist party in the early 1920s, headed by William Z. Foster.

Trade Union Unity League (TUUL): Trade union arm of the CPUSA in the late 1920s and early 1930s, successor to the TUEL.

Trotsky, Leon [Lev Davidovich Bronstein] (1879–1940): Second only to Lenin in the Bolshevik Revolution, Trotsky was defeated by Stalin in the struggle to succeed Lenin. He was accused of ultra-revolutionary left deviation from Marxism-Leninism and was later assassinated by a Soviet agent while living in exile in Mexico.

Trotskyists (Trotskyites): Followers of Leon Trotsky; accused of left-wing ultra-revolutionary ideological deviation.

United Communist Party (UCP): Title chosen for the organization formed when the Communist Labor Party merged with a faction of the Communist Party of America in 1920. The UCP then merged with the remaining portion of the Communist Party of America in 1921, under the name Communist Party of America.

United Front: A term used to describe an alliance, generally temporary and organized around a single issue or cause, between Communists and noncommunists.

United Toilers of America: The title of the above-ground arm of a faction of the underground Communist Party of America in 1922.

Van Kleeck, Mary (1882–1972): Prominent social worker in the 1930s and 1940s who was strongly aligned with the Communist party.

VKP(b): Vsesoiuznaia Kommunisticheskaia Partiia (Bolsheviki) (All-Union Communist Party [Bolshevik]). See RCP(b).

Wallace, Henry (1888–1965): Secretary of agriculture (1933–1940), vice president (1941–1944), and secretary of commerce (1945) under President Roosevelt; fired from the Cabinet by President Truman in 1946. Wallace became the presidential candidate of the Progressive Party in 1948.

Weinstone, William (1897–1985): A leading figure in the Communist party from the 1920s onward, Weinstone was a CPUSA representative to the Comintern. In the early 1930s he was an unsuccessful rival to Earl Browder for the leadership of the party.

Workers Party of America: One of the titles for the CPUSA in the 1920s. Also called the Workers (Communist) Party of America.

World Tourists, Inc.: A travel agency secretly owned by the CPUSA and run by Jacob Golos, a leader of the party's underground operations.

YCL: Young Communist League, youth arm of the CPUSA.

Zinoviev, Grigory (1883–1936): A prominent Bolshevik and close associate of Lenin's, Zinoviev was the first head of the Comintern. Bested by Stalin in the struggle to succeed Lenin, Zinoviev was accused of left-wing deviation and later executed in the Great Terror.

Chronology of American Communism

1917 Lenin and the Bolsheviks seize power in Russia.

1919 Communist Party of America and Communist Labor Party founded in the United States. Both parties go underground in emulation of the conspiratorial Bolsheviks and in response to government harassment.

1921 Under pressure from the Communist International (Comintern), the two American parties merge and form the Workers Party, later renamed the CPUSA, controlled by the underground.

1924 After considering supporting Robert La Follette for president, the Communist Party of America nominates William Z. Foster instead.

1925 Comintern prevents Foster from becoming party leader and gives control to Charles Ruthenberg.

1927 Ruthenberg dies; Jay Lovestone succeeds him as party leader.

1928 Followers of Leon Trotsky expelled from CPUSA. Comintern proclaims new era of revolutionary upsurge (the Third Period).

1929 CPUSA leaders Jay Lovestone and Benjamin Gitlow expelled from CPUSA on Stalin's orders.

1930 Communists take the lead in demonstrating against unemployment in America.

1931 Communists lead fight for the Scottsboro Boys, focus attention on plight of Southern blacks.

1932 Calling for a Soviet America, Communists on a ticket led by Foster get 102,991 votes in the national election. Secret apparatus established under the direction of J. Peters.

1934 Earl Browder becomes general secretary of the CPUSA.

1935 Georgi Dimitrov proclaims Popular Front against fascism at the Seventh Congress of the Communist International.

1936 Communists help form the Congress of Industrial Organizations (CIO) and begin to support President Roosevelt and his New Deal.

1937   Communists organize Abraham Lincoln battalion to fight in the Spanish
        Civil War. Communists are active in many civic and political organizations
        whose membership is chiefly noncommunist.

1938   House of Representatives' Special Committee on Un-American Activities
        charges widespread Communist infiltration of American life.

1939   CPUSA claims that its membership approaches 100,000, but actual registered
        members number about 66,000. After Nazi-Soviet Pact destroys Popular
        Front, liberals abandon Communist-dominated organizations.

1941   Popular Front resuscitated after German attack on USSR.

1943   Stalin disbands Comintern as gesture to Western allies.

1944   Browder leadership restructures the CPUSA as the Communist Political Asso-
        ciation.

1945   Article published under the name of Jacques Duclos leads CPA to remove
        Browder as leader and to reconstitute itself as the CPUSA.

1946   Eugene Dennis becomes general secretary of the CPUSA. U.S. code breakers
        of the Army Security Agency break the first coded World War II cables of
        Soviet intelligence agencies, which show extensive Soviet espionage and
        Communist collaboration in espionage against the United States during
        World War II. This becomes known as the Venona project.

1947   Truman administration creates loyalty program for government employees.
        CPUSA leaders, including Eugene Dennis, are indicted for violating the
        Smith Act, under which it is a criminal offense to conspire to teach and ad-
        vocate violent overthrow of the government.

1948   Communist effort to enter mainstream politics through the Progressive Party
        and the presidential candidacy of Henry Wallace fails. Elizabeth Bentley
        names numerous government employees as Soviet agents. Whittaker
        Chambers accuses Alger Hiss of Communist ties and espionage.

1949   J. Peters is deported to Hungary. Hiss is convicted of perjury.

1950   Senator Joseph McCarthy charges that Communists have infiltrated the State
        Department. Julius and Ethel Rosenberg are charged with atomic espio-
        nage. The CIO expels Communist-led unions.

1951   Supreme Court upholds constitutionality of the Smith Act. Several Commu-
        nist leaders jump bail and go underground. Anticipating the coming of
        American fascism, the CPUSA creates an elaborate underground apparatus
        to hide its cadre.

1953   Rosenbergs executed.

1956   Soviet leader Nikita Khrushchev denounces Stalin's crimes. The CPUSA is
        torn apart by Khrushchev's speech and by Soviet suppression of the Hun-
        garian Revolution.

1957   Supreme Court makes prosecution of Communists under the Smith Act vir-
        tually impossible.

1958   CPUSA membership falls to 3,000; hard-liners win control of the party.

1959   Gus Hall replaces Eugene Dennis as party leader.

1989   Gus Hall criticizes Soviet leader Mikhail Gorbachev; USSR cuts off secret subsidies to the CPUSA. Party membership, which has been increasing slowly, declines after collapse of communism in Eastern Europe.

1991   Nearly half of CPUSA's 3,000 members quit after Gus Hall supports attempted hard-line Communist coup against Gorbachev.

1992   Anti-Hall Communists form Committees of Correspondence and proclaim themselves democratic Socialists.

1996   CPUSA has about 1,000 members.

The Soviet World of American Communism

Introduction

From its founding in 1919 to the present day, the Communist Party of the United States of America (CPUSA) has attracted somewhere between a half and three-quarters of a million members. At its height in mid-1939, it had 66,000 registered members and perhaps ten times as many sympathizers, and it had played a major role in several of the great social upheavals of the 1930s. Indeed, until around 1950, Communists, in numbers that were far out of proportion to the size of the party, could be found in leading or supporting positions in the civil rights movement, in labor organization, in student movements, and in intellectual circles.

To their admirers and defenders, American Communists have usually been seen as idealistic and committed radical populists. They built unions, fought for racial and social equality, and battled fascism, often prodding their reluctant fellow citizens to live up to America's democratic ideals. But communism in America has always had more enemies than friends. Anti-Communists of various degrees have exposed, denounced, or opposed the efforts of Communists to advance their political agenda. To their enemies, American Communists were "soldiers of Stalin," committed to a totalitarian philosophy and willing to alter their political stance whenever it suited the foreign policy needs of the Soviet Union.

1

Early in the Cold War, the battle between Communists and anti-Communists became one of the defining arenas of American public debate. It has generated a vast literature on the nature of both communism and anticommunism and their place in American life that is evidence not only of the importance of the issue but also of its still highly contested nature.

One of the keys to understanding the grounds of this debate lies in defining the relation of the CPUSA to the Communist International, better known as the Comintern, the directing body for the various national Communist parties. On one side are those who insist that the American Communist party was a creature of the Comintern and, through it, of the Soviet Union, an American political organization whose primary loyalty was not American.[1] On the other side are those who maintain that American communism was a home-grown political movement with deep roots in this country.[2] The fierceness and the viciousness of the debate lie in precisely

[1]. Among the chief works to take this approach are Irving Howe and Lewis Coser, *The American Communist Party: A Critical History, 1919–1957* (Boston: Beacon Press, 1957); Theodore Draper, *The Roots of American Communism* (New York: Viking Press, 1957); Theodore Draper, *American Communism and Soviet Russia: The Formative Period* (New York: Viking Press, 1960); Max Kampelman, *The Communist Party vs. the C.I.O.: A Study in Power Politics* (New York: F. A. Praeger, 1957); Harvey Klehr, *The Heyday of American Communism: The Depression Decade* (New York: Basic Books, 1984); and Harvey Klehr and John Earl Haynes, *The American Communist Movement: Storming Heaven Itself* (New York: Twayne Publishers, 1992). Draper summarizes his views and replies to critics of this interpretation in Theodore Draper, "American Communism Revisited," *New York Review of Books* 32, no. 8 (9 May 1985); Draper, "The Popular Front Revisited," *New York Review of Books* 32, no. 9 (30 May 1985); and Draper, "The Life of the Party," *New York Review of Books* 41, no. 1 (13 January 1994).

[2]. Chief among these works are Maurice Isserman, *Which Side Were You On? The American Communist Party during the Second World War* (Middletown, Conn.: Wesleyan University Press, 1982); Mark Naison, *Communists in Harlem during the Depression* (Urbana: University of Illinois Press, 1983); Ellen W. Schrecker, *No Ivory Tower: McCarthyism and the Universities* (New York: Oxford University Press, 1986); and Fraser M. Ottanelli, *The Communist Party of the United States from the Depression to World War II* (New Brunswick, N.J.: Rutgers University Press, 1991); and the essays by various writers in Robert W. Griffith and Athan Theoharis, eds., *The Specter: Original Essays on the Cold War and the Origins of McCarthyism* (New York: New Viewpoints, 1974), and in Michael Brown, Randy Martin, Frank Rosengarten, and George Snedeker, eds., *New Studies in the Politics and Culture of U.S. Communism* (New York: Monthly Review Press, 1993). Isserman presents the case for the revisionist argument in Maurice Isserman, "Three Generations: Historians View American Communism" *Labor History* 26, no. 4 (Fall 1985): 517–45.

this problem: the issues it raises go beyond arcane academic inter-
pretations to questions about basic American values and our understanding of our own political culture.

If American popular culture in the 1950s was unabashedly anti-
Communist—with television shows like "I Led Three Lives" and a
host of melodramatic anti-Communist films—there has been a significant turn-around in the 1970s and 1980s. "McCarthyism,"
often used as a synonym for anticommunism of any kind, has been
increasingly depicted as one of the great evils of the twentieth century, the worst manifestation of a period that gave the lie to the
professed commitment of the United States to democracy, civil
liberties, and intellectual openness. From being villains, Communists and their allies have been recast as martyrs and victims.

Indeed, many historians now claim that the domination of late
twentieth-century America by right-wing, corporate capitalist interests can be blamed on the repression of the left, a process that
purportedly began in the McCarthy era. If the universities had not
been purged, if left-wing labor unions had not been expelled from
the Congress of Industrial Organizations, if leftist civil servants had
not been driven out of government, if Hollywood had not instituted
a blacklist, the American left would have been able to prevent the
worst excesses of the succeeding decades. This argument equates
communism with other leftist movements as the victim of a sen-
atorial bully, who persecuted patriotic Americans simply because
they criticized social and political conditions.

The CPUSA's defenders, including those who had little or no
sympathy for its views, generally regard American Communists as
a courageous and idealistic band of rebels. Many have simply ignored or downplayed the party's Soviet connections, attributing
them to ideological sympathy or declaring them to be little more
than pro forma professions of faith. Stories of the "Moscow gold"
that financed the party or of mysterious Comintern emissaries who
oversaw it have been dismissed as the product of paranoid fears
created by third-rate spy novels.

But Senator Joseph McCarthy was not the first person, and
hardly the most knowledgeable, to charge that the American Communist party was a tool of the Soviet Union. Almost from the day of
its creation, both the party's ideological opponents and govern-

ment agencies, convinced that the CPUSA was illegally tied to a foreign power, have searched for evidence to support this belief. Although that evidence was scarce in the 1920s and 1930s—when government agencies paid little attention to Communists—surveillance, wiretap, and cryptological evidence that accumulated from World War II onward provided documentation on Soviet financing of the CPUSA, as well as on the involvement of American party members in espionage.

Yet until the 1990s, most of the primary evidence that bore on this relationship was hidden or classified, buried in Soviet and American files.[3] With the collapse of the Soviet Union in 1991, however, the Soviet archives of both the Comintern and the CPUSA were made available to scholars by the Russian Center for the Preservation and Study of Documents of Recent History (RTsKhIDNI).

The bulk of the Comintern and CPUSA files concern prosaic matters; such is the nature of any archive of a large organization. But among these tens of thousands of documents in the RTsKhIDNI files are thousands that illuminate the relation of the CPUSA to the Comintern. For this book, we have selected documents that illustrate the different facets of that relation, focusing on those that reveal previously unknown or unexpected aspects of it or that contain items of particular historical interest.

As we shall see, these documents demonstrate that at every period of the CPUSA's history, the American Communists looked to their Soviet counterparts for advice on how to conduct their own party business. But there was more to it than that: these documents show that the CPUSA was never an independent political organization. There were moments when it was less strictly controlled by Moscow than at others, but there was never a time when the CPUSA made its decisions autonomously, without being obliged to answer to or—more precisely—without *wishing* to answer to Soviet authority. Historians who maintain that the American Com-

3. American involvement in espionage was discussed in Harvey Klehr, John Earl Haynes, and Fridrikh Igorevich Firsov, *The Secret World of American Communism* (New Haven: Yale University Press, 1995). The Venona files, Soviet cables dealing with espionage that were decrypted by American intelligence, will be the subject of a future volume in Yale University Press's Annals of Communism series.

munist party made its decisions as a result of a complex interaction between local events and conditions, on the one hand, and international supervision, on the other, simply state a commonplace without addressing the real issue: Which of the two was more important? The documents we have found demonstrate that the dictates of the Comintern almost invariably superseded policies offered on the basis of local conditions.

Although local American Communist units often took initiatives, these actions had to accord with national policy. Local party organizations were not given a free hand in choosing their own leaders or agendas; they could be—and often were—called to account by the New York party leadership for their decisions. And while mistakes might be tolerated, insubordination was not.

It was this commitment to the party and its leadership above all else that differentiated hard-core members of the CPUSA from the far larger numbers of people who passed through the party. Most of those who joined left within a year or two. They objected to the party discipline, the lack of democracy in its organization, or the amount of time members were expected to give. Idealists who joined the CPUSA because they believed that it was committed to a particular social agenda—antifascism, say—discovered that party policy could shift, and often did. These people remained with the party only as long as it supported their agenda. Their loyalty was to the policy, not the party.

Short-term party members may not have realized more than that the CPUSA expressed admiration and support for the Soviet Union. But anyone who remained in the party for more than four or five years could not ignore the fact that its fealty—at least ideologically—was given to the Soviet Union. Not everyone knew about the Soviet funding. Even fewer people were aware of the espionage. But long-time party members would not have been surprised or disconcerted to learn about these things. Dedicated Communists understood the importance of the Soviet Union in the revolutionary worldview. Moreover, most long-time party cadres, who numbered in the thousands through the 1950s, had been personally involved in either Comintern operations or the CPUSA underground apparatus, or they knew people who had.

This picture of the relation between the CPUSA and the Comintern does not justify or vindicate McCarthyism. Senator McCarthy proved, ironically, to be one of the greatest hindrances to the cause of anticommunism. In his often inaccurate charges, "supported" by exaggerated, distorted, misleading, and sometimes entirely false evidence, he equated Communists with Soviet spies, fellow travelers with Communists, and liberal anti-Communists with fellow travelers. By persuading many liberals that anticommunism was synonymous with demagoguery and opposition to the New Deal, McCarthy turned anticommunism into a partisan political issue. But the emerging picture of the relation between the CPUSA and the Comintern does provide the context for the broader anti-Communist sentiment in the United States as the Cold War developed. As the American branch of a foreign organization, the CPUSA was not regarded by most Americans as a legitimate political party. There was a clear sense in which it was "un-American." And when the Soviet Union and the United States came into conflict after World War II, it is hardly surprising that the American arm of Soviet Communism should have come under attack. Especially after the United States became involved in Korea, and American soldiers began dying in a war against two communist regimes, many Americans came to regard American Communists as disloyal.

In this book, we look at various aspects of the connection between the CPUSA and the Comintern. Created in 1919, ostensibly as an international coordinating center for world revolution composed of political parties from around the globe, the Communist International in fact functioned as the instrument of a single sovereign nation, the Union of Soviet Socialist Republics. It was headquartered in Moscow, financed by the Soviet Union, and dependent on the Soviet government for technical support and resources. In addition, the ideological prestige of having created the first successful socialist state guaranteed Soviet dominance of the Comintern.

In fact, the ultimate authority throughout the Communist world from 1918 until the rise of the People's Republic of China in the late 1950s was the Soviet Union. Communists who challenged Moscow's hegemony over the world Communist movement or any of its branches quickly became ex-Communists. Many were expelled.

Some continued to call themselves Communists and joined groups that the Soviet mainstream labeled heretical—Lovestoneites and Trotskyists.[4] And finally, thousands of Communists simply left the party when they recognized the futility of challenging the Soviet viewpoint.

The constituent parties of the Comintern, therefore, possessed only nominal independence. The second world congress of the Comintern, held in 1920, adopted twenty-one conditions for membership, several of which demanded organizational and political conformity with conditions imposed in Moscow. The intent, openly avowed in the statutes of the Comintern, was that "in reality and in action the Communist International must be a single universal Communist Party, the parties in each country acting as its sections."[5]

The American Communist movement emerged in 1919, funded in part by Soviet money. For a time a number of small, squabbling sects competed for recognition from the Comintern as its official representative in the United States. But once unity had been achieved in 1921—largely as a result of Comintern pressure and threats—the American Communist party became a valued member of the Comintern and remained so until 1940. In November of that year the CPUSA formally severed its ties to the Comintern to avoid being subject to the Voorhis Act, which required organizations under foreign control to register with the attorney general and provide detailed information about their officers, contributors, and activities. But the decision to disaffiliate was a sham, taken with the approval of the Comintern: the relationship of the American party to Moscow did not really change.

Even Stalin's decision to dissolve the Comintern altogether, as a gesture to his wartime allies in 1943, did little to alter that relationship. The lack of a formal organizational mechanism made it harder for the CPUSA to determine precisely what the Soviets

4. Taken together, these sects made up a tiny group that posed a negligible threat to Soviet communism. But ideologically, they obsessed the Soviet Union, which, as we shall see, devoted enormous resources to persecuting and combating them.

5. "Statutes of the Communist International," in *Theses, Resolutions, and Manifestos of the First Four Congresses of the Third International* (London: Ink Links, 1980), 124.

wanted it to do, but the close emotional and ideological bond remained, and so did Moscow's funding of the American movement. The Americans remained acutely attentive to the desires and needs of world communism—as defined by the USSR.

The Communist Party of the United States of America was, then, a domestic organization unlike any other American political group. Composed of American citizens and immigrant aliens, who ran candidates for office and attempted to influence American life, culture, and society, it had extraordinary and unprecedented ties to the ruling political party in a foreign power. Those ties were not static; they changed over the years as both the Comintern and the CPUSA changed. But until 1991 American Communists, regardless of why they joined the CPUSA or what activities they engaged in as members, or even how aware they were of the fact, belonged to an organization that was subservient to another.

When the Comintern was created, revolutionary hopes still ran high. Inspired by the Russian Revolution, revolutionaries in Moscow imagined that a worldwide Communist uprising was within their grasp. By the mid-1930s, they had become sobered by the rise of fascism and daunted by the resilience of world capitalism. Although the Comintern had never been a democratic body or an organization of equals, in this era it became even more an instrument of the Soviet state, as Stalin consolidated his power in the late 1920s and 1930s. The CPUSA in its turn changed dramatically. Throughout the 1920s it remained a small group, torn apart by internal strife that required frequent intervention from the Comintern. In the 1930s party membership began to grow. Communist leaders, moreover, learned a number of lessons during the 1920s that encouraged them to conform to Comintern directives; those who refused to do so were expelled.

In any battle with Moscow, foreign Communists who defied the Comintern were outgunned.[6] When the Comintern took on a national Communist party or some faction of its leadership, it was armed with its prestige as an official organization of the Soviet

---

6. We refer here to the Comintern era (1919–1943). After World War II, Communist governments in China, by virtue of its sheer size, as well as in Yugoslavia and Albania, strategically located between the Soviet bloc and the West in the early Cold War, were able to defy Moscow and establish autonomous Communist regimes.

Union, home of the world's only successful socialist revolution. As the universally accepted interpreter of Marxism-Leninism, the Soviet Union, through its creation the Comintern, was sacrosanct. In addition, the Leninist principle of democratic centralism conditioned Communists to accept decisions emanating from the body that, theoretically, stood at the apex of the world revolutionary movement.

This prestige gave the pronouncements of the Comintern an authority that American Communists were predisposed to obey. Of course, not every move the CPUSA made originated in Moscow. Although the Comintern often micromanaged the internal activities of the American Communist party, there were many occasions when it contented itself with simply setting the policy; the CPUSA would then decide how to carry that policy out. Particularly in the 1920s, before Stalinist orthodoxy was imposed, the Comintern's leaders often disagreed among themselves and, within limits, allowed conflicting viewpoints to be voiced during debates, thus enabling factions within the CPUSA to find patrons to advance their interests. And during the 1920s, as long as all the factions in the American Communist party pledged their loyalty to the Comintern and obeyed Comintern instructions, the Comintern tolerated their existence.

Throughout the Comintern's history its commissions and secretariats provided private forums for discussion and debate about American party tactics or activities. Although there are many examples of Comintern commissions that went against advice from American Communists, frequently CPUSA leaders made the tactical decisions, given their familiarity with local conditions. In all such cases, however, the assumption—usually unspoken, but occasionally stated clearly and forcefully—was that the ultimate judge of the proper tactics and strategy was the Communist International.

The leadership of the CPUSA acknowledged the importance of the Comintern by making frequent trips to Moscow to report to and consult with the Comintern's leadership. Not a year went by without one or two, and usually many more, CPUSA leaders making the trek to the Soviet Union. In the 1920s, the constant factional squabbling in the CPUSA led to frequent and prolonged meetings of the contending parties in Moscow. In the 1930s, with internal disputes largely squelched, Earl Browder still made annual trips to Moscow. Only the outbreak of World War II put an end to these pilgrimages.

American and Soviet Communists communicated in other ways as well. A joke within party circles in the 1920s was that the CPUSA was like the Brooklyn Bridge: it was supported at both ends by cables. In the 1920s and 1930s these flew back and forth across the Atlantic Ocean and Europe at a prodigious rate. Some were in plain text, others in code; some went to covert mail drops set up by the CPUSA. In the late 1930s the Comintern ordered the visiting Earl Browder to obtain a short-wave radio set and instructed him on the times and frequencies to use. After the signing of the Nazi-Soviet Pact in August 1939, the Comintern and the CPUSA communicated in this fashion. Meanwhile, couriers, often sailors, carried such material as microfilms of the minutes of important party meetings to the Soviet Union. Although snippets of these communications have previously been available, only since 1992 and the opening of Russian archives have fuller details of the links between the two parties been made public.

Such clandestine means of communication between the two public bodies were supplemented by yet more secret ties to more shadowy organizations. From its founding, the Comintern had maintained a special department, responsible for covert communication, money transfers, and foreign travel. The OMS (Otdel mezhdunarodnykh svyazei, Department of international relations) ran what was in effect an intelligence service. The OMS reported to the Comintern's Illegal Commission, which supervised its illegal operations. During the 1920s Mikhail Trilisser, head of foreign espionage operations of the OGPU (Obedinennoe gosudarstvennoe politicheskoe upravlenie, United political directorate of the state), the Soviet secret police and predecessor to the KGB, sat on the Illegal Commission as one of the OMS's supervisors. The OMS placed covert "station chiefs" in key countries, including the United States. In the mid-1930s, Osip Piatnitsky, head of the OMS since its founding, was purged. His replacement was Trilisser. The close cooperation between the Comintern and Soviet intelligence agencies increased during World War II, and Communist leaders in the

United States used Soviet intelligence channels to maintain communications with the Comintern.

Party leaders were not the only human links between the CPUSA and the Comintern. Particularly in the 1920s and 1930s, a steady stream of Americans flowed back and forth between the United States and the Soviet Union. Many were connected to the Soviet Union by family and ethnic ties. Others saw the country, particularly in the Depression-wracked 1930s, as a place where they could obtain employment. A few found it a refuge from legal troubles in the United States. The CPUSA and the Comintern monitored this traffic and attempted to make use of it. The CPUSA retained officials in Moscow as party representatives to the Comintern. In addition, from half a dozen to several dozen American Communists could usually be found working in Moscow at Comintern staff jobs or attending Comintern schools. For its part, until the mid-1930s the Comintern stationed representatives in the United States. These foreigners played a key role in the history of American communism. The prestige of the Comintern "reps" was quite high: even a hint that someone represented the international movement increased his or her authority and gave him or her a (sometimes undeserved) cachet. Indeed, several foreign Communists inflated their Comintern credentials to claim far greater authority over American Communist affairs than Moscow had intended.

But American Communists received direction from the Comintern in a variety of ways. Speeches and articles published in *Pravda* or other Soviet journals or carried in one of the Comintern's several publications indicated the correct public stance on matters of ideology and political policy. When American Communists learned that the tack they were taking on an issue differed from Moscow's, they would swiftly shift direction. But many organizational questions and subtleties of policy did not lend themselves to public broadcast. For these matters Moscow provided detailed directions tailored to American needs.

American Communists looked to the Comintern for guidance at every stage of their history. Soviet Communists settled American leadership disputes; they funded American movements and programs; they directed American ideology. And they always placed the national interests of the Soviet Union above those of other countries. And American Communists who did not do the same were not welcome in the party. This in large part accounts for the continued controversy: many leftists, including many former Communists, are unwilling to acknowledge that an organization that seemed to speak to the most disenfranchised of the American people, that argued for American values of equality, acceptance of outcasts, and respect for labor, was so tied to a foreign power that it could neither choose its own leaders nor set its own agenda. Except for a few key moments in history (the signing of the Nazi-Soviet Pact, the turn to Cold War policies), when Communists were forced to accept the party's Soviet allegiance—and when thousands who could not do so left—the rank and file could try to ignore what they preferred not to see. But the documents in this book prove that there was never a time when the leaders could blind themselves to the fact that their acceptance of the Soviet line had to be complete and unswerving. And even the rank and file could not miss the key aspects of Soviet domination.

Most of the documents in this book date from the 1920s to the 1940s. World War II disrupted communications between the CPUSA and the Comintern, and in 1943 the Comintern was itself dissolved. The International Department of the Central Committee of the Communist Party of the Soviet Union (CPSU) took over the supervision of foreign Communist parties, and we include several documents concerning the relationship of the CPSU and the CPUSA during the 1940s. By 1950, however, the CPUSA was under legal attack in the United States, and most of the party leadership was under indictment, in prison, or in hiding; American Communists therefore had less contact with the Soviet Union. In addition, access to more recent documents has been restricted. The documents that we reprint here from the 1980s, detailing the financial support given to the CPUSA by the Soviet Union, were released by the Yeltsin government as part of a campaign to discredit the Communist regime. As yet, no other material relating to the CPUSA has been made public.

The documents have been organized around the various kinds of ties that bound the CPUSA to the Comintern. In chapter 1, we explore the written Comintern policy and organization directives and the American responses to them. Chapter 2 documents the financial support that Moscow offered the CPUSA from its inception until the breakup of the Soviet Union, as well as the purposes for which that money was earmarked. In chapter 3 we look at the individuals who formed the human links between Moscow and the United States: the Comintern representatives who came to America and the American Communists who were stationed in Moscow. Chapter 4 deals with a specific aspect of the Comintern's influence on the CPUSA: the way the Comintern persuaded American Communists to accept (even approve) Stalin's purges and the terror of the 1930s. This last leads us in the conclusion to reflect on the extent to which the documents demonstrate the Sovietization of the American Communist movement.

CHAPTER ONE

Orders from the Comintern

THE COMMUNIST INTERNATIONAL sent thousands of written instructions to the Communist Party of the United States of America. Some were short, only a paragraph or two, while others went on for pages. Some were general enough to allow American Communists to interpret them to suit local conditions, while others were highly detailed, leaving no room for variation. To be sure, not all the Comintern's orders were carried out. It was not unusual for Moscow to order the CPUSA to do something, or even to do many things simultaneously, that the party did not have the personnel, the resources, or, most important, the popular support to accomplish.

But failure on the part of the CPUSA was rarely due to *unwillingness* to obey the orders; rather, it was the result of an inability to do so. On the few occasions when CPUSA officials objected to a Comintern order, they usually pleaded that the Comintern did not understand the situation or that a particular Comintern representative had exceeded Moscow's mandate. One finds no documents in the Soviet archives, either in the records of the Communist International or in those of the CPUSA, that show American Communist leaders refusing to carry out Comintern orders as a matter of principle. There are no American assertions of independence from Soviet authority; no minutes from the CPUSA's Political Bureau, Central Committee (CC), or national convention attest to debate over American autonomy. Instead, the archives contain unqualified assertions of American Communist loyalty to the "first land of socialism."[1]

In this chapter, we reprint Comintern orders from the early 1920s to the mid-1940s. Although most historians agree that the Comintern basically controlled every aspect of American party affairs during the 1920s, some scholars have asserted that after that time, as the CPUSA matured, the movement became "Americanized," and the party exercised a large degree of autonomy. These post-1970s historians maintain that American Communists of the 1930s and 1940s generation were essentially democratic in their outlook and that, although they still honored the Soviet Union symbolically as the first and most powerful socialist country, the CPUSA was neither Stalinist nor totalitarian in outlook or conduct.

But as the documents in this chapter show, even in the 1930s, Moscow decided how the American Communist movement would be run in matters of policy, organization, and choice of personnel. The Comintern not only guided the overarching strategy of the American Communist party but selected the party's leaders, rescheduled CPUSA conventions to suit Comintern needs, and ordered that a ranking American Communist official whose personal habits were deemed unacceptable be disciplined. These documents also show that although the Comintern's micromanagement of American affairs did decline during the 1930s, the essential nature of the relationship between the two groups remained unchanged.

In the Beginning: The 1920s

The Consolidation of the American Communist Party

On 31 August 1919 John Reed, Benjamin Gitlow, and a group of pro-Bolshevik delegates who had been ejected from the national convention of the Socialist Party founded the Communist Labor

1. "First land of socialism" and "great land of socialism" were common terms for the USSR used by American Communists. For an example of the first, see Gilbert Green, speech to the CPUSA antiwar conference, 31 May 1940, RTsKhIDNI 515–10–4178; for the second, see below, document 17.

Party. The next day, Charles Ruthenberg and Louis Fraina, joined by left-wing Socialists and other radicals who had boycotted the Socialist Party convention, created the Communist Party of America. Both parties announced their loyalty to the principles of the Bolshevik Revolution and to the leadership of the newly formed Communist International.

Two American Communist parties were one too many, and the Comintern ordered the two to merge. In January 1920 Grigory Zinoviev, head of the Comintern, dispatched a courier to America with written instructions demanding that the parties unite and giving guidance for the organizational structure of the new party. A supplemental order even specified the name: United Communist Party. The courier was arrested and his papers confiscated as he was trying to cross Latvia. But the Latvian government released the messages to the press, and they were effectively delivered when the New York *World* published them.

In the United States, both Communist parties promised obedience to the Comintern, but personal and organizational rivalries were so intense that the union was repeatedly delayed, as various factions maneuvered for supremacy. So bitter was the in-fighting that the Communist Party of America, the larger of the two original parties, split into two more groups, each of which claimed the name Communist Party of America. One of the splinter groups, led by Ruthenberg and Jay Lovestone, proceeded to merge with the Communist Labor Party in 1920 under the name United Communist Party. This new party, however, was no larger than the remaining Communist Party of America, which, under the leadership of Nicholas I. Hourwich and Alexander Bittelman, continued to be its hostile rival. There were still two American Communist parties.

The Communist International was planning to hold its third congress in June 1921. It did not want the occasion to be marred by the presence of competing American delegations. Therefore, in the spring of 1921 the Executive Committee of the Communist International (ECCI) issued an ultimatum to American Communists, demanding that they settle their differences. **Document 1** is the actual text of this ultimatum. Note that it is not a plea for unity; rather, it is a blunt assertion of the supremacy of the Comintern, containing the declaration that further delay constitutes a "crime against the Communist International" and that the American failure to achieve unity is an "injury of the authority of the Communist International." To press the point, the Comintern threatens to deny both groups representation at the congress and actually voids their representation in the ECCI until they achieve unity.

The Communist, the journal of the United Communist Party, carried a toned-down sequel to the ultimatum in its April 1921 issue, along with detailed Comintern instructions about the format of the unifying convention. *The Communist* unquestioningly accepted the Comintern's assertion of authority, proclaiming: "*The Communist International has acted! . . .* It is *binding* on the convention and on the representatives themselves. There will be no modification. . . . The highest authority of the Communist movement has spoken."[2] The convention met in May, and the two parties formally merged under the name Communist Party of America.

Soon afterward, factionalism once more rent the movement. At the third Comintern congress in June, Lenin had announced a shift in Communist policy. Asserting that expectations of an immediate, widespread proletarian revolution were an illusion, he insisted that Communist parties worldwide begin a lengthy period of proselytizing. Their first task would be to win organizational and ideological control over the industrial workers. American Communists found the new Comintern policy hard to accept. Most of them had abandoned the Socialist Party because it had failed to support immediate revolution, and the Communist Party of America had specifically organized itself on the Bolshevik model as an underground insurrectionary movement. Now, the American party found itself under Comintern orders to surface and undertake the slow task of organizing American workers. Nonetheless, the majority of the American party's Central Executive Committee (CEC, at that time the party's highest body) created an above-ground party, the Workers Party of America, at a convention held on 23–26 December 1921.

A minority of the CEC balked, however. They refused to recognize the new party, called an underground party convention, and proclaimed themselves the legitimate Communist party. All the evidence suggests that this dissident, underground convention attracted the support of a majority of rank-and-file American Communists. The dissidents did not see themselves as acting indepen-

2. *The Communist* (United Communist Party), 16 (April 1921): 3. Emphasis in the original.

dent of the Comintern, nor did they believe that they were defying Moscow. Rather, they thought that they were allowed some latitude in interpreting the Comintern's directives. As a concession to the Comintern's demand for an above-ground organization, they created the United Toilers of America as a legal front. Once again there were two Communist parties, each with an underground and an above-ground arm.

Both factions sent telegrams and delegations to Moscow justifying their actions and requesting Comintern recognition as the legitimate Communist party. After hearing out the rival delegations, the Comintern issued **document 2**. This order, addressed to "All Members of the Communist Party of America," drove home the point that the American party possessed only such latitude as the Comintern chose to give it. The order ignored the issue of which faction could claim the greater support. Instead, the key question was which faction was "in harmony with the Theses of the Third Congress . . . sent to the American Party as an instruction." The Comintern repudiated the United Toilers faction for its "refusal to abide by the decisions of the C.I." As an extra show of its power, the Comintern required John Ballam (whose pseudonym in document 2 is Moore), the chief figure in the United Toilers faction, to personally undertake the dissolution of his organization. The only concession granted Ballam's faction was a promise that if its adherents obeyed the order within thirty days, they could remain in the American Communist party. (In addition, as will be documented in chapter 2, their debts were picked up by the Comintern.)[3]

Faced with the Comintern ultimatum, the United Toilers faction, despite its rank-and-file backing, collapsed. Ballam toured the United States speaking to Communist groups and urging his supporters to embrace Moscow's decision. Overwhelmingly, they did so. The experience was an early and forceful lesson to American Communists on the nature of their relation to the Comintern. An American party convention, held in August 1922 and supervised by a three-member Comintern delegation, ratified the new arrangement.

3. See document 23, line item reference "Former Opposition Convention Expenses."

Document 1

From M. [Mikhail] Kobezky, secretary of the Executive Committee of the Communist International, 17 March 1921, RTsKhIDNI 495–1–26. Original in English. The document was printed on a small, thin swatch of silk for easy concealment by the courier who took it to America.

The Executive Committee of the Communist International having listened to the reports of the United Communist Party and the Communist Party of America, hereby declares that the further postponement of the unification of the two Communist groups is a crime against the Communist International.

At the moment when the great economic crisis (four million unemployed) and the savage persecutions prevailing in the United States are creating a most favourable ground for propaganda and organisation, at that moment a few thousand Communists are wasting their time in inter-organisational squabbles which have no political significance and only result to the injury of the authority of the Communist International.

Should the two groups fail to unite by the time the Third Congress is convened, the Executive Committee will propose that neither of the two groups be allowed representations at the Congress.

The Executive Committee hereby welcomes the desire for unity expressed by the rank and file members of both parties, and calls upon the comrades to unite in spite of the leaders should the latter continue to sabotage the cause of unity.

The Executive Committee further declares that the present representation of the American parties in the Executive Committee will be regarded as void till the time the union of both groups is brought about.

[illegible stamp]

Secretary Executive Committee Communist International:

Moscow, 17/III–21.   M. Kobezky

Document 2

From the ECCI "To All Members of the Communist Party of America: After Hearing the Claim of Comrade Moore . . . ," RTsKhIDNI 495–1–26. Undated, but context puts it in March or April 1922. Original in English; it is a typed draft with editing changes in ink. "Moore" is John A. Ballam, "Henry" is George Ashkenudzi, and "Dow" is Charles Dirba, all leaders of the United Toilers faction. "Lewis" is William Weinstone, "Marshall" is Max Bedacht, and "Carr" is Ludwig E. Katterfeld, all leaders of the Workers Party faction. Charles Ruthenberg was the head of the latter faction but at this time was serving a prison sentence for criminal anarchy in New York. Weinstone served as the party's executive secretary during Ruthenberg's absence.

TO ALL MEMBERS OF THE COMMUNIST PARTY OF AMERICA.

After hearing the claim of comrade Moore, that his group should be recognized as the Communist Party of America, the Executive Committee of the Communist International, decides as follows:

1. The Executive Committee of the Communist International recognizes as its American Section, only the Communist Party of America of which Lewis is at present Secretary, Marshall—returning delegate, and Carr—representative in the E.C. of the C.I.

2. The E.C. of the C.I. approves the action of the Majority of the Central Executive Committee of the Communist Party of America in forming a legal Party in harmony with the Theses of the Third Congress and the Theses on this subject, adopted by the E.C. of the C.I. last November, and sent to the American Party as an instruction.

3. The E.C. of the C.I. repudiates, the actions of the Minority Group, headed by Moore, Henry, and Dow, and severely reprimands them for their refusal to abide by the decisions of the C.I. and their destructive breach of Communist discipline.

4. The E.C. of the C.I. specifically prohibits this group, or any of its followers, from using the name of the C.P. of A., section of the C.I., or the Communist emblem, and prohibits them from issuing any further literature purporting to represent the C.I.

5. Regarding the threat of appeal to the Fourth Congress, the E.C. of the C.I. states that only members of a recognized section of the C.I., who obey its decisions, have a right to appeal. Those that place themselves outside the organization cannot appeal to the International Congress.

6. The E.C. of the C.I. instructs all members of the faction led by Moore, Dow, and Henry, who desire to remain members of the Communist International, to put themselves in good standing in the regular C.P. of A. organization, at once. This means, that every member must pay dues through the regular Party channels, and must comply with the decisions of the C.E.C. of the C.P. of A., and the Theses of the C.I. in regard to joining also the Legal Party.

7. All members that comply with this instruction within thirty days from the time that this is sent out by the C.E.C. of the C.P. of A. are to be accepted as members with full membership rights immediately, including the right to participate in the election of delegates to the C.P. of A. Convention this spring.

8. The C.P. of A. Convention must be held on such a date, that the members and branches, which comply with the above, can participate within their Sections in the choice of electors for picking the Convention delegates.

9. Any members of this "minority" that do not place themselves in good standing in the regular C.P. of A. within the time specified, are expelled from the Communist International, and cannot be readmitted to any section of the Third International, except as new members.

10. *Moore is instructed to return to A. at once and do his best to help carry out these decisions.*

The Comintern Sets American Party Policy

American Communists not only accepted Comintern intervention, they sought it, as **document 3** shows. In this 1924 letter Charles Ruthenberg, executive secretary of the Workers Party of America, informs Israel Amter, the party's representative to the Comintern, that the party will be sending a delegation to Moscow to ask the Comintern to decide "our Labor Party policy."

Ruthenberg also refers to divisions within the American Communist movement concerning the 1924 third-party presidential candidacy of U.S. Senator Robert La Follette (Republican, Wisconsin). The broad liberal and leftist backing for La Follette, particularly that of major unions in the American Federation of Labor (AFL), suggested that he might have a chance to change America's reliance on a two-party system. This center-left coalition, organized as the Conference for Progressive Political Action (CPPA), planned to hold a national convention at which they would nominate La Follette for president.

Communist leaders thought that the La Follette campaign offered a way for them to gain entry into organizations with large constituencies. How they approached the La Follette candidacy, however, was bound up with the party's still severe internal factionalism. At this point the Workers Party of America was divided into three groups, two large and one small. Ruthenberg and John Pepper led one of the major factions. Ruthenberg, of course, had been a leading figure in the American Communist movement since its inception.

Pepper, a Hungarian, had arrived in the United States as a member of the three-man Comintern delegation that had supervised the 1922 convention. He had stayed on, using his Comintern status to insinuate himself into the leadership of the American party. Citing the Comintern's support for "united front" tactics, he urged American Communists to move aggressively into mainstream politics. Opposing Ruthenberg and Pepper was the largest faction, led by William Z. Foster, head of the party's labor arm (the Trade Union Educational League), and James Cannon, the party's chairman. Foster and Cannon thought that Communists should make their move into mainstream labor and liberal groups gradually, establishing a solid base of support before attempting to influence these organizations. They regarded Pepper's tactics as too aggressive and liable to provoke a backlash. Ludwig Lore, head of the German immigrants, led a small third faction. Lore took a more leftist position, disdaining the shift away from an explicitly revolutionary position.

Communists sought entry into the third-party movement through an arrangement with leaders of Minnesota's Farmer-Labor Party. This state party had displaced the Democratic Party in Minnesota as the chief rival to the Republicans in 1918; in 1922 the Farmer-Labor Party had supplied both U.S. senators and two members of the House of Representatives. In 1924 it sought to spread its call for a leftist "cooperative commonwealth" (to be achieved by nonrevolutionary means) beyond Minnesota. William Mahoney, head of the Minnesota Farmer-Labor Federation, the organizing body of the Farmer-Labor Party, enthusiastically backed La Follette but tried to nudge the campaign to the left by making him the candidate of a national farmer-labor party rather than of the more centrist CPPA. With that in mind, Mahoney and the Minnesota Farmer-Labor Federation called a founding convention for a national farmer-labor party. Mahoney felt that if sufficient trade union, farmer, and independent leftist groups supported the convention, it could shape La Follette's campaign.

Communists approached Mahoney and offered their support. Thanks to its Moscow subsidies (documented in chapter 2, below), the Communist party and its affiliated ethnic, labor, and single-issue front groups employed several hundred organizers. Communist support guaranteed that the Farmer-Labor convention would receive public endorsement from these groups, as well as hundreds of delegates. Mahoney accepted the aid, believing that Communists were now ready to deal with other leftists on an equitable basis.

Both the Ruthenberg-Pepper and the Foster-Cannon factions agreed to enter the third-party movement via Mahoney's Farmer-Labor convention. Lore considered the idea ill-advised. The disagreement between the dominant factions was simply a matter of tactics. But as document 3 shows, even this minor, domestic-policy issue was referred to Moscow for resolution, on the initiative of the American Communist leadership.

In Moscow, Comintern leaders listened to the Americans' arguments and rendered a decision.[4] Their judgment was made not on the basis of American political realities but according to internal Soviet needs. Lenin, who had been gravely ill for more than a year, had died in January 1924, and the fight over who was to succeed him was well under way. Grigory Zinoviev was one of the leading contenders for the position. Leon Trotsky, who had been the early favorite but was now losing ground, sought to discredit Zinoviev by criticizing the Comintern's version of the united-front policy as opportunistic. Trotsky charged that the American Communist plan to back the reformist La Follette showed how soft policies led to the abandonment of revolutionary principle. Rather than argue about which of them was the more revolutionary, Zinoviev performed a tactical left-turn and ordered foreign Communists to pull back from close alliances with nonrevolutionary groups.

The Comintern delivered its decision on 20 May 1924. In it, the Soviets chastised both the Ruthenberg-Pepper and Foster-Cannon factions for offering excessive support to La Follette. The Comintern sent Foster back to America with orders for a drastic shift in the Communist stance at the upcoming Farmer-Labor convention, scheduled for 17 June in St. Paul, Minnesota. **Document 4** is the draft of a cable sent to Communist leaders in America while Foster was still in transit. In this cable, the Comintern orders a "sharp campaign against LaFollette" and instructed American Communists to urge the convention to found a national farmer-labor party with a Communist as its presidential candidate. If they are unable

4. In document 3 Ruthenberg tells Amter to expect a delegation of five: himself and Pepper from his faction, Foster and Cannon from their chief rivals, and a member of Lore's group. Later Ruthenberg decided to stay in the United States. To keep the delegation balanced, Cannon was also dropped. The final delegation consisted of Pepper, Foster, and Moissaye Olgin from Lore's group.

to stop the convention from supporting La Follette, they must sabotage the effort by attaching impossible conditions to the convention's support, namely, that La Follette break with capitalist organizations and accept control of his campaign by the new Farmer-Labor Party.

William Foster carried back a more detailed version of the Comintern decision. In its last paragraph, document 4 referred to the text of this decision ("sent with Bill") and included instructions for changing the wording in two lines. Foster's text, modified to make it appear American in origin, was formally adopted by the American Communist party and published in its press.[5]

As one member of the party's CEC noted, the Comintern decision confronted American Communists "with the necessity of completely reorienting ourselves practically within 24 hours."[6] But they did it. More than five hundred delegates from thirty states attended the 17 June Farmer-Labor convention. Many represented genuine, if small, farmers', labor, progressive, and radical organizations. Several hundred, however, were Communists, attending as delegates from the party's many affiliates and fronts. The covert Communists, as directed, argued for the immediate creation of a national farmer-labor party with a radical presidential ticket. When Mahoney and other noncommunists resisted, Communists reverted to the fallback position outlined by the Comintern in document 4: a "reliable worker president, working farmer vice-president." Under Communist pressure the convention nominated Duncan Macdonald, a mine-workers unionist, for president, and William Bouck, a radical farmer, for vice president. To win Mahoney's endorsement, Communists gave vague assurances, which Mahoney considered binding, that the ticket would be temporary, pending La Follette's nomination by the CPPA.

However, again in accordance with document 4, Foster also warned Mahoney that Communists would acknowledge La Fol-

---

5. Theodore Draper, *American Communism and Soviet Russia: The Formative Period* (New York: Viking Press, 1960), 461. A detailed account of the Communist involvement in the La Follette campaign is given in chapter 5 of Draper's book. Pepper claimed that the Comintern decision was actually drafted by Karl Radek, a German who headed the Comintern's American commission (Pepper to Dear Comrade, 5 July 1925, RTsKhIDNI, 515–1–273).

6. Alexander Bittelman, "Report of the Party's Executive," *Daily Worker*, 29 August 1925, magazine supplement, p. 2.

lette as the Farmer-Labor candidate only if he accepted the new party's radical platform and its control of his campaign, conditions that La Follette was unlikely to agree to. In fact, La Follette had already denounced Communist participation in the 17 June convention. After the CPPA nominated La Follette for president on a Progressive Party ticket on 4 July, Communists moved swiftly. The June convention had elected a National Executive Committee, which held a secret Communist majority. This majority met on 10 July and withdrew the Macdonald-Bouck ticket—not in favor of La Follette, as Mahoney had originally planned, but in favor of the just-announced ticket of the Communist party, William Foster and Benjamin Gitlow.

The Comintern's decision regarding the La Follette campaign thus had several results for American Communists. First, they passed up a chance to participate in the impressive, if unsuccessful, La Follette campaign. Even without Communist support, La Follette received 4,825,000 votes. The Communist party, on the other hand, retained its status as an isolated radical sect on the margin of American society; Foster received only 33,300 votes. Minnesota's Farmer-Labor Federation, badly scarred by the Communist manipulation, expelled scores of Communists from its ranks. When Communists reentered the state farmer-labor movement in the mid-1930s, William Mahoney, who had never forgiven their derailing of his dream of a national farmer-labor party, became their most determined enemy.[7]

A surprising casualty of the Comintern's decision was Ludwig Lore. On the surface, the Comintern had upheld Lore's ideological objections to Communist entry into the La Follette campaign. But despite its appearance, the Comintern's decision to order a pull-back from the campaign was not a matter of principle. In reality it was an anti-Trotsky ploy by Zinoviev. Lore was an admirer of Trotsky's; consequently, document 4 ordered American Communists to adopt a position that was closer to Lore's while simultaneously announcing: "Lore position repudiated. Comintern severely rep[r]imands Lore." Soon afterward, in 1925, Lore and

7. Mahoney's role as a leading anti-Communist within the Minnesota Farmer-Labor Party in the 1930s and early 1940s is discussed in John Earl Haynes, *Dubious Alliance: The Making of Minnesota's DFL Party* (Minneapolis: University of Minnesota Press, 1984).

other Communists who were deemed guilty of "Loreism" were expelled from the party.[8]

Document 3

Ruthenberg to Amter, 18 February 1924, RTsKhIDNI 515–1–307. Original in English.

FEBruary 18 1924

#25

I Amter
Moscow Russia

Dear Comrade Amter

You will find enclosed herewith the minutes of the meeting of the Central Executive Committee of our Party for February 15th and 16th from which you will see that a very deepgoing difference of opinion has developed in our Committee in reference to our Labor Party policy[,] which is made more dangerous for our Party in view of the factional situation which has developed as indicated in the minutes of this meeting.

The C E C has decided to send a delegation consisting of Comrades Pepper, Cannon, Foster and Ruthenberg and a representative of the Anti-Third Party tendency to Moscow immediately to present the whole question to the Executive Committee of the C I in an effort to secure a decision and avoid a factional controversy in our Party which would endanger the work and our achievements of the past year.

The points to be brought before the Comintern are the following:

1 Are the policies outlined in the November thesis of the C E C in regard to our relation to a Third Party correct?

2 Is the decision of the minority that we must take a decisive stand immediately for organizational crystallization of the class farmer labor forces thru a convention on May 30th so that the class farmer labor forces may act as a unit in relation to the July 4th Third Party convention correct?

3 The protest of the minority against removals of Party workers for factional reasons.

8. Moissaye Olgin, who went to Moscow as spokesman for Lore's position, turned on his colleague and published a series of denunciations of Lore after he returned to America.

Document 3 *continued*

I do not know just how soon the delegation will be able to leave but we will hasten the matter in every way possible. I hope that the delegates can be gotten off within two or three weeks' time.

We are writing you in advance of the arrival of our delegation so that you can bring the whole matter before the E C of the C I and have the necessary preparations made so that we can present the case as quickly as possible. It is very essential in view of the critical situation in regard to our Labor Party policy and the general situation in regard to the Farmer Labor movement that some of the members of the delegation return to this country as quickly as possible in order to participate in the various conventions which are planned for May 30th and July 4th and in the negotiations in relation to these conventions.

It is not likely that all of our delegation will be able to remain for the meeting of the enlarged executive committee owing to the situation as outlined above and it is our request that preparations be made to act upon the controversy immediately upon the arrival of the delegation in Moscow.

We have sent you the minutes of our various committee meetings from time to time and also various documents and we trust that these are on file in Moscow so that they will be available in submitting the controversy to the Executive Committee of the C I. We will send today additional copies of the various documents so that all the papers will be available.

Fraternally yours,

Executive Secretary

CER:PEB
OEA 12755

Document 4

Kolerov to CPUSA, "C. I. Decision . . . ," 1924, RTsKhIDNI 515–1–255. Original in English with annotations in Russian script. The annotations date the telegram as before 17 June, and the text itself indicates that it was probably sent before 4 June. Magnus Johnson was a U.S. senator from Minnesota and a leading figure in the Farmer-Labor Party. "Bill" was William Foster. "Kolerov" was Vasil Kolarov, a Bulgarian Comintern official.

the telegram signed by Kolarov
        (Before 17.VI.1924)

C. I. Decision: Must carry on sharp campaign against LaFollette, Magnus Johnson. Not for publication: Go June 17th Workers Party warn workers

На телеграмме
подпись Коларова.

[Рим 17.VI.1924]

     C. I. Decision: Must carry on sharp campaign against
LaFollette, Magnus Johnson. Not for publication: Go June 17th
Workers Party warn workers farmers against all alliances Third
Party. Must strive form Farmer-Labor Party. Nominate Communist
President, vice-President. If rejected propose reliable worker
president, working farmer vice-president. Program contain
demands city rural workers toiling farmers. Ifxproposxixxrejexted

If proposals rejected Communists support LaFollette only if breaks
with capitalist parties and makes clear declaration accept full
farmer-labor program and control, come to convention, accepts

farmer-labor control campaign funds. In case split C. E. C.
decide if masses leaving with us warrant campaign under
farmer-labor workers Party. Must nominate candidates and make
energetic campaign important states industrial workers
exploited farmers.

     Lore position repudiated. Comintern severely repimands
Lore. Kolerov.

     Bill arrives about June 4th. *****sent with Bill. Page
four lines sixteen change word third into petty bourgeoise. Line
seventeen change combine into make alliance with.

DOCUMENT 4. Kolerov to CPUSA, "C. I. Decision . . . ," 1924.

farmers against all alliances Third Party. Must strive form Farmer-Labor Party. Nominate Communist President, vice-President. If rejected propose reliable worker president, working farmer vice-president. Program [should] contain demands [of] city rural workers [and] toiling farmers. If proposals rejected Communists support LaFollette only if breaks with capitalist parties and makes clear declaration accept full farmer-labor program and control, come to convention, accepts farmer-labor control campaign funds. In case split C. E. C. decide if masses leaving with us warrant campaign under farmer-labor workers Party. Must nominate candidates and make energetic campaign [in] important states [of] industrial workers [and] exploited farmers.

Lore position repudiated. Comintern severely rep[r]imands Lore. Kolerov.

Bill arrives about June 4th. ***** sent with Bill. Page four line[] sixteen change word third into petty bourgeois[i]e. Line seventeen change combine into make alliance with.

Comintern Intervention in American Party Meetings

In addition to soliciting Moscow's aid to resolve internal dissension, American Communists sought Comintern approval of policy statements and even (the height of micromanagement) the scheduling of national conventions. This subservience robbed the conventions themselves of any independence and turned them into forums at which party members ratified decisions that had already been made by their leaders under Comintern supervision.

In 1927 the American party wanted to hold a national convention and sent a delegation to Moscow to discuss the policies to be adopted at this meeting. In **document 5** the Comintern ordered the American leadership to hold a plenum (a meeting of its leading officials) to adopt a draft set of policy statements before the delegation left Moscow. The Comintern reminded the Americans that the plenum's statements could not be "considered as final without ratification" by the ECCI and "shall not be published before such ratification." The second requirement was imposed so that modifications ordered by Moscow would not be too obvious.

The American party held the plenum, and in **document 6** the Comintern criticized the plenum's policy statements for discussing factional disagreements before dealing with matters of international policy. The criticism was an indication that Moscow was planning to demand that the statements be modified. The Comintern also scheduled the American party national convention, for 10 July 1927. Finally, this document specified who would be allowed to represent the American party in Moscow to discuss the plenum's draft statements.

Document 5

Kuusinen cable, 27 April 1927, RTsKhIDNI 515–1–929. Original in English with brief German and Russian annotations. Otto Kuusinen, a Finn, was a leading Comintern official who headed its American commission for several years. "WOPAT" stands for Workers Party, an early name for the CPUSA. The "POLBURO" was the Political Bureau, also called the Politburo, the highest executive agency of the American party.

WOPAT

CHICAGO

WE ARE OF OPINION THAT THE PLENUM OF CENTRAL MUST BE HELD IMMEDIATELY AND BEFORE DEPARTURE OF DELEGATION STOP HOWEVER THE DECISIONS OF CENTRAL PLENUM ARE NOT TO BE CONSIDERED AS FINAL WITHOUT RATIFICATION BY ECCI AND SHALL NOT BE PUBLISHED BEFORE SUCH RATIFICATION STOP OUR DECISION ABOUT COMPOSITION OF DELEGATION AS TELEGRAPHED TO YOU REMAINS IN FORCE UNCHANGED STOP CONSEQUENTLY OTHER COMRADES THAN THOSE WHOM POLBURO DECIDED UPON WITHIN THE RIGHT WHICH WAS GIVEN IT IN LAST TELEGRAM OF ECCI SHALL NOT COME STOP COPIES OF THIS TELEGRAM TO ALL MEMBERS POLBURO STOP ECCI KUUSINEN

From: Department [O]MS.
        Mochowaja 16.
27.IV.27.

Document 6

Presidium of the ECCI to Workers Party, 6 May 1927, RTsKhIDNI 515–1–929. Original in English with brief German and Russian annotations.

3633   6.V.27
[Illegible Russian script]

Telegramm

WOPAT   CHICAGO

PRESIDIUM ECCI DECIDES FIRST PRESIDIUM HOLDS TO BE INCORRECT THE CENTRAL PLENUMS MAJORITY CONDUCT COMMA ACCORDING TO TELEGRAPHED COMMUNICATION OF POLBURO COMMA PUT[T]ING AS FIRST ORDER OF BUSINESS INTERNAL PARTY PROBLEMS COMMA INSTEAD OF THE MOST VITAL PROBLEMS OF WAR IN CHINA NICARAGUA ETC STOP SECOND PRESIDIUM DE[C]IDES COMMA BECAUSE OF SPECIAL RESOLUTION OF CENTRAL PLENUM COMMA TO INVITE WEINSTONE AND CANNON

Document 6 *continued*

TO SESSION OF ECCI STOP THIRD PRESIDIUM DECIDES TO CALL THE PARTY CONVEN-
TION FOR JULY TENTH STOP THIS THIRD POINT CAN BE PUBLISHED STOP COMMUNI-
CATE CABLE TO ALL MEMBERS OF POLBURO STOP PRESIDIUM ECCI

Fr: Dept. OMS ECCI
Mochowaja 16 Moskaw

6.5.–27

Communism in Its Heyday: The 1930s

The 1936 Presidential Campaign

Contrary to many current historical accounts, the Comintern's frequent intervention in internal CPUSA affairs continued into the
1930s, and American Communists continued to willingly acqui-
esce to Comintern directives. Moscow, for example, scheduled
American party conferences throughout the decade. In 1936 the
Comintern, concerned about CPUSA plans for the presidential
campaign, sent this coded cable message to the CPUSA: "Consider
advisable questions party convention election tactics in view extreme importance discuss with you before convention. . . . Therefore recommend postpone convention to June. . . . Wire answer
immediately and when Earl [Browder] Bill [Foster] can come."[9]
Browder duly rescheduled the convention to June, and he and Foster visited Moscow in March to discuss CPUSA tactics.

Once in Moscow, Browder discovered that the Comintern's policies had recently shifted. Following the Communist International's
seventh congress in 1935, the CPUSA had sought to create a national center-left third party, which would be either a labor party or
a farmer-labor party. Communists hoped to achieve this by uniting
several constituencies that were pushing President Franklin Roosevelt's New Deal from the left: Minnesota's Farmer-Labor Party,
Wisconsin's Progressive Party, the EPIC (End Poverty in California) movement, New York's American Labor Party, and the Wash-

9. Dimitrov and Marty to Browder, 13 February 1936, RTsKhIDNI 495–184–
35, 1936 file.

ington and Oregon "Commonwealth" federations. Although the Minnesota Farmer-Labor Party had been in existence since 1918, the others were products of the political turmoil of the early 1930s. Each advocated a militant reform program that was somewhere to the left of the New Deal, but each also accepted America's constitutional order and rejected violent revolution and Marxism-Leninism. In the early 1930s Communists had scorned these movements as "social fascist" precisely because they were nonrevolutionary. (The CPUSA's use of the concept of social fascism is discussed in chapter 4.) After the Comintern adopted its Popular Front stance in 1935, however, American Communists had begun exploring ways to work with or to enter these center-left movements.[10]

These state-level movements were of some political weight. At the height of its power, in the mid-1930s, the Farmer-Labor Party held both of Minnesota's U.S. Senate seats, half of its U.S. House seats, the governorship, and all but two of the other nine elected offices statewide. In neighboring Wisconsin, the Progressive Party held one U.S. Senate seat, the governorship, and several U.S. House seats. In New York, then the nation's most populous state, the American Labor Party won sufficient votes that by supporting either Republican or Democratic candidates or by running its own, it affected the balance of power between the two parties. In California, the second most populous state, the EPIC-movement candidate for governor had won the Democratic Party primary in 1934, although he later lost the general election. Were these groups to unite into a national third party and form a presidential ticket in 1936, they could drain millions of angry radicalized voters away from President Roosevelt's reelection effort.

Initially, American Communists were indifferent to the threat a national third party might pose to Roosevelt's reelection. Their putative allies, however, viewed such a party with caution. Gover-

10. The state-level third parties that Communists either took part in or initiated are surveyed in Hugh T. Lovin, "The Persistence of Third Party Dreams in the American Labor Movement, 1930–1938," *Mid-America* 58, no. 3 (October 1976); Hugh T. Lovin, "The Fall of Farmer-Labor Parties, 1936–1938," *Pacific Northwest Quarterly* 62, no. 1 (January 1971); Hugh T. Lovin, "The Ohio 'Farmer-Labor' Movement in the 1930s," *Ohio History* 87, no. 4 (Autumn 1978); and Hugh T. Lovin, "The Automobile Workers Unions and the Fight for Labor Parties in the 1930s," *Indiana Magazine of History* 77, no. 2 (1981).

nor Floyd Olson, head of the Minnesota Farmer-Labor Party, supported Roosevelt's reelection. Senator Robert La Follette, Jr. (Progressive, Wisconsin), like his father, deeply distrusted any effort
that involved Communists and distanced Wisconsin's Progressive
Party from any Communist proposals. Most important, Sidney
Hillman and John L. Lewis of Labor's Non-Partisan League
wanted Roosevelt reelected. Labor's Non-Partisan League was the
political arm of the nation's leading unions, and a major supporter
of the American Labor Party in New York; its support was vital to
the success of a center-left third party. So by early 1936, American
Communists realized that their strategy of unifying the state-level
third parties was not working very well.

Meanwhile, Moscow was seeking closer ties with the Western
democracies against the threat of Nazi Germany; the Soviet Union
regarded Roosevelt as sympathetic to international opposition to
Nazi aggression. Concerned that a Roosevelt defeat in 1936 would
not serve Soviet interests, the Comintern had ordered the CPUSA
convention postponed and summoned Browder and Foster to Moscow for consultation.

In Moscow the Americans and the Comintern leaders considered
various options. If the plan for a national farmer-labor party were
dropped, should the CPUSA run a candidate of its own? If the
object were Roosevelt's reelection, would a Communist endorsement of Roosevelt cost him more votes than it would gain? The
matter was still unresolved when Browder and Foster returned to
the United States, but before their departure, Georgi Dimitrov,
head of the Comintern, informally told Browder that although the
details were up to him, Moscow did not want Roosevelt's reelection endangered.

After Browder's return, the American Communist party began to
change its stance. It continued to criticize Roosevelt's policies but
adopted a milder tone and backed away from supporting a third-
party candidate against him. Meanwhile, Dimitrov and Browder
continued to exchange messages about the situation. On 9 and 10
May Browder called a meeting of key party leaders to consider a
redirection of strategy. The plan he laid out was based on a lengthy
cable he had received from Dimitrov that ordered: "Concentrate
fire against Republican party—Liberty League reactionary bloc

same time criticizing Roosevelt's home and foreign policy. . . . Consider inadvisable put up independent FLP [Farmer-Labor Party] presidential candidate in present elections." Dimitrov also noted that he would let Browder decide whether the CPUSA should run its own presidential ticket.[11]

The party's policies for the rest of the campaign coincided with those laid out in Dimitrov's cable. In late May the Minnesota Farmer-Labor Party called a national meeting of those interested in a national third party. Through representatives, Governor Olson made it clear that although his Minnesota party supported the creation of a national farmer-labor party in the future, he was not interested in the promotion of an alternative to Roosevelt in 1936. In turn, Browder announced that the CPUSA was dropping its push for the national farmer-labor party. The conference adopted a resolution that essentially ended the campaign to create a new party in 1936.

After quietly abandoning its third-party efforts, the CPUSA ran Browder as the Communist candidate for president, but his candidacy was a charade. At the party convention in June, Browder mildly criticized Roosevelt for lack of vigor in pursuing the New Deal agenda, then went on to say: "The Communist Party declares without qualification that the Landon-Hearst-Wall Street ticket is the chief enemy of the liberties, peace and prosperity of the American people. Its victory would carry our country a long way on the road to fascism and war."[12] For the rest of the campaign the Communist party continued, while nominally opposing Roosevelt and backing Browder, to direct its fire at Republican Al Landon and to urge voters to make Landon's defeat their chief priority. And, as even loyal Communists knew, the only way to ensure Landon's defeat was to elect Roosevelt.[13]

This was not the last occasion on which the Comintern controlled both the timing and the content of a CPUSA national convention. In January 1938 Browder sent a memo to the Comintern

11. Dimitrov to Browder, 9 May 1936, RTsKhIDNI 495–184–34, 1936 file.
12. Earl Browder, *The People's Front* (New York: International Publishers, 1936), 24.
13. The CPUSA's role in the 1936 presidential campaign is described in Harvey Klehr, *The Heyday of American Communism: The Depression Decade* (New York: Basic Books, 1984), 186–206.

informing it that the CPUSA wanted to call a national convention; he asked for Comintern permission to hold the meeting and requested a review of the policies to be adopted by the convention: "We raise the question now of agreement by the ECCI to the Convention Call, agreement upon the approximate date . . . , and the proposals of the ECCI on the formulation of the agenda."[14] Browder also submitted a series of draft policy statements for Comintern approval.

Document 7 contains the Comintern's reaction to the statements. In general, the Comintern approved the proposals, which were later formally adopted by the CPUSA. Most of document 7, however, deals with criticism of Browder's policies that had been made by William Foster. The year 1938 marked the zenith of the party's Popular Front policy. Under Browder's leadership this policy had won American Communists a measure of respect and some influence on the left wing of the broad New Deal coalition, as well as in the new Congress of Industrial Organizations (CIO). The Comintern was pleased that the American Communist movement had, at last, achieved some clout. It certainly approved of the Popular Front policy; that, after all, had been initiated by Dimitrov in 1935. Foster, however, believed that Browder had allowed the program to get out of hand by offering excessive support to Roosevelt and John L. Lewis.

By this time the factionalism that had disrupted the party in the 1920s had been resolved. Browder's position was so dominant that a minor cult of personality, a pale reflection of the Soviet Union's near-deification of Stalin, had developed around him. The only CPUSA leader who dared challenge him on policy issues was Foster. By 1938 Foster was in poor health, he no longer headed a faction, and his authority in the party was limited to advising on trade union policy. He posed no direct threat to Browder's leadership. Indeed, he retained his position in part because he was the only senior party official with a credible record as a labor leader. Before becoming a Communist, Foster had led tens of thousands of Chicago-area packinghouse workers in a successful union-organizing drive in 1918. In 1919 he had, with AFL backing, taken more than 350,000 steelworkers out on strike in an impressive, though

14. Browder to Dimitrov, 19 January 1938, RTsKhIDNI, 495–74–466.

ultimately unsuccessful, attempt to unionize them. Now, Foster supported the Popular Front policy, as he did all Comintern-approved policies, but he criticized Browder for taking it to extremes, of "tailism" in Communist jargon: making the Communists into the "tail," or follower, of the New Deal.[15]

In document 7, the Comintern rejected Foster's arguments, claiming that they reflected Foster's "fear of involving the Party in a broad joint movement." The Comintern worded its criticism gently, however, and did not suggest ousting Foster from CPUSA leadership. And although it rebutted Foster's criticism that Browder's policy had degenerated into tailism, it commented that Browder, in responding to Foster, had "displayed a certain inclination towards a one-sided and exaggerated evaluation of Roosevelt's political role" and that there was some "danger of tailism." Moscow thus endorsed Browder's policies while cautioning him about getting carried away.

A few months after it issued document 7, the Comintern followed up on its warning by directing the CPUSA to drop its most successful Popular Front slogan: Communism Is Twentieth-Century Americanism. In **document 8** Sidney Bloomfield, CPUSA "referent" (liaison) in the Comintern Secretariat of André Marty, wrote to Dimitrov that on the orders of Boris N. Ponomarev he had informed the CPUSA of Comintern disapproval of the slogan.[16] But he was afraid that dropping the popular slogan without explanation would cause confusion. Ponomarev, a member of Dimitrov's Secretariat, had not told Bloomfield why it was to be dropped. Bloomfield took a guess of his own but wondered whether the Comintern could confirm his opinion. We cannot locate an explanation from Dimitrov (although the CPUSA did drop the slogan), and it may be that there was none. As Bloomfield had predicted, however, the abrupt cancellation of an appealing slogan

15. The best biographies of Browder and Foster are James Ryan, *Earl Browder: The Failure of American Communism* (Tuscaloosa: University of Alabama Press, 1997), and Edward P. Johanningsmeier, *Forging American Communism: The Life of William Z. Foster* (Princeton, N.J.: Princeton University Press, 1994).

16. Boris Ponomarev (spelled "Panamarov" in this document) held a mid-level Comintern post. After the Communist International was dissolved in 1943, Ponomarev transferred to the international department of the Communist Party of the Soviet Union and eventually became its head. In that position he helped supervise the American Communist party until his retirement in 1985.

caused confusion among American Communists. Questions about why it had been dropped persisted so long that Browder finally offered a justification at a December 1938 plenum of the Central Committee, and a version of his statement was published in the party's ideological journal, *The Communist*. But Browder's reasoning was unimpressive and seemed to be aimed chiefly at putting an end to the discussion.[17] The party's rank and file were not told that the slogan had been dropped on Moscow's orders.

Document 7

"Decision of the Secretariat of the ECCI," 2 February 1938, RTsKhIDNI 495–20–509. Original in English, with partially illegible handwritten German annotation.

"5"
968/4   <u>Confidential.</u>
Trans. Russ. Lev.
rc copy.
2.2.38

<u>DECISION OF THE SECRETARIAT OF THE ECCI.</u>

Considering the political line of the CPUSA in the main correct and placing on record the successes achieved by the Party in its work both in the trade union movement as well as in the development of a wide political front of all democratic and progressive forces against reaction and fascism, the Secretariat of the ECCI resolves:

1) To approve in the main the following drafts submitted by the delegation of the CPUSA: (a) On Building the Democratic Front Against the Danger of Fascism; (b) On Congressional Elections of 1938; (c) On Building a Mass Party of the CPUSA with the condition that these drafts will be made the basis for the decisions of the coming CC Plenum. On this basis the Party must with all its energy continue to carry out the line of the VIIth Congress of the CI, at the same time carefully watching all changes and events which may arise in connection with the development of the economic crisis and the sharpening of the international situation.

2) To call the Party's attention to the necessity of avoiding a one-sided evaluation of Roosevelt's policy in the sense of representing his home and foreign policy as being consistently progressive and genuinely democratic. The Party must clearly and openly point to the difference between Roosevelt's

---

17. Pat Toohey report to the Comintern, "Plenum of the CC CPUSA," 29 March 1939, RTsKhIDNI 495–14–124; Earl Browder, "Concerning American Revolutionary Traditions," *The Communist* 17, no. 12 (December 1938): 1079–85.

progressive and democratic statements which he repeatedly made in the recent period, and the actual policy of his administration. While boldly supporting the really progressive and democratic slogans advanced by Roosevelt, the Party must simultaneously come out with business-like criticism of every step of his administration which contradicts these slogans and must call upon the masses of people to demand from the Government and from Congress that the demands of the democratic anti-fascist front program be carried out in life and by means of joint mass struggle of all progressive forces and organisations to ensure the carrying out of such a program both in the home and foreign policy of the USA.

3) To consider it necessary in the interests of unity and collective work of the CC CPUSA to fully liquidate all political differences which have recently cropped up between Comrade Foster on the one hand, and Comrade Browder and the majority of the PolBureau on the other. In these differences Comrade Foster gave expression, in the opinion of the Secretariat of the ECCI, to certain remnants of sectarianism, i.e., to a certain fear of involving the Party in a broad joint movement with the petty-bourgeois, progressive and democratic forces, a fear that the Party will lose its independence and purity in questions of principle; at the same time these differences were sharpened and deepened by Comrade Browder having displayed a certain inclination towards a one-sided and exaggerated evaluation of Roosevelt's political role and of the democratic character of his policy. Comrade Foster was not correct in accusing the Party leadership of tailism in respect to movements and organisations adhering to Roosevelt, but the danger of tailism undoubtedly exists in connection with the Party's mass policy and the Central Committee in its documents must warn the Party of this. The main danger in the present stage does not however consist in this, but in a possible isolation of the Party because of remnants of sectarianism. The danger consists also in that all sorts of "leftist" and Trotskyite elements in the American labour movement try to utilise the remnants of sectarianism among members of the Communist Party for their own splitting and counter-revolutionary aims.

4) To call the attention of the Party leadership to the necessity of a fully critical attitude towards the weaknesses and shortcomings in the work of the Party and the Central Committee. Although the Party has recently achieved considerable success in comparison to the past, not for a moment should it forget that the tasks confronting it as well as the possibilities for the movement in the USA are so enormous and complicated, that they require the overcoming of even the smallest manifestations of self-satisfaction, require constant improvement in the Party's work and the systematic mobilisation of all its forces for making the most energetic efforts in carrying out the tasks confronting the Communist movement of the USA.

5) The Secretariat of the ECCI considers the proposal of Comrade Browder and others to call a Convention of the Party for the first half of 1938 advisable

and recommends that the CC conduct the most thorough-going preparations for this Convention, as a Convention which in the name of the entire working class should show the way and means of establishing the broadest democratic front against reaction and fascism and ensure the further rapid development of the Party and the consolidation of its positions in the ranks of the mass working people's movement of the USA.

Document 8

Bloomfield to Dimitrov, 12 August 1938, RTsKhIDNI 495–74–466. Original in English.

"8"
5882/1
rc copy.
16.8.38

August 12, 1938.

Dear Comrade Dimitroff:

A short while ago I was called in by Comrade Panamarov who told me to inform the comrades back home about the attitude here to the slogan of the C.P.U.S.A., "Communism Is Twentieth Century Americanism."

I told Comrade Panamarov that I would write to the comrades and convey to them the information, which I did. I also told him that while I surmised the reason for this attitude, I would however, like to have a little more clarification[,] which could come from a discussion of the matter[,] and I would particularly like to hear your views.

I informed Comrade Panamarov that this is one of our popular slogans which has influenced large masses. It serves as the main theme under which the Party claims and carries forward the revolutionary and democratic traditions of America. This slogan can be found in all our literature and agitation since the 9th Party Convention of June 1936. This slogan has fired the imagination and revolutionary idealism of the movement and the wider masses supporting it. On the basis of this slogan or the ideas implied by it the whole movement was spurred on to Americanise itself in the spirit of the 7th World Congress of the Communist International.

For these reasons I asked for more information in order to be more clear. However, I think that the reason for the position taken here against this slogan is that it is unscientific. Communism is the classless society in which the exploitation of man by man has been abolished; in which the state has withered away; in which the economic and other material conditions of life are on such a high level that the relations between m[e]n are on a high idealistic plane based upon the contribution of the individual to society according to his ability and from which the individual receives according to his needs; that Communism, which is the highest development of Socialism (which can be realised in one country) is universal. Now, since Americanism has not yet shown any sign of any society higher than capitalism, and since even in its development (in one country) the most it possibly could develop to, would be Socialism, therefore to call it "Communism" (regardless of which century) would be incorrect from a Marxian standpoint.

I have had no adequate explanation for the position here on the slogan. Therefore I can only conclude that what I have here stated as the possible reason for objection is correct. Perhaps the comrades in the U.S.A. will also think as I do in search of an explanation. A further explanation would clear up matters.

However, I would like to call to your attention the following important literature which may throw light on the slogan insofar as one can thereby see the reasons for its use by the Party:

1) "The Democratic Front for Jobs, Security, Democracy and Peace". Page 86, Chapter VI entitled "The American Tradition and Socialism".

This is the pamphlet containing Comrade Browder's report to the 10th Convention of the Party in May 1938.

2) "The Revolutionary Background of the United States Constitution", by Earl Browder in "The Communist" for September 1937, or in "The People's Front", the book by Browder, on Page 249.

Comradely yours,
Sidney Bloomfield
Referent, CPUSA,
Secretariat, Marty.

The Comintern and the Leadership of the CPUSA

That the Comintern intervened in the 1920s to select the leaders of the American Communist party, often overturning choices made by American Communists, has long been known. For this decade, the RTsKhIDNI archives simply add to primary sources already available in the United States. But what has been less well-documented is that in the 1930s, the heyday of American Communism, Moscow continued to select the leaders of the CPUSA. And American Communists went along with those decisions.

When, in 1934, the CPUSA wished to enlarge its Political Bureau (Politburo)—the highest authority in the party—by adding younger members, American Communists sent a proposal to Moscow, along with their choices for the new membership. The Comintern, however, rejected the request and specified that the American Politburo should be limited to five full members and three "candidate" (junior) members. The Comintern also picked the slate, naming Browder, Foster, Roy Hudson, Jack Stachel, and James Ford full members and Clarence Hathaway one of the candidate members. Moscow allowed the American party to choose the two remaining candidate positions, with the proviso that one of them represent the Young Communist League (YCL) and the other live in New York City.[18]

The CPUSA requested more leeway in deciding how large the Politburo should be. None was forthcoming. The Comintern cabled Browder and Gerhart Eisler (a German Communist who was serving as the Comintern representative to the CPUSA) that "we remain by previous opinion regarding number of members in Polburo. . . . Consider Enlargement Polburo unexpedient. . . . To include Polburo members . . . outside New York also unexpedient."[19] With that Moscow ended the matter.

Early in 1936 the American Communist party once again tried to enlarge the Politburo. Solomon Mikhelson-Manuilov, the Comintern's OMS (Department of international relations) station chief in the United States, cabled Moscow that the CPUSA was "provisionally proposing in agreement with leading comrades that you consider as members of next Political bureau following Foster, Earl, Stachel, Hathaway, Ford, Hudson, Bittelman. Candidates: Green, Krumbein, Berry most capable young Negro."[20] In **document 9** André Marty, a French Communist member of the ECCI, evaluated the American slate for his Comintern colleagues. He offered no information about Browder and Foster because the two had spent a great deal of time in Moscow and were known to

18. Comintern Political Commission to Edwards and Earl [Browder], 2 April 1934, RTsKhIDNI 495–184–24, 1934 file. "Edwards" was the alias of Gerhart Eisler.

19. Comintern Political Commission to Browder and Edwards [Gerhart Eisler], 5 April 1934, RTsKhIDNI 495–184–24, 1934 file.

20. Kraft [Mikhelson-Manuilov] cable, 1 February 1936, RTsKhIDNI 495–184–33, 1936 file. The proposed slate for full members of the Politburo was William Foster, Earl Browder, Jack Stachel, Clarence Hathaway, James Ford, Roy Hudson, and Alexander Bittelman. The proposed candidate members were Gilbert Green, Charles Krumbein, and Abner (A.V.) Berry.

Comintern leaders; their retention on the American Politburo was not in question.

Marty described the backgrounds of Ford and Stachel and concurred with the Americans' request to keep both in the Politburo. He also endorsed Roy Hudson, a militant maritime unionist who had risen swiftly in the party, as a full Politburo member. Marty, did feel, however, that Hudson had not yet "sufficiently justified" his high status and recommended that he be assigned work in one of the coastal districts in order to develop his capabilities and justify his continued position in the Politburo.

Marty also accepted Gilbert Green, the head of the YCL, as a candidate member. But he objected to the rest of the CPUSA's choices. He wondered whether Clarence Hathaway ought to be promoted from candidate to full member, noting that Hathaway "drinks a bit, with occasional lapses in his responsibility toward his duties." Marty conceded that Hathaway's "candidacy would raise no doubts whatsoever" were there not an unspecified—and "unverified"—irregularity in his record (see below). Marty was even more negative about Alexander Bittelman, whom he considered lacking in knowledge of the masses, with a tendency toward abstractness and chronic illness. Marty suggested making him a candidate member and judging from his performance whether he was up to the position of full member. Marty considered the proposed addition of Abner Berry premature and supported the nomination of Charles Krumbein as a candidate member. In fact, Marty suggested that if Bittelman were dropped from the slate of full members, Krumbein might be substituted.

Document 10 shows that Dimitrov and the other Comintern leaders accepted Marty's recommendations with only minor adjustments. Two days after Marty's memo, the Comintern cabled its decision to the CPUSA. Foster, Browder, Ford, and Stachel had been approved, as well as Green for candidate member. Hudson was also to remain; he would be given a major maritime district to run. But the Comintern vetoed Bittelman as full member and Berry as candidate member; the former was not a leader of the masses, the latter was too new. Moscow did approve of Krumbein. In fact, the Comintern offered the CPUSA the option of promoting him from candidate to full Politburo member, should the Politburo be enlarged (which was also permitted). In document 9 Marty had suggested that the CPUSA be allowed to substitute a more experienced black leader for Berry. This was done: Harry Haywood became the new candidate member. Haywood, who had lived in Moscow from 1926 to 1930, attended both Moscow's University for the Toilers of the East and the International Lenin School, and become a member of the Soviet Communist party, stood well with the Comintern. As for Hathaway, the Comintern blocked his promotion to full member but allowed him to be kept on as a candidate member of the Politburo.

Moscow's concern about Clarence Hathaway extended beyond his qualifications for full membership in the Politburo. Hathaway was an influential member of the American Communist party, with a number of coups to his credit. He had established a Communist presence in the International Association of Machinists in the early 1920s and been elected vice president of the AFL's Minnesota Federation of Labor in 1923. In the 1930s he served as the CPUSA's representative to the Comintern, chief editor of the *Daily Worker,* the main CPUSA newspaper, and candidate member of the Politburo. Hathaway also supervised the Communist party's reentry into the Minnesota Farmer-Labor Party and established an alliance with senator and later governor Elmer Benson; he even helped elect a secret Communist, John Bernard, to the U.S. House of Representatives as a Farmer-Labor member. Given his record, it is not surprising that other CPUSA leaders had wished to reward him with a promotion.

The Comintern's personnel department did not see matters in the same way. In addition to blocking the 1936 promotion, in 1939—as **document 11** shows—the director and the secretary of the department, L. A. Gulyaev and A. G. Stetsenko, prepared an extensive report on Hathaway.[21] They summed up his history in the American Communist movement with special attention to his alcohol problem, citing among other incidents a drunken fight with a Moscow policeman (militiaman). They also noted that Hathaway's former wife had once claimed that Hathaway had been a police agent (informer). (Probably this was the unverified irregularity to which Marty had referred in document 9.) Gulyaev and Stetsenko

21. Gulyaev and Stetsenko were both Russians. Gulyaev headed the personnel or "cadre" department of the Comintern from May 1939 to October 1941. Stetsenko had special responsibility for Anglo-American cadres from 1938 to 1940.

noted that Hathaway had been cautioned about his personal behavior, but apparently he had not changed. (The 1936 Comintern cable—document 10—contained an explicit warning about Hathaway's personal conduct. This was crossed out of the draft, but the warning was probably conveyed verbally.) Gulyaev and Stetsenko concluded: "We consider it necessary to suggest that the U.S. Communist party Central Committee should consider the issue and decide whether it is possible to keep Hathaway in a leading party position in the new circumstances."

Gulyaev and Stetsenko's report ended Hathaway's career as a party leader. In 1940 Hathaway's fellow CPUSA leaders not only removed him from the Politburo and the editorship of the *Daily Worker* but expelled him from the party altogether. They cited personal irresponsibility (his drinking) as the reason, but Moscow had been the real catalyst. Because of document 11, American Communist leaders expelled one of their most experienced and successful comrades.[22]

Document 9

"Information on Candidacies Nominated for the PB CC CPUSA," signed "M" [André Marty], 7 February 1936, RTsKhIDNI 515-1-3966. Original in Russian. "PB CC CPUSA" stands for Political Bureau of the Central Committee of the CPUSA. The Trade Union Unity League was the radical trade union arm of the CPUSA in the late 1920s and early 1930s. See below, "Moscow and American Communist Labor Policy."

[illegible script]

0251 8 FEB 1936 [stamp]

1706/3/fr. orig./A.B.   Top Secret.

7.II.36

Information on candidacies nominated for the PB CC CPUSA (in connection w/dispatch fr/Robert. (from Secretariat Com. Marty)

1. FOSTER, William—mem. PB
2. BROWDER, Earl—mem. PB

22. After his expulsion, Hathaway returned to Minnesota. There he reorganized his private life and got his drinking under control. Hathaway remained a Marxist-Leninist, and, because his expulsion had been for personal rather than ideological failings, American Communists continued to deal with him. He became a successful organizer for the United Electrical and Machine Workers (CIO) and a valued ally of the CPUSA within the Minnesota CIO. His continued loyalty and reformed private life led to his readmittance into the party in the late 1940s. He rejoined the national leadership in 1959.

3. FORD, James—mem. PB, nominated member of new PB. Negro, b. 1893, in party since 1926, was a worker/steel founder, then postal clerk, no party penalties, a leader of Negro comrades, currently secretary of a Negro area of New York, Harlem, has acquitted himself well in that work, his candidacy raises no objections.

4. STACHEL, Jack—mem. PB, nominated member of new PB. A Jew from Poland, born in 1899, in the party since 1923, was a worker/hatter, until 1929 one of the chief leaders of majority fraction, was second secretary of Trade Union Unity League, a leading party comrade, now practically the second secretary of the CC, no objections to him.

5. HUDSON, Roy—mem. PB, nominated member of new PB. American, born in 1901, in the party since 1930, worker seaman, was secretary of a revolutionary sailors' union. Was promoted to the CC and the PB at VIII party conference in 1934. His promotion was put through by way of the workerization and Americanization of the CC and the PB. But as yet it has not sufficiently justified itself. Hudson has no special popularity and brings nothing essential to the work of the PB. However, it would be inexpedient, in view of the same considerations that motivated his promotion, to leave him at present outside the PB. At the same time it definitely must be recommended to the CC to change Com. Hudson's position by giving him one of the coastal districts, where he can both develop and prove himself, and demonstrate whether he can continue as a member of the PB.

6. HATHAWAY, Clarence—candidate for the PB, nominated member of the new PB. American, born in 1894, in the party since 1919, was a worker. A leading party comrade, was secretary for several critical party districts, has for several years been chief editor of the "Daily Worker," a strong worker, drinks a bit, with occasional lapses in his responsibility toward his duties. However, at the "D.W.," H. is carrying on tremendous work, and if [not] for a single—true, an unverified—moment [in his record], then his candidacy would raise no doubts whatsoever.

7. BITTELMAN, Alexander—mem. CC, nominated mem. new PB. A Jew from Poland, born in 1891, in the party since 1919, by profession an engineer, until 1929 was one of the chief leaders of minority fraction, then worked out of the country, currently the director of agitprop for the CC and editor of "Communist." B. is a leading party comrade, politically capable and full of initiative, however his knowledge of the masses is inadequate, he suffers somewhat from abstractness, is often ill. It is inexpedient to promote him immediately to membership in the new PB. One may concur with promoting him to candidate of the PB. Subsequent experience will show whether he can remain at all within the staff of the PB and become a member of the PB.

Instead of Bittelman it is expedient to promote the PB member Krumbein, currently nominated candidate for the PB.

8. KRUMBEIN, Charles—mem. CC, nominated candidate for the new PB.

American, born in 1894, in the party since 1919, was a worker. One of the leading party comrades. Recently was secretary of the largest New York party district and acquitted himself well at that work. At present temporarily in prison in connection with passport issues raised by his work along our lines outside the country. His candidacy raises no objections.

If Bittelman's candidacy to PB membership falls away, and no other candidacy is found, then Com. Krumbein is perhaps the best candidate for membership in the PB, and in that case it would be expedient to promote him from candidate for PB, as he is currently nominated, to membership in the new PB.

9. GREEN, Gilbert—candidate for PB, nominated, as before, candidate for the new PB as well. A Jew, b. in 1906, in the party since 1925, was a worker, secretary of Young Communist League USA and ECCYI [Executive Committee of the Communist Youth International], his candidacy raises no objections.

10. BERRY, A. V.—nominated candidate for the new PB. Negro, born in 1902, in the party since 1929, was a worker, currently secretary of sectional organization in the *Chicago* district. Even disregarding the experience with Com. Hudson, who was promoted to the PB without sufficient preparation, this promotion of Com. Berry to the PB is still inexpedient. Com. Berry is a comparatively young member of the party, without broad political experience or the experience of serious leadership work, and, of course, he does not possess the corresponding authority either within the party or in the country. If the American comrades have not yet developed a different pair of new comrades for promotion to the PB, that is no grounds for premature promotions to an institution like the PB. If Com. Berry is a developing comrade of PB staff caliber, then it is expedient, bearing this in mind, to give him more important work than he has now, to help him develop further and show himself capable of being in the supreme governing organ of the party, and later promote him to the PB.

The American comrades must be advised either to select a different Negro comrade as a candidate for the PB or to promote one of three or four proven party workers of stature like [John] Williamson, secretary of the Cleveland district, [Robert] Minor, [Max] Bedacht, or [Jack] Johnstone. In view of certain considerations also of an internal party nature, it is inexpedient, perhaps, for the time being to put forward the candidacy of Com. [William] Weinstone, who has acquitted himself well as secretary of the Detroit district and is a proven comrade, politically capable and full of initiative.

M.

7.1.36

Document 10

"Re Proposal Polburo . . . ," 11 February 1936, RTsKhIDNI 515–1–3961. Original in English, with handwritten annotations in English and Russian. These annotations indicate that the document, the draft of a cable, was sent.

USA

178
2 11 II 1936 [stamp]

"8"–11.2.36
SS/2

0283 10FEB 1936 [stamp]

Re proposal polburo we accept Foster Browder Ford Stachel c[an]didate Green stop Hudson remain polburo but be assigned an important maritime district *stop* if polburo is to be enlarged our opinion add Krumbein and *candidates* comrades from nearby district characteristics popular with masses American able organiser stop re Hathaway we propose he remains candidate with warning discussion[1] regarding personal conduct stop Bittleman remain only as member CC because not American mass leader consider Berry too new for polburo first needs experience CC and more leading work avoid too rapid unprepared promotion stop if convention postponed we desire opportunity better discussion with Earl Bill

give back to [illegible]

1. Before crossing out the entire warning notice, someone apparently suggested replacing the word "warning" with "discussion."

Document 11

Gulyaev and Stetsenko to Dimitrov, 26 November 1939, RTsKhIDNI 495–74–472. Original in Russian. The "Michigan group" refers to socialists in Michigan who helped found the Communist Party of America but who withdrew in 1920 to form the Proletarian Party. "Kautskian" refers to the doctrine of Karl Kautsky, a German Marxist theoretician whom Lenin scorned for not being sufficiently revolutionary. "AUCP(b)" stands for the All-Union Communist Party (Bolshevik), the official title of the Soviet Communist party. "ILS" stands for the International Lenin School. Cannon and Dunne were James Cannon and William Dunne, prominent American party figures in the 1920s.

To the General Secretary of the ECCI

Comrade Dimitrov:

As you know, the candidate for the Politburo of the Central Committee of the U.S. Communist party, the editor of the "Daily Worker," Clarence Hathaway, was not elected to the Politburo by the last Congress of the U.S. Communist party because of violations of party ethics.

Comrade Hathaway was warned that if such actions were repeated in the future, he would be expelled from the Central Committee of the U.S. Communist party.

After joining the Communist party in 1919, comrade Hathaway was expelled in 1920 for his support of a group that deserted the Comintern line. In the same year his membership was reinstated, however, he lost his [illegible].

From 1919 to 1922 he supported the so-called Michigan group that founded the still-existing Kautskian "proletarian" party.

In 1923 he took part in the internal factional strife in the U.S. Communist party, he belonged to the Foster group, and then joined the Cannon-Dunne group in 1925.

During his stay in Moscow in the ILS, Hathaway, being a member of the AUCP(b) received a strict reprimand with a warning from the Khamovniki AUCP(b) Committee for drinking and for beating a militiaman.

According to his autobiography, in 1912 Hathaway volunteered and joined the National Guard of Minnesota, the main reserve of the regular army, which was used for suppressing workers' riots and as strike breakers during strikes. After being a member of the National Guard for three months, Hathaway quit.

Hathaway's first wife, whom he left with three children (now all adults) claimed in one of her letters to the wife of a member of the U.S. Communist Party Central Committee, comrade Bill Dunne, that Hathaway was a police agent.

According to the information given by the comrades who recently arrived from the USA (for example, Comrade Keller, a responsible member of the U.S. Communist party), Hathaway's behavior did not improve. We consider it necessary to suggest that the U.S. Communist party Central Committee should consider the issue and decide whether it is possible to keep Hathaway in a leading party position in the new circumstances.

THE DIRECTOR OF PERSONNEL, ECCI, Gulyaev (GULYAEV)

THE SECRETARY OF PERSONNEL, ECCI, Stetsenko (STETSENKO)

"26" November 1939
2 copies.ak
No. 29/SS

The CPUSA in the Labor Movement

The scope of Comintern control over the CPUSA is illustrated by Moscow's influence on party involvement in the trade union movement. For Communists, trade unions offered a prime area of activity because Marxism-Leninism taught that industrial workers were the key to the revolutionary transformation of society. Communists needed to build and expand their influence in the labor movement if they were to make use of it, however, and they devoted their greatest resources to the task. From 1919 until 1935, Moscow dictated the CPUSA's labor policy and oversaw its implementation. But although American Communists in the mid-1930s began to take initiatives of their own, they still needed to present them to Moscow for Comintern approval.

At its founding, most of the members of the American Communist movement regarded the American Federation of Labor with disdain, preferring the revolutionary Industrial Workers of the World (IWW), which was overtly radical and sought to supplant the AFL. Nevertheless, in 1920 the second Comintern congress ordered the Americans to work within the AFL, over the objections of John Reed, the United Communist Party representative. Louis Fraina, representative of the rival Communist Party of America, accepted the Comintern decision without protest, although some of his comrades in the United States later grumbled at his failure to object. At the congress, William Haywood, the long-time leader of the IWW who had fled to the Soviet Union to avoid a prison term for opposition to World War I and had become a Communist, denounced the decision as a betrayal of America's radical unionists. But the Comintern insisted, and soon afterward American Communists abandoned the IWW and committed themselves to working within the reformist AFL.

In 1921 the Red International of Labor Unions (RILU), better known as the Profintern from its Russian abbreviation, held its first congress in Moscow. Attending as an observer was William Z. Foster, who had long believed that radicals needed to work within the existing trade union structure. As noted earlier, Foster had led several massive strikes by American workers in 1918 and 1919. In 1920 he founded the Trade Union Educational League (TUEL) to promote radicalism from within existing unions. Foster feared that unions dedicated to supplanting the AFL—thus creating dual unions—were doomed to failure and only strengthened the position of employers. By the time he left Moscow, Foster's TUEL had been named the Profintern's American affiliate, and Foster had secretly joined the Communist party. The Profintern provided covert subsidies to the TUEL and, over the objections of American Communist leaders, assigned Foster a leadership position in the American party. By the mid-1920s Foster was one of the American Communist party's top leaders. The TUEL, meanwhile, gained some influence within the AFL, but its success was limited and its progress slow.

In several documents the CPUSA makes it clear that its trade union policy reflects Comintern decisions. In 1926, for example, the Politburo declared: "The main line for our work in the trade unions has been correctly laid down by the Comintern and Profintern. . . . Our task now is to locate the source of the theoretical and practical errors in our work and to find the most practical and effective methods of applying the tactics of the Comintern and Profintern to the concrete situation in the American Trade Union movement today."[23]

What the Comintern and Profintern had given, they could take away. In 1928 the Comintern initiated a sharp left turn in Soviet policy. At Stalin's direction, the Comintern announced that the world was entering a new period of capitalist crisis and, consequently, revolutionary possibilities. Known in Communist parlance as the Third Period, this new era demanded that Communists drop the united-front policies that had prevailed since 1921 and take a more explicitly revolutionary stance. The Profintern told the TUEL that it needed to shift its emphasis from working within mainstream AFL unions to promoting independent revolutionary unions that would directly challenge the AFL. This, of course, was in direct opposition to Foster's long-held position against dual unions. Foster acquiesced, although he was slow in implementing the new policy.

Compliance with Moscow's orders meant that the TUEL had to be dissolved, and that its allies in the AFL, developed with such effort, had to be abandoned. A promising alliance of Communist activists with reformers in the United Mine Workers union—which at one time seemed strong enough to challenge union president John L. Lewis—had to be jettisoned. The Profintern monitored the transition carefully. As **document 12** indicates, at one point the

23. CPUSA Political Bureau, "Resolution of the Trade Union Work of the Party," 1926, RTsKhIDNI 515-1-612.

Profintern ordered the Americans to postpone the convention designed to transform the TUEL into a dual union federation—the Trade Union Unity League (TUUL)—because they were insufficiently prepared for the change. The rescheduled convention met in Cleveland, Ohio, from 31 August to 1 September 1929 and there created the TUUL as a federation of new, revolutionary industrial unions. Profintern leader Solomon Lozovsky and the Comintern continued to direct a stream of detailed orders and guidance to the Americans.[24] A 1930 Comintern policy statement reminded the CPUSA that the TUUL must be "an irreconcilable enemy of the AF of L. Its task is to mobilise the masses, to win them to its side, to organize them in its ranks, in order to destroy the American Federation of Labour—this most reliable support of American imperialism."[25]

Labor unrest during the Depression led, in the early 1930s, to the explosive growth of independent unions, company-sponsored unions, and AFL unions. But despite high expectations, the TUUL unions remained small. Clearly frustrated, the Comintern demanded a change of strategy. In February 1934 the Comintern decided that the American Communists should help form a new, independent trade union federation that would bring together three groups: the affiliates of the TUUL, various independent unions, and unions in the AFL that were headed by progressives unhappy with the AFL's moderate leadership.[26] The CPUSA quickly responded: in April the party publicly announced that its union organizations would "struggle for an Independent Federation of Labor." But in June, before much had been done along these lines, the

24. See, for example, [Lozovsky] to Foster, 17 September 1929, RTsKhIDNI 534–6–138; "Resolution of the Political Secretariat of the ECCI on the Situation and Tasks of the CPUSA," 12 October 1930, RTsKhIDNI 495–3–231; Lozovsky, Mingulin, and Piatnitsky comments in "Notes on the Meeting of the Political Commission. Held, Jan. 1, 1930, On the American Question," RTsKhIDNI 495–4–9. The document is undated.

25. Anglo-American Secretariat, "The TUUL and the Tasks of the Party," sent to the CPUSA 16 March 1930, RTsKhIDNI 495–72–96.

26. "On the Work of Forming an Independent Federation of Labor in the USA," 21 February 1934, RTsKhIDNI 495–20–508. The order was prepared by a three-member committee of the Anglo-American Secretariat, consisting of I. Mingulin, Joel Shubin, and Otto Kuusinen. Minutes of Anglo-American Secretariat, 13 January 1934, RTsKhIDNI 495–72–257.

Comintern modified its strategy still further by ordering the CPUSA to put greater emphasis on work within the AFL.[27]

The CPUSA did not change course as rapidly as Moscow wanted, and the Comintern showed its displeasure. On 28 August 1934 the *Daily Worker* published an editorial criticizing John L. Lewis and the AFL leaders who were urging the AFL to organize the millions of unskilled and semiskilled workers in the steel, auto, and other basic industries. Since 1929 the CPUSA had insisted, in line with Comintern policy, that this effort would be fruitless if undertaken under the aegis of the AFL, with its moderate unionism. But after the Comintern policy changed, the American representative to the Comintern informed his comrades that the Comintern was sending them an article "correcting" the *Daily Worker* editorial, explaining that it was now Moscow's view that with regard to Lewis and the AFL "our position must be that the industrial union would be a step forward for the workers."[28]

By December, Moscow had moved still further in the direction of the AFL, and the Comintern decided that the despised organization should once again become the focus of Communist trade union activity. The Comintern announced that "the main task of the party in the sphere of trade union work should be the work in the AFL unions." As for the revolutionary unions into which the CPUSA had thrown its resources since 1929, they should now "join the AFL or its unions wherever there exist parallel mass AFL trade unions, or the Red Trade Unions can join the AFL directly." The TUUL, whose chief function had been abolished by this directive, could remain for a short time as "a propagandist center" to promote labor unity as well as a temporary home for unions trying to join the AFL. In addition, the new directive observed that "the tone used in the press with regard to the AFL must be changed."[29]

27. "The Way Out: A Program for American Labor" (New York: Workers Library Publishers, 1934), 50: manifesto and principal resolutions adopted by the Eighth Convention of the Communist Party of the United States of America, held in Cleveland, Ohio, 2–8 April 1934, and published as a pamphlet; Sherman to Dear Friends, 14 June 1934, RTsKhIDNI 515–1–3412. "Sherman" was the pseudonym used to designate the CPUSA representative to the Comintern. At this time it was probably William Schneiderman.

28. Sherman to Dear Friend, 19 October 1934, RTsKhIDNI 515–1–3412.

29. Comintern to Dear Friends, 20 December 1934, RTsKhIDNI 495–20–508. From 1929 to 1934, in accordance with the earlier Comintern stance, American Communist papers had consistently referred to the AFL in critical or contemptuous terms.

This time, American Communists got the message. In March 1935 a party trade union leader reported to Moscow that

> the Auto Workers Union [TUUL] no longer exists as a separate organization. Its members have all transferred into the various American Federation of Labor Unions. The Steel and Metal Workers Industrial Union transferred the steel members into the A.F. of L. union known as the Amalgamated Association of Steel, Tin and Iron Workers. . . . The TUUL has dissolved and the unions that formerly were affiliated to the TUUL have joined together in a committee known as the Committee for Unification of the Trade Unions: their object being to assist each other in carrying through the unification of those unions that still are outside of the AF of L into the AF of L in their respective industries.[30]

By late 1935, in response to Comintern direction, Communists had succeeded in inserting the majority of their TUUL cadres and membership into the American Federation of Labor.

One of the oddities of history, however, is that no sooner had Communists entered the AFL than the industrial unionists decided to get out. Led by Lewis, AFL leaders who supported an aggressive drive to organize the mass-production industries formed the Committee for Industrial Organization in November 1935 and were soon in direct conflict with the AFL's craft-union leaders. Within two years the renamed Congress of Industrial Organizations had become a powerful rival union center, sweeping millions of industrial workers into new unions.

In yet another policy shift, American Communists followed the CIO, and in 1937 the American representative to the Comintern, Eugene Dennis, announced that the CPUSA had achieved "decisive political influence" within twelve newly organized CIO unions and "important influence" in four others.[31] Dennis was not exaggerating. By the end of World War II, Communists led or helped lead eighteen CIO affiliates. In all, CIO unions with Communist-aligned leaders represented some 1,370,000 members, about a fifth to a quarter of the CIO's total membership. There was also a Communist-led faction in the ruling coalition of the million-member United

30. Jack Stachel to Dear Comrades (International Committee of the Metal Workers), 19 March 1935, RTsKhIDNI 515–1–3914.
31. T. Ryan [Eugene Dennis], "C.I.O. National Conference," 15 November 1937, RTsKhIDNI 495–20–519.

Auto Workers, its largest affiliate.[32] The CPUSA's role in the CIO helped the party transform itself from a vocal but marginal group into a significant force in American life. The CPUSA was, above all, a political enterprise rather than a union organizer—but it was the party's base in the CIO that gave its political activities clout.

Why and how did the anti-Communist John L. Lewis become the means by which Communist influence in the American labor movement reached its peak? Scholars have never been able to say with certainty. Most historians have seen the relationship as an unspoken, arm's-length understanding between Lewis and the Communists. Although a handful of scholars have asserted that face-to-face meetings and direct negotiations took place between CIO leaders and the Communist party, their chief evidence has been recollections and reminiscences offered many years afterward.[33] The Comintern archive at the RTsKhIDNI provides the first documentary evidence that Lewis and the Communist leaders negotiated directly about the Communist role in the CIO. Comintern reports also indicate that the CPUSA decided to pursue the CIO—and were allowed to proceed—despite doubts within the Comintern about the initiative.

When Lewis and his cohorts formed the Committee for Industrial Organization, the CPUSA had just abandoned the TUUL and reentered the AFL at the Comintern's bidding. Having cited the need for labor unity as their reason for these actions, Communists were cautious about embracing a cause (the CIO) that might split the labor movement. Moreover, Lewis and the other early CIO

32. On the strength of Communists in the CIO, see Max Kampelman, *The Communist Party vs. the C.I.O.: A Study in Power Politics* (New York: Praeger, 1957), and Judith Stepan-Norris and Maurice Zeitlin, " 'Who Gets the Bird?' or, How the Communists Won Power and Trust in America's Union: The Relative Autonomy of Intraclass Political Struggles," *American Sociological Review* 54, no. 4 (August 1989): 503–23.

33. Among the few who see a direct relation between the CPUSA and the early CIO are Harvey Klehr, *The Heyday of American Communism: The Depression Decade* (New York: Basic Books, 1984), 229–30, and Mark Naison, "Remaking America: Communists and Liberals in the Popular Front," in *New Studies in the Politics and Culture of U.S. Communism*, ed. Michael Brown, Randy Martin, Frank Rosengarten, and George Snedeker (New York: Monthly Review Press, 1993), 49. Other works that examine the Communist role in the CIO are Bert Cochran, *Labor and Communism: The Conflict That Shaped American Unions* (Princeton, N.J.: Princeton University Press, 1977), and Harvey A. Levenstein, *Communism, Anticommunism, and the CIO* (Westport, Conn.: Greenwood Press, 1981).

leaders had a long record of hostility to communism. But the CPUSA had enthusiastically supported industrial unionism and had long agitated for the organization of the mass-production industries, tasks that Lewis and the CIO were undertaking. In addition, in late 1935 Lewis gave an exclusive interview about his hopes for the CIO to the *Daily Worker,* a signal that he was willing to cooperate with Communists.

Document 13 offers a detailed account of early CIO-CPUSA relations, one that resolves much of the mystery about it. The document is a transcript of a September 1936 report delivered by Clarence Hathaway to the Marty Secretariat of the Comintern, reviewing the history of CPUSA involvement in the CIO. From the report's content, and even more from its tone, it is clear that American Communists, rather than Soviets, initiated the move to the CIO. Although the Comintern had allowed the CPUSA to proceed on this course, the Soviets still had doubts about the change. Consequently, Hathaway does not merely report on the party's actions but defends its decision to back the CIO.

Hathaway refers to several meetings between members of the Politburo and Lewis and Sidney Hillman, "the two outstanding leaders of the CIO," regarding CIO strategy and the role of Communists in the organization. These meetings were advantageous to the party, reports Hathaway: "I met with Lewis and raised the question of the reinstatement of all Communists and militants who had been expelled by the Tighe leadership of the American [Amalgamated] Association of Iron, Steel and Tin Workers. He asked for a list of those names. We provided him with it and immediately, all were reinstated." (The Amalgamated Association was later absorbed into the CIO's Steel Workers Organizing Committee.) Hathaway goes on: "Then, we raised the question of placing a number of Communists and militant workers on the paid organising staff. . . . Here again, he asked us for our recommendations, and Comrade Stachel estimated, the day before I left, that we now have approximately 45 or 50 Communists on the full-time organising staff of steel. All this shows not only that they [Lewis and the CIO] have shown a readiness to cooperate in discussions and words, but that they have brought our people in everywhere."

Hathaway's report showed that Lewis and Hillman rejected the

Communists' suggestions on several key policy issues concerning the CIO response to AFL demands to disband. (The report deals with late 1935 and early 1936, before the split between the AFL and the CIO became final.) On these issues, the Communists deferred to Lewis and Hillman's judgment. Hathaway observed that American Communists believed that "we are due for a period in the U.S. when there will be a divided trade union movement" and that the CPUSA had decided upon "boldly and aggressively going along with the drive the CIO is making." He noted, however, that the CPUSA was urging Lewis to keep the CIO as a center for new industrial unions and avoid setting up dual unions in competition with the AFL.

Other documents found in Moscow reinforce the account in document 13. In April 1936 Browder traveled to Moscow for consultations with the Comintern. In response to a sharp question from the Profintern's Lozovsky, Browder defended his decision to support the CIO in testimony to a Comintern commission:

> I do not think it is correct, for example, to say that Lewis has used us, and not we have used Lewis. I do not think it is correct to say that we are at the tail of this movement. Let us suppose that the Committee for Industrial Organization and Lewis had not taken up this fight. Well, then we would be at the head of the whole movement for industrial unionism; we would not be at the tail-end then, but would we really be any better off than we are today? No. I think we are much stronger and better off because Lewis is at the head of the movement and organized this whole number of unions for us, and if Lewis is using us in this way, I wish William Green [head of the AFL] would use us in this way too.
>
> I do not think we have to be afraid of the breadth of this movement; I do not think we should immediately cry, we are losing the leadership, when some of these big bureaucrats come in and take the leadership of a big movement we have created. They may ride this horse very high, and ride for a while, but when they get on this horse of ours, they are riding for a fall because it is our horse and they cannot steal it.[34]

In mid-August 1936 Browder sent a cable to the Comintern that set out in abbreviated form the same arguments Hathaway presented in more detail a month later in document 13. The cable ended by noting that because of the decision to go with the CIO,

34. Browder testimony, 10 April 1936, RTsKhIDNI 495–14–63.

Communists had been chosen as key organizers of the steel union in a number of important districts:

> Party members elected as organizers for all Steel industry centers. . . . In one case half of the organizers, as for example, in the Chicago district, are Communists, and there are also significant numbers of the latter in Pittsburgh and Ohio, as in other centers including the South. Approximately fifty Party members are full-time organizers in the Steel industry campaign. Together with a large number of volunteer organizers the Party plays a decisive role in organizing fraternal and Negro organization and in stimulating the work of women and young people. There is direct contact with all the leading workers of the CIO charged with work in the Steel industry campaign, discussing jointly with us all the issues. . . . CIO workers and Lewis acknowledge this work of the Party and understand our potential capabilities in the whole battle.[35]

In spite of Browder's arguments, the Comintern continued to fret about who was using whom in the CIO. **Document 14** shows that Comintern leaders remained uneasy about the CPUSA's CIO strategy. Here one I. Mingulin, a senior Comintern official, writes Dimitrov that he still fears that "we are, as it were, forced to follow in Lewis's footsteps." Mingulin adds: "It is possible that this is not completely the case, and also that party policy in this matter is completely correct. But we do not have sufficient information." Because of the press of the upcoming presidential election, Browder and other CPUSA leaders were not scheduled to come to Moscow until December, but Mingulin felt that the issue needed immediate attention. He urged the Comintern to order Hathaway, who was traveling to Europe on other business in September, to come to Moscow and give a full account of the CIO situation. A handwritten note on the memo indicates that Dimitrov approved Mingulin's suggestion. (Hathaway's account is document 13.)

So we can see from this episode that although the CPUSA on this occasion took the initiative, there were clear limits on its independence. Responding to an unexpected opportunity, the party placed its organizers at the disposal of John L. Lewis in return for entry into the CIO and a measure of toleration. Although risking a split with the AFL—in contravention of Comintern orders—the deci-

35. Earl [Browder] via Stack [or Stock] to Randolph, 15 August 1936, RTsKhIDNI 495–184–3, 1936 file.

sion was in line with words of approval coming from Moscow about Lewis and was tempered by the fact that there was as yet no irrevocable break between the CIO and the AFL. When Comintern officials expressed concern about the decision, American party leaders were summoned to Moscow to justify their actions. Neither in Hathaway's report nor Browder's cable (nor, for that matter, in any other document) does the CPUSA declare that Americans were the best judges of the local situation and that the decision should rest with them. American Communists may have won approval of their policies, but they still had to ask for it.

Document 12

Losovsky [Lozovsky] to TUEL, Browder, and Ballam, 18 May 1929, RTsKhIDNI 534–6–138. Original in English. "Bills return" refers to William Foster, who was then in Moscow but preparing to return to the United States.

TELEGRAMME

TUEL   NEWYORK   BROWDER   BALLAM

EXECUTIVE CONSIDERS NECESSARY FOR BETTER PREPARATION POSTPONE TUEL CONVENTION SEVERAL MONTHS FINAL DATE WILL BE FIXED AFTER BILLS RETURN

LOSOVSKY

18.V.29

Document 13

Excerpt from Clarence Hathaway, "Report of Situation in U.S.A. and Work of Party," given to a meeting of the Marty Secretariat, 15 September 1936, RTsKhIDNI 515–1–3967. Original in English. The remainder of the report deals with CPUSA activities in the 1936 elections.

CONFIDENTIAL

MEETING OF SECRETARIAT OF COMRADE MARTY.
September 15, 1936.
Steno: Scherer/3.

Speaker: HATHAWAY - Report of Situation in U.S.A. and Work of Party.
    I propose to take up only two major questions—the question of the situation in the A.F. of L., and the election campaign.

Document 13 *continued*

I would say at the outset that I only received word last night that the report was to be delivered today at 12 o'clock, and for that reason, my report will not be organised in a form that would ordinarily be the case, but will rather be a more general discussion of our problems that I think will bring out the main points and will open the way for questions.

I shall start with the situation in the AFL. I do not think it is necessary here to go into the general background of the present situation. I think all the comrades are familiar with the fact that the unions of the Committee for Industrial Organisation have been suspended from the AFL, unions that involve a membership of close to 40% of the entire AFL, and not only that, but are unions that embrace the mass production industries of the country.

This is the result of a long struggle in the AFL that began at the San Francisco convention two years ago and came to a head at the last convention in Atlantic City, following which the CIO was organised, a bloc to carry on the fight for industrial unionism and for organisation of the unorganised.

The chief problem before us now is what to do in the present situation. The C.C. of the Party is fully agreed that it is our job and the job of all militants in the trade union movement to develop the broadest and most aggressive fight for the unification of the AFL. The question that confronts us is the problem of how best that fight for reunification can be carried on.

In order to discuss that question, I think that, at the outset, we must bear in mind that we are not dealing with a division in the ranks of the AFL or in the trade union movement that is comparable with the division that existed when the left wing had their own unions outside the AFL. If we were to consider this in the sense of Communist or left unions being outside and the main body of the workers inside, and approached it from the viewpoint of our past tactics and strategy, we would be making a most serious mistake in this case. We must bear in mind that in this case unions have been suspended, and ones most decisive in the American trade union movement. To begin with, there is the United Mine Workers, in the most basic industry, with 400,000 members, the largest in the AFL. The other unions are the Amalgamated Clothing Workers, the International Ladies' Garment Workers, the United Textile Workers, Rubber Workers, Automobile Workers, etc. This gives a character to this struggle quite different than previous struggles for unity within the AFL.

Secondly, we must take into consideration the issues around which the suspension of these unions took place. At the AFL convention, these unions had put the issue squarely, first, of the organisation of the unorganised in the mass production industries. It was their contention, and correctly, that the American trade union movement could not be a power until the basic industries of the country were organised, and they charged the Executive Council with responsibility for the matter of organisation in these industries and insisted that a course be pursued of bringing the workers in those mass production industries into the AFL. They furthermore pointed out, on the basis of experience, that these industries could not be organised except on the basis of industrial unionism.

The AFL convention rejected such a policy and, immediately following the convention, these unions formed a bloc in the AFL to independently carry forward the drive to organise the unorganised on the basis of industrial unionism.

In the period since the CIO was organised, it has achieved very great results in doing what the AFL had itself failed to do. To their credit, the Automobile Workers' Union was definitely established as an international union in the AFL, and has been built up to some 45 or 50 thousand members, as compared with a scattered group of federal locals at the time of the Atlantic City convention. In the case of rubber, there also, the federal locals have been crystallised into an international union and tremendous gains had been made in organising the unorganised. In a number of other instances, there are very direct gains to be shown as a result of the activities of the CIO.

The biggest task set by the Committee was the drive to organise the steel industry. There, after a long battle with the reactionary officials of the Amalgamated Association of Iron, Steel and Tin Workers, they finally forced its leadership into line, succeeding in setting up a special committee to organise the steel industry. They put up $500,000 for the beginning of the campaign, set up committees in steel and have since put on a large staff of organisers, and the campaign at present is well under way with very substantial achievements to be recorded.

This shows very clearly that, in approaching this present division in the AFL, one can only approach it in relation to these basic questions—organisation of the unorganised, and one must bear in mind the successes the CIO has already achieved and the aggressiveness with which they are pushing forward the policy it adopted at the AFL convention.

In approaching the question of the policy, there are a number of other things that must be taken into consideration, including the role played by the various groups in the AFL during the period preceeding the actual suspension order on August 5th. We had a number of discussions in the P.B. on the question, and following those discussions, we also had discussions with Lewis and Hillman, the two outstanding leaders of the CIO.

During the entire period following the Atlantic City convention, the CIO had made their struggle entirely within the framework of the upper bodies of the AFL. At no time had they directed any appeals to the local unions, to the central bodies, such as the Federations of Labor, etc., that is, appeals of a public character, calling upon them to join with the policies of the CIO and against those of the Executive Council. We were of the opinion that the CIO should have made such appeals, and we took it up with them.

It should be pointed out that the Party, throughout the entire period, had appealed to the local unions, to the central bodies, the State Federations of

Labor, and had introduced resolutions in these bodies calling for endorsement of the steel drive and of the general drive to organise the mass production industries and against the threats of a split being made by the Executive Council.

In placing this question before Lewis and Hillman, they took the position that it was quite all right for us to issue these appeals, that they appreciate the efforts we were making to rally the lower organisations of the trade unions, but their contention was that if they undertook to make these direct appeals to local bodies, it would further prejudice their case and give a weapon to the Executive Council that it was unnecessary to give them.

Whether or not this policy on their part was correct is, of course, a matter of debate, but at any rate, they insisted, and pursue consistently a policy of limiting their activities to setting up of organising committees, building of unions, etc., to the fight at the top of the AFL, without such appeals at the bottom.

As the question approached a climax, when they were summoned to appear before the Executive Council to answer charges of insubordination, dual unionism, etc., there again, the question arose as to the tactics that should be followed. We had discussions in the P.B., and at the outset, there were some who thought that we should publicly urge the CIO to accept the summons, appear before the Executive Council, make their fight there, and, in that way, try to prevent the expulsion from taking place, or, at least, to arouse sentiment against the suspension. This also was discussed with Lewis and Hillman and they were absolutely opposed to such a policy. They contended, and correctly, that if they appeared before the Executive Council in response to the summons issued, it would already legalise the proceedings being carried out by the Executive Council, would indicate on their part acceptance of the whole procedure being followed, and that, under the constitution of the AFL, the whole action of the Executive Council is quite contrary to both the letter and spirit of the constitution. The constitution specifically states that no union can be suspended or expelled from the AFL except by a two-thirds vote of the convention, and it was their opinion that, to go before the Executive Council and there argue the case, was already to grant that the Executive Council had power that the constitution specifically failed to give them, and also that, considering that the Executive Council is stamped so completely against them, with only one vote for the CIO group, despite the fact that they have 40% of the membership, and that there are about 13 or 14 for the reactionary group, it is clear this would have prejudiced their case completely.

Secondly, there was the question as to whether or not the CIO would already declare its intention of going to the convention in Tampa, that will be held at the end of November, and there carry on a fight for a seat in the convention, despite the suspension order, or whether they will ignore the Tampa convention. There again, in our discussion, there were those of us who took the position that one cannot lay down the rule as a dogma that, in any and all circumstances, the fight must be carried at the Tampa convention; that it is something that will have to be determined by the relationship of forces, by the response in the local unions, in the state conventions of the federations of labor, in the various international unions, etc., and the fight is carried to Tampa only providing there is a real opportunity there to develop the fight on a basis that will further the movement and discredit the policies of the Executive Council.

There were some comrades, particularly Comrade Foster, who thought we must come out and criticise the CIO for not already declaring its intentions of taking such a course. Then, there was the question of legal action. There again, Comrade Foster was of the opinion that we should publicly call on the CIO to throw the whole thing into the courts, challenging the power of the Executive Council to carry out its suspension order, and undertaking to win such a court battle.

Without in any sense being against court action as a matter of principle, we were against any public declaration that would already put us in the position of appearing to attack the CIO leadership at the very moment that the Executive Council was attempting by every means to justify this suspension order by placing the blame on them.

We discussed all of these question with Lewis, and we discussed also a declaration that had been made by [David] Dubinsky, one of the CIO leaders, that could only be accepted as implying a determination on their part to set up a new center, a new parallel AFL.

On the first question, the question of going to Tampa. Lewis took this decision—that they were going to do nothing that would commit them to Tampa, nor would they do anything that would prejudice their fight at Tampa, if such a fight could be made. He said that it was their intention to strive to influence every convention that was held between the date of the first suspension order and the Tampa convention, and in each case they would exert the maximum of their influence to get this convention to go on record against the action of the Executive Council. If, in this work prior to the convention, it appeared there would be those forces which would have a voice in the AFL who would carry forward the fight there against the suspension order and for their reinstatement, they would consider sending all of their forces there to join in such a fight from the outset, but, he said, if those developments did not take place, and we who are outside the AFL would not be given a voice on the floor of the convention and would never get our people inside the hall, if we go to Tampa then and stand around the corridors for a few weeks, every capitalist newspaper in America will ridicule us and say we came to Tampa, stood around in the corridors begging to be heard, were laughed at by everyone, and finally picked up our bags and started to walk back to New York. He said this would discredit us in the eyes of large masses of workers and make it appear that, instead of being powerful unions that could stand on their own feet and dictate terms to this group that is deliberately wrecking the unions, we would be in quite the opposite position—of begging them in a most unprincipled manner to get in. He did not think, under such circumstances, that it would be the correct policy to follow.

Secondly, as to legal action, he pointed out that in this case it could be taken any time up to within six months after the convention of the AFL took place at Tampa, and that certainly they were not closing the door to possibilities of such action, but there again, they were not going to take the position of throwing this into the courts at this time because, in doing so, in their opinion they would hamper the development of their struggle inside other unions, because the Executive Council could declare, they are taking an inner-union controversy into the courts and attempting to settle it there without giving the convention membership an opportunity to make their decision.

As for the question of setting up a new center, I think we should understand that if this split continues, inevitably the Lewis group will set up a new center. But the question that arises, and that was discussed with them, was the steps that would be taken now—whether this center would be set up immediately in this period, thereby closing the door to a great extent to the development of struggle inside the AFL, or whether this would come as the culmination of a real struggle for reunification of the movement on the basis of the principle issues the fight started over..

Lewis suggested that we should not lose sight of the fact that, with the suspension order by the Executive Council, the fight only began in the AFL; this was in no sense the culmination of the fight, but the beginning, and then he went on to illustrate practically what he meant by this declaration. He pointed out that the Executive Council will have to go before the convention and there submit its whole policy for ratification; that, in the convention, regardless of the form it takes, there will be a big battle there; he doubts whether the CIO will be able to get a majority against the Executive Council in the convention, but, majority or no majority, there will be a big fight on this issue.

I might say in parenthesis that, since the suspensions took place, the international union of Hotel & Restaurant Employees met in Rochester, N.Y. It is a union that has not been associated with the CIO and was considered one of the more conservative unions in the AFL. This union, with only one dissenting vote, went on record against the policy of the Executive Council and for withdrawal of the suspension order against the CIO.

The Teachers' Union met in Philadelphia and took similar action. So, at least those two international unions which met since the decision had both gone on record against the Executive Council.

As for the State Federations of Labor, some 18 had met before I left and 16 of these had gone on record against the policies of the Executive Council and for the policies of the CIO.

If one considers the central bodies, then the biggest central bodies in the country, in all decisive cities, have gone on record endorsing the policies of the CIO, except in New York, but even there the CIO is making an approach to the leadership, as is shown by the fact that they met with the president of the State Federation of Labor, and with [Joseph] Ryan, secretary of the Trades Assembly, both of whom came into the American Labor Party and are working there with the CIO.

In such circumstances, it is clear that Lewis is absolutely correct in emphasising the fact that, quite aside from the position the CIO unions will occupy in relation to Tampa, whether there in person or not, there will be a tremendous fight at the convention around this issue, but he points out that even at the convention, assuming it endorses the policy of the Executive Council, the fight is by no means over, because the Executive Council must then proceed to instruct every central body, every State Federation of Labor, to purge itself of those unions that have been suspended. Lewis also points out that just as soon as they go down to the lower ranks, to the local central bodies, State Federations of Labor, etc., there, a purge will not and cannot take place. He points, for example, to Pennsylvania, which is a state controlled by the United Mine Workers, the Amalgamated, International, etc., etc., and if you purge those, they have no more labour movement left in the state. The same is true of Indiana, Ohio, Illinois, Kentucky, whole mining regions in the south, etc. The same is true of New York—if there is a purging of all the Needle Trades Unions, they have not much of a labour movement left there. So, if you consider it just in that sense and try to push this policy, and must go to the lower bodies and rank and file, they will meet with obstacles they cannot overcome.

In this connection, you must bear in mind the strength and influence of the unions they are attempting to expel, but you must also bear in mind that the unions, the leadership of which is trying to carry through the expulsion, are themselves split wide open on this question.

A few illustrations. For example, the Painters' Union in New York, which is one of the bodies that would be called upon to purge itself; also the Needle Trades Workers. But the whole Painters' District Council is under our leadership and is committed to left policies, in opposition to the national leadership. Take also in New York a local like the Musicians' Union, which is one-half the membership of the National Musicians' Union. This local in New York is committed 100% to our policy, and the other half that controls the national administration is allied with [William] Green and the Executive Council. An[d] so it is in union after union. In no case are these unions solid in support of the policies of the Executive Council, but it is safe to say that the unions of the CIO are solid in support of their policies, which is evidenced by the conventions held of the Miners', Amalgamated Clothing Workers, where, to a man and with tremendous enthusiasm, the unions rallied in support of their policies. This, I think, is of tremendous importance in determining the perspectives of the struggle.

One other point of utmost importance to bring out, and that grew out of conversations with Lewis, is that Lewis emphasised that there was another thing that had to be taken into consideration in connection with this whole fight—and that was the election campaign; that the reactionaries of the Republican Party, the Liberty League, etc., would inevitably try to exploit this whole division in the AFL to line up the reactionaries of the Executive Council behind the Landon-Liberty League campaign, by attempting to show that a victory for Roosevelt would be a victory for the Lewis group in the AFL and would virtually mean the policy of the administration in destroying the Executive Council leadership. He said, for that reason, they were consciously trying to avoid taking any course that would sharpen the struggle to the point where [William] Hutcheson, [Matthew] Woll and some individual Republicans in the Executive Council would be able to line up the whole Executive Council for their policies.

At any rate, he stressed that, in considering the question of legal action, in considering the question of forming a new center, and all other questions of that kind, they were doing this always with the election campaign in min[d] and with the objective of avoiding an issue that would throw votes away from Roosevelt to Landon. Incidentally, the correctness of emphasising this at the outset was made very clear by the speech of Landon on Labor Day, when he went out of his way to express his regrets at the division that had taken place in the AFL, his hopes for a united AFL, etc. It is well worth looking up this speech to see how cleverly they exploited it at the first opportunity.

Another point Lewis emphasised, which we think is of decisive importance, is that, under no circumstances must this inner-fight in the AFL be permitted to take on a character, or to overshadow the carrying forward of the steel campaign. He pointed out that the whole success of the CIO, a thing that would determine whether it won or lost its fight, would not be a mere battle, or whether or not they appeared at the Tampa convention, but it would be determined by whether or not they organised the steel industry. If they were successful in their steel campaign, it did not make any difference what the policy of the Executive Council was—that policy would be broken by the sheer weight of the developing mass movement around a successful steel campaign. But if, on the contrary, they failed in their steel drive, this would defeat them in the AFL more decisively than any action that might be taken by the Executive Council, and they could then justify their entire policy. He pointed out that the greatest danger was that a course be pursued to transfer all energies and attention to the inner fight to the neglect of carrying forward this campaign. He pointed out another thing in this connection, namely, that, if among the unorganised workers in the steel industry, in auto, rubber, etc., the whole issue became whether the AFL is right or whether the CIO is right, and became not a fight mainly against the steel corporations around the conditions of the workers, but carrying forward the batter [battle?] between the different groups in the AFL, this would have a confusing effect among the workers and set back the whole thing.

I cite this to show that both in our consideration of the question, in our discussions with the leaders of the CIO, the problem of the tactics being followed was approached not from the viewpoint of just unity in the abstract, but in relation to the indications of the whole fight, which includes the election campaign, the drive to organise the steel industry, the carrying forward of the principle fight in the AFL for class policies, etc.

After these discussions, we discussed the thing further in the P.B. and we came to this conclusion—that the fight for the reunification of the movement must be carried on in a manner that could in no way contribute, directly or indirectly, to giving weapons to the Executive Council; that we would not make any calls for Lewis or Hillman or the CIO as such to do this, that or the other thing in relation to the struggle, if, in so doing, this implied that we were attacking the general line of the CIO in the fight. It is our opinion that, in the main, taking into consideration the position of this group, they have waged a generally correct fight since the Atlantic City convention; that our fight is chiefly that of reaching the local unions, the central bodies, State Federations of Labour, building up of the militant forces in the various conventions that take place, and in each case, working in cooperation with the forces of the CIO in carrying on the fight.

It is our opinion also that, under no circumstances, should we advocate a policy directly or by implication that would mean the giving up of the issues of the organisation of the unorganised, of industrial unionism, or the liquidation of the CIO. There, the question was discussed: should we advise a course that would mean the liquidation of the CIO as an organised bloc in the AFL. We came to the conclusion—No, because if you liquidate the CIO and turn back to the Executive Council, the job of carrying on the work of organising the unorganised on any basis, we know from many years of experience, that not one single step would be taken in that direction, and through the dissolution of the CIO, you would make it impossible for any of the unions which are now carrying forward that fight to continue.

So, it is our opinion that the fight must be to win the AFL membership and the unions of the AFL for a unified trade union movement on the basis of the carrying forward of this campaign of organising the unorganised on an industrial union basis. We believe that any other course would weaken the whole fight and play into the hands of the Executive Council.

If you ask us our perspective, we say quite frankly that we believe that we are due for a period in the U.S. when there will be a divided trade union movement. We do not believe that the Executive Council, made up of the Greens, Wolls, Hutchesons and that group, will yield; we do not believe they will accept the CIO unions, because these people are fully conscious that if the CIO unions carry forward their present policy and are successful in organising these basic industries, it means the political death of these people who are in control of the AFL. There is no doubt but that the suspension was carried through because they knew they were reaching the end of their rope, where they would be destroyed as the leadership, and they are perfectly willing to split the movement in two, or even further, if, by doing so, they can hold on.

I do not think any manoeuvre that will be carried through can overcome such a situation as that, and that the fight for a unified trade union movement can best be served by boldly and aggressively going along with the drive the CIO is making. The one thing we should be on guard against and should press Lewis, Hillman and the others to avoid, is that, in the setting up of a center that will inevitably follow during the course of the next 6 or 8 months that will unite those unions that are suspended, we must avoid any policy that will mean the bringing of all forces of the AFL from the other unions out into this bloc. For example, if, in Pennsylvania, the Pennsylvania State Federation of Labor refuses to purge itself of the CIO unions, the question there is: should Lewis, Hillman, etc., take the whole Pennsylvania labour movement, which would include carpenters, plasterers, barbers, etc., into the CIO, thereby bringing about a split in every international union of the CIO? We say, No; that inside the unions still in the AFL, unity must be maintained and the fight carried on inside these unions and inside the AFL as well for unity, on the basis of the carrying forward of the policies that the CIO at the moment typify.

Certainly, under no circumstances, would we pursue a policy of indifference when our holding them together[1]

The question now is whether the CIO, in holding its own forces together, should call to its banner other trade unions that support its general policies, or whether it should carry forward the fight within the AFL unions in support of its general policies and for unity.

It is our opinion this latter course should be adopted, and, from the discussions we had with Lewis, it would appear, at least now, that they are ready to follow such a policy.

There are many secondary questions arising with this whole situation, but I think, in the main, this presents our viewpoint. (In answer to question by Mingulin:)

Lewis agreed to this in the conversations I had with him less than a week before I left. I would say that, so far, the differences between Lewis and us are that Lewis, Hillman, and their group have limited their activities in mobilising support for their fight to the more or less apparatus connections within the AFL. For example, at the Hotel and Restaurant Employees' convention, Lewis and Hillman had approached a whole group of the leading people there, whereas we had approached a series of local unions and we had a strong fraction and left-wing group. At the convention, on this, we had a common policy with those who had been lined up by Lewis, working in his way, and this line-up by us, working in our way, but generally, our role has been to carry on the fight at the bottom, whereas theirs has been limited to carrying it on at the top. But, to an increasing degree, during the past period, they have shown a readiness to consult with us and make known their policy.

To show the degree to which they have shown a friendliness towards us, I can cite a few things. For example, at the beginning of the steel drive, on instructions of the P.B., I met with Lewis and raised the question of the reinstatement of all Communists and militants who had been expelled by the Tighe leadership of the American [Amalgamated] Association of Iron, Steel and Tin Workers. He asked for a list of those names. We provided him with it and immediately, all were reinstated. Then, we raised the question of placing a number of Communists and militant workers on the paid organising staff, contending that only to the degree that militants, who had the confidence of the workers, were on the staff, could the campaign be successful. Here again, he asked us for our recommendations, and Comrade Stachel estimated, the day before I left, that we now have approximately 45 or 50 Communists on the full-time organising staff of steel.

All this shows not only that they have shown a readiness to cooperate in discussions and words, but that they have brought our people in everywhere.

I might also add that, on this question of inner-union democracy in the Miners', Lewis is carrying through elections, real honest elections, honest as compared with what existed in the Miner[s]' Union before; he is opening up regular nominations in the local unions and carrying through regular elections. In some districts they have not seen them since 1920 or 1921. Yet, this is being done, not in all districts yet, but, nevertheless, he is yielding to the point where he sees the necessity of granting in his own union what he is demanding for himself in the AFL. I might also add that in a whole series of miners' locals, during this period and in these elections, Communists have been elected into the leadership, and this in no sense without his knowledge. As for reinstatements in the Miners' Union also, a whole series of our comrades have been reinstated.

. . .

1. The page ends here, in the middle of the sentence. The next page begins a new paragraph. The pages are numbered consecutively, and none appear to be missing.

of the steel drive, on instructions of the P.B., I met with Lewis
and raised the question of the reinstatement of all Communists and
militants who had been expelled by the Tighe leadership of the
American Association of Iron, Steel and Tin Workers. He asked for
a list of those names. We provided him with it and immediately,
all were reinstated. Then, we raised the question of placing a
number of Communists and militant workers on the paid organising
staff, contending that only to the degree that militants, who had
the confidence of the workers, were on the staff, could the campaign be successful. Here again, he asked us for our recommendations, and Comrade Staćhel estimated, the day before I left, that
we now have approximately 45 or 50 Communists on the full-time organising staff of steel.

                                        they have
     All this shows not only that ~~he has~~ shown a readiness to
cooperate in discussions and words, but that they have brought
our people in everywhere.

     I might also add that, on this question of inner-union
democracy in the Miners', Lewis is carrying through elections,
real honest elections, honest as compared with what existed in
the Miner' Union before; he is opening up regular nominations in
the local unions and carrying through x regular elections. In
some districts they have not seen them since 1920 or 1921. Yet,
this is being done, not in all districts yet, but, nevertheless,
he is yielding to the point where he sees the necessity of granting in his own union what he is demanding for himself in the AFL.
I might also add that in a whole series of miners' locals, during
this period and in these elections, Communists have been elected
into the leadership, and this in no sense without his knowledge.

DOCUMENT 13. Page 17 of Clarence Hathaway, "Report of Situation in
U.S.A. and Work of Party," given to a meeting of the Marty Secretariat, 15
September 1936.

Document 14

Mingulin to Dimitrov, 25 August 1936, RTsKhIDNI 495–14–55a. Original in Russian with handwritten annotation. "D.U. (USA)" probably refers to the *Daily Worker*, of which Hathaway was chief editor. Because the British party newspaper had the same name, "USA" would be needed.

File: The issue has already been resolved favorably

Georgi Mikhailovich! *(D)*

You have probably already read Browder's telegram about the situation in the AFL.

I agree completely with your answer to my note concerning Comrade Hathaway's coming here for discussion of the work of the D.U. (USA). In fact, that will be hard to do without discussing other issues with the Central Committee delegation. But in connection with Comrade Browder's telegram two other issues arise. One thing is clear from the telegram: we are, as it were, forced to follow in Lewis's footsteps and have linked ourselves too closely. It is possible that this is not completely the case, and also that party policy in this matter is completely correct. But we do not have sufficient information.

The delegation from the Central Committee will be able to be here only after the elections, i.e., at the beginning of December. This is after the AFL congress, the most important congress in the AFL's history. For there to be a maximum guarantee of correct policy in relation to the AFL, I think it would be essential to make use of Hathaway's trip to Europe and listen to his information about the situation in the AFL and our tactics.

This also relates to the development of the Farmer-Labor Party. This matter seems to have really gotten started with the formation of a workers' party in New York by the trade unions. The right wing of the Socialist Party has already entered this party. This party is also the work of Lewis's movement, and the plan is that after the elections it is supposed to become a party of national dimensions. For now, it will put up candidates for Congress and others from New York; in 1938, candidates from other states; and in 1940, a presidential candidate. The party decision makers declare that they will not allow Communists in. Our comrades are urging the trade unions to join this party. Browder asks us in the telegram to give our opinion on this matter. But again, from here, in print, one cannot get a full picture of the situation. Hathaway would be able to give information about this issue as well.

Thus I propose that Hathaway come here exclusively for information, which is extremely necessary. In September it will have been half a year since Browder and Foster left, and we still have another three or four months until the next delegation; for this reason, and in view of two or three important issues on which it would be extremely useful and urgent to receive detailed information, a trip by Hathaway for this purpose would be useful.

These are my thoughts in brief. I await your instructions.

(I. MINGULIN) *I. Mingulin*

25.VIII.1936

The Nazi-Soviet Pact and Its Aftermath

The Nazi-Soviet Pact

On 23 August 1939 Nazi Germany and the Soviet Union signed a nonaggression treaty that divided Central Europe between them and facilitated the Soviet Union's supply of fuel and raw material for the German war machine. Although officially neutral, the Soviet Union became a de facto nonbelligerent ally of Nazi Germany. When Hitler followed this pact up by invading Poland on 1 September, American Communists found themselves faced with what seemed to be an ideological impasse. Since 1936, the CPUSA had been calling for an anti-Nazi alliance comprising Britain, France, the United States, and the Soviet Union to oppose Hitler, as well as for a domestic center-left alliance behind President Roosevelt and his New Deal program. The Popular Front had been a tremendous asset to the growth of the American Communist movement. At a time when most democratic leaders seemed reluctant to confront Hitler, Communists appeared to stand as moral exemplars in the fight against fascism.

There are few more telling illustrations of the loyalty of American Communists to Stalin than their reaction to the Nazi-Soviet Pact. There was never any question that the CPUSA would support the pact; the only problem seemed to be an initial confusion over how to show that support, for the Comintern had not given the rest of the Communist world any advance warning, nor had it laid the groundwork for the Soviet Union's abrupt reversal of policy.

The Nazi-Soviet Pact severely damaged the CPUSA's alliance with New Deal liberals. Many of the Popular Front organizations collapsed when the Communists insisted that the groups support

the pact. Under Communist pressure the Hollywood Anti-Nazi
League changed its name to the Hollywood Committee for Democratic Action and ceased calling for an anti-Nazi alliance; the organization lost much of its movie-industry support, along with its
ability to raise money for Communist-backed causes. When the
League of American Writers supported the pact, it lost so many of
its prominent liberal members that its letterhead had to be dis-
carded. In the CIO, Communist trade union leaders found themselves on the defensive when pro-Roosevelt workers reacted angrily
to Communist attacks on the president's policies.

The party itself also suffered a significant loss of members.
The CPUSA was often secretive or vague about actual membership, and the opening of the Moscow records provides a much-
needed documentary base for assessing its size. But even with
these records it is difficult to develop a consistent set of figures
because the party used different definitions of membership at different times. For example, on 1 January 1939, party records
show an "enrolled" membership of 88,000. However, of these,
only 66,000 were "registered," that is, had renewed their membership with a party club. Further, of these registered members,
only 46,000 were "dues-paying" members during the first seven
months of 1939. But however one measures it, these figures
show rapid growth during the Popular Front period. Using comparable figures, we find that on 1 January 1937 there were
38,000 registered members, increasing to 54,000 on 1 January
1938, and peaking at 66,000 on 1 January 1939.[36]

After the Nazi-Soviet Pact, the party lost members for two years.
Its registered membership dropped to 55,000 in January 1940 and to
50,000 in 1941. Only some of these losses, however, were due to
disillusionment with the Nazi-Soviet Pact. Nearly half of the loss
occurred when the party dropped 7,500 immigrants who had not
applied for U.S. citizenship to protect them from the risk of deportation. And some of the losses were undoubtedly due to other causes.
Therefore, at most, only about 13 percent of the party membership

36. Nat Ross, "Organisational Status and Organisational Problems of the CPUSA,"
27 August 1939, RTsKhIDNI 515–1–4083; "Report of J. W. [John Williamson,
CPUSA organizational secretary]," 27 May 1941, RTsKhIDNI 515–1–4209.

could be said to have left in reaction to the pact. This means that about 87 percent took the pact in stride. John Williamson, the CPUSA organizational secretary, estimated that the loss of dues-paying members was even less significant: for the twelve-month period from September 1939 to August 1940, membership averaged 44,000, only 2,000 fewer members than the monthly average for 1939 before the pact. These figures suggest that antifascism, sometimes said to have been a defining characteristic of rank-and-file Communists, was less important to them than loyalty to the Soviet Union.[37]

The first weeks after the signing produced confused statements from American Communists who were uncertain about what Moscow wanted them to say. Several attempted to reconcile the pact with the party's antifascist stance by presenting it as a clever ruse on Stalin's part to restrain Nazi aggression. The day after the signing was announced, Earl Browder told the *New York Times* that the pact made "a wonderful contribution to peace," and the *Daily Worker* proclaimed that "German fascism has suffered a serious blow."[38] Hitler's invasion of Poland put a stop to this rhetoric.

Some Communists, on the other hand, while defending the pact as a practical necessity for Soviet survival, stuck to the party's earlier aggressive anti-Hitler stance, calling for a broad alliance against the Germans. For a few days they applauded the Polish resistance to the blitzkrieg. This was not what Moscow wanted, however, particularly after 17 September, when the Soviet Union took advantage of Poland's war with the Germans in the west to attack from the east; the Soviet Union soon occupied the eastern half of Poland.

Although it had given them no warning, once the attack had begun, the Comintern was free to give American Communists clear instructions about the appropriate response. Earlier, in December 1938, Browder had visited Moscow, at which time the Comintern instructed him to acquire a short-wave radio, on which the Soviets

37. T. Ryan [Eugene Dennis], "The Organizational Position of the CPUSA," 1 April 1941, RTsKhIDNI 515-1-4091; "Report of J. W.," 27 May 1941, RTsKhIDNI 515-1-4209. In his 1941 report, Dennis estimated that the January 1939 registered membership was 65,000, rather than the 66,000 reported above.
38. *New York Times*, 24 August 1939, 9; *Daily Worker*, 23 August 1939, 1.

could send him coded messages. (Browder's aide was to tune in to a prearranged frequency at specific times.)[39] But no messages came until a week after the Nazi-Soviet Pact, when Dimitrov sent a brief warning by coded cable: "According to the new situation I propose that the automobile man start to work with us from the tenth this month."[40] ("Auto" or "automobile" work were codes for short-wave radio operations; "automobile man" referred to the radio operator.)

Shortly thereafter, CPUSA leaders received a series of messages that instructed them to make a sharp break with past policies. **Document 15** is one of these messages; in it, the Comintern informs Browder of the new CPUSA stance toward the war. Years later Browder gave an abbreviated version of this message to Philip Jaffe, who published it in his *Rise and Fall of American Communism* (1975). But the book omits a section in which Browder was personally chastised for remaining "a captive of tenets that were correct before the European war but are now incorrect." The complete text is printed here for the first time. Although there are many minor wording and stylistic dissimilarities between document 15 and Jaffe's text, they probably reflect nothing more than the difference between the original Russian text (which we have translated here) and the text Browder gave Jaffe, which was both translated and deciphered.[41]

In this message, the Comintern informed American Communists that "any basis for contrasting 'bourgeois democracy' and fascism is disappearing. By the same token, the prerequisites for a 'democratic' front have been undermined." Communists used the name Democratic Front in 1939 for what had originally been called the Popular Front. Dimitrov is here telling Browder that the Popular Front is over. The CPUSA was also directed to "stop following Roosevelt's lead." This was painful news for Browder, who had invested himself heavily in an alliance with Roosevelt; nonetheless,

39. Philip J. Jaffe, *The Rise and Fall of American Communism* (New York: Horizon Press, 1975), 40.

40. Brother to Son and Earl [Browder], 1 September 1939, RTsKhIDNI 495–184–8, 1939 file. "Brother" and "Son" were cover names for Dimitrov, head of the Comintern, and Rudy Baker, head of the CPUSA underground.

41. The text Browder gave Jaffe is in Jaffe, *Rise and Fall of American Communism*, 44–47.

he obeyed the order.[42] In the late fall of 1939 the CPUSA began sharply criticizing Roosevelt, and in 1940 the party tried to block his reelection.

Document 15 also deals with the appropriate stance the United States should take toward the combatants. The U.S. neutrality law of the 1930s provided that in the event of war the United States would impose an embargo on sales of military goods to belligerents. In accordance with this law, when the Spanish Republic faced a revolt by the forces of General Francisco Franco in 1936, the United States refused to sell badly needed supplies to the Spanish government—even as Nazi Germany and fascist Italy provided Franco's forces with ample aid. Antifascists were determined that the U.S. law should differentiate between aggressor and victim; they did not wish to see the United States refuse to sell military supplies to the next victim of Hitler's aggression. Before the Nazi-Soviet Pact, Communists, as warriors in the antifascist cause, had been ardent supporters of this modification to U.S. neutrality law.

In paragraph "a" of document 15, the Comintern states that all belligerents are equally at fault: "Who started the war is not an issue." The policy had now been clarified, and the CPUSA immediately dropped its insistence that the law differentiate between aggressor and victim. When President Roosevelt, eager to aid the countries that were fighting Hitler, proposed that the neutrality law's embargo provisions be repealed, American Communists denounced him.

The new position was elaborated in another Comintern document, dated 28 October 1939 and entitled "Proposals Concerning the Work of the C.P. USA." Most of the document repeats points made in document 15, but it expands on one matter. The British navy had effectively cut Germany off from American trade, while Britain and France were able to buy American goods for their war industries, despite the fact that the United States remained officially neutral. This situation met with President Roosevelt's approval, for it allowed the United States to maintain official neutrality while in reality functioning as a nonbelligerent ally of Britain and France

42. The awkwardness Browder displayed in adjusting to the new policy is discussed in detail in James Ryan, *Earl Browder*, 159–69.

against Hitler. The arrangement was unacceptable to the Soviet Union, however, with its new relationship with Germany. The Comintern demanded that American Communists "agitate for a real and genuine neutrality by the USA, one which strictly prohibits the shipments of arms and war materials, or the granting of credits and loans."[43] Given the financial condition of Britain and France, a denial of credits and loans would have meant the end of their ability to support their war efforts with American industrial supplies. Had the United States adopted the policy, it is doubtful that Britain could have withstood the Nazi onslaught of 1940–1941.

From 31 May to 1 June 1940, immediately preceding its national convention, the CPUSA held a special antiwar conference in New York City that was attended by about 2,000 party officials and delegates. A microfilmed transcript of the proceedings was sent to Moscow. Every party leader of note and many local members spoke at length, opposing either assistance to Britain and France or American military preparation. Gilbert Green, a member of the Politburo, reminded the audience that one of the CPUSA's most important tasks was "to defend the first land of Socialism, the Soviet Union, and to win the wide masses for an understanding of its consistent socialist peace policy." Milton Wolff, the commander of the Communist-aligned veterans' organization of Americans who had fought with the International Brigades in Spain, assured the conference that those who had fought the fascists in Spain were opposed to any assistance to Britain and France. He denounced Vincent Sheean, an American journalist who had been a prominent backer of the Republican side in the Spanish Civil War, for "stabbing [Republican] Spain in the back" by supporting aid to countries that opposed Hitler. Wolff falsely accused a group of International Brigade veterans who supported aid to Britain and France of desertion during the Spanish Civil War.[44]

Jim West, a party organizer in Seattle, discussed the influential Communist role in the Washington Commonwealth Federation, at that time the leading New Deal political organization in the state

43. "Proposals concerning the Work of the C.P. USA," 28 October 1939, RTsKhIDNI 495–20–538.

44. Gilbert Green transcript, Milton Wolff transcript, antiwar conference, 31 May–1 June 1940, RTsKhIDNI 515–1–4178.

and a political power within the state Democratic Party. West reported proudly that "in Washington the W.C.F. was one of the first state organizations which correctly understood the changes which took place and transformed the program and methods of work to make the peace the central question confronting them."[45] By this, West meant that the federation had quickly followed the Soviet line and moved from supporting American aid to antifascist powers before the Nazi-Soviet Pact to opposing such aid afterward.

West noted that in early 1939 the Washington Commonwealth Federation had been "the first organization to launch the Draft Roosevelt Movement" (for a third term as president) but had responded to the pact by "putting on the brakes with rapidity and going on a new road of broad struggle against war and American involvement."[46] Before the Nazi-Soviet Pact, labor unions and political groups with a strong Communist presence had been among the earliest and most vocal advocates of Roosevelt's running for a third term, despite the tradition of two-term presidencies. As West boasts here, after the Nazi-Soviet Pact, these groups reversed course. He also noted that federation-backed candidates for local offices had defended the recent Soviet invasion of Finland; he praised this as a sign of the success of Communist work in Washington state politics.

(At a companion conference of Communist union organizers held at the same time, a CIO unionist spoke of how the party was aligning its work in the union movement to conform to its stand against Roosevelt's foreign policy. Reporting on Communist activity in the Minnesota CIO, the unionist noted that "we all understand the main fight is a fight against this war, we show no quarter to those people who have a tendency to line up the trade union movement in support of this [pro-Roosevelt] war program, but we must fight them and expose them all the way down the line.")[47]

Robert Minor, a veteran party leader and Browder's chief aide, delivered the keynote speech at the antiwar conference. Minor de-

45. Jim West transcript, antiwar conference, 31 May–1 June 1940, RTsKhIDNI 515–1–4178.
46. Ibid.
47. Transcript [speaker's name illegible], industrial conference, 31 May 1940, RTsKhIDNI 515–1–4180, p. 31.

voted his address to a defense of the Nazi-Soviet Pact. He dismissed Poland, which had been written out of existence by the pact, as simply a land mass with "artificial borders." (This accords with document 15, which describes Poland as "a reactionary multinational state built on the oppression of Ukrainians, Belorussians, and Jews.") He also quoted Stalin; "fascism is not the issue," he claimed, in one's response to Hitler's Germany. Rather, the chief villain is "British and French imperialism." Minor prophesied that the pact would "be looked upon by future centuries as a great landmark in the struggle against war."[48] (It should be noted that in the months immediately preceding Minor's speech, Hitler had invaded and conquered Denmark, Norway, the Netherlands, and Belgium. As Minor was speaking, German armies were completing their conquest of France.) Minor, then, apparently did not even try to reconcile the Soviet line with the party's own past pronouncements—or with unfolding current events—he simply accepted it, offering an open declaration of support.

Document 16 illustrates another way in which the CPUSA tried to accommodate itself to Comintern wishes. It is a 1940 memo written by Nat Ross, American referent in the Marty Secretariat and de facto American representative to the Comintern. Moscow had instructed the CPUSA to convince prominent noncommunists to write brochures and make statements defending the Nazi-Soviet Pact. Ross requested more precise guidance about what the CPUSA was supposed to do, commenting: "The best results would be obtained if the CC CPUSA were informed in essence of what type of brochures the ECCI considers necessary, and on that basis the CC would be able to decide which prominent noncommunists among the intelligentsia and the trade union movement could best write such brochures for wide mass consumption and mass influence."

As possible authors, Ross suggested Theodore Dreiser, one of the country's leading novelists: "I am inclined to believe he would write it and undoubtedly with the assistance of the Party." Dreiser had aligned himself closely with the Communists since the late 1920s but did not officially join the party until 1945. In 1941 (after

48. Robert Minor transcript, antiwar conference, 31 May–1 June 1940, RTsKhIDNI 515–1–4175.

Ross's memo was written) he published *America Is Worth Saving,* a pamphlet that argued that the United States had no interest in the outcome of the war between Nazi Germany and Great Britain and should neither intervene nor provide aid to countries fighting Hitler.[49]

Ross commented that another potential pamphlet writer, the prominent journalist Anna Louise Strong, had been "somewhat confused on the meaning of Soviet-German relations"—a delicate reference to the bewilderment felt by some of the party's allies at the rapid shift in the Communist attitude toward Nazi Germany. Nonetheless, Ross believed that Strong "would write only what is okayed by the CP USA." He also discussed the Rev. Harry F. Ward, Corliss Lamont, Mary Van Kleeck, and Frederick Vanderbilt Field as possible authors.

Ward and Lamont were then and remained throughout their lives two of the most prominent noncommunists to consistently defend Soviet communism. Ward was a member of a vocal group of socially active Christian clergy who supported Soviet causes. In 1940 he chaired the American Civil Liberties Union (ACLU) as well as the American League for Peace and Democracy, an organization that brought together liberals, leftists, and Communists behind a Popular Front political program. Lamont, one of the founders of the National Council for American-Soviet Friendship, also served on the national board of the ACLU. Although both Ward and Lamont had signed a statement, published 14 August 1939, asserting that it was a "fantastic falsehood" to say that Nazi Germany and Soviet Russia had anything in common, each supported the pact without apparent reservations.[50] The American League for

49. Theodore Dreiser, *America Is Worth Saving* (New York: Modern Age Books, 1941). Dreiser believed that the United States should expend neither men nor money to save the British Empire, which he considered evil.

50. This public statement was signed by four hundred Popular Front intellectuals and activists; it denounced those who claimed parallels between Soviet Communism and Nazism. This statement was a response to a spring 1939 public letter from the Committee for Cultural Freedom, an organization of anti-Communist liberals and leftists, that had declared both Communists and fascists to be enemies of democracy. See William L. O'Neill, *A Better World: The Great Schism; Stalinism and the American Intellectuals* (New York: Simon and Schuster, 1982), 14–15; Guenter Lewy, *The Cause That Failed: Communism in American Political Life* (New York: Oxford University Press, 1990), 50–53.

Peace and Democracy dropped its support for an antifascist foreign policy. This move caused so many liberals to leave the organization that it collapsed, but Ward and Lamont adopted a stance that opposed Roosevelt's attempts to aid the anti-Nazi belligerents.

Mary Van Kleeck, a leading social worker, also signed the 14 August statement and also accepted the Nazi-Soviet Pact from the first. In late 1939 Van Kleeck gave an important speech in New York City to social workers about how the profession should view the war in Europe. Her speech was published in *Social Work Today,* a journal backed by Communist-led social workers unions, and in 1941 (soon after Ross wrote document 16) it was turned into a pamphlet, entitled "Social Work, Peace, and the People's Well-Being." Van Kleeck condemned American assistance to the anti-Hitler belligerents, defined the Nazi-Soviet Pact as a "new basis for collective security in . . . Europe," and denied that the Soviet annexations of Estonia, Latvia, and Lithuania were acts of conquest; rather, they resulted from "pacts of peace and economic cooperation."[51]

Field, a scion of the Vanderbilt family, had taken on the task of organizing the American Peace Mobilization, the peace front adopted by the CPUSA during the Nazi-Soviet Pact period. Field remained closely aligned with the CPUSA throughout his life: he even went to prison in 1951 for defying a court order to hand over records of a Communist-aligned organization to a federal judge. But he continually denied being a member of the party until 1983, when he admitted in his autobiography that he had been a secret Communist since 1934.[52]

---

51. Mary Van Kleeck, "Social Work, Peace, and the People's Well-Being," *Social Work Today,* pamphlet no. 7 (February 1941). The text was also printed in the March 1940 issue of *Social Work Today.* Van Kleeck's role as a leader of left-wing social workers is discussed in John Earl Haynes, "The Rank and File Movement in Private Social Work," *Labor History* 16, no. 1 (1975): 78–98.

52. Frederick V. Field, *From Right to Left: An Autobiography* (Westport, Conn.: Lawrence Hill, 1983).

Document 15

To Browder, "Despite the Fact That Since Our Telegram . . . ," RTsKhIDNI 495–74–469. Original in Russian. This document is not dated, but internal references place it in late September 1939.

Dear Comrade Browder:

Despite the fact that since our telegram you have taken some steps to correct the erroneous position of your party as regards the European war, your speech in Cleveland demonstrates that you nevertheless remain a captive of tenets that were correct before the European war but are now incorrect. It is not simply that we Communists characterize that war as imperialist, but rather that the war is bringing about such radical changes in the entire international situation, changes that compel Communists of all countries to make a radical shift in the tactics of Comparties. What are these changes? First, the war plunges the capitalist world into a state of acute and profound crisis. At issue here is not only fascism, but the very existence of the entire capitalist system. The issue of fascism is secondary; the main and fundamental issue is the struggle against capitalism, against bourgeois dictatorship, irrespective of which political guise it assumes or which hypocritical slogans it employs to conceal its imperialist aims in both the belligerent and the neutral countries. Second, war is the most virulent manifestation of imperialist dissipation and reaction. In wartime the bourgeoisie of so-called bourgeois-democratic states pattern their own regimes after fascism (consider, for instance, the dispersal of the Communist party in France). The bourgeoisie of these countries have now assumed a stance toward the Soviet Union [literally, "the land of the Soviets"] more hostile than that of the fascist states. The ruling classes of the belligerent states are equally waging an imperialist war, equally acting as both the defending and the attacking parties in that war, equally stepping up bourgeois-dictatorship terror campaigns. Consequently, any basis for contrasting "bourgeois democracy" and fascism is disappearing. By the same token, the prerequisites for a "democratic" front have been undermined. Don't think that the USA will be an exception in this regard. Even remaining neutral, the USA with its powerful financial oligarchy take the same route as belligerent Europe—the path of intensified reaction, if for no other reason than that its bourgeoisie realizes that the war jeopardizes its continuing dominance. Third, workers can now contemplate prospects far broader than simply defending the remnants of "bourgeois democracy." We would be pedants, rather than revolutionaries, if we were to cling to the old slogans of a "popular" or "democratic" front at a time when the very underpinnings of capitalism are vulnerable. Moreover, the more the idea of a frontal assault against capitalism takes hold of the consciousness of the masses, the faster the higher-ups of the so-called democratic parties, too, will defect to the reactionaries' camp.

The task of American Communists is now to realize a militant unity of proletarian activities, to strengthen proletarian union with the farmers by independently mobilizing the masses against reaction and the intensification of capitalist exploitation.

We therefore think that the CPUSA should stop following Roosevelt's lead and instead take independent positions on all fundamental domestic and foreign policy issues. American Communists are against involving the American people in the war because they do not want the masses to die to benefit their imperialist exploiters. But is this position really identical with the American bourgeoisie's position of "neutrality"? Is "neutrality" really anti-imperialist? This neutrality was dictated by the predatory aspirations of American capital to use the European war to strengthen its own imperialist positions, to drive its competitors out of the market, to dominate the seas and oceans, and to become the all-powerful ruler over nations ravaged by the effects of the war. The American bourgeoisie are lifting the embargo because they hope to get rich off the poverty of other nations. But you, Comrade Browder, in your Cleveland speech, showed solidarity with this position instead of exposing its greedy imperialist character. You did not even find it necessary to remind the audience that the American bourgeoisie, proclaiming the defense of "democracy" against fascism, are Japan's primary military suppliers in its imperialist war against the Chinese people. We also feel you should take a more independent position with regard to [John L.] Lewis. We do not at all recommend that American Communists behave in such a way that they begin to be excluded from industrial trade unions. On the contrary, you must do everything in your power to thwart the reactionaries who wish to throw Communists out of industrial trade unions. But Communists should firmly defend their principled views and appropriately criticize the half-heartedness of the industrial trade union higher-ups, making clear to the masses the differences between the Communist party and Lewis.

In a few days, we will publish our position on the war and the changes in Communist party tactics. The arguments developed therein will allow you to understand the new tactical aims, which come down to the following:

a) The current war is imperialist, unjust, and equally reactionary for all warring capitalist powers. This is not a war of democracy against fascism, but a war between reactionary imperialist Germany and the reactionary imperialist states of England, France, and Poland. Who started the war is not an issue here. What is fundamental is that this war is being waged by states run by imperialist cliques. This is a war for imperialist supremacy.

b) This war is a continuation of the struggle between the rich powers (England, France, the USA), which are the backbone of the entire capitalist system, and the cheated states (Germany, Italy, Japan), who in their struggle for a new world order deepen and aggravate the crisis in the capitalist system.

c) The bourgeoisie of England and France rationalize this war of pillage by claiming it to be antifascist in character; Germany, by [claiming] it is fighting against the unjust remnants of the Versailles peace.

Document 15 *continued*

d) Poland was a reactionary multinational state built on the oppression of Ukrainians, Belorussians, and Jews. It decayed because of the corruption of the ruling classes. The international proletariat has no interest in the existence of such a parasitical state.

e) The Soviet Union, in coming to the aid of western Ukrainian and Belorussian workers, saved 11 million people from a capitalist hell, brought them into the ranks of socialism, assured their national and cultural development, and with all of its might secured them from foreign enslavement.

f) The war has created a new international order. As a result, the tactics of a single workers' and people's front loses its significance.

g) At the present stage of the war the Communists' task is to boldly, as befits Bolsheviks, fight against the war, vote against credits in belligerent and non-belligerent countries alike, concentrate their fire against the bourgeois dictatorship in their own countries, mercilessly expose social democracy, which has crossed over to the camp of imperialist reaction; in the neutral countries (above all the United States) to expose the bourgeoisie as profiteers and marauders of war and to hold high the banner of proletarian internationalism.

That's all for now.

Shaking your hand[1]

1. This is a standard friendly closing.

Document 16

Ross to Yovchuk, 20 December 1940, RTsKhIDNI 495–14–137. Original in English.

To Comrade Yovchuk;
Copy Marty Secretariat:

December 20, 1940.

With regard to prominent Americans (non-Communists) who would write effective brochures explaining and defending the peace policy of the Soviet Union and answering the arguments of the enemy, the following three stand out:

1. <u>Theodore Dreiser</u>. He would be the best choice because a brochure by Dreiser would reach and influence wide circles of the labour movement and the middle class. The question is whether Dreiser would undertake to write such a brochure since he has not written at length on such a question before. I am inclined to believe he would write it and undoubtedly with the assistance of the Party.

2. Anna Louise Strong. She returns to the USA in January with the advantage of having just spent a few months in the Soviet Union and having visited a

number of European countries since the outbreak of the war. The question with Strong is that she has herself been somewhat confused on the meaning of Soviet-German relations. I believe, however, she would write only what is okayed by the CP USA and she could write a good brochure.

3. Corliss Lamont. He has been for many years a leader of the Friends of the Soviet Union movement in the USA, and is the author of a number of books on the Soviet Union. The fact that he is the son of Thomas Lamont of J.P. Morgan and Company and has taken such a good position has also helped to give him a considerable mass reputation. Lamont is very competent to write a good brochure.

Both Strong and Lamont could reach a broad audience beyond the left wing circles but not as broad as Dreiser. There are a number of others who are qualified to write such brochures (Dr. Harry F. Ward, Mary Van Kleeck, Fredrick Field, etc.).

However, I believe that the best results would be obtained if the CC CPUSA were informed in essence of what type of brochures the ECCI considers necessary, and on that basis the CC would be able to decide which prominent non-Communists among the intelligentsia and the trade union movement could best write such brochures for wide mass consumption and mass influence.

Ross.   *Ross*

The "Just War of Defense"

In the spring of 1941 Eugene Dennis, a senior CPUSA official, arrived in Moscow to discuss the party's policies. After receiving Dennis's reports (described in chapter 3), the Comintern prepared instructions for the CPUSA. One draft, dated 18 June 1941, with annotations indicating that Dennis had helped prepare it, bore the title "On the Work of the Young Communist League of the USA." In it the Comintern acknowledged that "thanks primarily to the activity of the Communist Party and the Young Communist League of the USA Roosevelt and the American imperialist bourgeoisie have not been able to date to win the majority of the organized, progressive youth for their imperialist and reactionary policies." The Young Communist League was instructed to "intensify to the maximum its struggle on the ideological front by explaining patiently and reasonably to the broad sections of the American youth the imperialist nature of Roosevelt's policy, especially exposing his antifascist and national defense demagogy." Moscow further called on the YCL "to intensify the work in the trade unions and in the factories, combining legal with illegal forms of work."[53]

On 20 June the Comintern leadership wrote a "Draft Resolution on the American Question" (**document 17**) for transmittal to the United States. The document called for continued opposition to Roosevelt's program of aid to Britain, insisting: "It is of considerable importance that the party is continuing to wage the most systematic struggle and gathering the workers and the people to struggle against the aggressive imperialist policies of the Roosevelt administration and the ruling circles of monopolistic capital, which are prepared to bring the country totally into the war in the near future." The Comintern reminded the CPUSA of the need to carry on work within the American armed forces, both to promote the party's anti-intervention message and to gain military training for young Communists: "It is just as necessary that the party and the Young Communist League broadly popularize the Leninist stance of the struggle against the imperialist war and against militarism, and carry out serious work within the army and navy, as well as among the reserve officers of the training cadre (ROTC) and the civilian training centers for youth (CCC), and also make sure that the members and cadres of the party and the YCL receive military training and master military art and science."

Then, on 22 June, Germany invaded the Soviet Union. The Comintern dropped the 20 June draft, and on 26 June, Dimitrov sent the CPUSA the outline of an entirely different policy. This message—marked "Please decipher at once!"—stated that "the aggression of German fascism against Soviet Union has basically changed whole international situation and character of the war itself." Dimitrov informed the CPUSA that the anti-capitalist and anti-imperialist rhetoric of the Nazi-Soviet Pact period no long applied; the war was now to be seen as "neither a class war nor a war for socialist revolution" but a "just war of defense."[54]

---

53. "On the Work of the Young Communist League of the USA," 18 June 1941, RTsKhIDNI 495–73–106. A typewritten note on the document says it is "from Ran," probably a typographical error for Ryan, Eugene Dennis's pseudonym.

54. Dimitrov to New York, "The Aggression of . . . ," 26 June 1941, RTsKhIDNI 495–184–3, 1941 file.

Another coded Comintern cable reinforced the point that Marxist-Leninist slogans would be dropped for the time being. American Communists were urged to "keep in mind that at the given stage the question is about defense of peoples against fascist enslavement and not about socialist revolution."[55] And, as Dimitrov had explained in his cable of 26 June, the change of rhetoric must accompany a change of strategy: "This basic change of situation and of character of the war requires also a change in tactics of the Party. The main task now is to exert every effort in order to secure the victory of Soviet people and to smash the fascist barbarians. Everything must be subordinated to this main task. From this follows; first that the Communists and the working-class in America . . . with all forces and all means, must resolutely raise struggle against German fascism. Secondly, they must demand from the American government all aid to the Soviet people."[56]

As soon as news of the invasion reached the United States, American Communists knew that they would be changing their antiwar policy. But, as before, they were initially unsure of the line Moscow planned to take toward Britain and its allies. Consequently, their initial statements, while calling for the defense of the Soviet Union, did not at the same time urge assistance for those countries that had been fighting Hitler since 1939. The day after the invasion, for instance, the *Daily Worker* warned that the German attack on the USSR could lead to a new "Munich," a peace between Nazi Germany and Great Britain that would leave the Soviet Union alone to face Hitler.[57] Dimitrov dealt with this issue in his 26 June message. He ordered the CPUSA to drop its opposition to aid for Britain, explaining that Communists must "support all measures of the government which makes possible the continuation of the struggle of the Anglo-American bloc against fascist Germany; because this struggle itself is actually a help to the just war of the soviet people."[58]

55. "Perfidious Attack against . . . ," RTsKhIDNI 495–184–3, 1941 file. The date on this cable is partially illegible. The year (1941) and the month (June) are clear; the first digit of the day is a 2, but the second digit cannot be read. The attack was on 22 June; this cable was therefore sent between 22 and 29 June.
56. Dimitrov to New York, "The Aggression of . . . ."
57. *Daily Worker*, 23 June 1941, 1.
58. Dimitrov to New York, "The Aggression of . . . ."

The CPUSA adjusted its position as instructed. On 28 June the party adopted a program entitled "People's Program of Struggle for the Defeat of Hitler and Hitlerism" that complied with Dimitrov's directives. The statement denounced Nazi Germany as a menace not only to the Soviet Union but also to "the American people, the British people and the people of the world." Earlier opposition to aid for Britain vanished; instead, the CPUSA now demanded that all possible assistance be given to all countries fighting Hitler. The party then set about reviving its Popular Front coalition and presenting itself as an ardent backer of President Roosevelt.

The policies and behavior of the American Communist party during the period of the Nazi-Soviet Pact described here force modification of the conventional view that American Communists were ardent and committed antifascists. Certainly, they were leaders in the antifascist movement of the mid-1930s. The Popular Front was an effective tool for promoting the antifascist cause in the United States (and one of the party's best recruiting aids). But when Stalin allied himself to Hitler in 1939, American Communists did everything in their power to block American assistance to those fighting Nazi Germany. Even after Hitler invaded the Soviet Union, the CPUSA awaited a Comintern order before it supported aid to Britain. The essence of American communism was loyalty to Stalin.

Another point must be made regarding the behavior of the CPUSA during this period. In 1940 the party publicly severed its membership in the Communist International. This action was taken in response to the Voorhis Act. The CPUSA and the Comintern agreed that formal disaffiliation was preferable to compliance with the act. With private Comintern approval—the Comintern went so far as to provide the draft language used by the CPUSA to proclaim its independence—the formal disaffiliation took place at a special CPUSA convention on 16 November.[59] On 21 November Nat Ross, the CPUSA referent, reported on the proceedings to the presidium of the Comintern. He assured the Comintern that the CPUSA regarded the disaffiliation as a sham and that "in essence and in fact the entire Party membership . . . will be

59. The draft of the statement is found in Comintern cable, "If It Is Absolutely . . . ," 16 November 1940, RTsKhIDNI 495–184–15, 1940 file.

drawn still more closely under the banner of the Communist International."[60]

Document 17

"Draft Resolution on the American Question," 20 June 1941, RTsKhIDNI 495–20–513. Original in German. An abbreviated English-language version with the same title, dated 19 June 1941, was found in the same file. The Dies Committee was the House of Representatives' Special Committee on Un-American Activities, headed by Martin Dies.

> 5   Outgoing No. 51
> 21/VI 1941 Insert No._____[stamp]

"8"

Confidential!

6047/7/F
Copy
20.6.1941

Draft Resolution on the American Question

1) A characteristic feature of the present political situation in the United States consists of the struggle that is developing between two imperialist groups in the ranks of American finance capital in which each of these groups strives to realize the imperialist war aims and to strengthen the world domination of American imperialism.

In this situation, where American imperialism has already been deeply drawn into the war, [and] lengthens and spreads it, it is of considerable importance that the party is continuing to wage the most systematic struggle and gathering the workers and the people to struggle against the aggressive imperialist policies of the Roosevelt administration and the ruling circles of monopolistic capital, which are prepared to bring the country totally into the war in the near future.

At the same time it is the duty of the party to significantly strengthen its exposure of the equally imperialist policies of the so-called isolationist and appeasement groups of finance capital and to mobilize the masses against these groups, which advocate an agreement with German imperialism and, more openly than the Roosevelt forces, carry out an anti-Soviet and reactionary international policy. The party must make clear that these two most important imperialist groups, represented by Roosevelt-Willkie and Hoover-Lindbergh, pursue reactionary policies in both foreign and domestic areas

---

60. "Meeting of the Presidium of E.C.C.I. on the American Question," 21 November 1940, RTsKhIDNI 495–20–540.

Document 17 *continued*

that are against the national interests, welfare, and future of the American people, despite their differing tactical orientation to the question of whether to come to an agreement with English or with German imperialism about the redivision the world. Both groups follow warmongering and anti-Soviet policies; both groups are attempting to achieve the hegemony of American imperialism on a world scale. The party must make every effort, in contrast to both the imperialist groups and [their] plans, to solidify the growing antiwar and anti-imperialist people's front movement under the leadership of the workers and to create a third front, the front of the people, which is against the imperialist war and capitalist reaction, which wants to save the American people from the war, strives for a people's peace, and endeavors to protect the welfare and freedom of the American people.

2) Today more than ever, every decision, every action of the party, particularly the struggle for a people's peace, the establishment of friendly relations with the great land of socialism, must be based on the defense of the daily demands and the real national interests of the American people, and more than ever must it be expressed particularly clearly that they spring from those same things. In order for the party to be capable of mobilizing and decisively influencing the broad masses and for it really to strengthen, broaden, and lead the developing people's front of the struggle against the imperialist war and reaction, it is necessary that the party act still more effectively as a truly national party of the American working class, as the best defender of the happiness, welfare, and peace *of its* people and *its* nation, as an independent American party guided by the teachings of Marxism-Leninism, and develop itself as such.

3) As an organic component in the struggle against capitalist reaction and against America's being drawn into the war, everything must be done to bolster and expand the mass movement for the defense of the legal existence and democratic rights of the party. For this it is necessary for the party to consolidate its political influence and its links with the crucial strata of the working masses, that it strengthen still more the connection of the struggle for the defense of the party and the liberation of Comrade Browder and all jailed workers with the mass movement for the maintenance of the rights to organize and strike, for the protection of civil freedoms and toward guarding against the American people's being drawn into the war; that the party present itself even more energetically as the irreconcilable enemy of all **imperialists**—the German and Japanese just as much as the American and English—that it expose the reactionary international connections and role of the Morgans, Du Ponts, and Fords, the Catholic hierarchy, and such agents as the Dies Committee; that the party more tellingly expose the activity of the Nazi Bund, the Italian Fascists, the Christian front, the KKK, and other fascist groups at home and abroad and organize resistance against them.

4) In view of the growing persecution of the CPUSA and the efforts to place

it outside the law, it is also of definitive importance that the party, with particular decisiveness, overcome certain legalistic tendencies that still exist in its ranks and that it more thoroughly prepare itself to work even under conditions of the utmost difficulty. The party must turn its greatest attention to protecting the leading cadres from arrest and imprisonment—to really examining all cadres—vigilantly expose, fight, and be on the alert for spies and provocateurs and other agents of the enemy, and in the same way to organizing its most important work among the masses within and through the unions and broad mass organizations. At the same the party must see to it that on a countrywide scale as well as in the various states where the party stands in danger of being made illegal, timely provisions are undertaken for the building of all new legal mass organizations that may be necessary. In this regard it is advisable to pay particular attention to exploiting the existing possibilities of supporting in diverse forms the developing movement for independent political action by workers and farmers.

5) In carrying out the work of strengthening and leading the antiwar and anti-imperialist people's movement, it is urgently necessary that the party carry on a systematic ideological and political struggle against the social democratic and bourgeois reformist influence of the workers and progressive movement. In this connection it is necessary that all pacifist illusions and influences in the broad mass movement be energetically opposed as well as that all vestiges of pacifism be eradicated from the ranks of the party. While much attention is to be dedicated to the organizing of a broad people's movement, legal work among the masses, and the defense of the standard of living and the civil rights of mobilized youth and the working population, the democratization of the armed forces, and so forth, it is just as necessary that the party and the Young Communist League broadly popularize the Leninist stance of the struggle against the imperialist war and against militarism, and carry out serious work within the army and navy, as well as among the reserve officers of the training cadre (ROTC) and the civilian training centers for youth (CCC), and also make sure that the members and cadres of the party and the YCL receive military training and master military art and science.

6) At the present time the party is obliged to display the greatest political initiative and firmness in order to strengthen its vanguard role as well as its connection with the masses, in order to solve the new and complicated problems boldly and independently, in order independently, as Bolsheviks, to think and act in the interests of its own people and the working class, in the interests of proletarian internationalism and socialism. To carry this out, to guarantee that the party is up to these great obligations that now confront it, it is necessary today more than ever that the bolshevik unity of the party be maintained and strengthened at any price. All this demands above all that all factional elements be ruthlessly opposed and extirpated, that the party act in unity and in the comradely spirit of bolshevik self-criticism, and that genuine

political unity and collective work be established in the Politburo and in the CC under the leadership of comrades Browder and Foster.

The Downfall of Earl Browder

Although Stalin officially dissolved the Communist International in 1943 as a gesture of goodwill to his new allies, the staff of the Comintern's headquarters remained in operation as several secret "institutes" that were later integrated into the apparatus of the Communist Party of the Soviet Union (CPSU) in 1945. During this period Dimitrov and Browder had a policy disagreement, the outcome of which illuminates the nature of the CPUSA-Comintern relationship, all public pronouncements notwithstanding.

The roots of the disagreement lay in the events of June 1941, when, with Moscow's urging, Browder had thrown the CPUSA fully behind the war policies of President Roosevelt. American Communists now attempted, with considerable success, to convince the country to forget the party's behavior during the Nazi-Soviet Pact and to see them as loyal American leftists. The Popular Front was revived, and Communists resumed their weakened position in the CIO and on the left wing of the New Deal coalition. The Roosevelt administration also adjusted its policies. In view of the CPUSA's enthusiastic support for the war, authorities relaxed their use of internal security regulations against Communists. In May 1942, as a gesture of goodwill during the visit of Viacheslav Molotov, Stalin's minister of foreign affairs, Roosevelt commuted Browder's sentence for passport fraud and released him from prison.

By the end of 1943 the American Communist party had recovered from its setbacks during the Nazi-Soviet Pact period. Exhilarated by the party's growth, by Roosevelt's personal intervention in his case, and by the wartime atmosphere that allied communism with patriotism, Browder announced "the greatest, most important turning point in all history." This was the November 1943 meeting between Roosevelt, Winston Churchill, and Stalin at Teheran, where the three Allied leaders reached a series of agreements on military cooperation, strategy for the war in Europe, and conditions of the postwar peace. These accords were evidence, Browder claimed, that the ruling classes of the United States and Great Britain had put aside their hopes of destroying communism and had come to accept the Soviet Union as a full partner in world affairs. (This view and the lessons he drew from it came to be known as Browder's "Teheran doctrine.")[61]

Reflecting on the dissolution of the Comintern and on the Soviet insistence, quoted above, that the war was "not about socialist revolution," Browder believed that Stalin had decided not to renew the campaign for world revolution after the war. In addition, the leader of American communism saw little likelihood of a postwar social revolution in America and judged that even Europe would "probably . . . be reconstructed on a bourgeois-democratic, non-fascist capitalist basis, not upon a Soviet basis." In this situation Browder felt that Communists should work to prevent reactionaries from sabotaging long-term Soviet-American cooperation. The CPUSA should not "raise the issue of socialism in such a form and manner as to endanger or weaken national unity"; rather, it should be "ready to cooperate in making this capitalism work effectively."[62]

In his 1944 pamphlet *Teheran and America*, Browder offered a new (for Communists) analysis of America's domestic political system. Rather than seeing the two major parties as organs of the bourgeoisie, Browder decided that "these parties are parties only in a formal and legal sense; they are not parties in the sense of representing well-defined alternative policies. They are coalitions of local and regional interests, diverse tendencies of political thought, and institutionalized politics. . . . The two-party system [consists] in fact [of] coalitions of many groups that in most other countries would be separate parties."[63]

Although Communists had worked within the New Deal coalition in the late 1930s, the CPUSA had been careful to maintain its

61. Earl Browder, "Teheran—History's Greatest Turning Point," *The Communist* 23, no. 1 (January 1944): 3.

62. Ibid., 7, 19.

63. Earl Browder, *Teheran and America* (New York: Workers Library Publishers, 1944), 29, 40.

formal independence. In the minds of American Communists, the Popular Front was a tactical alignment, not a permanent strategy, and the party's formal independence was a sign that it kept as an option the possibility of opposing the Democratic Party. Browder called for a change, noting that "if the lesser group takes the name of party and becomes one of the so-called 'minor parties,' it is regarded as a sect which has withdrawn itself from the practical political life of the nation."[64] In effect, Browder condemned CPUSA independence as politically ineffective.

In line with these views, Browder ordered a sweeping restructuring of the American Communist movement. The Young Communist League dissolved and reformed as the American Youth for Democracy (AYD). This group presented itself as a broad, liberal-left organization of progressive youth: the AYD advocated neither Marxism-Leninism nor socialism. In May 1944 the Communist Party of the United States of America itself dissolved and reconstituted itself as the Communist Political Association (CPA). For Browder, Communists would now form the militant left wing of a broad progressive coalition; the CPA would function as a strong Marxist-Leninist advocacy group within the existing two-party system.

Browder announced his plans to dissolve the CPUSA at a January 1944 meeting of the party's National Committee, as the Central Committee was then called. Most of the leadership supported Browder's plans—at least, no one offered any serious criticism—and the National Committee unanimously voted to reorganize the CPUSA. Most of the party's rank and file also accepted Browder's dramatic recasting of Communist thinking without argument. Two senior Communists, however, had private doubts about the Teheran doctrine: Sam Darcy, the district organizer for eastern Pennsylvania, and William Z. Foster. Foster and Darcy prepared a letter to the party's leadership, signed only by Foster, that criticized aspects of Browder's new line. They did not attack Browder's plan to convert the CPUSA to a political association; rather, they took issue with Browder's vision of the postwar world. Browder proph-

64. Ibid., 40.

esied that big business would continue its wartime cooperation with the Roosevelt administration; Foster foresaw the inevitable breakdown of that cooperation and the need for Communists to take a more adversarial stance toward business in the future.

Browder did not allow the Foster letter to be published in the party press and limited its circulation to the Politburo and a few of the party's leading figures. At a February meeting of the Politburo, Browder and the rest of the CPUSA leadership attacked Foster and Darcy. The group voted to reject the letter, with only Foster and Darcy themselves dissenting. Browder had made it clear that Foster faced expulsion from party leadership if he continued to cause trouble, and Foster pledged to carry the matter no further. Darcy refused to submit, however, and as a test of Foster's loyalty, Browder ordered him to chair the commission that expelled Darcy from the CPUSA.

The only concession Browder allowed Foster was that he did send Dimitrov a cable, at Foster's request, that summarized Foster's letter. He also transmitted the entire text to Moscow through the Soviet diplomatic pouch. (At this point the CPUSA was referring a disagreement within its top leadership to a Soviet organization that on paper no longer existed and from which it had in any case disaffiliated itself.) Browder told Foster and other CPUSA leaders that in reply Dimitrov had urged Foster to withdraw his criticism. When the CPUSA met in convention on 20 May 1944 Foster, the figurehead chairman of the party, presided over a unanimous vote to dissolve the party. The delegates then proclaimed themselves the founding convention of the Communist Political Association and unanimously elected Earl Browder president. (His CPUSA title of general secretary was dropped as part of an effort to make the organization sound more American. In the same vein, the CPUSA Politburo became the CPA national board.)[65]

65. Browder's new policy and the Foster-Darcy dissent are discussed in James Ryan, *Earl Browder*, 217–36; Maurice Isserman, *Which Side Were You On? The American Communist Party during the Second World War* (Middletown, Conn.: Wesleyan University Press, 1982), 187–97; Jaffe, *The Rise and Fall of American Communism*, 57–63; and Harvey Klehr and John Earl Haynes, *The American Communist Movement: Storming Heaven Itself* (New York: Twayne, 1992), 103.

The CPA continued under Browder's unchallenged leadership until the following spring. Then, in April 1945, *Les Cahiers du communisme*, a theoretical journal of the Communist Party of France, published an article by Jacques Duclos, a senior French party official, entitled "On the Dissolution of the American Communist Party."[66] Duclos stated flatly that Browder's beliefs concerning the direction of the postwar world were "erroneous conclusions in no wise flowing from a Marxist analysis of the situation" and that his "notorious revision of Marxism" had led to the "liquidation of the independent political party of the working class." The article denied that the wartime Soviet-American agreements could be interpreted as laying the foundation for "a political platform of class peace in the United States in the postwar period" or that there was "the possibility of the suppression of the class struggle in the postwar period." Instead, the Teheran agreement was only "a document of a diplomatic character."[67]

When the Duclos article reached the United States, in May 1945, American Communists concluded that it was a message from Moscow: Duclos had no other reason to concern himself with the American party. Furthermore, he had quoted from Foster's letter, which was secret; it had been sent only to Moscow.

At this time Earl Browder was the undisputed leader of the American Communist party and had been so since the early 1930s. Virtually every major party official, and many of the minor ones, owed their positions to his approval. Indeed, most rank-and-file members had joined the party after he assumed office and had no memory of any other party leader. None of this counted when Moscow, however indirectly, repudiated him. In the Duclos article, Moscow was perceived to have spoken, and in June the Communist Political Association stripped Browder of his executive power; in July an emergency convention dissolved the CPA and reconstituted itself as the Communist Party of the United States of America. Later, the

66. Jacques Duclos, "A propos de la dissolution du P.C.A.," *Cahiers du communisme*, nouvelle série, 6 (April 1945): 21–38. For an English translation, see "On the Dissolution of the American Communist Party," *Political Affairs* 24 (July 1945): 656–72.
67. Duclos, "On the Dissolution of the American Communist Party," 656, 670.

CPUSA denounced its former leader as "an unreconstructed revisionist . . . a social-imperialist . . . an enemy of the working class . . . a renegade . . . [and] an apologist for American imperialism." In early 1946 the CPUSA expelled him from the party.[68] Browder's former allies abandoned him. Eugene Dennis, whom Browder had brought into the top leadership, denounced him and after a brief transition became the new general secretary.[69]

Such is the generally accepted history of the upheavals in the party during 1944 and 1945. Although a few historians dispute the point,[70] both American Communists and a majority of scholars agree that the Duclos article was intended as a message from Moscow. Opinions have differed more widely over whether the article was actually written by someone in Moscow or by Duclos at Moscow's direction. **Documents 18, 19, and 20** offer new proof that the article was not only written but published in Moscow in Russian; it was then translated into French and given to Duclos for attribution.

These documents were found in the archive of Institute 205 of the Department of International Information of the Central Committee of the CPSU. Institute 205 was one of the surviving sections of the Comintern's central staff that was incorporated into the CPSU's International Information Department. Comintern chief Dimitrov continued to supervise this organization until he became the head of Bulgaria's newly established Communist government in December 1945. At that time Andrei Zhdanov took over the International Information Department of the CPSU and completed the absorption of the Comintern into the CPSU bureaucracy.[71]

68. "CP Raps Press Hubbub on Browder," *Daily Worker*, 30 April 1946, 2.

69. Foster, whose health was poor, took the lesser post of party chairman.

70. M. J. Heale, for example, in *American Anticommunism: Combating the Enemy Within, 1830–1970* (Baltimore: Johns Hopkins University Press, 1990), accepts only that the Duclos article was "apparently reflecting the views of Moscow" (134).

71. Institute 205 was concerned with the assessment and analysis of foreign information. Two other Comintern groups that were also incorporated into the CPSU's International Information Department were Institute 99 (recruitment of Communist cadres for work among prisoners of war held by the Soviet Union) and Institute 100 (foreign radio broadcasting and covert short-wave radio links). We know that as late as November 1944 at least one American, Elsa Feinstein, the daughter of CPUSA leader Max Bedacht, worked for Institute 205. (See Reichman to Dimitrov, 9 November 1944, RTsKhIDNI 495–74–485.)

Document 18 is an excerpt of the Russian text from which the Duclos article was translated. It consists of typeset page proof, complete with pagination and minor handwritten edits. The French translation (document 19) is typewritten, and it incorporates the handwritten corrections from the Russian page proof. This indicates that the Russian text was the original. Further research in the RTsKhIDNI archives revealed that the article excerpted in document 18 is, in fact, corrected page proof for the January 1945 issue of the *Bulletin of the Information Bureau of the CC VKP(b)* subtitled *Issues of Foreign Policy*; at the beginning of document 18 we reprint the cover of this journal.[72] The bulletin was an internal Soviet publication that circulated only within a select group of senior CPSU and Soviet government officials; every issue carried on its front cover the designation "SECRET."

Document 20 is the last piece connecting the French and Russian articles: it is the cover letter from the translator, dated 19 January 1945, accompanying his return of the original Russian and the French translation. The French article appeared under Duclos's name in the April 1945 issue of *Les Cahiers du communisme*. (No author is listed for either document 18 or document 19.) There are a few differences, none major, between the article printed in *Les Cahiers du communisme* and the drafts found in Moscow, but these changes probably reflect editing and revision—largely stylistic—of the January draft. The version published in *Les Cahiers du communisme* contains several opening sentences by some unknown author (probably the French editor), explaining, rather unconvincingly, why Duclos would be commenting on American Communist affairs: "Many readers of *Cahiers du communisme* have asked us for clarification on the dissolution of the Communist

72. This issue is found in RTsKhIDNI 17–128–50. "VKP(b)" is the Russian acronym for AUCP(b), the All-Union Communist Party (Bolshevik). The text published in the secret journal contains the handwritten corrections found in the document; this suggests that the document was the final page proof for the January 1945 issue (no. 2) that was given to the translator. (The corrections appear on later pages in the article, which are not reproduced as part of document 18.) No author is listed. We would like to thank Jonathan Brent for calling our attention to the fact that document 18 is typeset page proof, Edward Mark for suggesting that it might be from an issue of the bulletin, and Sergei Listikov for locating the issue in the RTsKhIDNI files.

Party of the U.S.A. and the creation of the Communist Political Association . . . "[73] The article also contains a page and a half of assurances that the French party is not guilty of any of the ideological deviations that have just been charged to Browder. This material, added at the end of the essay, is not found in either the Russian original or its French translation.

These documents, along with **document 21**, require us to modify the history of the Browder-Foster conflict slightly. Document 21 is a message from Dimitrov to Molotov, the Soviet foreign minister, dated 8 March 1944. In it, Dimitrov quotes Foster's objections to Browder's Teheran doctrine and offers the text of a cable he has drafted to be sent to Browder. In this cable Dimitrov did *not,* as Browder told his colleagues and as historians have since believed, endorse Browder's views over Foster's. Instead, the cable is a clear warning to Browder. Dimitrov notes: "I am somewhat disturbed by the new theoretical, political, and tactical positions you are developing. Are you not going too far in adapting to the altered international situation, to the point of denying the theory and practice of class struggle and the necessity for the working class to have its own independent political party? Please reconsider all of this and report your thoughts." To underline the seriousness of his concern, he adds: "Confirm receipt of this message." Before sending the cable, Dimitrov requested Molotov's "opinion and guidance." No written reply has been located, but Dimitrov's diary reproduces the text given in document 21 and indicates that he sent it.[74]

Considering that Dimitrov regarded the matter as important enough to raise with the Soviet foreign minister and directed Browder to confirm receipt of his cable, we have good reason to conclude that Browder received the warning. Apparently, he disre-

73. Duclos, "On the Dissolution of the American Communist Party," 656. France had been liberated from Nazi occupation in mid-1944, and in early 1945 it was in political turmoil. It is doubtful that many French Communists had even heard of what had been happening within the CPUSA.

74. Georgi Dimitrov diary entries, 7–8 March 1944, RTsKhIDNI 146-2-13. The Dimitrov diary will be published as part of the Yale University Press Annals of Communism series. The Dimitrov cable is also discussed in James Ryan, *Earl Browder,* 229.

garded it and concealed the message from his colleagues, assuring them that Dimitrov supported him. Surely, had Foster seen Dimitrov's cable, he would never have agreed to stifle his objections. Nor would Eugene Dennis and the other CPUSA leaders who supported Browder in 1944 have endorsed his Teheran doctrine. Document 21 also shows that when Browder sent Foster's letter to Moscow, he was not, in fact, making a concession to Foster; Dimitrov mentions here that he had requested Foster's comments.

Many years after he was expelled, after he had given up all hope of being restored to the Communist party, Browder called the Duclos article "the first *public* declaration of the Cold War."[75] It did have something of that quality. Browder had reorganized the Communist party on the assumption that postwar Soviet-American relations would be based on peaceful coexistence. In light of the Duclos article, the party reversed its strategy from cooperation with established liberal and labor leaders to a policy of opposition to anyone who did not support American accommodation of Stalin's postwar goals. By the late summer of 1945 the American Communist party was repositioned to fight a Cold War that on the surface had not yet begun.

Was Browder right in calling the Duclos article a public declaration of the Cold War? Or was the shift in CPUSA policy simply fortuitous? In mid-1945 Raymond Murphy, a senior State Department official, suggested to his colleagues that the Duclos article might be a harbinger of increased Soviet aggressiveness.[76] Murphy, however, had long viewed Soviet communism as malevolent, and because his was a minority view in the State Department, his warning was ignored.

Several historians and commentators on the Cold War have echoed Browder and Murphy in their assessments of the Duclos article. Those who regard the United States as the initiator of the

75. Earl Browder, "How Stalin Ruined the American Communist Party," *Harper's*, March 1960, 45.

76. Raymond E. Murphy memorandum, "Possible Resurrection of Communist International, Resumption of Extreme Leftist Activities, Possible Effect on United States," 2 June 1945, in *Foreign Relations of the United States: The Conference of Berlin (The Potsdam Conference), 1945*, vol. 1 (U.S. Department of State, Washington, D.C.: Government Printing Office, 1960), 267–80.

Cold War reject this view, of course, as do those who doubt the Soviet origins of the article.[77]

Why did the Soviets publish this article secretly in Moscow and then send it to Paris for open publication as an ostensibly French essay? Perhaps they feared that publication in a Soviet source would be too blatant a signal that Stalin was preparing for a confrontation with the West. By arranging for French Communists to deliver the rejection of Browder's policy of Soviet-American cooperation, the Soviets may have hoped to avoid alerting American leaders prematurely to the anticipated change in Soviet policy.

Documents 18, 19, and 20, by demonstrating the wholly Soviet origins of the Duclos article, lend additional weight to the view that it constituted the first salvo in Stalin's confrontation with the West. In addition to preparing the CPUSA for the Cold War, the article was alerting Western European Communist parties to the coming shift in Stalin's policy.

Document 18

Cover of БЮЛЛЕТЕНЬ БЮРО ИНФОРМАЦИИ ЦК ВКП(б): ВОПРОСЫ ВНЕШНЕЙ ПОЛИТИКИ (Bulletin of the information bureau of the CC VKP[b]: Issues of foreign policy), along with the first four paragraphs of the hand-corrected page proof for О КОММУНИСТИЧЕСКОЙ ПОЛИТИЧЕСКОЙ АССОЦИАЦИИ США (On the Communist Political Association of the United States), an article that was published in this issue, January 1945, RTsKhIDNI 17–128–754. The page proof for this article was attached to a cover letter (document 20) dated 19 January 1945. A translation of the text and that of document 19 follows document 19.

77. See Arthur Schlesinger, Jr., "Origins of the Cold War," *Foreign Affairs* 46 (October 1967): 43–44, and Jaffe, *Rise and Fall of American Communism*, 206–10, 230. Among those who do not view the Duclos article as a harbinger of the Cold War are Gabriel Kolko, *The Politics of War: The World and United States Foreign Policy, 1943–1945* (New York: Random House, 1978), 441–42; Harvey A. Levenstein, *Communism, Anticommunism, and the CIO* (Westport, Conn.: Greenwood Press, 1981), 185–87; Maurice Isserman, *Which Side Were You On?* 219; Malcolm Sylvers, "Left-Wing New Dealers, Moderate Communists, and Enlightened Bourgeois: Progressive Capitalism as a Program for the Postwar U.S.A.," in *Economic and Strategic Issues in U.S. Foreign Policy*, ed. Carl-Ludwig Holtfrerich (Berlin: Walter de Gruyter, 1989), 244–45; and Fraser M. Ottanelli, *The Communist Party of the United States from the Depression to World War II* (New Brunswick, N.J.: Rutgers University Press, 1991), 211–12.

Document 18 *continued*

БЮЛЛЕТЕНЬ
БЮРО ИНФОРМАЦИИ ЦК ВКП(б)
ВОПРОСЫ ВНЕШНЕЙ ПОЛИТИКИ
№ 2
Январь 1945 г.

М О С К В А

BULLETIN OF THE
INFORMATION BUREAU OF THE CC VKP(b)
ISSUES OF FOREIGN POLICY
No. 2
January 1945

MOSCOW

О КОММУНИСТИЧЕСКОЙ ПОЛИТИЧЕСКОЙ АССОЦИАЦИИ США

На состоявшемся 20 мая 1944 г. в Нью-Йорке съезде коммунистической партии Америки было принято решение о росписке компартии США и о создании Коммунистической политической ассоциации (КПА).

Причины роспуска компартии Америки и принятия "нового курса" в работе американских коммунистов изложены в официальных документах КП и в ряде выступлений бывшего генерального секретаря коммунистической партии Америки Браудера.

В речи, посвященной итогам Тегеранской конференции и политическому положению США, 12 декабря 1943 г. в Бриджпорте, опубликованной в журнале "Коммунист" в январе 1944 г., Браудер впервые обосновал необходимость изменения курса американской компартии.

Отправным пунктом в обосновании изменения курса американской компартии для Браудера, по его заявлению, послужила Тегеранская конференция.

. . .

О КОММУНИСТИЧЕСКОЙ ПОЛИТИЧЕСКОЙ АССОЦИАЦИИ США

...состоявшемся 20 мая 1944 г. в Нью-Йорке ...коммунистической партии Америки было при... решение о роспуске компартии США и о со... ...и Коммунистической политической ассоциации ...А).

...чины роспуска компартии Америки и приня... ...нового курса» в работе американских комму... ...ов изложены в официальных документах КП и ...де выступлений бывшего генерального секрета... ...оммунистической партии Америки Браудера.
...речи, посвященной итогам Тегеранской конфе... ...нии и политическому положению США, 12 де... ...я 1943 г. в Бриджпорте, опубликованной в жур... ...«Коммунист» в январе 1944 г., Браудер впервые ...новал необходимость изменения курса амери... ...кой компартии.

...правным пунктом в обосновании изменения ...а американской компартии для Браудера, по ...заявлению, послужила Тегеранская конферен... ...Однако, правильно подчеркивая значение Теге... ...ской конференции для победы в войне с фашист... ...Германией, Браудер сделал из решений кон... ...ренции целый ряд неверных, немарксистских вы... ...ов и по сути дела построил целую концепцию, ...равильно определяющую пути общественного ...вития вообще и, в первую очередь, обществен... ...о развития США.

...раудер заявил, что в Тегеране капитализм и со... ...лизм начали находить путь к мирному сосущест... ...ванию и сотрудничеству в рамках одного мира, что ...еранское соглашение о совместной политике ...дполагает и совместные усилия в сведении к ...нимуму или к полному устранению методов на... ...льственной борьбы в разрешении внутренних во... ...сов каждой страны в отдельности.

«Тегеранская декларация, — указывал Брау... ...дер в своей речи, — это единственная надежда ...на продолжение цивилизации в нашу эпоху. Вот ...почему я могу принять, поддержать и поверить ...в Тегеранскую декларацию, сделав ее исход... ...ным пунктом всех моих соображений насчет ...проблем нашей страны и всего мира».

...Исходя из решений Тегеранской конференции, ...раудер делает политические выводы в отношении ...облем всего мира и, особенно, в отношении внут... ...него положения США. Ряд этих выводов сви... ...льствует о том, что основные вопросы внутриполи... ...ческой жизни США должны разрешаться в ...льнейшем путем реформ, так как «неограниченная ...утренняя борьба угрожает международному един... ...ву, установленному в Тегеране».
...Тегеранское соглашение, по мнению Браудера, ...начает, что большая часть Европы, лежащей к

западу от Советского Союза, вероятно, будет восстановлена на буржуазно-демократической базе, а не на фашистско-капиталистической или на советской базе.

«Но это будет такая капиталистическая база, — говорил Браудер — которая обуславливается принципом полного демократического права на самоопределение для каждой нации, права, обеспечивающего полную свободу мнений внутри каждого государства всем прогрессивным и созидательным силам, не терпящего никаких помех в деле развития демократии и социального прогресса, в соответствии с различными желаниями народов. Это сулит Европе перспективу доведения до минимума и даже до полной ликвидации угрозы гражданской войны после мировой войны».

Значение Тегеранской конференции конкретно для Америки, — указывает Браудер, — означает перспективу обеспечения непосредственно после войны расширенного производства, предоставления всем работы, перспективу укрепления демократии в рамках нынешней системы, создание широкого национального единства на многие годы, но не перспективу перехода к социализму, к которому американский народ не подготовлен.

«Мы можем поставить своей целью, — говорил Браудер на пленуме ЦК компартии 4 января 1944 г. — либо осуществление политики Тегерана, либо же задачу немедленного перехода США к социалистической системе. Не ясно ли, что мы не можем добиваться того и другого. Первая перспектива, несмотря на многочисленные трудности, определенно находится в пределах практически осуществимого. Вторая перспектива является по меньшей мере сомнительной, в особенности, если учесть, что наиболее прогрессивная часть рабочего движения Америки не обладает даже теми гуманными социалистическими идеями, какие свойственны лейбористской партии Англии. Следовательно, политика марксистов в США должна заключаться в том, чтобы со всей реальностью считаться с перспективой послевоенной капиталистической реконструкции США, оценивать все планы, исходя из этой перспективы, и активно сотрудничать с наиболее демократическим и прогрессивным большинством в стране, добиваясь национального единства, достаточно широкого и эффективного для осуществления политики Тегерана».

DOCUMENT 18. First page of the proof for О КОММУНИСТИЧЕСКОЙ ПОЛИТИЧЕСКОЙ АССОЦИАЦИИ США (On the Communist Political Association of the United States), an article that was published in БЮЛЛЕТЕНЬ БЮРО ИНФОРМАЦИИ ЦК ВКП(б): ВОПРОСЫ ВНЕШНЕЙ ПОЛИТИКИ (Bulletin of the information bureau of the CC VKP[b]: Issues of foreign policy), January 1945. Several pages of the article proof have hand corrections, one of which is visible here.

...jet de l'Association Politique Communiste des Etats-Unis

Le Congrès du Parti communiste d'Amérique, qui s'est tenu le
1944 à New-York, a pris la décision de dissoudre le Parti
...niste des Etats-Unis et de créer l'Association Politique Com-
...ste (A.P.C.)

Les raisons de la dissolution du parti communiste d'Amérique
...u "nouveau cours" dans l'activité des communistes américains
...exposées dans les documents officiels du P.C. et dans tout un
...bre de discours de Browder, ancien secrétaire général du Parti
...muniste d'Amérique.

Dans son discours consacré au bilan de la Conférence de Téhéran,
...la situation politique aux Etats-Unis, prononcé le 12 décembre
...3, à Bridgeport et publié dans la revue "Communiste" en janvier
...4, Browder a, pour la première fois, argumenté la nécessité du
...gement du cours du parti communiste américain.

Selon la déclaration de Browder, la conférence de Téhéran lui a
...vi de point de départ pour argumenter le changement du cours du
...i communiste américain. Cependant, tout en soulignant avec
...esse l'importance de la conférence de Téhéran pour la victoire
...s la guerre contre l'Allemagne fasciste, Browder a tiré des déci-
...ns de la conférences tout en nombre de conclusions fausses, non-
...istes et au fond a construit toute une conception définissant
...e manière fausse les voies de l'évolution sociale en général et
...remier lieu celles de l'évolution sociale des Etats-Unis.

Browder a déclaré qu'à Téhéran le capitalisme et le socialisme
...ient commencé à trouver la voie de la coexistence en paix et de la
...llaboration dans le cadre d'un seul et même monde, que les accords
...éhéran, concernant la politique commune, supposaient également
...efforts communs en vue de réduire au minimum ou de supprimer
...plètement les méthodes de la lutte par la force dans la solution

DOCUMENT 19. First page of "Au sujet de l'Association Politique
Communiste des Etats-Unis," a translation of document 18.

Document 19

Excerpt from "Au sujet de l'Association Politique Communiste des Etats-Unis," RTsKhIDNI 17–128–754. Undated, but attached to cover letter (document 20) dated 19 January 1945.

Au Sujet de L'Association Politique Communiste des Etats-Unis

Le Congrès du Parti communiste d'Amérique, qui s'est tenu le 20 mai 1944 à New-York, a pris la décision de dissoudre le Parti communiste des Etats-Unis et de créer l'Association Politique Communiste (A.P.C.)

Les raisons de la dissolution du parti communiste d'Amérique et du "nouveau cours" dans l'activité des communistes américains sont exposées dans les documents officiels du P.C. et dans tout un nombre de discours de Browder, ancien secrétaire général du Parti communiste d'Amérique.

Dans son discours consacré au bilan de la Conférence de Téhéran, et à la situation politique aux Etats-Unis, prononcé le 12 décembre 1943, à Bridgeport et publié dans la revue "Communiste" en janvier 1944, Browder a, pour la première fois, argumenté la nécessité du changement du cours du parti communiste américain.

Selon la déclaration de Browder, la conférence de Téhéran lui a servi de point de départ pour argumenter le changement du cours du parti communiste américain.

. . .

On the Communist Political Association of the United States of America

The Congress of the Communist Party of America, which met on 20 May 1944 in New York, decided to dissolve the Communist Party of the United States of America and create the Communist Political Association (CPA).

The reasons for dissolution of the American Communist party and for the "new course" in the activity of American Communists are set forth in official documents of the C.P. and in a number of the speeches of Browder, former general secretary of the American Communist party.

In his speech devoted to the results of the Teheran Conference and the political situation in the United States, delivered 12 December 1943 in Bridgeport and published in the journal "Communist" in January 1944, Browder, for the first time, argued for the necessity of changing the course of the American Communist party.

Browder stated that he took the Teheran Conference as his point of departure in arguing for changing the course of the American Communist party.

Document 20

Geminder to Shuklin, 19 January 1945, RTsKhIDNI 17–128–754. Original in Russian.

To Comrade SHUKLIN

I am sending you a translation of an article on the U.S. Communist Political Association. I am simultaneously returning the original to you.

(B. GEMINDER) *Geminder*

19.1.45

Document 21

Dimitrov to Molotov, 8 March 1944, RTsKhIDNI 495–74–482. Original in Russian.

<u>Personal</u>

To Comrade v. m. MOLOTOV:

In response to the question I put to Comrade Browder—What is the substance of his disagreements with Comrade Foster?—and to my suggestion that the latter state his point of view in his own words, I received the following reply from Comrade Foster:

> I agree with the overall assessment of Teheran put forward by Browder with the exception of his serious underestimation of the danger of American imperialism. I do not agree with several points as regards America, including the question of the Republicans' and Democrats' running a joint candidate in the elections, which would result either in the removal of Roosevelt or in the reduction of aid. I do not agree with assessing the role of major American capital as progressive, which leads to underestimating the danger of reaction in the U.S. I do not agree with the assumption that employers will voluntarily double their workers' salaries in order to keep their businesses in operation. I do not agree with having the regulation of foreign trade depend on monopolists. I do not agree that monopolists can be controlled only with their own consent. I do not agree with accepting the basic slogan of the major industrialists, the freedom of entrepreneurial initiative, since that would reduce to a minimum the necessity of social welfare, measures restricting monopolies and a government program for public works as a remedy for mass unemployment.
>
> I agree with maintaining national unity and carrying out a well-considered strike policy even after the war, but I do not agree with extending no-strike pledges into the postwar period. I agree that America does not at present face the problem of socialism, nor will it immediately after the war; but neither can I ignore the socialist lessons of the Soviet Union. I am drafting a full statement of my views. I will accept your advice.—Foster.

In this connection I consider it advisable to send Comrade Browder the following encrytped telegram:

Document 21 *continued*

To Browder: Received Foster's telegram. Please report which leading party comrades support his views. I am somewhat disturbed by the new theoretical, political, and tactical positions you are developing. Are you not going too far in adapting to the altered international situation, to the point of denying the theory and practice of class struggle and the necessity for the working class to have its own independent political party? Please reconsider all of this and report your thoughts. Confirm receipt of this message.

I would appreciate your opinion and guidance in this matter.

(G. DIMITROV)

8 March 1944

CHAPTER TWO

Moscow Gold

FROM VIRTUALLY THE MOMENT it was created, the Communist Party of the United States of America depended on financial support from the Soviet Union. "Moscow gold" enabled the fledgling American Communist movement to pay organizers, publish newspapers, and support a variety of fraternal, educational, and union activities. Unlike its rivals on the American left, which relied on funds raised by membership dues and donations from sympathizers, the CPUSA, emboldened by the deep pockets of its foreign sponsor, created an infrastructure and a public presence far greater than its members could support.

A combination of scarce domestic resources and ambitious, far-reaching goals persuaded American Communists to accept large subsidies from abroad in spite of the political and legal risks involved. To American Communists, Soviet contributions represented the international solidarity that the working classes of more fortunate countries owed their struggling comrades. For anti-Communists, however, Moscow's financial assistance underlined the CPUSA's role as a foreign agent: like anyone financially dependent on another, the CPUSA could not be wholly autonomous. With foreign money came foreign influence.

Even though American Communists privately saw nothing wrong with accepting Soviet subsidies, they recognized that public acknowledgment of these funds would adversely affect their image and might even hamper their efforts to raise money within the United States. American Communists vigorously denied that they received money from abroad, and they suppressed evidence of their financial relation with Moscow. As a result, although testimony by ex-Communists and exposés of the American Communist party frequently allude to the subsidies, there has been only limited documentary evidence that they ever existed.

But tales of "Moscow gold" persist, based on secondhand reports and oral testimony. Several of these center on the romantic figure of Michael Borodin, a hero of the early days of the Communist movement, when many thought that revolution was about to sweep the globe. In 1918 Borodin attempted to smuggle some of the tsar's jewels into the United States. Estimated at a value of $250,000, the diamonds were shuffled from courier to courier. The plan went awry, however, and their final destination has never been determined.[1]

One of the earliest to accuse the American party of being Soviet subsidized was Benjamin Gitlow, a leading Communist in the 1920s who became a vehement anti-Communist after his expulsion from the party in 1929. In books and congressional testimony, Gitlow charged that during his tenure the Comintern had regularly provided funding to the American party for presidential campaigns, union activities, and propaganda efforts like the *Daily Worker,* which was founded with Soviet money. Although Gitlow's figures would vary significantly at different tellings, he implied that on the average during the 1920s the Soviet subsidies amounted to close to $250,000 a year. Jay Lovestone, the party's general secretary during the second half of the decade—who was also expelled—disputed Gitlow's figures, testifying before the Dies committee that the Soviets provided about $25,000 a year, no small sum in the 1920s but only a tenth of Gitlow's

---

1. One story has it that after the jewels reached New York, Russian Communists used them as security for a loan from the Irish Republican movement and deposited them in a bank. Later transferred to Ireland, the jewels were finally returned to Russia in 1948 after the loan was repaid by the Soviet government. In another account, Borodin was accused of stealing them (or carelessly allowing one of his agents to steal them) and was forced to account for them to an angry Comintern. See Theodore Draper, *The Roots of American Communism* (New York: Viking Press, 1957), 236–41.

total. Neither man was able to support his testimony with documents.[2]

Other ex-Communists confirmed that Soviet subsidies were commonplace into the mid-1930s. In 1953 Earl Browder reluctantly admitted that during the first half of the 1930s the Comintern had provided at least 10 percent of the party's funds. Nat Honig, a onetime editor of *Labor Unity*, a publication of the party's Trade Union Unity League (TUUL), testified that the journal was heavily subsidized by Moscow in the early 1930s. By the end of the decade, however, the CPUSA had about 66,000 members and had developed substantial financial resources of its own. By some accounts, direct Soviet subsidies ceased at this time. Browder claimed that he was able to eliminate the subsidy by 1935.[3] As will be seen, this was not true.

In addition to direct payments via courier, the Soviets were suspected of using a variety of business fronts to subsidize the CPUSA indirectly. Dr. D. H. Dubrowsky, an American who represented various Soviet government agencies in the United States, broke with the Communists in 1935 and later testified before the House Special Committee on Un-American Activities. Dubrowsky claimed that the Soviet Union raised millions of dollars each year in the United States through rentals and sales of Soviet films, profits from the insurance and transport of goods between the United States and the USSR, charges on transferring the estates of Russian immigrants who died in America to relatives in the Soviet Union, and a variety of fees for doing business with Amtorg, the Soviet Union's state trading organization. A portion of this money, he testified, was funneled into the CPUSA by the Soviets, who directed these transactions through CPUSA-controlled enterprises.[4] One such enterprise was World

2. Theodore Draper, *American Communism and Soviet Russia* (New York: Viking Press, 1960), 202–8.

3. Harvey Klehr, *The Heyday of American Communism: The Depression Decade* (New York: Basic Books, 1984), 376–77. Testimony of Nat Honig, transcript of proceedings held before the Subversive Activities Control Board, in the matter of *Herbert Brownell, Attorney General, v. Communist Party*, 1951 (reprinted on microfilm in *Records of the Subversive Activities Control Board, 1950–1972* [Frederick, Md.: University Press of America, 1988], 440).

4. Klehr, *Heyday of American Communism*, 377; Dubrowsky testimony, House Special Committee on Un-American Activities, *Investigation of Un-American Propaganda Activities in the United States*, 76th Cong., 1st sess., 1939, 8:5137–71, 5206–57.

Tourists, a travel and shipping agency set up in the 1930s by CPUSA members with funds secretly provided by the Soviet Union. Soviet government agencies like Amtorg would direct businessmen and tourists who wished to travel to the Soviet Union to purchase their tickets or ship their goods through World Tourists. World Tourists would then turn the profits over to the CPUSA.[5]

Apart from charges by ex-Communists, however, for many years there was little direct evidence of Soviet subsidies, hardly any of it documentary. "Moscow gold" has been a term of derision: in 1926 a pamphlet denying that the Soviets had covertly funded the British General Strike ridiculed the idea of "Russian gold" and "Red money." In 1938 Earl Browder scoffed at rumors of Moscow gold while denying that the CPUSA accepted Soviet subsidies.[6]

The documentary evidence published here for the first time, however, confirms the substantial role Soviet funding played in the life of the CPUSA, from the origins of the party until the collapse of the Soviet Union. The RTsKhIDNI archives contain hundreds of documents that bear on financial matters. This chapter offers only a sampling, but it illustrates the many and varied facets of the financial ties between the Comintern and the CPUSA.

In 1919 and 1920, the Comintern gave four people gold and jewels valued at 2,728,000 rubles (the equivalent of several million U.S. dollars, an enormous sum at the time) to found a Communist movement in America. Included among the recipients was John Reed, one of the fathers of American communism. The full text of a Comintern account sheet that records these transactions has been reprinted in *The Secret World of American Communism*.[7]

---

5. World Tourists' ties to the Soviet government were so close that in 1940 the company and its chief officer, Jacob Golos, pleaded guilty to failing to register as agents of a foreign power. An account of World Tourists by Elizabeth Bentley, a company official who later broke with the CPUSA, can be found in Bentley, *Out of Bondage: The Story of Elizabeth Bentley* (New York: Devin-Adair, 1951). (Bentley and Golos were lovers.)

6. "Red Money: A Statement from the All-Russian Council of Trade Unions" (London: Labor Research Department, 1926); Earl Browder, letter transcribed in *Report of the Joint Legislative Committee to Investigate the Administration and Enforcement of the Law* (Albany, N.Y.: J. B. Lyon, 1939), 2:51–52. Browder's remarks are also reported in the *Daily Worker*, 30 June, 1938, 1, 4.

7. "Corresponding with Krumina's Receipts . . . ," RTsKhIDNI 495-82-1, in Harvey Klehr, John Earl Haynes, and Fridrikh Igorevich Firsov, *The Secret World of American Communism* (New Haven: Yale University Press, 1995), 22–24. The account sheet uses the word *tsennosti,* a term denoting valuables like jewelry, to

There are no details in the archive about how this enormous fortune was transported to the United States, although we know that Reed was caught smuggling jewels through Finland in 1920. It is possible that the jewels Borodin smuggled were part of this payment. Even if only a portion of the jewels managed to reach America, however, the money would have supported the fledgling Communist movement (which had fewer than 15,000 members, most of them poor, non–English speaking immigrants) in a number of activities that could not otherwise have been attempted.

The Comintern soon regularized the procedure for financing its foreign subsidiaries. In February 1923 a Comintern official wrote to the American Communist party that the Comintern's Budget Committee had just released $10,000 of its 1922 subsidy for the American party. The letter noted that $500 of this had been deposited to the American party's Moscow account; $1,000 each had been given to Ludwig Katterfield and Max Bedacht, senior American party officials, who were carrying the money back to the United States; and $3,750 each was being sent by unspecified means to Joseph Brodksy, the party lawyer, and Philip Rosenbliett, a New York dentist who was part of the underground organization. The letter further noted that the Budget Committee had retained $8,000 of the 1922 subsidy. This sum would be sent only after the Americans showed that they had carried out "the organisation by the C.P. of a book store and the publication of a definite quantity of printed matter."[8]

Document 22 indicates that the CPUSA has fulfilled this requirement, so Moscow is releasing the final $8,000 (actually $8,496, less $1,000 to go to Soviet famine relief; see below). In this document, a letter to the American Communist party, the Comintern states that it has initially allocated $37,500 to the American party for 1923 but that the party should appeal for more aid if this is insufficient. (It was: on 16 May 1923 "J. Miller," apparently an alias for party leader Charles Ruthenberg, advised Comintern official Osip Piatnitsky that "the sum for 1923 is far from being sufficient.")[9]

describe the subsidies. This account sheet is also discussed in Dmitri Volkogonov, *Lenin: A New Biography* (New York: Free Press, 1994), 346.

8. "To the Communist Party of America," 22 February 1923, RTsKhIDNI 495–19–608, in Klehr, Haynes, and Firsov, *Secret World of American Communism*, 26.

9. J. Miller to Piatnitsky, 16 May 1923, RTsKhIDNI 495–19–608.

In document 22 the Comintern also deals with the question of how the American party handled the money it had managed to raise by its own efforts. American Communists had collected money in the United States to help relieve famine in Russia. When the party requested permission to retain 40 percent of these relief contributions to fund American Communist activities, the Comintern had refused. To make sure that the Americans turned over the money, therefore, the Comintern announced that it would deduct the $16,000 the CPUSA had skimmed off the famine relief fund from the party subsidy and pay it directly to the fund.

In **document 23** the American party reported to the Comintern with details of how it had spent a Comintern subsidy of $30,950 received in December 1921, as well as two additional subventions totaling $49,429 that were received in June and July 1922. This was a lot of money: on the basis of various indexes, a reasonable calculation would put the value of the 1920s dollar at more than eight times that of a mid-1990s dollar. Using the consumer price index, for example, we find that the total subsidy of $80,379 mentioned in this document comes to more than $650,000 in 1995 dollars.

As the document makes clear, this money supported every area of party life: the retirement of old debts, the wages of party organizers and officials, overhead for the national office, convention expenses, newspaper publication expenses, labor union organization ("industrial work"), shortfalls in membership dues from the party's immigrant federations, and legal defense costs. Eleven hundred dollars of the Comintern subsidy was passed on to the Canadian Communist party. **Document 24** shows a more modest expenditure of Comintern funds: $44,864 for the first nine months of 1926. Again, all aspects of the American party's activities received Moscow's assistance. Every area in which American Communists were involved benefited substantially from Soviet subsidies.

What is not clear is what portion of the party's *total* budget came from Comintern coffers. The financial records in the Moscow archives are incomplete with regard to both total Comintern subsidies and the American party's annual budget. One document that comes close to being a listing of total annual expenditures is an account sheet labeled "Combined Cash Receipts and Cash Expenditures for Period Beginning December 1st 1923 and Ending July

31st 1924 of the Workers Party of America National Office, Liberator Publishing Company, National Defense Committee of the Workers Party of America, Farmer-Labor Voice." For this eight-month period the account sheet shows total expenditures by the CPUSA (or Workers Party of America, as it was then termed) of $117,270.50.[10] Although none of our sources cover precisely the same period, using documents 23 and 24 we can estimate the proportion of American Communist funds that came from Moscow in the 1920s. The $44,864 in Comintern funds spent during the first nine months of 1926 reported in document 24 comes to 38 percent of the total money spent during the eight months of 1923–1924. The $80,379 received from the Comintern in the eight-month period of December 1921 through July 1922, shown in document 23, is 69 percent of this amount. A fairly conservative conclusion, then, would be that in the 1920s "Moscow gold" accounted for at least a third and in some years more than half, or even two-thirds, of the budget of the American Communist party.

Document 22

Excerpt from a one-page letter, Piatnitsky to the Comparty America [the American Communist party] and Com[rade] Miller, RTsKhIDNI 495–19–608. Original in English. The document is undated, but internal evidence indicates that it was written sometime between late February and mid-May 1923. "Miller" is thought to be a pseudonym for Charles Ruthenberg. "Com. [A]mpter" is Israel Amter. "Munzenburg" is Willi Münzenberg, a German Communist who raised foreign money for Russian famine relief.

The Comparty America.
  Com. Miller.

On the arrival of Com. [A]mpter, the ECCI investigated your proposal that 40% of the sums collected on behalf of famine relief be left in your hands. The ECCI rejects this proposal on the grounds that these funds are subscribed by large numbers of non-Party people and such a measure as you propose may cause a considerable loss of confidence in the Communist Party on the part of

---

10. "Combined Cash Receipts and Cash Expenditures for Period Beginning December 1st 1923 and Ending July 31st 1924 of the Workers Party of America National Office, Liberator Publishing Company, National Defense Committee of the Workers Party of America, Farmer-Labor Voice," RTsKhIDNI 495–19–609. The document is undated.

those people. Arising out of this the ECCI has resolved, to reimburse Com. Munzenburg the 16,000 dols. which you retained from famine relief funds, out of the balance of the subsidy of 1922 and part of the subsidy for 1923.

. . .

The balance standing to your account for 1922 was 8,496 dols. You will see *therefore* that we have not sent you 1,000 dols.

You will gather from the above that we have accepted your list of the pamphlets you have published and we are therefore returning you the money for 1922. (Of course we are paying the money to Munzenburg out of your account. cf. above.)

The sum allocated to you for 1923 is 37,500 dols, of which part must be used for trade union work. If this sum is insufficient, send us an estimate of the additional sum you [r]equire and the purposes for which you require it, [and] the Budget Commission will examine the matter.

. . .

Piatnitsky

Document 23

J. Miller to ECCI, 6 March 1923, RTsKhIDNI 495–19–608. Original in English. Pseudonyms: "J. Miller" was probably Charles Ruthenberg; "Lewis" was William Weinstone; "LCWheat" was Jay Lovestone; "J. Moore" was John J. Ballam. (The $450 listed for Moore was probably to cover the expenses for the Comintern-ordered tour of the United States to dismantle the United Toilers. Similarly, "Former Opposition Convention Expenses" were the costs of liquidating the United Toilers faction; see chapter 1.) Fritzmann was a Comintern official. "CPA" is the Communist Party of America, "UCP" the United Communist Party, "N.O." the party's national office; "federation" and "federation bureaus" are the party's foreign-language immigrant affiliates; "Y.C.L. of A." stands for the Young Communist League of America and "LPP" for the Legal Political Party. In 1921, the underground Communist party established an above-ground organization, the Workers Party of America. In the Communist jargon of the time, the latter was the legal, as opposed to the illegal, Communist party.

LETTER #9 March 6, 1923

TO THE E.C. OF C.I. CONFIDENTIAL

[illegible Russian script]

> Encl. No. *466*
> Date *26.III* 1923
> The Secretariat E.C.C.I.

Dear Comrades:-

Some time ago we received a communication from Comrade Fritzmann requesting an account of certain receipts and expenditure which is to be submitted to the Budget Commission.

In compliance with this request we herewith enclose accounts which, for reference purposes, are referred to as "T#1" and "T#2 and 3"

In showing the disposition of the contributions, we have not included regular expenditures for the current month or months during which the contributions were received. We show only the payments made directly out of these particular accounts.

We call your attention to the notes at the foot of the statements which, we believe, are self-explanatory.

The accounts as shown on the statements enclosed do not of course show the only expenditures made by the National Office for the particular items indicated. During the course of the year, we have made additional contributions for such items as shown and also for others. These expenditures were made out of the regular receipts which the National Office obtained from the District organizations.

If there is any further information that you desire, we shall be glad to comply with your request for same.

Comrade Fritzmann, in the same letter, dated at Berlin, asks to know if we have his address about passports and enclosed therein his address. We are at a loss to understand what this matter refers to and we ask you to let us know.

[filing stamp]

Fraternally yours,
J. Miller
Executive Secretary, C.P. of A.

Document 23 *continued*

<u>DISPOSITION OF SPECIAL CONTRIBUTION T-#1 (LEWIS, EXEC. SECY.)</u>
<u>DECEMBER, 1921 . . . . $30,950.00</u>

<u>LPP Contributions</u>
   Pre-Convention (1st) Contributions (By N.O.
      direct and thru Districts) 850.00
   Convention (1st) Expense paid by CPA 2600.00
   Contributions since Convention 3750.00 $7,200.00

<u>English Language Press (LPP) Contributions</u> 1,390.00

<u>Foreign Language Press Contributions (Lithuanian)</u> 100.00

<u>Federation Bureaus - Contributions</u>
                    Jewish 400.00
                    Ukranian 250.00   650.00

<u>Federation Conferences (Paid by Nat'l Office): Russian</u> 250.00

<u>Propaganda Contributions</u>
               Negro 650.00
               Irish. 95.00   745.00

<u>Defense Contributions</u>
   Misc. - National 1000.00
   Misc. - Various 1000.00   2,000.00

<u>Industrial Department</u>
   Special Contribution - American Bureau (thru Cook) 1,000.00

<u>Old UCP Loans and Accounts</u>
   Loans & Expense. 7930.00
   Old Printing Bills 400.00   8,330.00

<u>Miscl. Old Loans & Accounts Repaid</u>. 2,835.00

<u>Federation Dues (Back Dues</u>. 1,800.00

<u>Back Wages</u>. 1,600.00
                                                TOTAL   27,900.00

Note: The difference between Receipts ($30950.) and $27900, or $3050. needed to meet Deficit due to Excess of Expenditures *over Receipts* of the National Office for the months of December, 1921, and January, 1922.

Document 23 *continued*

Periods immediately preceeding and following Conventions (in this case the 1st LPP Convention) show lower Receipts by the Districts, and consequently, lower Remittances to the National Office.

DISPOSITION OF SPECIAL CONTRIBUTIONS - T-2 AND T-3, JUNE-JULY, 1922

(LCWheat, Exec. Sec'y)	. . . .	$49,429.00
		468
		18 3

Defense Contributions		
District II Cases 1000.00		
Bruce Case. 150.00		
Miscellaneous (N.O.) .1800.00		$2,950.00
Industrial Work (Contributions)		
National. 9000.00		
Districts I, II, III 300.00		9,300.00
Press Service (Contributions)		1,000.00
LPP Contributions (N.O.).		5,000.00
W.L. Contributions for Election Campaign, Debts, etc. . .		1,000.00
English Language Press Contributions (LPP)		1,600.00
Foreign Language Press Contributions (LPP)		
Jewish 2500.00		
Russian 250.00		
Ukranian 50.00		2,800.00
Federation Bureaus (Contributions)		
Jewish. 375.00		
Polish 600.00		
Russian 800.00		1,775.00
Special Ukranian Organization Work.		250.00
Special Organization Work, Wages & Expenses (J.Moore)		450.00
International Delegates		
To C.I. (Trav. Expenses & Wages) 2585.00		
To Profintern (Spec. Contrib. to R.I.) 400.00		2,985.00

Document 23 *continued*

Special C. I. Expense.............................	150.00
C.P. of Canada - Contribution......................	1,000.00
Canadian Conference Expenses	100.00
Y.C.L. of A. Contributions........................	225.00
Deficit 2nd National Party Convention (Part paid by N.O.) ..	4,550.00
Former Opposition Convention Expenses...........	239.00
Advance to Districts	460.00
Old Accounts & Loans Repaid	4,175.00
Federation Dues (Back Dues	2,800.00
Back Wages......................................	2,200.00
Strike Donation	300.00
	TOTAL 45,309.00

(See Note [below])

Note:

The difference between the amount received ($49429.) and the amount expended as shown above ($45309.) was spent for General Organization Expenses during July and August, 1922, and the next two months following the 2nd National Convention of the CPA. While moneys were received from some of the Districts, this was insufficient, however, to meet the Current Expenses of the National Office. Hence, the difference of $4120.00, indicated as used for General Organization Expenses, was needed to meet the Deficit (or difference between Receipts & Expenditures) of the National Office.

LETTER #9   March 6, 1923

TO THE E.C. OF C.I.   C O N F I D E N T I A L

Lint. No. 466
Den 16. III   1923
Das Sekretariat E. K. K. I.

Dear Comrades:-

Some time ago we received a communication from Comrade Fritzmann
requesting an account of certain receipts and expenditure which is to
be submitted to the Budget Commission.

In compliance with this request we herewith enclose accounts
which, for reference purposes, are referred to as "T#1" and "T#2 and 3"

In showing the disposition of the contributions, we have not
included regular expenditures for the current month or months during
which the contributions were received. We show only the payments
made directly out of these particular accounts.

We call your attention to the notes at the foot of the statements which, we believe, are self-explanatory.

The accounts as shown on the statements enclosed do not of
course show the only expenditures made by the National Office for
the particular items indicated. During the course of the year, we
have made additional contributions for such items as shown and also
for others. These expenditures were made out of the regular receipts
which the National Office obtained from the District organizations.

If there is any further information that you desire, we shall be
glad to comply with your request for same.

Comrade Fritzmann, in the same letter, dated at Berlin, asks
to know if we have his address about passports and enclosed therein
his address. We are at a loss to understand what this matter refers
to and we ask you to let us know.

                                    Fraternally yours,

                                    Executive Secretary, C.P. of A.

DOCUMENT 23. J. Miller to ECCI, 6 March 1923.

DISPOSITION OF SPECIAL CONTRIBUTION T-#1 (LEWIS, EXEC. SECY.)

DECEMBER, 1921 .... $30,950.00

LPP Contributions
    Pre-Convention (1st) Contributions (By N.O.
        direct and thru Districts) 850.00
    Convention (1st) Expense paid by CPA 2600.00
    Contributions since Convention 3750.00 $7,200.00

English Language Press (LPP) Contributions 1,390.00

Foreign Language Press Contributions (Lithuanian) 100.00

Federation Bureaus - Contributions
               Jewish 400.00
               Ukranian 250.00   650.00
    Federation Conferences (Paid by Nat'l Office): Russian....   250.00
Propaganda Contributions
             Negro 650.00
             Irish 95.00   745.00

Defense Contributions
        Misc. - National 1000.00
        Misc. - Various 1000.00   2,000.00

Industrial Department
    Special Contribution - American Bureau (thru Cook) 1,000.00

Old UCP Loans and Accounts
    Loans & Expense 7930.00
    Old Printing Bills 400.00   8,330.00

Miscl. Old Loans & Accounts Repaid 2,835.00

Federation Dues (Back Dues 1,800.00

Back Wages 1,600.00

                                       TOTAL   27,900.00

Note: The difference between Receipts ($30950.) and $27900, or $3050.
        needed to meet Deficit due to Excess of Receipts over Expenditures
        of the National Office for the months of December, 1921, and
        January, 1922.
        Periods immediately preceeding and following Conventions (in this
        case the 1st LPP Convention) show lower Receipts by the Districts,
        and consequently, lower Remittances to the National Office.

DOCUMENT 23. continued

DISPOSITION OF SPECIAL CONTRIBUTIONS - T-2 and T-3, JUNE-JULY, 1922

(LCWheat, Exec.Sec'y) $49,429.00

Defense Contributions
District II Cases 1000.00
Bruce Case 150.00
Miscellaneous (N.O.) 1800.00 $2,950.00

Industrial Work (Contributions)
National 9000.00
Districts I, XXX II, III 300.00   9,300.00

Press Service (Contributions) 1,000.00

LPP Contributions (N.O.) 5,000.00

W.L. Contributions for Election Campaign, Debts, etc. ..   1,000.00

Polish Language Press Contributions (LPP) 1,600.00

Foreign Language Press Contributions (LPP)
Jewish 2500.00
Russian 250.00
Ukranian 50.00   2,800.00

Federation Bureaus (Contributions)
Jewish 375.00
Polish 600.00
Russian 800.00   1,775.00

Special Ukranian Organization Work 250.00

Special Organization Work, Wages & Expenses (J.Moore)   450.00

International Delegates
To C.I. (Trav. Expenses & Wages) 2585.00
To Profintern (Spec. Contrib. to R.I.) .. 400.00   2,985.00

Special C. I. Expense 150.00

C.P. of Canada - Contribution 1,000.00

Canadian Conference Expenses 100.00

Y.C.L. of A. Contributions 225.00

Deficit 2nd National Party Convention (Part paid by N.O.) ... 4,550.00

Former Opposition Convention Expenses 239.00

Advance to Districts 460.00

Old Accounts & Loans Repaid 4,175.00

Federation Dues (Back Dues 2,800.00

Back Wages 2,200.00

Strike Donation 300.00

              TOTAL   45,309.00

(See Note page 2)

DOCUMENT 23. continued

Note:

The difference between the amount received ($49429.) and the amount expended (as shown above ($45309.) was spent for General Organization Expenses during July and August, 1922, and the next two months following the 2nd National Convention of the CPA.   While moneys were received from some of the Districts, this was insufficient, however, to meet the Current Expenses of the National Office.   Hence, the difference of $4120.00, indicated as used for General Organization Expenses, was needed to meet the Deficit (or difference between Receipts & Expenditures) of the National Office.

DOCUMENT 23. continued

Document 24

Charles Ruthenberg, "Statement Recei[p]ts from Comintern Jan 1 to Sept 25th 1926," 8 October 1926, RTsKhIDNI 495–19–613. Original in English. "Tuel" stands for the Trade Union Educational League, "YWL" for the Young Workers League (predecessor of the Young Communist League), "YCI" for the Young Communist International, "Wopat" for the Workers Party. Dolsen is James H. Dolsen. "Indian students expense" refers to the cost of sending several Indians who were working in the United States to Moscow to study in Comintern schools before returning to work in India. "International publishers" refers to the party's publishing house. Overgaard is Andy Overgaard, a Communist labor organizer; Howat is Alexander Howat, a non-Communist who challenged John L. Lewis's leadership of the United Mine Workers and lost. The party backed Howat.

Attached to 6 mos report by Ruthenberg
1 copy Piatnitsky
1 copy Roy
1 copy [illegible]

Statement receits from Comintern Jan 1 to Sept 25th 1926 stop
Balance on hand Jan 1 as per previous statement 6664 dollars stop

Account third quarter 1925 comma 2 thousand dollars stop
4th quarter 1925 comma 6400 dollars stop
1st quarter 1926 comma 5000 dollars stop
Balance 1926 comma 3589 dollars stop
Lenin library fund comma 7500 dollars stop
For Tuel 5708 dollars stop
Canadian party comma 1500 dollars stop
YWL representative 400 dollars stop
YWL representative 400 dollars stop
YWL representative 500 dollars stop
For YWL 750 dollars
Account Host expense comma 1000 dollars stop
For Overgaard comma 353 dollars
Refund Dolsen expense comma 350 dollars stop
Refund account students expense comma 750 dollars stop
For CI representative 2000 dollars stop
Total receipts 14,864 dollars stop
Expenditures stop
Daily Workers 13000 dollars stop
International labor defense comma 4000 dollars stop
YCI representative comma 1555 dollars stop
Comintern representative comma 210 dollars stop
To YWL 750 dollars stop
To Canadian party comma 1500 dollars stop
Indian students expense comma 1792 dollars stop
International publishers comma Lenin library comma 1200 dollars stop

Document 24 *continued*

To Dolsen comma 300 dollars stop
To Overgaard comma 353 dollars stop
To Tuel *comma* 5717 dollars stop
Canadian party cable comma 66 dollars stop
Trade Union delegation to Srworc comma 1618 dollars stop
Expenses Yugoslav and Armenian comrades in Mexico comma 535 dollars stop
To Wopat for Howat expense comma 1000 dollars stop
To Wopat comma 9868 dollars stop
Total expenditures comma 44,864 dollars stop

Ruthenberg stop Oct. 8th 1926, 167 a-26.
[illegible script]

Designated Funds

The Comintern frequently earmarked money for specific purposes. **Document 25** is a 1925 letter from the Secretariat of the ECCI notifying the American party that it was sending $2,500 to finance a "Negro Labour Congress."[11] In addition to specifying the general purpose of the money—"The money appropriated for the Negro Labour Congress cannot be spent for any other Party purposes"— the Secretariat listed the exact amount designated for various expenditures, allocating, for example, $75 for advertising in the Negro press, setting a stationery budget of $50, ordering the party to produce one pamphlet (cost: $175) and two leaflets ($130). In addition, the Secretariat demanded a "detailed account" of all expenses, to be made after the meeting was over.

And the Comintern was not the only Soviet agency to subsidize the American Communist party. The Profintern (Red International of Labor Unions, or RILU), International Red Aid, and other Comintern-affiliated agencies each sent subsidies to their American counterparts, all of whom were part of the Communist movement. The accounts could become confused, as **documents 26, 27, and 28** indicate. Money intended for one purpose might be diverted to another. Document 26 indicates that Soviet money that was supposed to be spent on the Trade Union Educational League, the

11. The meeting was the founding convention of the American Negro Labor Congress, the party's organizing arm for black workers and farmers in the mid- to late 1920s.

124

party's trade union arm, was mistakenly spent on the *Daily Worker*. The party's regular subsidy, meanwhile, had been diverted in transit by Swedish Communists to their own party, rather than being transferred to America. The Americans had also, as document 27 noted, spent money sent to them from MOPR (International Red Aid) on the *Daily Worker*, which was in financial distress, because the courier who delivered the first $5,000 did not make it clear who had sent the money or that it was intended for MOPR's American counterpart, the International Labor Defense.[12] As we see from document 28, the Comintern accepted Ruthenberg's explanation of this financial tangle; here Ruthenberg summarizes their agreement about how to straighten the situation out.

Document 25

Secretariat of the ECCI to the CEC of the Workers Party of America, 3 February 1925, RTsKhIDNI 495–19–608. Original in English on Executive Committee of the Communist International letterhead with handwritten Russian annotations. The "CEC" is the Central Executive Committee. Note: the arithmetic in this document is off by $20: the total of the figures should be $2,480, not $2,500.

Ruthenberg wrote it down himself

No.   Moscow, February 3 1925

                                                    Strictly confidential

To the C.E.C. of the Workers'
Party of America.

Dear Comrades,

   To support the organizational work of the Negro Labour Congress we appropriated 2,500 dollars. The money will be sent to the C.E.C. of the W.P. of A. Your C.E.C. is responsible for carrying out the work as well as spending of the appropriated sum. The Budget Commission set up the following budget for the Negro Labour Congress:

12. MOPR (Mezhdunarodnaia organizatsiia pomoshchi revoliutsioneram), often called the International Red Aid in English, provided legal aid and assistance to Communist-backed strikes or to Communists and the families of Communists jailed by authorities.

The Executive Committee of the Communist International.

Address: Mokhovaia, 16. Address for telegrams: International, Moscow. Telephone No. 2-24-12, 56-71, suppl. 26.

Workers of all countries, unite!

No.   Moscow,   February 3   192_

Strictly confidential

For the C.E.C. of the Workers'
Party of America.

Dear Comrades,

To support the organisational work of the Negro Labour
Congress we appropriated 2,500 dollars. The money will be
sent to the C.E.C. of the W.P. of A. Your C.E.C. is responsible for carrying out the work as well as spending of the
appropriated sum. The Budget Commission set up the following
budget for the Negro Labour Congress:

		Dollars
A pamphlet expressing aims of the congress		175
Negro Press advertisement		75
Travelling expenses inorganisational work		375
Salary for two organisers for three months		780
Offices expenses for three months		475
Rgnt:	120 dol.	
Stenographer	325 "	
Stationary	50 "	
Two leaflets		130
Rental of halls for meetings		250
South African delegate		200
TOTAL		**2,500**

The money appropriated for the Negro Labour Congress
cannot be spent for any other Party purposes. We expect a
detailed account after the Negro Labour Congress.

With communist greetings,

Secretariat of the ECCI.

DOCUMENT 25. Secretariat of the ECCI to the CEC of the Workers Party of
America, 3 February 1925.

Document 25 *continued*

		Dollars
A pamphlet expressing aims of the congress		175
Negro Press advertisement		75
Travelling expenses in organisational work		375
Salary for two organisers for three months		780
Offices expenses for three months		495

	Rent:	120 dol.
	Stenographer	325 "
	Stationary	50 "

		Dollars
Two leaflets		130
Rental of halls for meetings		250
South African delegate		200
	TOTAL	2,500

The money appropriated for the Negro Labour Congress cannot be spent for any other Party purposes. We expect a detailed account after the Negro Labour Congress.

With communist greetings,

This document must
be enciphered

Secretariat of the ECCI.

Document 26

General Secretary, Workers (Communist) Party, "Statement Regarding Funds for T.U.E.L. Received by Party," 23 February 1926, RTsKhIDNI 515–1–629. Original in English. The reference to "files of the Omsk" refers to the OMS (Department of International Relations). The *Politiken* was a Swedish Communist journal.

Statement Regarding Funds for T. U. E. L.
  Received by Party

Moscow, Feb. 23., 1926

1 The Party receives its funds through connections seperate from the T. U. E. L. Funds for the T. U. E. L. have heretofore not been sent through the connections of the Party and the Secretary of the Party has never handled TUEL funds.

2 In May or early in June 1925 the Party received through its connections the sum of 7,250. At this time the second quarter of the 1925 allotment of the Party was due and this sum was considered to be this second allotment.

3 The Secretariat of the Party, which handled all matters concerning funds from the Comintern at the time of receipt of this $7,250 consisted of Comrades Foster, Bittelman and Ruthenberg.

4 Comrade Ruthenberg reported the receipt of this 7,250 to the Secretariat. The Secretariat voted the greater part of this amount to the Daily Worker Comrades Foster and Bittelman taking the initiative in the matter.

5 During the period of June, July, August, Comrade Ruthenberg, at the request of Comrade Foster, sent repeated coded cables, as can be substantiated by the files of the Omsk asking what had become of allotment of $7,500 and $1500 which the TUEL was expecting.

6 No replies were received to these cablegrams until early in September when a long cablegram was received listing all amounts sent to the Party in which it was stated $7,500 and $1500 had been sent to the Party for the TUEL. These funds at that time had all been voted by the Secretariat to the Daily Worker.

7 Comrade Ruthenberg then repeatedly cabled asking what had become of the second quarter allotment for the Party and received advice that this had also been sent. He replied that it had not been received. Upon his arrival in Moscow Comrade Piatnitzsky informed him that the second quarter allotment had been sent to Stockholm to be forwarded to the U.S.A. but that the manager of the Politiken had used the money for that paper to meet an emergency.

8 It appears therefore that the Politiken received the Party money and the Party received the TUEL money.

9 Additional confusion was caused by a cable from the Comintern stating that money for the Lenin Library had been sent. One of the sums received was taken for this amount, but it now appears that no remittance was made for the Lenin Library.

10 Similar confusion resulted in 1924, when Comrade Foster received and used for the TUEL $8,446 send for the Party, because $7,000 sent to the TUEL was not delivered. The Party received the $7,600 in 1925 (October), but the TUEL still owes $1,440 account this transaction.

11 The Party received and used for the Daily Worker by authority of the Secretariat, in which Comrade Foster and Bittelman were the majority

The sum of	$ 7,250	
and	1,500	
	$ 8,750	

Total due the TUEL from Party		8,750
The TUEL owes Party account		
1924 confusion	1,440	
The Party paid to		
TUEL in 1925	1,632.21	
The Party paid to		
Wangerin 1925	650.00	3,722.21
There is due the TUEL from Party		5,027.79

12 The Swedish Party recently remitted 2,000 of the Party funds which it withheld. It still owes approximately 4,000. The Swedish Party should be required to pay this 4,000 out of its 1926 allotment to the American Party and the American Party will transfer to the TUEL the 5,027.79 still due it from the funds it received which were intended for the TUEL and which were voted to the Daily Worker.

Fraternally submitted

General Secretary
Workers (Communist) Party

5027.79
750
5777 79
3974
1803.79

Document 27

Ruthenberg to Piatnitsky, 6 March 1926, RTsKhIDNI 515–1-594. Original in English.

Moscow, Mar.6,1926.

Dear Comrade Piatnitski:

During the year 1925 there was sent to our Party two items of $5,000 each by the Mopr which was to be delivered to the American Section of the Mopr, the International Labour Defense.

The first item of $5,000 which was received by the Party during the month of June, 1925, without any notice that it was intended for the Mopr was appropriated for the Daily Worker which was in financial difficulty by the Central Executive of the Party.

The second $5,000 we received at the end of 1925 and has been turned over to the International Labour Defense.

In regard to the first $5,000, after we were advised that this money was raised for the Mopr, the Party made arrangements and paid $1200 of this sum to the Mopr.

The total amount sent to the International Labour Defense by the Mopr was $10,000. and of this amount a total of $6200 has been turned over to the Mopr leaving a balance of $3800, which the Party is indebted to the Mopr.

The Mopr has requested that we authorise that this amount be paid out of our 1926 appropriation and we hereby authorise you to turn over to the Mopr $3800 and charge this amount to our account.

Fraternally yours,
C Ruthenberg
Secretary.
Workers Party of America.

Document 28

Executive Secretary, Workers Communist Party to Piatnitsky, 9 March 1926, RTsKhIDNI 515–1–629. Original in English.

Moscow, March 9, 1926.

Dear Comrade Piatnitski:

In accordance with the agreement made in the meeting of the sub-commission of the Budget Commission to take up the question of the adjustment of the money sent by the Profintern to the TUEL and the money used by the Swedish Party, I authorise you to pay from the account of the American Party the following sum:

Sent to TUEL		$7,250.00
" " " Railroad Department		1,500.00
Again sent to TUEL Railroad Department		750.00
	Total	$9,500.00

Deductions:		
Paid to TUEL	$1632.21	
" " " Railroad Dept.	650.00	
Due to Party from TUEL on account of receipt of Party funds by TUEL in 1924	1440.00	
Total	$3722.21	3,722.21
Balance due to TUEL $5,777.79		

Of this amount you are to collect $3974. from the Swedish Party and are to pay out of the account of the American Party $1803.79, making the total to be paid to the Profintern for the TUEL $5,777.79.

There is also to be adjusted the question of the funds of the International Red Aid which were received by the Party. On this account, $10,000 was received by the Party. The Party had paid to the International Labour Defence the whole of the last remittance of $5,000 and $1200 on account on the first remittance, making a total of $6200. This leaves $3800 due to the International Red Aid which we authorise you to pay to the International Red Aid and charge to our account.

Fraternally,

EXECUTIVE SECRETARY.
WORKERS COMMUNIST PARTY.

Not all the funds were sent by courier; many were laundered through various businesses, including that of Julius and Armand Hammer. **Document 29** is a cable, or possibly an internal memo, stating that the Comintern has just dispatched $6,495 for American party use; the money is to be paid directly to Armand Hammer at his Berlin office, and he will give further orders about its ultimate transfer to Ruthenberg. In **document 30** the Comintern informed Ruthenberg that a total of $14,777 was on the way; the money was to be subdivided as follows: $5,777 to assist the TUEL, $7,500 to publish an edition of Lenin's works in English, and $1,500 to pay part of the annual subsidy for the Canadian Communist party.[13] Again, these funds were to be transferred through the Berlin business office of Armand and Julius Hammer. In *The Secret World of American Communism* we reproduced documents showing that Julius and his oldest son, Armand, who later became a prominent American businessman, laundered Comintern money destined for America. Since that publication, Edward Epstein has published a biography of Armand Hammer that demonstrates, with the aid of additional documents from Russian archives, that not only did he carry money as a courier but his Russian business enterprises were fronts—money losers kept afloat by the Soviets in order to further covert activities in the United States.[14]

As we have seen, the numerous covert paths by which Comintern money flowed to the United States frequently caused confusion for those who were trying to keep the accounts straight. Some of this confusion involved the Hammers. **Document 31** contains Armand Hammer's reply to a Comintern query concerning how much money he had delivered to Joseph Moness, one of the Comintern's New York contacts, who was to pass it along for the use of the American Communist movement.

In answer to another Comintern attempt to set its books straight,

13. A number of the exchanges between the American party and the Comintern show that the Comintern regularly sent its subsidy for the Canadian Communist party through the American party. See documents 23 and 24, above, as well as Piatnitsky to Ruthenberg, 24 July 1926, RTsKhIDNI 495–19–613, and Alexander to Browder, October 1933, RTsKhIDNI 495–184–20, 1933 file.

14. Klehr, Haynes, and Firsov, *Secret World of American Communism,* 26–30; Edward Jay Epstein, *Dossier: The Secret History of Armand Hammer* (New York: Random House, 1996), 87–122.

in June 1926 (**document 32**) Ruthenberg explained that two couriers (designated number 1 and number 2) had delivered a total of $15,617; however, an expected $2,550 had not arrived, and the previous quarter's subsidies had been $400 short.

In addition to financing the American party's domestic activities, the Comintern usually paid the salary and expenses of its representatives stationed in the United States as American party supervisors. In document 32, Ruthenberg requested money for this purpose. **Document 33,** a May 1926 telegram from the Comintern, contains several orders concerning allocations of the $5,589 that has just been sent to America, $2,000 of which was to be used to pay "Comrade Henry," the Comintern representative in the United States. The Comintern had decided that the representative's salary must be equivalent to that of a member of the CPUSA Central Committee.[15] In **document 34,** dated 11 June 1926, Ruthenberg acknowledges receipt of the $5,589 and reports that $1,000 was used to reimburse the party for an earlier, covert subsidy given to Alexander Howat, a Communist-backed rival to United Mine Workers president John L. Lewis.[16] This did not represent an isolated case of Soviet funding of factionalism in American trade unions. **Document 35** is an extract from the minutes of a July 1926 meeting of the Comintern's Anglo-American Secretariat. The American party had requested money to support its campaign to unseat Lewis; the Secretariat reported that a favorable recommendation was being sent to the Budget Commission.

By the mid-1920s American Communists were so dependent on Soviet funding that they grew indignant when funds that had been promised did not materialize. **Documents 36, 37, and 38** all display irritation because money from Moscow has been delayed, thus crippling the activities of the International Labor Defense (document 36), work in Communist agricultural organizing (document 37), and the publication of one of the party's newspapers (document 38).

15. CPUSA Central Committee members were cadres who received a party salary.
16. The subsidy to Howat was also mentioned in document 24, above.

Document 29

"Make Arrangements to Pay . . . ," RTsKhIDNI 495–19–612. Original in Russian. Handwritten. Undated, but the context suggests 1925 or 1926. It is unclear whether this is a draft of a cable or an internal Comintern memo.

Make arrangements to pay <u>Armand Hammer</u> *personally 6,495 dollars in Berlin at the office of* <u>The United American Company</u> *(Alamerico)* <u>Augsburger Str. 47</u>, *and he will give orders, if necessary by telegram, for their New York office to pay this money to* <u>Moness</u> *for C. E.* <u>Ruthenberg</u>.

Document 30

Comintern to Ruthenberg, 13 April 1926, RTsKhIDNI 495–19–613. Original in English. Handwritten.

9–8–26

To comrade Ruthenberg

According to your demands, which have been mentioned in your letters of [illegible] 26, we send you today through Berlin—Julius Hammer—the following sums—$7.500 for the editions of Lenin's works (according to indications of comrade Bedacht, $5.777—your debt to Tuel (according to the demands of comrade Foster). Will you please transfer it to the addressee. We send you also $1.500 for the Com. Party of Canada. This sum is composed of the ballance of its last year's money and of the part for the first quarter of 1926. Please send it to our Canadian Party.

Thus we send alltogether the sum of $14.777. Please, confirm the receipt of the money sent and let us know, when and to whom you handed it out.

As for the sum for Lenin's editions, we beg you to make regularly corresponding accounts.

13.IV–1926
Ya Sheh[? initials]

Document 31

"Quotation from a Letter . . . ," 21 May 1925, RTsKhIDNI 495–19–612. Original in Russian. Handwritten. Because the Russian alphabet does not contain the letter H, this document follows the standard practice of using the nearest equivalent, a Cyrillic letter Romanized as G. "L." probably stands for Leningrad. A cable found with this document indicates that the total amount Hammer conveyed to Moness was about $18,000. (See "Telegram sent . . . ," 11 June 1925, RTsKhIDNI 495–19–612.)

Document 31 continued

Quotation from a letter from Comrade G.'s [Hammer's] oldest son from L., 21 May 1925 (This son passed money to Moness last year.)

Regarding Moness I am almost certain that I paid him the entire sum except for several hundred dollars about which there were no clear instructions in the telegram. Since I am not in a position to find out from here (from L.) I will not attempt to confirm, but I would have absolutely refused to pay them more money. If I am not mistaken, when I wrote to my father that I had given Moness this amount he answered me and said that I should have given him the rest of the money (about 800 dollars) as this made up the full amount. Meanwhile Moness left for Europe and there was no one for me to contact.

Document 32

Ruthenberg to Comintern, 7 June 1926, RTsKhIDNI 495–19–613. Original in English, followed by a handwritten Russian translation. In the margin are the handwritten Russian words "Must check [illegible]." Only the English is transcribed here.

We have received 14717 dollars sent through number 2 and 5 hundred and 4 hundred for YCI representative through number 1 stop 2050 and 5 hundred sent through number 1 in april not received stop Investigate stop 4 hundred short last quarter 1925 received stop How about funds for Comintern representative about we cabled twice stop Ruthenberg 7/VI

Document 33

Comintern to Ruthenberg, 25 May 1926, RTsKhIDNI 495–19–613. Original in English. The marginal notation is in handwritten Russian.

Sent 25.5.26 via Com. Mabar

Comrade Ruthenberg.

Your telegramm requesting subsidy received. You can take a loan of Dol. 5.000 from the Lenin works edition fund only if you will be able to return in time and if because of that the edition will not be postponed.

Regarding your request about a new subsidy of dol. 15.000 it is decided to refuse but to send you the remainder for 1926 a sum of 3.589 which goes to you to-day via Stockholm.

Besides that we are sending to-day by the same way dol. 2.000 for comr. Henry. [Turn?] them over to him and tell him that according [to] a decision of Secretariat his salary must be equal to the salary of a member of CC. Let him

Document 33 *continued*

send an account of money spent. The question of his staying will be decided additionally.

Alltogether we are sending dol. 5.589. Notify receipt.

Document 34

Ruthenberg to Comintern, 11 June 1926, RTsKhIDNI 495–19–613. Original in English, followed by Russian handwritten translation. Only the English is transcribed here.

Received 5589 through number 1 stop Cable items included and purpose also now received 750 for 8 stop 353 for Overgard and 1 thousand refund account advance to Howat stop 5 hundred for Wangerin still short Ruthenberg

11/VI

Document 35

"Extracts from Minutes of National Secretariat for America and Canada Meeting of July 7th, 1926," 7 July 1926, RTsKhIDNI 495–19–613. Original in English with Russian annotations. Roy is probably M. N. Roy, an Indian Communist.

EXTRACTS

FROM MINUTES OF NATIONAL SECRETARIAT FOR AMERICA AND

CANADA MEETING OF JULY 7th, 1926.

Discussed:

Decided:

1. Telegram of Comrades Foster, Ruthenberg and the representative of the ECCI asking for funds to intensify the campaign among the miners.

National Secretariat supports the demand for funds; to put the question to the Budget Commission requesting a quick and favourable decision; to request the Profintern to send financial aid.

[illegible Russian script]

Roy
Responsible Secretary.

Document 36

James Cannon to MOPR, 8 October 1926, RTsKhIDNI 495–19–613. Original in English. Cannon was a senior American party official who ran the International Labor Defense.

For MOPR stop Failure to send 3860 for conference and organisation expenses causing serious demoralisation our work stop Large expenses in curred on basis promised funds creates severe financial crisis stop Urgently request your cable funds immediately stop Answer Cannon 8–X–26

9–X–26 [illegible signature]

Document 37

Lovestone to Pepper, 15 October 1928? RTsKhIDNI 495–19–613. Original in English, with handwritten Russian annotations. Krestintern was the Red Peasant International, an organization for agricultural workers that was similar to the Profintern.

From New York   Insert No. 161.30
Received 15/10

For Pepper, Excursion money unreceived thus paralysing work wire date money cabled stop Piatnitzky must immediately cable our 17 hundred dollars he holding stop For Krestintern rush 5 thousand for agriculltural department war campaign, Lovestone,

[illegible script in Russian]

Document 38

Lovestone to Bukharin and Molotov, 26 September 1928, RTsKhIDNI 495–19–615. Original in English with handwritten Russian annotations. *Novyi mir* was the CPUSA's Russian-language newspaper.

From New York *sent 26/IX–28*   Insert No. 606.
received and deciphered 27/IX at 11 o'clock

Bukharin Molotov Insist you execute your promise rendering immediate substantial financial assistance Novy Mir cable money immediately. Lovestone. No 34.

D/2.
Copy in Russian sent to Molotov
(Bukharin not available)   7150 * 26.IX.1928 [stamp]

Bankrolling Depression-Era Activities

In January 1930 a Comintern representative in the United States, "H. Davis," sent a report (**document 39**) back to Moscow that analyzed the dismal state of the party's finances after the expulsion of Jay Lovestone in 1929 (see chapter 1). It is not altogether clear who Davis was: he may have been Boris Mikhailov, who arrived in New York in May 1929 as the chief Comintern representative. Mikhailov officially worked as a correspondent for the Soviet news agency Tass, but he became the de facto head of the CPUSA during its post-Lovestone reorganization. Mikhailov, however, usually used the pseudonym "Williams." Bertram Wolfe, the CPUSA representative to the Comintern at the time of Lovestone's expulsion, noted in his autobiography that Mikhailov brought two assistants with him.[17] Davis may have been one of the assistants, or the name may simply have been another pseudonym used by Mikhailov.

Davis estimated that there was a gap between CPUSA income from dues and private contributions and its expenditures of between $3,000 and $4,000 a month, but he claimed that the party was learning to live within its means. He placed the blame for earlier shortfalls on Lovestone and begged the Comintern to help the party clear debts of approximately $25,000, promising that no further subsidies would be required.

In spite of Davis's pledge, Comintern records indicate that Soviet money continued to flow into the CPUSA's coffers, albeit in reduced amounts, during the 1930s. In 1933 "Alexander," the alias of a Profintern officer named Keetagnian, sent Browder a cable informing him that "Francis" would be bringing $5,980 to the United States.[18] The cable indicated that $2,100 was a quarterly payment for "USA assistance 3 months"; another $1,000 was for the "USA reserve," and that "reserve [was] not to be spent without our indication." The Profintern allocated $1,500 to "San-Francisco assistance 3 months."[19] Very likely the latter was support for the San Francisco office of the Pan-Pacific Trade Union Secretariat,

17. Bertram D. Wolfe, *A Life in Two Centuries* (New York: Stein and Day, 1981), 527.

18. "Francis" was one Francis Bedrick. See Alexander to Browder, 11 February 1933, RTsKhIDNI 495–184–20, 1933 file.

19. Alexander to Browder, 2 February 1933, RTsKhIDNI 495–184–20, 1933 file.

a Profintern agency run by the American Communist Harrison George.[20] Smaller sums were allocated to pay the salary of one "Arturo" (unknown) and as a quarterly payment for an unspecified Profintern operation in Canada.

There are many other telegrams indicating that a number of couriers were delivering money to Browder throughout 1933 and 1934. In a cable of 12 July 1933, for example, Browder confirmed that Max Bedacht, head of the party-aligned International Workers Order, had brought $1,900 from Moscow and that one "Finkelberg" (unknown) had delivered $3,000, making a total of $4,900.[21] (After an inquiry from the Comintern, which had sent $3,000 via Bedacht, Browder agreed that Bedacht had actually delivered that amount.)[22] Browder's cable of 12 July also identified Abraham Heller, a wealthy Russian-born American Communist, as a conduit for party funds. Heller was the founder of an industrial oxygen business that he later sold for a considerable sum to Union Carbide. During the New Economic Policy period in the Soviet Union, he operated a profitable acetylene welding business.[23] Heller, a fervent Communist, sank more than $110,000 of his personal fortune into International Publishers, the CPUSA's publishing arm.

There are also a number of telegrams from party leaders in the United States recommending couriers. Bedacht made frequent delivery trips, and in January 1938 Earl Browder, who was in Moscow, sent a handwritten note to the Comintern (**document 40**) suggesting that Bedacht be used as a special courier. Browder's request went to M. A. Moskvin (Mikhail Trilisser), the Soviet intelligence officer who supervised the Comintern's covert activities. Moskvin then wrote a confidential memo (**document 41**) to Nikolai Yezhov, head of the NKVD, requesting that Bedacht be issued a Soviet visa so that he could perform courier duties.[24]

20. George's work for the Pan-Pacific Trade Union Secretariat is discussed in Klehr, Haynes, and Firsov, *Secret World of American Communism*, 49–60.

21. Earl [Browder] to Comintern, 12 July 1933, RTsKhIDNI 495–184–42, 1933 file.

22. "Bedacht Had from Us . . . ," 21 July 1933, RTsKhIDNI 495–184–20, 1933 file; Earl [Browder] to Comintern, 26 July 1933, RTsKhIDNI 495–184–42, 1933 file.

23. The New Economic Policy period was a span of a few years (1921–1925) after the Bolshevik Revolution in which Lenin allowed private enterprises to operate in selected sectors of the Soviet economy.

24. The NKVD (Narodnyi komissariat vnutrennikh del, People's commissariat

The annual subsidies from Moscow in the 1930s appear to have been between $10,000 and $15,000 (roughly $110,000 to $160,000 in 1995 dollars), although supplemental payments were made for such items as travel by Communist officials and special projects. The "Alexander" cable discussed above mentions a reserve of $1,000 in addition to a 1933 Profintern subsidy of $8,400 for Communist trade union work. A Comintern cable to Browder dated 13 November 1933 refers to a subsidy for CPUSA activities (not connected with trade unions) of $6,300: $4,200 is to cover expenses for the first six months and $2,100 those of the rest of the year. The cable noted that two couriers had already delivered the full amount. In addition, the Comintern cable stated that a third courier had been dispatched on 10 November with $720 to cover six months' salary for "Emil," presumably the alias of a Comintern operative.[25]

The combined subsidy for party and trade union work in 1933 came to $14,700, in addition to the $1,000 reserve. This total is only a fraction of the subsidy amounts recorded during the 1920s, but it is not trivial. In the 1930s, a blue-collar worker typically earned $1,000 a year, and many white-collar workers and lower-level professionals earned less than $2,000. Thus, $14,700 would have met the salary requirements of perhaps ten party organizers, and possibly more, for the party paid its lower-level cadre wages that were closer to blue-collar than to white-collar levels.

In 1934 the Comintern notified the CPUSA that a courier carrying $4,818 was already in transit; part of the funds were to be used to subsidize Communist trade union newspapers and part for work among black Americans.[26] In the same year, the Comintern cabled that "Black," the alias of Solomon Mikhelson-Manuilov, U.S. station chief of OMS, which oversaw covert activities, had complained that his wages were not being paid regularly. The CPUSA was reminded that the Comintern had already allocated funds for

---

of internal affairs) was the Soviet security and political police, successor to the GPU (Gosudarstvennoe politicheskoe upravlenie, State political directorate) and predecessor to the KGB (Komitet gosudarstvennoi bezopasnosti, Committee for state security). Yezhov is best known for the "Yezhovchina," the peak phase of Stalin's Great Terror, when Yezhov supervised the imprisonment and death of millions of Soviet citizens.

25. Andrew to Browder, 13 November 1933, RTsKhIDNI 495–184–19, 1933 file.

26. Andrew to Browder, 29 June 1934, RTsKhIDNI 495–184–24, 1934 file.

his salary in its subsidies.[27] Also in 1934 "Spector" (another of Mikhelson-Manuilov's cover names) reported to the Comintern that he and Browder had jointly confirmed with receipts the expenditures of $10,394 for various purposes that had been specified earlier. This message, however, did not break down the expenditures by purpose or recipient.[28] A 1935 Comintern cable directed that $3,000 be used to finance a training school for CPUSA organizers.[29]

There are also indications that, Browder's insistence to the contrary, annual Comintern subsidies continued beyond 1935. An undated telegram from 1936, addressed to the American, Canadian, and British parties—identified as "all parties and committees which receive subventions"—noted that while the 1937 subsidies would not be set "before we get cash-balance of party cash for 1936," three-quarters of the anticipated sum would be sent forthwith. True, this cable did not specify an amount for the CPUSA subsidy; it only indicated that there was such a subsidy.[30] Browder made a special appeal that year to the Comintern for $10,000 to help finance the party's electoral campaign.[31] He suggested that the money be taken from Alexander Trachtenberg, head of International Publishers. Trachtenberg was himself receiving Soviet subsidies to publish the many pamphlets and books promoting communism that issued from the publishing house.[32] Mikhelson-Manuilov suggested another way to launder the campaign funds:

27. Comintern to CPUSA, "Black Complaining . . . ," 19 March 1934, RTsKhIDNI 495–184–25, 1934 file.

28. Spector to Michael, "Financial Report December First . . . ," RTsKhIDNI 495–184–38, 1934 file. This document is not clearly dated and may be an early 1934 report about 1933 payments. We have been unable to locate the earlier document.

29. Michael to Kraft, 13 June 1935, RTsKhIDNI 495–184–28, 1935 file. "Kraft" was yet another alias for Mikhelson-Manuilov.

30. "Oral Communication to All Parties . . . ," RTsKhIDNI 495–184–37, 1936 file.

31. Earl [Browder] to Moskwin [Moskvin], 15 May 1936, RTsKhIDNI 495–184–33, 1936 file. Browder phrased the request as being for a loan rather than for a grant.

32. Confirmation of Comintern payments to Trachtenberg for publications include: Kraft to Comintern, 16 July 1934, RTsKhIDNI 495–184–38, 1934 file; Comintern to CPUSA, "Trachtenberg Must Hand . . . ," 26 November 1933, RTsKhIDNI 495–184–19, 1933 file; Son to Brother, 2 April 1942, RTsKhIDNI 495–184–19, 1942 file. "Son" was the code name for Rudy Baker, head of the CPUSA secret apparatus, and "Brother" was Georgi Dimitrov. Earl Browder was code-named "Father."

World Tourists could advance it to the CPUSA from its funds, and the Comintern would then reimburse Intourist, the Soviet state travel agency, which was owed money by World Tourists.[33]

In the 1930s the CPUSA had less need for Soviet subsidies than it had in the 1920s. The party had accumulated real property; it owned the necessary printing and other equipment for its activities; its membership was larger; and it received donations from a small group of wealthy members and sympathizers like Abraham Heller and Frederick Vanderbilt Field. But the supply of Moscow gold may not have decreased as much as our figures suggest. The Russian historian Dmitri Volkogonov, who has had access to Russian archives that are still closed to Western researchers, writes that in the 1930s Stalin reduced the Comintern's budget but increasingly directed that subsidies for foreign Communists move through NKVD channels and be assigned to the NKVD's budget. The smaller subsidies from the Comintern during the 1930s and early 1940s may misrepresent the reduction in Soviet support for the CPUSA because they do not reflect increases from Soviet intelligence agencies.[34]

Document 39

H. Davis to Esteemed Comrades, 13 January 1930, RTsKhIDNI 495–19–131. Original in handwritten Russian.

New York
13 January 1930
N5/W.

Esteemed comrades,

A grim legacy of the party's factional past was its <u>financial position</u>. Here mismanagement, a complete lack of planning, and the inclination to live "from day to day" were the rule. Sources from which the party could draw <u>extraordinary</u> funds were almost exclusively in the hands of Lovestone: no

33. Kraft to Miller, 15 May 1936, RTsKhIDNI 495–184–33, 1936 file.
34. Volkogonov, *Lenin,* 398–405. The archives of Soviet intelligence agencies are still closed.

one else had access to them or even knowledge of them. In times of financial difficulties—and these occurred very frequently—Lovestone would single-handedly exert pressure on these sources and come up with money, present-ing it to the party unexpectedly and with great flourish, as if to say, "See what a slick operator I am, and how I always manage to save the party in times of trouble." Furthermore, considerable funds were expended on factional struggle—the costs of organizing factional apparatus, communications, fa-cilities for factional meetings of both groups etc., etc.

When he left the party, Lovestone did not take very much with him: of the 165 people expelled during the period of the struggle with Lovestone, about a hundred are with him at present; however, he did take from the party many sources of financial support, sources with which only he had been connected or of which only he knew. And these sources had in the past been the main support of the party's finances.

During the first months following Lovestone's expulsion the party's finan-cial position was at times nothing short of catastrophic; September and Octo-ber were particularly difficult in this regard. The party was living from day to day, the question of where to get money was the principal question at every meeting of its leadership organs. Every four or five days the "Daily Worker" or "Freiheit" would face the threat of its next number's not coming out or of a strike by typesetters who were not receiving their wages, etc.

True, that same period saw the first benefits of the liquidation of factions and hence of factional expenses. But the mismanagement and chaos contin-ued. In September we raised the issue of putting the party's financial policy on firm footing. Organizationally, this took the form of creating a financial commission with extremely broad powers: to cut expenses and staff, to con-centrate the use of extraordinary [financial] sources—neither the Secretariat nor the Politburo was to incur the slightest expense of any significance with-out a prior resolution by the Financial Commission. The commission did not begin working immediately; its personnel had to be modified by the selection of stronger people, good "managers." By November or December the commis-sion's work was proceeding systematically; order and planning began to take shape.

Next, it was essential to reduce to a minimum the party's financial depen-dence on private, at times chance, sources—on which it had chiefly (if not almost exclusively) subsisted—to move the party over to regular mainte-nance by party and working masses, rather than by chance and quite capri-cious bourgeois "benefactors." Out of this necessity grew the reform of the dues collection system, which we began in November, running a campaign about it not only in the newspaper but in all leaflets, and which was intro-duced at the beginning of the new year. Here there was no avoiding a certain

amount of resistance, for the districts were loath to part with the old patri-
archal order in which they would take all the dues and all funds for themselves, giving nothing to the center. With the introduction of this system—
and in fact we had introduced it in a number of places as early as September
on a trial basis—it was possible to begin constructing a sounder party budget.
The development of the new budget, of course, went slowly; it had been
delayed; we hadn't finished it by year's end—and we have only now got its
draft ready, which is due for certain (minor, to be sure) changes.

Its basic feature is that it is to a much greater degree built on membership
dues rather than on private donations. We had the following proceeds from
membership dues in the past year:

for October $1,395.25
" November $1,730.12
" December $1,035.56

The new system of membership dues freely allows us to enter a monthly
income of $4,500 in the budget from membership dues for the coffers of the
CC. By contrast, so-called private donations account for no more that $1,000
a month in the budget.

The preliminary draft estimates party (CC) expenses at $8,600 a month,
including such subsidies from Central Committee coffers as the following:

to the newspaper "The Daily Worker" $2,000/month
to the magazine "The Communist" $100/month
for Youth $200/month
for the language groups' press $150/month

Aid to the districts from the CC—apart from the amount they receive from
membership dues and private sources—is entered in the draft as $200 a
month.

We will do some additional work on the draft in the Secretariat. I foresee the
possibility of (1) some reduction in general expenses—chiefly from cutting
funds for the apparatus—and (2) some increase in fundamental aid to districts; in any case, I will try to arrange this. But the essential aspect of the
budget remains: it is built exclusively on the funds of the party itself, without
any external support whatsoever, and this year the party will not ask for any
subsidies, either for the party or for the newspaper. Even such extraordinary
expenses as the convening of a party conference are provided for by the
budget and will be covered by the party's own funds.

One matter remains: debts. They have accumulated during the past two or
three years; currently, for instance, in January we are paying debts from the
last party conference, held in January of last year. The party's debts hang like
a millstone around its neck. They must be cleared because they could hamper
the orderly financial existence of a party without a deficit and without sub-

sidies; they might ruin the good order of our finances, which we have worked so hard to achieve.

The party's Financial Commission determined a total figure for the party's debts of $37,835.05. That, of course, is a bookkeeping figure, not a real one. It was already clear to me from a preliminary review of debts with the comrades from the Financial Commission that the party was not going to pay a number of these debts and that there was no need for it to pay them. The real figure, according to my preliminary calculations, will come to between $23,000 and $25,000.

Early next week the Secretariat will make the following request of the Budget Commission: the party is presenting its budget; that budget is such that this year the party is not requesting and will not request any sort of subsidies or extraordinary support; the party asks for help in paying off only old debts, to eliminate the grim factional legacy in the area of finances, to meet the obligations that have accumulated over the past two to three years.

That request is hardly asking too much. I trust, Com. Mikhail, that you will appreciate all the efforts we have made here to achieve the regularization of the party's finances. We did not pull it off without a struggle: we had to fight with grasping tendencies, with the view, for instance, that the Budget Commission is obliged to give us subsidies: "That's what it's there for, after all. No subsidies? What sort of internationalism is that?" With the help of the determined and reasonable comrades from the Financial Commission, we have demonstrated with numbers that the party is capable of existing completely independently and that, what's more, in a year or by the end of this year the party will be able to render certain regular assistance to fraternal parties in Cuba, the Philippines, and Mexico. That will be internationalism. I hope that you will approve and appreciate the firm resolve of the party leadership to live without subsidies, and that you will grasp the full meaning of the necessity of clearing our debts. We will furnish a precise figure for those debts in our report. And just as our budget was drafted without "grasping," I will make every effort to give you not some unfounded, "grasping" figure for our debts but the truthful, real sum of the party's actual obligations. I ask you to take that sum seriously rather than as an attempt to "overcharge" and extract as much as possible.

I hope that the Budget Commission will accommodate our party in its present need. For our part we will attempt to secure every guarantee that the sum obtained (and we will need to have it right away) will not be squandered on trifles, on other needs, but will actually go to pay off our debts.

With comradely greetings,
H. Davis

Document 40

Earl Browder, "I Recommend Max Bedacht . . . ," 24 January 1938, RTsKhIDNI 495–261–34. Original in English. Handwritten. "I.W.O." is the International Workers Order, a party fraternal organization.

Moscow, Jan. 24. 1938

I recommend Max Bedacht for special courier in connection with U.S.A., (but not for political reports); He is one of foundation members of CP. and is now Nat'l Secy. of I.W.O.

Earl Browder

Moscow, Jan. 24, 1938

Document 41

Moskvin to Yezhov, 2 February 1938, RTsKhIDNI 495–261–34. Original in Russian.

No. 20

2.2.1938

To the Secretary of the CC of the AUCP(b)
Com. N. I. Yezhov

I ask you to issue a tourist visa to enter the USSR for:

1.BEDACHT, Max (Amer. passp.) Born 1883, barber, member of the Swiss Social Democratic Party since 1905, member of the U.S. Socialist Party, 1908 to 1919. Since 1919, member of the CPUSA.
Member of the CC and the PB of the CPUSA since 1921.
Was a representative of the CPUSA at the ECCI in 1926.
Was a delegate to the 3d and 4th congresses of the C.I.
Recommended by the general secretary of the CPUSA, Comrade Browder, as a one-time courier.

Please send visa to New York.

M. A. (M. A. MOSKVIN)

SE/3   E.[?] Verm[?]

Fifty Years of Soviet Subsidies

The onset of World War II further complicated the logistical arrangements for delivering money but did not stop it from coming. Scattered documents indicate that the party's "secret apparatus," its covert arm, which was directed by Rudy Baker, received Soviet subsidies via mail drops. In February 1940, Baker and Browder cabled Georgi Dimitrov, head of the Comintern: "We propose you send several 1000 bill every 2 or 3 weeks, scilfully concealed inside cover english edition book published cooperative publishing society and addressed Mr. A. Spritzman 1709 Boston road Bronx New York." Baker repeated the suggestion in a second cable, saying, "Propose you again send additional 500d. or 1000 bill skillfully concealed in cover of book publisched in USSR and send to: Mrs. M. Steinberg 326 Beach N66 Street Arwerne New York."[35]

No direct reply to these requests was located, but in 1942 Baker reported to Dimitrov that he had "received during year 1941 85 of which gave Trachtenberg—35, Son—10"; he had distributed the rest to various other people.[36] Whether the figures refer to hundreds or thousands of dollars is unclear, but it is probably thousands, as is suggested by a 1942 year-end financial report of the CPUSA secret apparatus that Baker sent to the Comintern. It details what was spent in 1942 ($11,311) and what funds remain for 1943 ($18,834). The total came to $30,145 (approximately $250,000 in 1995 dollars).[37]

By the end of the 1940s, with the onset of the Cold War and the CPUSA's public support of Stalin, American Communists were once again on the defensive. The Soviet Union was called upon to finance a significant portion of the CPUSA budget in order to keep the party active. As the Congress and the public became increasingly vocal in their anticommunism, however, and as Communists

35. "Several 1000 bill" means several thousand dollars and "500d. or 1000 bill" means five hundred or a thousand dollars. Father and Son to Brother, "We Discussed . . . ," 13 February 1940, and "Propose You Again . . . ," both in RTsKhIDNI 495–184–4, 1939–1940 file. "Propose You Again . . . " is undated.

36. Son to Brother, 2 April 1942, RTsKhIDNI 495–184–19, 1942 file.

37. "Son Financial Statement for 1942," in Son to Brother, RTsKhIDNI 495–74–480. The document is undated. The complete text of the year-end report, which includes the financial statement, is reprinted in Klehr, Haynes, and Firsov, *Secret World of American Communism*, 206–15. It is not clear whether this financial report was for Baker's entire secret apparatus or for a single network.

were subpoenaed, questioned, and shunned for their perceived ties to the Soviet Union, the CPUSA felt even more pressure to conceal that the party funding was largely supplied by a foreign power. Subsequently, the denial of Moscow gold has become a public party stance—one that began to be accepted among scholars as well in the 1970s and 1980s. But in fact, after 1950, Soviet subsidies became an important component of the annual CPUSA budget.

In 1950 the Soviet Union established a new system for subsidizing foreign Communist parties. Funded by contributions from the USSR, Eastern European satellites, and China, the International Trade Union Fund for Aid to Leftist Workers' Organizations was set up under the aegis of the Romanian Trade Union Council. The first listing of a contribution to the CPUSA that we have located came in 1958, when $210,000 was sent. In 1959 the CPUSA received $250,000, and International Publishers was sent an additional $50,000. By 1962 the subsidy was $475,000. In 1963 the CPUSA asked for a million dollars and received $500,000. In 1965 the CPUSA received its first million-dollar subsidy.[38]

One of the most unusual operations in this long and profitable relationship involved Morris and Jack Childs, two brothers who were senior members of the CPUSA. For more than twenty years they were couriers, transferring Soviet funds to the CPUSA. Secretly, however, they were U.S. government agents: in the early 1950s the FBI had successfully recruited them. Beginning in 1958, Morris Childs made trips to Moscow to pick up funds, while Jack Childs received cash from Soviet couriers in New York City or Canada. Between 1958 and 1980 they delivered more than $28 million in Soviet subsidies to the CPUSA, reporting the while to the FBI.[39]

Additional information about Soviet funding of the CPUSA came to light shortly after the break-up of the Soviet Union in 1991.

38. A large number of documents bearing on Soviet funding of foreign parties can be found in *Fond 89: The Soviet Communist Party on Trial* (London: Chadwyck Healey, 1986), microfilm, reel 14.

39. The annual amounts delivered by the Childs brothers are listed in appendix B of John Barron, *Operation SOLO: The FBI's Man in the Kremlin* (Washington, D.C.: Regnery, 1996). Barron's account, while generally reliable, contains no citations and is careless about some of the details. On the strengths and weaknesses of the book, see Theodore Draper, "Our Man in Moscow," *New York Review of Books,* 9 May 1996, 4–7. The role of the Childs brothers as FBI informants was first revealed in David J. Garrow, *The FBI and Martin Luther King, Jr.: From "Solo" to Memphis* (New York: Norton, 1981), 21–77.

In his memoirs, published in 1994, Oleg Kalugin, a retired KGB general who had served as a Soviet intelligence officer in the United States, makes several references to such subsidies. Kalugin writes that when he served in the KGB's New York office during the 1960s, "one of our KGB case officers was assigned full time to the American Communists, delivering money and instructions from Moscow." He also reports on KGB assistance and cash subsidies that went to a publishing firm headed by Carl Marzani, a veteran Communist who concealed his party membership for much of his life, as well as to two left-wing American political journals.[40]

The most dramatic evidence of continuing Soviet subsidies, however, came out of an investigation by Russian prosecutors into the use of state funds by the Communist Party of the Soviet Union to subsidize foreign Communist parties. Deputy Prosecutor-General Yevgeny Lisov uncovered a top secret budget account dated 3 December 1989 and signed by V. Falin, International Bureau Chief of the CPSU Central Committee, in which, noted Lisov:

> The International Fund for Assistance to Leftist Workers' Organizations has for many years been formed from the generous dues of CPSU and a number of other socialist countries' Communist parties. . . . The CPSU dues allocated to the International Fund for Leftist Workers' Organizations in 1989 amounted to (reference number P144/129 dated 29 December 1989) 13.5 million "hard" rubles, or 22,044,673 U.S. dollars. . . . Seventy-three Communist parties, workers parties and revolutionary groups received aid from the CPSU fund in 1989.

Lisov announced that during the 1980s the "amount received by all foreign parties for the ten-year period totaled over 200 million dollars."[41]

The investigation revealed that the subsidies to the CPUSA had been particularly large throughout the 1980s. Lisov turned over material documenting these subsidies to the *Washington Post* Moscow bureau chief, Michael Dobbs, as well as to several Russian newspapers. **Document 42** is one of these: an undated letter from

40. Oleg Kalugin, with Fen Montaigne, *The First Directorate: My Thirty-Two Years in Intelligence and Espionage against the West* (New York: St. Martin's Press, 1994), 49–54.

41. Yevgeny Lisov, "Investigation: Greens for Reds," *Ogonyok* 9 (February 1992): 6. At this time, the new Yeltsin government was trying to discredit the CPSU by exposing its subsidy of foreign Communist parties and presenting the practice as an illegal diversion of state funds for private party purposes.

Gus Hall, head of the CPUSA from 1959 to the present day, to Boris Ponomarev (spelled "Ponamarev" here), a member of the Secretariat of the CPSU Central Committee who was in charge of CPSU relations with Communist parties in noncommunist countries. Internal references suggest that the letter was written in the late summer or fall of 1981. It contains a plea for financial aid, although it does not mention a specific amount. Most striking is Hall's attempt to lay the groundwork for increased subsidies by arguing that the current American political life offers great possibilities for increased Communist influence—this in the first years of Ronald Reagan's presidency. Hall urges that this opportunity not be wasted for lack of money. Two years later, Hall remained optimistic about the CPUSA's opportunities. He wrote to Moscow asserting that he was "convinced that the potential of the mass upsurge can be turned into a reality if we can reach the eyes and ears of the millions with our message" and reiterated that "our one single-most serious obstacle to doing this is the lack of financial means."[42]

By 1987 Hall had apparently concluded that his predictions of imminent Communist gains were wearing thin; it was better to stress the importance of the party in an increasingly imperialistic country. At this time, as **document 43** indicates, the American Communist party was receiving an annual subsidy of $2 million. It was not enough, insisted Hall, who complained that despite record fundraising, the party's fixed costs were rising: it had been forced to cut back on its publishing ventures, Communist election campaigns were becoming more expensive, and members had even been forced to mortgage homes. He asked for an additional $2 million, justifying the 100 percent increase by noting that "because our Party works in the decaying heart of imperialism whatever we do in influencing events in the United States has an impact on world developments."

It may have been too late in the fiscal year for Moscow to accede to Hall's request: **document 44,** a handwritten, signed receipt from Hall, dated 14 March 1987, indicates that he received only the regular allocation of $2 million. **Document 45,** however, is another

---

42. Hall to Dear Comrades, reproduced in John E. Haynes and Harvey Klehr, "'Moscow Gold,' Confirmed at Last?" *Labor History* 33, no. 2 (Spring 1992): 287–88.

handwritten, signed receipt, this one dated 1988, which shows that the subsidy had been increased to $3 million. Accompanying the latter item is **document 46,** a memo from N. S. Leonov, deputy head of the KGB's First Chief Directorate (foreign intelligence arm), to Anatoly Dobrynin, former Soviet ambassador to the United States and Ponomarev's successor in the CPSU Secretariat, confirming that Hall has received the money and passing along the receipt.

According to Lisov, Soviet subsidies to the CPUSA continued until 1989, when Hall's criticism of Mikhail Gorbachev's reforms led to a cut off. Losing this money probably created a serious financial crisis in the CPUSA. We know that in 1990 the party newspaper, the *People's Daily World,* was forced to reduce its publication schedule from five days a week to two days and finally to one, when it was renamed the *People's Weekly World.* The size and physical quality of the paper declined as well. The party also scaled back its other publications, laid off staff, and showed further signs of fiscal stress.

Throughout the 1970s and 1980s, while it was receiving secret Soviet funding to support its activities and run its electoral campaigns, the CPUSA enjoyed legal exemption from most U.S. campaign-finance laws requiring disclosure of the names of political contributors. In addition, the CPUSA was able to avoid many similar state laws through either special legislation or legal appeals. Agents for the Democratic and Republican parties who accepted under-the-table contributions were indicted for violation of finance-disclosure laws; the Communist party successfully argued that disclosure of its contributors would expose these individuals to political harassment. Yet throughout this period, the party repeatedly violated U.S. laws concerning currency, customs, foreign-agent registration, and political contributions. Holding CPUSA candidates to the same legal standards enjoined on other candidates would not only have exposed the party's criminal acts, it would have uncovered the millions of dollars the party received annually from the Soviet Union.

During this period there was only one government prosecution of an American leftist who accepted illegal Soviet subsidies. In 1989 the Rev. Alan Thomson, executive director of the National Council of American-Soviet Friendship, a CPUSA-aligned organization, was arrested for bringing $17,000 in undeclared currency into the

United States. Thomson had been given the money by the Soviet counterpart of the council while on a visit to the Soviet Union. Upon arrival in the United States—where he did not declare the money to Customs—he turned the cash over to a colleague for laundering. The colleague, however, was an FBI informant, and the FBI had secretly videotaped Thomson's instructions to the woman concerning the series of bank transactions that would be necessary to hide the source of the funds. Thomson pleaded guilty in 1992 to violating U.S. currency laws.[43]

Document 42

Hall to Ponomarev. Original in English. Undated, but internal evidence suggests it was written in the late summer or fall of 1981. The authors thank Michael Dobbs, *Washington Post* Moscow bureau chief, for making this letter available.

Comrade Boris Ponamarev,

I want to express our thanks and appreciation to the Central Committee of the Communist Party of the Soviet Union for the very fine vacation and health visit we have had here. Also our Party places a high value on the ideological vacations [taken by] the two groups of our comrades who have been in the U.S.S.R. this year.

I greatly appreciated your visit to Barvicka and your very deep and helpful analysis of some of the current world developments and especially your assessment of U.S. Imperialism and the motivating factors behind its present policies of aggression. It will be very helpful in building the mass movement against its criminal policies.

It is in this connection that I want to restate and emphasize what in my opinion is both a responsibility but also an unprecedented opportunity for our party.

There are a number of objective developments, that are reaching qualitative levels, that together are creating the most favorable situation for our party being able to influence the mass upsurge, and political development generally. More than at any moment in recent history. I am convinced that our party can be an important factor in slowing down, stopping and reversing the present reactionary policies of the Reagan Administration.

Tens of millions have become disillusioned. They are moving towards mass actions, and millions are in an ideological flux. Our party can be an important and even a decisive factor in influencing and moving these masses.

43. *U.S. v Alan Thomson*, U.S. District Court, Western District of New York, June 1992.

Document 42 continued

Not since the days of the organization of the mass production workers into the C.I.O. unions has our party had such working relation[s] with all levels of the Trade Union movement.

The developments in the peace movement, the womens and youth movements and especially the new potencional [potential] are reaching new levels.

And as I indicated in our discussions I believe the 1982 Congressional elections—which start by the New Year, have the possibilities of making a qualitative change in the composition of Congress.

To be able to take full advantage of the new possibilities, especially in the industrial Midwest it is necessary to publish the Daily World both in New York and Chicago—and at a later date also in San Francisco.

And as you Comrade Ponamarev more than anyone else is fully aware that for our party to be able to take full advantage of these new objective developments, depends on our ability to reach the millions with our message, and how big a force we can support.

And this to a large extent depends on our financial resources. Needless to say the continuing escalation of inflation is creating serious problems for us.

In this kind of a situation there is no question a few hundred dollars can make the difference between victory or defeat in a number of Congressional campaigns.

Because of the unprecedented possibility of making a turn in the political developments, and the importance of making a maximum effort I can only urge special consideration for the financial problems that we will face in the coming year,

Comradely,
Gus Hall

Document 43

Hall to Dobrynin, 14 January 1987. Original in English. The authors thank Michael Dobbs, *Washington Post* Moscow bureau chief, for making this letter available.

January 14, 1987

Central Committee, CPSU
Comrade Dobrynin

Dear Comrade,

I don't like to raise the question of finances, but when the "wolf" is at the door one is forced to cry out.

As I indicated before, our special financial crunch at this moment is the result of a number of special developments that were forced on us simultaneously.

First, we are forced to establish a new print shop outside New York City. This is an expensive operation, but we had no choice. We know the FBI had a hand in creating this situation.

Secondly, the initial cost of starting to publish the People's Daily World, both in New York and San Francisco simultaneously, turned out to be a much more expensive proposition than was originally estimated. Had we known the initial cost we most likely would not have undertaken the task. But there is no way we can undo it now without serious political consequences for our Party.

And, thirdly, we went all out in the last Congressional elections, which in my opinion paid off very well. However, as I am sure you are aware, no matter how tightly one holds the purse strings election campaigns are a costly business.

Of course, what we spend in comparison to bourgeois candidates is peanuts compared to the average campaign expense for a U.S. Senator, which is now about $20 million.

The fact is we were influential and even the deciding factor in the defeat of some of the extreme Reaganite candidates.

And of course, because of inflation, the cost of everything we do keeps going up.

The taxes and the upkeep of our headquarters building goes up every year. Selling the building, which I have often given thought to, would also be a serious political setback for the Party.

And the truth is that in spite of the fact that our Party raises about twice as much money now than at any time in our history, we still face a serious crisis.

We have been forced to cut back in a number of areas. For example, we have been forced, most reluctantly, to end the publication of Labor Today, a left trade union newspaper, because of the increase in the cost of production. This, in spite of the fact that its circulation has continued to increase.

So, in a real sense I cannot overemphasize that the "wolf is at the door."

During the past months we have coped with the crisis largely by borrowing from everyone we could and even mortgaging homes. And of course going into debt.

Thus, the cold facts are that we have been able to function in the past years because of the very generous contribution of approximately $2 million per year. Once or twice there have been smaller, special additional contributions for very specific purposes.

In order for us to continue functioning effectively on the present level, -the $2 million is needed. But, for us to get out of the special crisis because of the special developments, we have to find an additional $2 million.

I have some idea about the problems, including the financial requesdts, you comrades must face. And I am sure everyone believes their problems are most important.

I can only argue that because our Party works in the decaying heart of

Document 43 *continued*

imperialism whatever we do in influencing events in the United States has an impact on world developments. And, because of the crisis of the Reagan presidency, which is deep and chronic now, our Party's work has had and continues to have a growing impact on the politics of our country.

Therefore, in the context of the struggle against U.S. imperialism and the policies of the Reagan Administration, our Party must be seen as an important, and even indispensable, factor.

I can only hope that in the midst of all the pressures and activities that you can give this problem your most serious and urgent consideration.

With best wishes for the New Year,

> Comradely,
> *Gus Hall*
> GUS HALL

Document 44

Receipt from Gus Hall, 14 March 1987. Original in English. Hand printed, signed. The authors thank Michael Dobbs, *Washington Post* Moscow bureau chief, for making this receipt available.

RECEIVED $2 000 000 (TWO MILLION) DOLLARS USA
14/3/87

> *Gus Hall*
> 0929 [stamp]
> 9APR87 00306 [Russian stamp]

Document 45

Receipt from Gus Hall, 19 March 1988. Original in English. Hand printed, signed. Reproduced in Yevgeny Lisov, "Investigation: Greens for Reds," *Ogonyok* 9 (February 1992): 7.

RECEIVED $ 3 000 000
(three million US dollars)

> *Gus Hall*

> *19.03.88*

January 14, 1987

Central Committee, CPSU
Comrade Dobrynin

Dear Comrade,
    I don't like to raise the question of finances, but
when the "wolf" is at the door one is forced to cry out.
    As I indicated before, our special financial crunch
at this moment is the result of a number of special
developments that were forced on us simultaneously.
    First, we are forced to establish a new print shop
outside New York City. This is an expensive operation, but
we had no choice. We know the FBI had a hand in creating
this situation.
    Secondly, the initial cost of starting to publish the
People's Daily World, both in New York and San Francisco
simultaneously, turned out to be a much more expensive
proposition than was originally estimated. Had we known the
initial cost we most likely would not have undertaken the
task. But there is no way we can undo it now without serious
political consequences for our Party.
    And, thirdly, we went all out in the last
Congressional elections, which in my opinion paid off very
well. However, as I am sure you are aware, no matter how
tightly one holds the purse strings election campaigns are a
costly business.
    Of course, what we spend in comparison to bourgeois
candidates is peanuts compared to the average campaign
expense for a U.S. Senator, which is now about $20 million.
    The fact is we were influential and even the deciding
factor in the defeat of some of the extreme Reaganite
candidates.
    And of course, because of inflation, the cost of
everything we do keeps going up.
    The taxes and the upkeep of our headquarters building
goes up every year. Selling the building, which I have often
given thought to, would also be a serious political setback
for the Party.

DOCUMENT 43. Hall to Dobrynin, 14 January 1987.

And the truth is that in spite of the fact that our Party raises about twice as much money now than at any time in our history, we still face a serious crisis.

We have been forced to cut back in a number of areas. For example, we have been forced, most reluctantly, to end the publication of Labor Today, a left trade union newspaper, because of the increase in the cost of production. This, in spite of the fact that its circulation has continued to increase.

So, in a real sense I cannot overemphasize that the "wolf is at the door."

During the past months we have coped with the crisis largely by borrowing from everyone we could and even mortgaging homes. And of course going into debt.

Thus, the cold facts are that we have been able to function in the past years because of the very generous contribution of approximately $2 million per year. Once or twice there have been smaller, special additional contributions for very specific purposes.

In order for us to continue functioning effectively on the present level,—the $2 million is needed. But, for us to get out of the special crisis because of the special developments, we have to find an additional $2 million.

I have some idea about the problems, including the financial requesdts, you comrades must face. And I am sure everyone believes their problems are most important.

I can only argue that because our Party works in the decaying heart of imperialism whatever we do in influencing events in the United States has an impact on world developments. And, because of the crisis of the Reagan presidency, which is deep and chronic now, our Party's work has had and continues to have a growing impact on the politics of our country.

Therefore, in the context of the struggle against U.S. imperialism and the policies of the Reagan Administration, our Party must be seen as an important, and even indispensable, factor.

I can only hope that in the midst of all the pressures and activities that you can give this problem your most serious and urgent consideration.

With best wishes for the New Year,

Comradely,

GUS HALL

DOCUMENT 43. continued

RECEIVED $2 000 000 (TWO million)

DOLLARS USA

14/3/87

Gus Hall

0929

9.АПР87 00306-ол

RECEIVED $ 3 000 000

(three million US dollars)

Gus Hall

19. 03. 88

DOCUMENTS 44 AND 45. Receipts from Gus Hall, 14 March 1987 and 19 March 1988.

Document 46

Leonev to Dobrynin, cover letter with receipt, 14 April 1988. Original in Russian. Reproduced in Yevgeny Lisov, "Investigation: Greens for Reds," *Ogonyok* 9 (February 1992): 7.

Top secret

Personal

USSR Committee of State Security   CC of the CPSU

First Main Directorate   To comrade A. F. Dobrynin
14.04.88 No. 157/609

Moscow

Routing of receipt:

We are forwarding herewith a receipt for the transfer to the leadership of the Communist Party of the United States of 3,000,000 (three million) dollars US against funds allocated for 1988.

Said transfer is executed in compliance with resolution P–97/48 of 30.12.87.

Enclosure: receipt on 1 sheet, unnumbered, dated 19.03.88, top secret, in English.

Deputy director of First
Main Directorate   *N. S. Leonov*   N. S. Leonov

20 APR 88 00690 [stamp] [various signatures and dates; two notations reading *To the archive*]

The Significance of the Moscow Gold

What difference did Soviet subsidies make? How much would have have been different had the CPUSA been forced to rely on its own resources, as other American political parties were? Although no one can really answer this question, we can see from **document 47** and other sources something of the extraordinary reach of the Moscow gold into every facet of American Communist life.

Document 47 returns us to the 1930s, the era of the CPUSA's greatest expansion and influence. It illustrates the extent to which the publishers, youth organizers, union organizers, and technicians who did the work of the CPUSA and disseminated the (Soviet) Communist message depended on Soviet subsidies.

The document is an excerpt of testimony from two senior American Communists before the Anglo-American Secretariat of the Comintern in 1932. The first speaker is Clarence Hathaway, the CPUSA representative to the Comintern. The second is Joseph Peter (better known as Peters), who had headed the CPUSA's organizational department in 1930 and 1931 and was at this time in Moscow for high-level Comintern training.

Hathaway reported that the CPUSA had 232 "functionaries" (paid party staff) in New York alone and that although it had only 800 members in the Minnesota district, "we now have 26 full time functionaries: These are the functionaries of the Party, the TUUL, the WIR [Workers' International Relief] and so forth." Peter supplemented this testimony:

> I will go to a small section in Newark. . . . Here we have 130 dues paying members and we have the following full time functionaries, a section organizer, Organizational Secretary, Trade Union Organizer, ILD [International Labor Defense] organizer, W.I.R. Organizer, Daily Worker Agent, Election Campaign Manager, one full time comrade in New Brunswick, one full time comrade in Elizabeth altogether 9, then the technical helpers in the ILD, WIR, a full time YCL Organizer, so that we see in a small section with 130 dues paying members, 18 or 20 full time comrades.[44]

When Hathaway declared that the twenty-six Minnesota functionaries had "to be paid by 800 Party members," he was complaining about the party's top-heavy bureaucracy. His statement that funds to pay for party staff come from members' dues is probably not meant to be taken literally and is, in any case, impossible. As late as 1936 the average party member paid dues of no more than $6 a year. By this measure, the Minnesota district generated less than $5,000 a year in dues, a significant portion of which was forwarded to the party's national headquarters. Party dues in Minnesota could barely have covered the salaries of a fifth of the cadre

44. For reasons of readability, the large number of typographical errors in the original have been corrected in this extract. The transcribed document, however, reprints the original text.

actually employed, and this would have left nothing for the Minnesota party's other expenses.[45]

A similar story of overstaffing is told in a 1932 report from the CPUSA's Philadelphia district that lists the following full-time party employees in the city: district organizer (party head), organizational secretary, agitprop (agitation and propaganda activities) director, clerical worker in the party office, YCL organizer, two TUUL organizers, Communist Shoe Workers Union organizer, Communist Marine Workers Union organizer, two Unemployed Council organizers, ILD organizer, WIR organizer, organizer for the Friends of the Soviet Union, *Daily Worker* distributor and stringer, and *Morning Freiheit* distributor and stringer. This totaled sixteen full-time salaried party employees in a district of only a few hundred members.[46] The CPUSA's paid staff in Philadelphia alone exceeded the entire, nationwide paid staff of most of the rival American radical organizations. No other group on the left or even the liberal-left could afford a paid staff that approached the size of the CPUSA's.

The CPUSA staffs, though large, were not particularly well paid. Most local functionaries received salaries that were equivalent to those of upper-level blue-collar workers. Even the highest officials of the party were paid no more than the lower ranks of middle-class professionals. The records of the CPUSA contain numerous complaints from staff members that their salaries had been paid late or that they had received only partial paychecks at the end of a budget cycle to make the books balance; and there are many irritated exchanges concerning expense accounts. Few of the hundreds of people employed by the CPUSA or one of its affiliates could be said to have prospered, but during the Depression, jobs at even these modest salaries were highly valued.

Its large professional staff allowed the CPUSA to produce a core of activists at any political or public event. The party's district organizer (DO) had the authority to mobilize the cadre whenever necessary: if a union picket line needed reinforcements, the DO

45. On party dues, see Klehr, *Heyday of American Communism*, 375.

46. L. P. Lemley to [Charles] Dirba, 6 April 1932, RTsKhIDNI 515-1-2772. Lemley noted that he had not listed the employees of the Philadelphia office of the Russian Beneficial Association, a party-controlled fraternal insurance company.

could order the agitprop director, the YCL organizer, and the ILD organizer to show up, preferably accompanied by a few rank-and-file party activists. If demonstrators were needed at a local city council meeting to raise their voices against a proposed budget cut, the DO could assign the WIR, Friends of the Soviet Union, and TUUL organizers to grab their placards and go. If a party-backed candidate needed envelope stuffers and people to distribute campaign literature door to door, the local clerical staff, the Unemployed Council organizer, the ILD organizer, and the newspaper distributors were dispatched to campaign headquarters. These people were not volunteers; they were doing their jobs. No other radical political group and few liberal or conservative political groups could guarantee to produce live bodies with the same assurance as the CPUSA. A number of historians have written about the grass-roots activity of the American Communists. Only a few of them noted that much of the "grass-roots" activity was carried out by paid staff.[47]

The large number of paid party staff also reinforced the CPUSA's extreme centralization. Both in theory and in practice the American Communist party sought uniformity of activity and ideology. The national headquarters' control over the paychecks of its widespread professional cadre helped promote conformity and undercut the possibility of local autonomy.[48]

All of this money, much of which came from Moscow, contributed to the party's loyalty to the Soviet Union. Unless they had private means, most Communist leaders and active party militants were on salary, either from the CPUSA or one of its affiliates. Leaving the movement meant finding a new job and starting a new

47. One of the few historians to note the extraordinary number of paid party staff is Mark Naison in "Remaking America: Communists and Liberals in the Popular Front," in *New Studies in the Politics and Culture of U.S. Communism*, ed. Michael Brown, Randy Martin, Frank Rosengarten, and George Snedeker (New York: Monthly Review Press, 1993), 68. On the other hand, Fraser Ottanelli, in *The Communist Party of the United States from the Depression to World War II* (New Brunswick, N.J.: Rutgers University Press, 1991), makes no mention of the size of the paid staff.

48. In the early 1920s the immigrant language federations had possessed a measure of organizational autonomy. But this independence was destroyed in the "Bolshevization" campaign ordered by the Comintern in 1925 and stamped out in the last holdout, the Finnish Federation, in 1931. See Draper, *American Communism and Soviet Russia*, 153–71.

life. Loyalty to Moscow, on the other hand, brought economic security, as well as a sense of certainty. A break with Moscow was not merely ideological, it was financial. The Soviet subsidies helped ensure economic and psychological loyalty to the Soviet Union. We do not claim that they were the primary source of that loyalty; many party cadre were talented people who sacrificed a great deal materially for communism. Cadre were far less likely than ordinary rank-and-file Communists to leave the CPUSA. But the financial ties made it easier for dedicated Communists to remain committed to the movement.

Document 47

Excerpt of Clarence Hathaway and Joseph Peter, testimony to Anglo-American Secretariat, 7 January 1932, RTsKhIDNI 495–72–168. Original in English. Evidently, the typist had a tendency to confuse the letter z with the letter y.

. . .

[Speaker Hathaway]

I want to deal with the tendency of the Central and the district apparatuses to grow even when the Party has the tendency to remain at 10,000. This constantly rose and   and the most important thing is that there is quite a tendency for this apparatus to separate itself from the Party. For example, in Pittsburg we find that according to the reports distributed, that we have an apparatus the members of which are not attached to the nuclei of the Party, and do not in any way participate in leading the work of the lower units, but they have their own unit in the office composed of the functionaries and the stenographers. Such a situation as this takes on rather a crystalised form in Pittsburg, but I think in many districts of the Party, we have this tendency in practice. My opinion is that in this also, it is necessary to wage the sharpest struggle, and I think that this apparatus has to be reduced. For example we have distributed a letter by Comrade Bedacht which tells us that in the Minnesota district, we now have 26 full time functionaries. These are the functionaries of the Party, the TUUL, the WIR and so forth, and all of these functionaries have to be paid by the 800 Party members in the district.

This has to be paid bz 800 Partz members and the effect of this politicallz, organizationallz and financiallz and in everz other waz is to demoraliye the work of the Party and not to strengthen the work of the Party. I cite Minnesota because Comrade Bedacht happened to write about Minnesota. In the New Zork District Comrade Peter informs me that there are onlz 232 functionaries, but comrades all of these things in the Party have to be examined, we have to

Document 47 *continued*

examine this inner Party situation, and we have to find out what prevents us from drawing the Party into mass work.

. . .

[Speaker Peter]

. . . I will bring in concrete examples. Comrade Hathaway said in New York we have 232 full time functionaries. I will go to a small section in Newark. There are 130 dues pazing members in this section, here we have a 130 dues pazing members and we have the following full time functionaries, a section organiyer, Organizational Secretarz, Trade Union Organizer, ILD Organizer, W.I.R. Organizer, Dailz Worker Agent, Election Campaign Manager, one full time comrade in New Brunswick, one full time comrade in Eliyabeth altohether 9, then the technical helpers in the ILD, WIR, a full time YCL Organizer, so that we see in a small section with 130 dues paying members, 18 or 20 full time comrades. Comrades, what is the situation with these functionaries, as soon as a new campaign comes up a new comrade put at the head, for a Madison Square Garden meeting a comrade put in charge, a staf of 5 put in charge of the Daily Worker Bayaar, not to mention how many functionaries we have had. Comrade Lenin said good to have as many full time functionaries as possible.

. . .

CHAPTER THREE

Communists Abroad

IN ADDITION to the chains of gold that linked the CPUSA to the Comintern, there were human bonds as well. From the first, American Communist party leaders traveled constantly to Moscow to meet with Soviet leaders and officials of the Communist International. These conferences and meetings, lasting anywhere from a few days to several weeks, enabled the Soviets, as leaders of the international movement, to acquire firsthand information from their affiliates and to give detailed advice and instructions in return.

These brief visits were not the only human connections between Moscow and the United States. Many American Communists went to the Soviet Union for longer periods of time: for training in Comintern schools, for work in Comintern agencies, and to represent the CPUSA in what was viewed as the center of world revolution. And a number of foreign Communists—Russians, Germans, Britons, Finns—were dispatched to the United States to assist the CPUSA, to oversee its activities, and, if necessary, to mediate among its quarreling factions.

Comintern "Reps"

Among the twenty-one conditions of membership in the Comintern were requirements that national programs be approved by the Executive Committee of the Communist International (ECCI) and that "all the decisions" of the Comintern be "binding on all parties belonging to the Communist International."[1] To ensure the latter, the Comintern chiefly relied on the ideological subordination of foreign Communists to the Soviet Union. But up until the late 1930s, it also sent representatives to the foreign parties to monitor activities and enforce Comintern orders.

The Plenipotentiaries

The Comintern sent many different kinds of representatives to the United States. Most had limited mandates. A representative might be charged with providing political guidance to a party-aligned foreign-language newspaper or reorganizing party training of cadre or serving as a liaison between the Young Communist International and its American branch. A few, however, came to America with a larger mandate: their job was to act as the official representative of the Communist International in the United States. Although the extent of their powers varied somewhat during the 1920s and 1930s, the plenipotentiary reps dealt directly with the political leaders of the CPUSA: they were consulted on all important matters of policy; they intervened in factional disputes—and they communicated regularly with the Comintern, offering the Soviets advice on Comintern decisions affecting the CPUSA's leadership, policies, and activities.

These representatives had the power to lay down the law according to Moscow, and in a few crucial periods they did just that. When the CPUSA was split between the mutually hostile factions led by Charles Ruthenberg and William Z. Foster in 1925, it was a Comintern representative, Sergei Gusev, who ordered the Foster faction, which held a clear majority, to turn control of the party over to the Ruthenberg faction; stunned and dismayed, Foster's group nonetheless obeyed. A year later, an ECCI letter spelled out to its representative the role that he was required to play in the affairs of the American party. In May 1926, that role was plenipo-

---

1. "Theses on the Conditions of Admission to the Communist International," in *Theses, Resolutions, and Manifestos of the First Four Congresses of the Third International* (London: Ink Links, 1980), 96.

tentiary: "to intervene in cases of important differences between the Political Bureau and the Trade Union Commission of the Workers' Party, in order to bring about an understanding or, should this be impossible, to decide the question." The representative was instructed to ensure that the American party was not "being deprived of the services" of either the Foster group, which controlled the Trade Union Commission, or the Ruthenberg group, which controlled the Political Bureau.[2]

In early 1929 a Comintern delegation consisting of the German Philip Dengel and the Englishman Harry Pollitt demanded that party leader Jay Lovestone step down in favor of his arch-rival Foster. Lovestone's faction held an overwhelming majority, and, unlike Foster, Lovestone appealed the decision directly to the Comintern. The Comintern representatives sent a telegram to Moscow (**document 48**) complaining that the American Communists were resisting the ECCI line and implying that the representatives did not know how to handle the situation. Lovestone rushed off to Moscow to make his appeal in person. There he learned the price of defying the Comintern representative.

Joseph Stalin himself sat on the Comintern commission that considered Lovestone's appeal. Responding to protestations by Lovestone and his co-leader Benjamin Gitlow that their faction had won the support of 90 percent of the American party members, Stalin pointed out the brutal truth:

> You declare you have a certain majority in the American Communist Party and that you will retain that majority under all circumstances. This is untrue, comrades of the American delegation, absolutely untrue. You had a majority because the American Communist Party until now regarded you as the determined supporters of the Communist International. And it was only because the Party regarded you as the friends of the Comintern that you had a majority in the ranks of the American Communist Party. . . . There have been numerous cases in the history of the Comintern when its most popular leaders, who had greater authority than you, found themselves isolated as soon as they raised the banner against the Comintern. Do you think you will fare better than these leaders? A poor hope, comrades! At present you still

2. Secretary of ECCI to the Representative of the ECCI in America, 24 May 1926, RTsKhIDNI 515–1–587.

have a formal majority. But tomorrow you will have no majority and
you will find yourselves completely isolated if you attempt to start a
fight against the decisions of the Presidium of the Executive Committee
of the Comintern.[3]

The Comintern summarily demoted Lovestone, Gitlow, and their
allies and, a short time later, ordered them expelled from the party.
Stalin was proven correct; barely two hundred people followed
their exiled leaders out of the Communist party. It was a clear
lesson to American Communists that the representatives spoke
for Moscow—and Moscow spoke for the American Communist
party.

With the example of Lovestone before them, American party
leaders were eager to display their deference to Comintern guidance. As noted in chapter 2, in mid-1929 the Comintern sent a
three-man delegation to the United States, headed by Boris
Mikhailov (pseudonym "Williams"). **Document 49,** dated 21 November 1929, is a report by one of the two unidentified assistants
on what responses he received when he queried the American party
leaders about whether they would like the Comintern to send another representative when he and Williams/Mikhailov returned to
Moscow, as they were scheduled to do. (The second assistant may
already have left.) Max Bedacht insisted that "there should always
henceforward be a representative of the C.I. in America." Earl
Browder considered it "essential that there should be a representative" for several more months. William Weinstone felt "that either
Williams or [the assistant] must be present," and Robert Minor
agreed. Only Foster suggested that "the need of the moment was
for the Party to stand on its own legs without Comintern representatives to depend upon." It was hardly an accident that Foster,
arguably the best-known Communist in America, was never allowed by the Soviet Union to become general secretary of the
CPUSA. Ironically, Lovestone, Bedacht, and Browder—each of
whom was chosen as party leader in preference to Foster—were
later expelled for ideological differences with the Soviet Union,
while Foster remained a loyal Communist all his life.

3. Joseph Stalin, *Speeches on the American Communist Party* (San Francisco:
Proletarian Publishers, n.d.), 30–31.

For part of 1932 the Comintern representative was Joel Shubin, a Russian and the husband of the American writer Anna Louise Strong. In the summer of 1933 Gerhart Eisler, a German Communist, replaced Shubin. Interestingly, when Eisler returned to Moscow for the seventh Comintern congress in 1935, he went as a CPUSA representative to the Comintern congress (even though he was officially the Comintern representative to the CPUSA and not a member of the American party at all). On the seventh congress's delegate lists he is carried as CPUSA representative "John Gerhart."[4] Browder, well pleased that Eisler was using his Comintern authority to support Browder's policies, appealed to Georgi Dimitrov that "Comrade Gerhart return to America, at least until our Party Congress early in 1936."[5] Eisler did come back, but he left the United States after the 1936 party congress; he was probably the last Comintern representative with plenipotentiary powers.[6]

4. Seventh Congress of the Communist International delegate list for America and John Gerhart registration sheet (with photograph), 1935, RTsKhIDNI 494–1–467. The authors thank Peter Huber for finding these documents.

5. Browder to Dimitrov, 2 September 1935, RTsKhIDNI 495–74–463, reproduced in Harvey Klehr, John Earl Haynes, and Fridrikh Igorevich Firsov, *The Secret World of American Communism* (New Haven: Yale University Press, 1995), 62.

6. Eisler returned to the United States in June 1941: he received a sixty-day entry visa when he told immigration authorities that he was a refugee from Nazism—though not a Communist—and wished only to pass through on his way to Mexico. But he remained in the country illegally, receiving a covert stipend under the name Julius Eisman from a CPUSA front. As Eisman, he wrote for party publications under the pseudonym "Hans Berger" and consulted with CPUSA officials. In 1946 his sister, a former Comintern official who had broken with communism, denounced him as a Soviet agent. He was called before the House Committee on Un-American Activities and was convicted of contempt because of his evasive testimony. He also faced prosecution for having used a fraudulent American passport in the 1930s. But while he was free on bail, Eisler evaded FBI surveillance, and in May 1949 he slipped onto a Polish ship and escaped to East Germany, where he became a government official. Some writers have described Eisler in this World War II period as *the* Comintern representative to the CPUSA. It is very likely that Eisler was engaged in Comintern work, but given the nature of the Comintern's operations during World War II, it is doubtful that his role was that of the classic Comintern Rep of the 1920s and 1930s. Eisler's activities in the 1940s are summarized in Earl Latham, *The Communist Controversy in Washington: From the New Deal to McCarthy* (Cambridge: Harvard University Press, 1966), 103–4, and Herbert Romerstein and Stanislav Levchenko, *The KGB against the "Main Enemy"* (Lexington, Mass.: Lexington Books, 1989), 237–42.

Document 48

Telegram from the "Duet" of ECCI to Kuusinen, 4–5 March 1929, RTsKhIDNI 495–19–133a. Original in English. The "Duet" is Philip Dengel and Harry Pollitt. The cable is signed "Victoria," who was probably the Englishman, Pollitt.

Telegram received on the night of 4th–5th March 1929.
Moscow to Kuusinen from New York. Telegram to the "Duet" of ECCI.

Our instructions known in America in the middle of February. Working under impossible conditions. 90% of the delegates of the Convention are organising resistance to the line of the ECCI. The majority of the CEC, under the leadership of Lovestone, accepted the Open Letter with considerable reservations, rejecting organisational measures. Lovestone stated that the instructions of the ECCI express running sore in the apparatus of ECCI. We ask whether, in view of this situation, Lovestone can make the political report to the convention. The weakest part of our instructions is in relation to Foster, whom it is absolutely impossible to trust, and casts a shadow on our mission. The work of the convention is postponed. Wire immediately instructions

Victoria.

Document 49

Comintern representative to Dear Comrades, 21 November 1929, RTsKhIDNI 495–19–133a. Original in English.

November 21, 1929.

Dear Comrades:—

In view of my approaching departure for the Party Congress and the possibility that I might be reporting to the Comintern, I asked a number of identical questions of several of the leading comrades in private conversations had with each of them.

Those questions were:

1. As to whether I could inform the CI that there was real inner consolidation of the Party and of the leadership.

2. Whether, if I were not to return after the Party Congress, I should recommend the Comintern to send another representative.

3. In that case whether it should be an Englishman, German or a Russian—having in mind the technical difficulties with regard to the last of these.

4. As to whether Comrade Williams should stay here for some time longer.

5. Finally, if they wished him to stay, whether he should work in the Party headquarters or in the districts; and, if in Party headquarters, should he work as now or take up some special work such as the Organization Department of New York City, or Negro Department, or T.U.U.L., etc.

I give their answers seriatum.

Comrade Bedacht said—yes, that assuredly there was inner consolidation and much better than he had anticipated. The only sign he could think of against this inner consolidation was the development of a criticism of Comrade Foster among leading comrades of the former minority.

He said that there should always henceforward be a representative of the CI in America, and, indeed, in other parties as well was his general view. Until the coming convention it was essential to have a representative. It is true there are special difficulties in the case of a Russian working illegally here, but that a German or Englishman did not suffer from these difficulties and either would be good, but that an Englishman would probably be the best.

There was no need for Williams to go with me across to report because whichever of us went would present the same line, since we appeared to have no differences. Of course for a full comprehensive report it was absolutely essential for Williams to go, but he stipulated that if no other representative were coming immediately then Williams must stay; for the situation in the Party was still not entirely settled.

That if Williams stayed, he should be partly in the districts and partly in the Party headquarters, but when at headquarters should, as before, work along with the Polburo and the Secretariat. If there were time for other work, he should devote himself to the Daily Worker.

Comrade Browder said—that there was real inner consolidation, especially below in the basic units of the Party, but also in the Secretariat where there had been very good cooperative working between himself, Comrade Bedacht and Comrade Minor.

He said that it was <u>essential</u> that there should be a representative in the CPUSA until two months after the coming convention. When asked his choice of three possible nationalities, he said emphatically, a German.

In his opinion if I were to go to Moscow and report, then six weeks later Williams could go and make a second report, but in that case only after the new representative arrives.

He said that if here, Williams should work three weeks of each month in the districts, work in which was now of the utmost importance; and one week he should be in New York. That in New York he should work either in the T.U.U.L., or, next most important, in the Party headquarters itself; that he should not work in the Daily Worker in which outside help could not avail much and to which Browder himself would, as head of Agitprop, now begin to give more attention.

Comrade Weinstone said—that yes, real inner consolidation of the Party was steadily developing and more than he expected, but the tempo was still rather slow. He said a representative was essential until the coming convention at least. But why should not Williams be the representative? Any technical difficulties about a Russian comrade could be satisfactorily got over.

He said there was no need for Williams to go now; that either Williams or myself _must_ be present; that the situation in the Party was not at all stable and required the presence of someone from the Comintern. If there was a fundamental discussion of the question at Moscow then Williams should be there, but no such fundamental discussion seemed very likely, though there were important questions to be settled such as that of the Labor Party.

He thought that Williams should work not in the districts—apart from the benefit of seeing them at first hand, they were not of such importance as the work in the center. What the Party required now was strong work in the center giving the drive to all the districts. That in the center Williams should devote himself to the Daily Worker, as Comrade Minor required political help as editor of the Daily Worker.

Comrade Foster said—that there had been a real inner consolidation, especially throughout the ranks of the Party. That here in the top bodies he could discern still the lines of the previous factions showing themselves faintly, but even there steadily fading away.

He did not think there should be another representative. The need of the moment was for the Party to stand on its own legs without Comintern representatives to depend upon. That the leading bunch must begin to feel their own responsibility; must begin to develop the responsibility of leadership; and that the Party, too, must learn to walk on its own legs; that the Party was like a convalescent who must more quickly learn to walk on his feet.

Document 49 *continued*

That if the CI did send another representative he should be either an Englishman or Russian; that the Russians had a wonderful way of getting to understand the problems confronting the Party. And that the English, because of their common language and certain common traditions in the labor movement and general likeness, were also very well able to act as representatives—but that the Germans did not seem to catch hold properly of the American situation. That, therefore, if there had to be a representative he should be Russian or English.

He then said, in response to my 4th question—that Williams must stay. That the situation in the Party was still difficult in the districts and among the functionaries especially; and even in the Secretariat he could see there might possibly be difficulties in common collective working.

That Williams should work entirely in the districts, concentration on which was now very important.

That if there were any fundamental discussion of the American question in Moscow, then of course Williams must be there too.

Comrade Minor considered there was emphatically real inner consolidation, but that the tempo of this was still too slow.

That a representative of the CI must always be with the parties whenever the situation was even in the least degree critical, and certainly here now. That any such representative should be Russian or German; that he doubted if the German CP could find the type of comrade required.

That the staying of Williams was essential; and that he should both work in the districts and at headquarters, and that there he should take care of the Negro Department.

Other Functionaries

In addition to the Comintern, other Soviet agencies sent representatives to the United States. The Young Communist International, International Red Aid, and other Comintern-affiliated organizations frequently stationed representatives there. Moreover, because of the many foreign-language subgroups in the CPUSA, the Comintern or other national Communist parties often sent representatives of a specific nationality to work with the appropriate subgroup. **Document 50** is a 1930 letter from Max Bedacht to the Comintern's Political Secretariat asking for reliable foreign functionaries who could work with the various foreign-language subgroups. Recognizing that other Communist parties might take this opportunity to exile a troublesome figure of their own, Bedacht asked that the foreign parties "consider rather the capability of the candidates than their readiness to get rid of the candidates."

A representative carrying a mandate from Moscow was someone whose authority and influence greatly impressed American Communists. Particularly in the 1920s, self-assured foreign Communists arriving in America were sometimes able to claim broader authority than the Comintern had intended.

In 1922, for example, the Comintern dispatched a delegation to America to resolve a bitter struggle inside the American Communist movement over whether the party should be legal or illegal (underground). When two of the delegates, Henryk Walecki and Boris Reinstein, returned to the Soviet Union, the third, a Hungarian named Joseph Pogany, remained behind. Although his assignment had apparently been limited to working with the immigrant Hungarian federation attached to the American party, Pogany, using the name John Pepper, quickly convinced the American Communists that he was the official Comintern representative. Within a year, he was, according to the leading scholar of the party's early history, "the de facto leader of American Communism."[7]

By the late 1920s, though, Pepper was in political trouble in Moscow. Along with his protégé, Jay Lovestone, he had been closely identified with Nikolai Bukharin, the Soviet leader then under attack by Joseph Stalin. The Comintern recalled Pepper to Moscow and, after Lovestone's ouster, expelled him "for refusing to submit to instructions of the ECCI and for deceiving the Communist Party of America and the Comintern, for his role in the American Party where together with Lovestone he was the leader of the Majority faction and where he instigated his followers to carry on factional work the object of which was to enforce his opportu-

7. Theodore Draper, *American Communism and Soviet Russia: The Formative Period* (New York: Viking Press, 1960), 61.

nist line."[8] In 1937 Earl Browder went to Moscow, where he paid a visit to Gosplan, the Soviet economic planning agency. There he met Pepper, who held an obscure job in the agency. Soon afterward, Pepper disappeared. In 1996 it was learned that he had been arrested by Stalin's security police and executed.[9]

Document 50

Bedacht to Political Secretariat, 18 March 1930, RTsKhIDNI 495–4–19. Original in English. *Novyi Mir* was the CPUSA's Russian-language newspaper.

March 18, 1930

To Political Secretariat.

Dear Comrades,

In the work of the Party in America we require a number of agitators and other capable Party functionaries of different nationalities. I have been instructed to submit to the ECCI a request for such Party workers. At the same time I want to ask that in the selection of these workers our brother Parties of these nationalities should be made to consider rather the capability of the candidates than their readiness to get rid of the candidates.

The Party needs: 1) An Italian comrade with abilities as agitator and editor; 2) a Russian comrade to edit "Novi Mir"; 3) a Jugo-Slav Comrade capable as organiser and editor; 4) a Polish comrade, capable as organiser and editor especially important are his qualifications as an organiser; 5) a Hungarian comrade, capable for editorial work and 6) a Finnish comrade who also is required to be an organiser and editor. The latter comrade should, if possible, be a rather authoritative comrade.

I submit this request hoping that immediate steps be taken to secure assignments from our brother Parties. If at all possible it would be advisable that the candidates can read English, but if this is impossible without impairing their

8. "Decision of the ICC on Pepper's Case," 4 September 1929, RTsKhIDNI 495–3–153.
9. For Browder's story, see Draper, *American Communism and Soviet Russia,* 435. Associated Press reporter Alan Cullison told John Earl Haynes in a 20 August 1996 interview that he had located Pepper's daughter in Moscow; she stated that her father had been shot in 1937.

qualities as organisers or editors, we prefer the good organiser to the good linguist.

Fraternally yours,
Max Bedacht

The CPUSA Challenges the Mandate
of a Comintern Representative

As Jay Lovestone learned, the Comintern's plenipotentiary representatives could not be defied, but the Comintern's lesser representatives were not accorded the same status, although their influence was still great. There were several disputes in the early 1930s over the mandates of various foreign Communists dispatched to America for special purposes.

One of these was Aino Kuusinen, a Finnish Communist and the wife of Otto Kuusinen, one of the Comintern's most powerful men. In 1930 the Comintern sent Aino Kuusinen, along with Kullervo Manner, a prominent figure in the Finnish Communist party, to the United States to help resolve a major conflict among Finnish-American leftists. Finnish-American Communists had lost control of a large consumer cooperative organization when a sizable number of their comrades had broken with the CPUSA. The Comintern dispatched Kuusinen to deal with the confusing and bitter struggle for control of the Finnish-language Communist newspapers and other ethnic institutions. She was also required to help enforce the ultra-radical Third Period line within the Finnish-American Communist movement. In document 50 Bedacht had asked for a Finnish representative who would "be a rather authoritative comrade." In Aino Kuusinen, CPUSA leaders got more than they bargained for. From the moment she arrived until she returned to Moscow in 1933, Kuusinen, known as Comrade Morton, was at the vortex of a bitterly divided Finnish-American Communist movement.[10]

10. For details about Aino Kuusinen's mission to the United States, see David John Ahola, *Finnish-Americans and International Communism: A Study of Finnish-American Communism from Bolshevization to the Demise of the Third International* (Lanham, Md.: University Press of America, 1981), 162–182; Aino

Whenever she was challenged by her enemies within the Finnish Workers Federation, Morton/Kuusinen referred to her mandate from Moscow. She also had an ally in the person of "Comrade Allen," the American alias of Niilo Karlovich Virtanen, another Finnish Comintern official. Allen/Virtanen undertook missions to Canada and the United States in the late 1920s and early 1930s as an organizational instructor, and his position in the Comintern was deputy head of the ECCI Secretariat.

Earl Browder, just establishing his leadership over the CPUSA, soon became concerned that Morton/Kuusinen was promoting people and stances that were not in line with what he wanted. In September 1932 he wrote to the Comintern on the increasing conflict within the Political Bureau of the CPUSA. Browder himself was under attack by William Weinstone and Jack Stachel, charged with being too left-wing. He also faced criticism from Allen/ Virtanen concerning organizational issues. Browder was cautious in his criticism of Allen/Virtanen, who had, Browder noted, "on the whole, been a stabilizing influence in the Polburo and has been of the most tremendous help to us." Although Allen/Virtanen was a man "whose opinions I value highly and with whom I very much dislike to disagree," Browder wanted the Comintern leadership to see his side of the dispute. (It is significant that Allen/Virtanen, a so-called Orginstructor who was not even a plenipotentiary Comintern representative, nonetheless participated in meetings of the Politburo, the most powerful agency in the American Communist party.)[11]

Allen/Virtanen sent a stream of reports and letters to the Comintern in 1932 and 1933 that were critical of the CPUSA and its activities, charging the Americans with slackening their efforts among the unemployed and mishandling the veterans' Bonus March. At one point he caustically concluded that "our party does not yet know how to properly approach American workers with its agitation and propaganda." He also criticized the party's poor

---

Kuusinen, *The Rings of Destiny: Inside Soviet Russia from Lenin to Brezhnev* (New York: Morrow, 1974), 82–102.

11. Browder to Piatnitsky, Manuilsky, and [Otto] Kuusinen, 23 September 1932, RTsKhIDNI 495–19–619.

results in recruiting African-Americans, especially in Harlem.[12] In **document 51** Allen/Virtanen blasted Israel Amter, the leader of the party in New York, as "chemically pure of all what we call political understanding" and also warned Moscow that some African-American Communists displayed anti-Semitic attitudes. Allen/Virtanen noted that he regularly attended the meetings of the party's top leadership but that his lack of a full Comintern mandate reduced his effectiveness. He concluded that the Comintern should send "here a real Ex.R. [Extraordinary Representative] with necessary authority."[13]

By early 1933 Browder and other American party leaders, believing that Allen/Virtanen and Morton/Kuusinen were meddling in matters beyond their Comintern mandate, exploded at a Politburo meeting. Allen/Virtanen was not present; Morton/Kuusinen was. The minutes show that she did not back down. She defended Allen/Virtanen, noting that "the good, as well as the bad deeds, of Comrade Allen, will be discussed in the ECCI when he returns there." She emphasized: "I have been sent here by decision of the ECCI to do Finnish work in America for a long period of time. This is the statement stated in the Open Letter of the C.I. to the Finnish workers, altho the names are not mentioned because I am illegally here."[14]

In response to Morton/Kuusinen's charge that the Politburo was flouting the will of the Communist International, Browder replied: "This is not the situation. The Polburo is very sensitive to the desires of the Comintern. We don't wait for instructions to carry them out and one word is sufficient—a suggestion from the Comintern is sufficient to get all measures necessary by the Polburo." He counterattacked: Morton/Kuusinen, he claimed, was lying about

12. Allen to Dear Comrades, 18 July 1932, RTsKhIDNI 495–19–619. The veterans' Bonus March was an attempt by World War I veterans to force Congress to speed up promised bonus payments. The Communist party had tried unsuccessfully to influence the march.

13. Allen/Virtanen made other criticisms, urging the Comintern to appoint a fully mandated representative: see document 51 and Allen to the Anglo-American Secretariat, 15 September 1932, RTsKhIDNI 515–1–2611. The Extraordinary Representative would have had the powers of a plenipotentiary. At that time there was no fully mandated representative: Joel Shubin had been in the United States as a Comintern representative in 1932; Gerhart Eisler did not arrive until mid-1933.

14. Minutes of Polburo Meeting, 4 January 1933, RTsKhIDNI 515–1–3130.

her Comintern mandate. "The leaders of the C.I. informed me that they have no political representatives in America; that everyone who is sent to America is sent to work under direction of the Polburo; that they hold the Polburo responsible for the work of these comrades. . . . The Polburo is the representative of the Comintern in America. There is no other representative. I hope this is clear."[15]

The CPUSA remained on the offensive against Morton/Kuusinen and Allen/Virtanen. **Document 52** is a 1933 letter from Earl Browder to Osip Piatnitsky charging the representatives with "misusing the name of the Comintern, claiming special authority from the CI for their actions." The American Politburo ordered Morton/Kuusinen to leave the United States in June 1933.[16] The Comintern also recalled Allen/Virtanen to Moscow. The Comintern formally reviewed his activities in **document 53** and faulted Allen/Virtanen ("Comrade V.") for correcting the CPUSA leadership in a manner that "exacerbated relations between him and the party leadership." Even so, his criticisms of the CPUSA leaders were judged to be correct, and Allen/Virtanen remained active in the Anglo-American Secretariat, which sat in judgment on CPUSA affairs.

The activities of Allen/Virtanen and Morton/Kuusinen in the United States give a clearer picture of the role of the Comintern representatives in America. They both had power and influence in the CPUSA; Allen/Virtanen even participated in the meeting of the party's Politburo, something only a handful of American Communists could claim. But neither had plenipotentiary powers, and American Communist leaders now knew the difference between the Comintern's chief representative and those who were given lesser authority. Nonetheless, the Comintern did not explicitly endorse Browder's claim that Morton/Kuusinen and Allen/Virtanen were subject to the authority of the CPUSA. But Browder, while asserting that authority, readily conceded that the Comintern had the power to do whatever it wanted.

Part of the trouble between Allen/Virtanen, Morton/Kuusinen,

---

15. Ibid.
16. To Comrade Morton, 12 June 1933, RTsKhIDNI 515–1–3141.

and the CPUSA leadership developed because there was no plenipotentiary Comintern representative during this period. When
Gerhart Eisler arrived in mid-1933 to take up this position, he put
the weight of the Comintern behind Earl Browder, and the paral-
ysis within the CPUSA leadership about which Allen/Virtanen had
complained ended.

Document 51

Allen to the Anglo-American Secretariat, 12 August 1932, RTsKhIDNI 495–72–201.
Original in English.

New York, August the 12th 1932.

To the Anglo American Secretariat.

27 AUG. 1932 * 6061 [stamp]

Dear Comrades.

Some remarks as to the things in New York district an[d] in the Centre.
1. New York district had its district convention in the middle of June. I happened to be in our other concentration districts at that time, and can not speak
about the proceedings of the convention on basis of my own observations. But
the resolution of the convention was bad, as you have seen in "Daily Worker".
And as the result of the convention you cannot see any improvement in the
district. For some time ago the Polbuero took up the matters in N.Y. district in
the course of preparation of the district committee meeting which was held on
August the 7th. The preparatory district buero meetings revealed a complete
lack of politics in the district leadership. The discussions touched only petty
organizational matters. It is [true] that the comrades in district buero exercised
a severe self criticism and openly admitted that the prestige of the district
leadership has considerably gone down since the district convention, but the
only way out they were inclined to see [was] in the new appointments here
and there and in some new organizational schemes. So, for in[s]tance comr.
Zack who is the member of district secretariat and the leader of party's trade
union work in New York long time bitterly fought as the main remedium for
the situation for a certain curious idea according to which the street units
should be composed on the basis of the trade of the comrades, and so composed units should then have as their main task the concentration in the

various factories. Only after a very strong intervention on behalf of the Polbuero Commission was this rather imaginary idea as to the work in the shops
dropped.

For the preparation of the district committe meeting there was also arranged a
joint meeting of district buero and Polbuero. Several negro comrades attended, and the meeting revealed that there are very serious anti-semitist
tendencies among our negro comrades in New York. One of the most developed negro comrades (Comr. Briggs, co-editor of the "D.W.") even stated that
the negro comrades are considering the party and especially its leadership in
New York as a "jewish corporation." Such anti-semitist tendencies have of
course their objective reasons. For instance the Garveyists are in their agitation carrying out a very intensive anti-semitist campaign to victims of which
even our negro comrades have fallen to a certain extent. But on the other hand
there is a lot of subjective reasons (wrong approach to the negros, command-
ism, buerocracy etc.) on the part of our party functionaries who in most cases,
and especially in New York happen to be jews/ to their nationality. And it is
quite sure that such anti-semitism can be found in New York not only among
the negros but also among the members of various language organizations
which are under the influence of our party, and even among the party-
members belonging to these various nationalities. And it is of course a problem the party should bravely try to settle. Unfortunately the comrades seem to
have the inclination rather to evade such problems. Further the negro comrades are very dissatisfied with the appointments of negro comrades on behalf
of the party. Before the district convention there was a negro comrade in the
district office as leader of the negro department. But after this comrade was
put into Harlem as a section organizer the district office remained without any
negro comrade. A certain change was made in this regard at the district committee meeting by putting a negro comrade as a member of district secretariat.
By the way, about the same comrade I was told *some weeks earlier* by the
members of N.Y. district secretariat that he is an outspoken "anti-party element". I think that this example better than many explanations illustrates the
bad relationships and mutual distrust prevailing between the N.Y. party leadership and the negros. I must further state that the appointments and dis-
missals of the negro party functionaries are quite curious ones especially here
in New York. In Harlem section we had before the district convention as
section organizer one politically very well developed negro comrade who was
at the last plenum co-opted as a member of CC. This new member of CC is now
leader of unem[p]loyed work in Harlem and as a section organizer there is
another negro comrade who politically is much weaker in the opinion of all.
Another negro comrade, Maude White, also a CC member after the last

plenum has worked in our needle trades union. But for some weeks she was dismissed without any further ceremonies. After such examples it is quite clear that the general distrust the leading negro comrades seem to have to the N.Y. district leadership as well as to the PB. is not decreasing but on the contrary increasing.

I am convinced that the things in N.Y. district will not improve very much before there are made considerable changes in the district leadership. Comrade Amter seems to be chemically pure of all what we call political understanding. And that is of course a change which must take place the sooner the better.

2. Since my last letter there has been little more collective work in national secretariat. I have been regularly invited to secretariat meetings which also have been attended by comr. Stachel and Hathaway. But the unhealthy tension, mentioned in my previous letter, between Weinstone and Browder continues as before. This makes the work very difficult. The smallest matters have the inclination to become to the most complicated problems, like for instance the division *of* work in the department which has to take care of literature. Many times after lengthy and empty discussions no decision is reached. I have considered it as my task to *try to* maintain a certain equilibrium in the secretariat. Nothing else can be done in my opinion for the time being. Anyhow, taking into the consideration the general logic of the development in such cases like this, I would repeat my request of sending here a real Ex.R. with necessary authority. I have privately spoken with W. as well with B. of such a possibility, and both of them seem to be of the opinion that it would to a certain extent improve the situation. In the meantime I would appreciate very much if you could give me certain advices as to what is to be done. In two weeks we will have the C.C. meeting. I have proposed and the comrades have agreed that we should have at this meeting as a special point in the agenda the question of the inner situation in the party. Such a discussion can of course have its bad as well as good sides. What I am driving at is that we should at least among the members of the CC. bring about a quite open and detailed discussion as to the weaknesses *and* shortcomings of the Central Party leadership along the lines the discussion was carried out in the enlarged Polbuero meeting in July. The fact remains that accusations are made everywhere in districts against the PB. as well as against the individual members of it, but these accusations are not discussed in an organizational manner in the respective party instances. Such a very curious an[d] in my opinion unhealthy

Document 51 *continued*

conception prevails that the names, weaknesses and shortcomings of the party leaders can not even be mentioned in the discussions. And such a conception has until now hindered all critisism from below. If we could break down this conception and carry through at the CC. meeting a real open discussion some things at least would be remedied even without any organizational changes. Such a discussion on behalf of the rank and file members certainly would serve as a more or less imperative directive to the secretariat and PB to try to do their work better than what the case is now.

Yours <u>Allen</u>

Document 52

Browder to Piatnitsky, 7 May 1933, RTsKhIDNI 495–19–616. Original in English. We have not reprinted the Finnish letter and its translation to which Browder refers.

REGARDING COMS. MORTON, ALLEN, AND FINNISH QUESTION

Dear Comrade Piatnitsky:—

Herewith attached you will find a copy of a letter in the Finnish language, with an English translation, which was sent to Hans Johnson (secretary of the Finnish Federation, now in Moscow) by C. Paivio, leader of the largest Finnish district in the U.S.A. Paivio was one of those who were drawn into the struggle against the C.C. under false pretenses. He has been disillusioned by his own experiences with Com. Morton, which he describes in this letter. His letter is a complete answer to all the questions you asked at the meeting of the Political Commission at the time we were considering the telegrams on the Finnish question.

On the basis of the information contained in these letters, and the experiences I have already reported, I feel that it is my duty to bring formal charges against Comrades Morton and Allen, and demand that disciplinary action be taken against them.

I charge these two comrades with playing the leading role in
(1) Establishing a fraction to fight against the line of the CPUSA and of the CI, especially against the policy of the united front;
(2) Trying to change the leadership of the CPUSA through factional struggle and by raising the threat of further faction fights;
(3) Mobilizing all the old remnants of right-wing factionalism in the Finnish Federation, and the old federationist tendencies, as the basis of their faction against the Central Committee;

(4) Misusing the name of the Comintern, claiming special authority from the CI for their actions;

(5) Developing the struggle of their faction, which began against the Central Committee, into a struggle against all Finnish comrades who wish to follow the line of the CPUSA and the CI, and endangering the existence of the whole Finnish communist movement in America.

It is necessary to point out, also, that while Comrade Hans Johnson, secretary of the Finnish Federation, was undoubtedly misled by the claims of Coms. Morton and Allen to special authority from the CI, that he was also a conscious participant in the violation of the cabled instructions of the CI regarding the removal of Com. Morton from Finnish work, and bears full responsibility in this question.

It is also necessary to declare that Comrades Weinstone and Bedacht, despite the unanimous decisions of the Politburo and the CC Plenum of the CPUSA, have followed a conciliatory policy towards Morton and Allen, and evidently speculated upon this opposition, if they did not directly collaborate with it.

With Communist greetings
Earl Browder
Earl Browder

Moscow, May 7, 1933.

Document 53

"On Comrade V.'s Work in the CPUSA," 25 May 1933, RTsKhIDNI 515–1–3093. Original in Russian. The document shows signs of handwritten editing, most of which is illegible. "Comrade V." is Niilo Karlovich Virtanen; Puro is Henry Puro, a Finnish-American Communist leader.

Mingulin
2136   25 May 1933 [stamp]   Return within 7 days [stamp]

Secret

"8"
5001/4/s4935/da.
25.V.33

ON COMRADE V.'S WORK IN THE CPUSA (8).

1. During his stay in the country, Comrade V. has done significant, positive work.

Document 53 *continued*

From April 1932, i.e., since the XIVth plenum of the Central Committee of the party, until September 1932, i.e., through the XVth Central Committee plenum, Comrade V. worked for the most part in the center and in essence became part of the party leadership. Aiding the work of the Central Committee Secretariat, where at this time acute differences had developed among its members, Comrade V. alone made it possible for this leading organ of the Politburo of the party to do any work whatsoever. It must be noted, however, that this work, although it gave direct positive results, cannot be looked on as the instructor's main task.

After the XVth Central Committee plenum, Comrade V. worked for the most part in concentration districts, where his work showed certain practical results—in Detroit, in preparing the automobile workers' strike, and in Chicago, in stimulating and improving the work of the local party organizations.

2. Comrade V., struggling to enact the decisions of the Comintern regarding the CPUSA and for the most part correctly criticizing the party leadership for not enacting the most important directives of the XIVth Central Committee plenum, did this before the XVIth Central Committee plenum in such a form that it exacerbated relations between him and the party leadership, which at the XVIth plenum led him to a standoff with the party Politburo on the Finnish question, as well as on the general issue of the party's position and its leadership:

a) Being connected and adequately informed about the situation of the Finnish organization and its leadership, Comrade V. did not see and did not warn the Central Committee in a timely fashion about great shortcomings in the work of Comrade Puro in the leadership of the Finnish organization and about the growing dissatisfaction among the senior Finnish comrades regarding Comrade Puro. Having learned from the protocols of the Bureau of the Executive Committee of the Finnish organization of these sentiments and of the intention to remove Comrade Puro, a Politburo member, from the leadership of the organization, Comrade V. sent a letter to the Finnish Bureau of the Central Committee, in which he supported the proposal to remove Comrade Puro from the leadership of the Finnish organization. Only two days after this, Comrade V. wrote about this same letter to the Politburo. Such a method of action, although with an essentially correct proposal regarding Comrade Puro, could not help warn about and eliminate the conflict. As the conflict developed, Comrade V. in exactly the same way did nothing to help eliminate it, although the Finnish comrades referred to him in their speeches at the 19 November session of the Finnish bureau, naming him along with Comrade Morton.

b) Comrade V. spoke at the Politburo before the XVIth Central Committee plenum, making a number of basically correct critical comments regarding the party's nonfulfillment of the extremely important decisions of the XIVth Central Committee plenum and the party leadership's work. But the form in which this criticism was made, as well as certain excesses and ambiguities in it, were such that it could have been interpreted as a statement against the party leadership and, specifically, against Comrade Browder, designed to isolate him in the party leadership. ~~This was precisely how the Politburo interpreted this statement and it condemned it. In spite of this, however,~~ Comrade V. gave approximately the same speech at the Central Committee plenum a week later, which ~~condemned his speech in precisely the same way.~~ ~~Although~~ Comrade V. informed the Comintern Executive Committee of his opinion regarding the party leadership, ~~in the sense of the need to remove it,~~ essentially, he did not receive a directive to carry out ~~such~~ a line of action and did not address himself to the XVIth plenum with such inquiries. Doubtless, however, the exacerbation of tensions between Comrade V. and the Politburo is explained by the Politburo's and the subsequent Central Committee plenum's erroneous assessment of the party's achievements and shortcomings.

c) It must be noted that Comrade V.'s instruction about his tasks and obligations in America was completely insufficient and that a number of his letters went unanswered.

A Comintern agent in the United States whose stay was less controversial than that of Aino Kuusinen or Niilo Virtanen was Solomon Vladimirovich Mikhelson-Manuilov, the Comintern's OMS station chief in the United States from 1933 to 1938. Born in eastern Latvia in 1893, Mikhelson-Manuilov had lived from 1912 to 1916 in London, where he was active in the politics of exiled Russian Marxists and joined Lenin's Bolshevik Party in 1914. In 1916 he moved to New York, where he worked in the garment trade as a shop assistant and joined the American Socialist Party. He returned to Russia in mid-1918 to assist the new Bolshevik regime. In 1919 he was sent to Odessa to direct a network of émigré Bolsheviks who had returned from the United States and England and operated covertly in Ukraine during the Russian civil war. In 1929 he joined the Comintern and became the OMS station chief in Berlin, a position he held until 1932. During his U.S. stay the CPUSA awarded him American party membership, which was back-dated to 1919, thus conferring founding-member status on him. A number of coded cables between Moscow and Mikhelson-Manuilov (many cited in this volume under the code names "Kraft," "Spector," and "Black") show him supervising the distribution of Comintern funds to the United States, overseeing the movements of CPUSA and Comintern couriers, and answering queries from Moscow concerning CPUSA activities.[17]

The CPUSA and International Comintern Operations

At times the United States acted as the center for Comintern operations elsewhere in the world. In particular, the Comintern ran its Asian operations from the San Francisco area. During the 1920s and 1930s, the United States was one of the Western powers that had been granted special extraterritorial rights in the International Settlement in Shanghai, and American citizenship therefore provided a margin of immunity from the often harsh anti-Communist policies of Chinese police loyal to the Nationalist government of Chiang Kai-shek. In **document 54** the Comintern directs William Z. Foster, who was in charge of trade union work, to ask Robert Dunn to head a "formally independent economic research institute in Shanghai" that in addition to the research would provide "cover for Panpacific Trade Union Secretariat." The Pan-Pacific Trade Union Secretariat, an arm of the Comintern's Red International of Labor Unions (Profintern), worked both overtly and covertly to organize Communist trade unions in East Asia. Dunn, an economist, denied his membership in the Communist party throughout his life, although he was a prominent figure in the Labor Research Association, a left-wing economics think tank. After his death in 1977, however, the *Daily World* printed a CPUSA eulogy for Dunn that praised him as "part of us for virtually all his adult life," a claim that is confirmed by this document.[18]

The well-known American writer Agnes Smedley, who also never admitted to her relationship to the Comintern, likewise did Comintern work in China. Smedley was in the USSR in early 1934, when the Comintern ordered her to Shanghai. She did not travel directly to China from the Soviet Union, which would have been literally a red flag to Shanghai authorities, but by way of Europe, where she

17. The authors thank Fridrikh Igorevich Firsov, former Comintern historian at the RTsKhIDNI, for this biographical sketch of Mikhelson-Manuilov.

18. Si Gerson, eulogy for Robert Dunn, *Daily World*, 8 February 1977; see also Harvey Klehr, *The Heyday of American Communism: The Depression Decade* (New York: Basic Books, 1984), 476n.20.

stopped in several places, and the United States. Shortly after she left the USSR and was en route to the United States, the Comintern cabled Earl Browder with a message: "We have sent Smedley through America to China. She will come to you. Transmit her following message which we received for her from China: Society should not be incorporated in USA. After arrival Shanghai Isaak will hand over immediately printing office through American Consul. Question concerning Chinese printer you will decide after arrival."[19]

The cable was referring to Comintern plans to create a new Shanghai-based, English-language journal on Chinese affairs to replace *China Forum,* a covertly Communist-aligned journal that had been published by Harold Isaacs until early that year, when it ceased publication. The line in the cable "Society should not be incorporated in USA" was an instruction to Smedley not to incorporate the magazine in the United States. Isaacs planned to turn over the printing plant through the American Consul; because of the extraterritorial status of Shanghai's international zone, legal instruments were registered with one of the controlling foreign powers.

In June the Comintern reminded the CPUSA that it needed to notify Moscow when Smedley left the country.[20] In July, however, the Comintern sent an urgent message to the CPUSA: Browder was to tell Smedley "she must not leave" the United States when she had planned to, "but must wait for our instructions."[21] A few weeks later Browder was instructed to inform Smedley once again: "Don't leave for China." The cable, from Pavel Mif, the Comintern's China specialist, explained that the Shanghai police had arrested a number of Communists and, perhaps more troubling, "Isaac[s] refuses to hand over printi[n]g house."[22] Isaacs had become increasingly sympathetic toward Trotskyism and correspondingly unwilling to cooperate with the Comintern.[23] Shortly

19. Comintern to Earl [Browder], 22 April 1934, RTsKhIDNI 495–184–24, 1934 file. For biographical details about Smedley, see Klehr, Haynes, and Firsov, *Secret World of American Communism,* 60–64.

20. Comintern to CPUSA, 27 June 1934, RTsKhIDNI 495–184–24, 1934 file.

21. Comintern to CPUSA, 9 July 1934, RTsKhIDNI 495–184–24, 1934 file.

22. Comintern to CPUSA, 14 August 1934, RTsKhIDNI 495–184–24, 1934 file. Mif's real name was Mikhail Firman.

23. In 1938 Isaacs published *The Tragedy of the Chinese Revolution* (London: Secker and Warburg, 1938), in which he took a critical view of the effects of Stalinism on Chinese communism. In 1935 Smedley, then in Shanghai, sent a warning to the Comintern via Earl Browder that Isaacs had completed the manuscript of this

after this the Comintern cabled the CPUSA to "inform Sm[e]dley printing press stolen and soled [sold] by Isaac[s]." "Nevertheless," the cable continued, "paper must be started," and "in the meantime Sm[e]dl[e]y will work independently." The cable went on to add that the crackdown on Communist activities in Shanghai was so severe that "due tense situation impossible at present to make connections between Sm[e]dl[e]y and Chinese party or European comrades in Shanghai." Instead, the CPUSA was directed to find someone "politically developed and legal with real passport american as her coworker or partner" in the planned publication.[24] Smedley finally left for Shanghai in October 1934, but she encountered great difficulties establishing the new journal, *Voice of China*, until Browder was able to send her two CPUSA professionals, Grace and Max Granich, to assist with the work.[25]

Smedley proved undisciplined, however, and in 1936 she failed on several occasions to adhere to Comintern instructions. Her continual refusal to follow orders finally led the Comintern to sever its connections with her. One matter over which Smedley and the Comintern disagreed was Smedley's close relationship to Madam Sun, the widow of Sun Yat-sen, founder of the Chinese republic. Madam Sun was sympathetic to the Communist cause, and the Comintern was anxious for its relations with her to be handled with great care. In July the representative of the Pan-Pacific Trade Union Secretariat in Shanghai, Rudy Baker, warned the Comintern that contrary to instructions, "Smedley continue[s] maintain contact with Party union and foreign com[r]ade using Madam Sun and foreign non-Party person as translator for Party work." Baker indicated that Smedley's combining Comintern work with internal Chinese Communist party activities and involving Madam Sun was dangerous. He urged the Comintern: "Recall her otherwise serious trouble."[26]

book and was en route to Europe to find a publisher. See Earl to Comintern, 14 August 1935, RTsKhIDNI 495–184–34, 1935 file.

24. Comintern to CPUSA, 5 September 1934, RTsKhIDNI 495–184–24, 1934 file.

25. Browder promised to provide CPUSA assistance for Smedley in Browder to Dimitrov, 2 September 1935, RTsKhIDNI 495–74–463, reprinted in Klehr, Haynes, and Firsov, *Secret World of American Communism*, 62–63.

26. Johnson and Betford to Wang-Ming, via Browder, 31 July 1936, RTsKhIDNI 495–184–3, 1936 file. "Betford" was Baker's alias during his service with the Pan-Pacific Trade Union Secretariat. "Wang-Ming" was the pseudonym of Chen Shao-

In addition to maintaining close relations with Madame Sun, Smedley publicly attacked the Chinese Nationalist leader Chiang Kai-shek when the Communists were negotiating with him about creating a united front, an act that further exasperated the Comintern professionals. Early in January 1937 Browder cabled Moscow that American Communists working for the Comintern in Shanghai had asked the CPUSA to "publicly repudiate" Smedley's position on Chiang because it was in conflict with the Chinese party's policy. As ever, Browder relied on Moscow: "We must have your agreement before we can intervene. Telegraph at once advice."[27] The Comintern replied that it was "necessary" to "publicly repudiate Smedley. Declare that she does not represent the Communists attitudes and is not authorized to act in its name." On 29 January 1937, the *Daily Worker* carried out Moscow's directive and denounced Smedley.[28]

Document 54

Alexander and Earl to Foster, 11 July 1928, RTsKhIDNI 534–6–137. Original in English. At this time Browder was working for the Comintern and serving as the first general secretary of the Pan-Pacific Trade Union Secretariat. "Alexander" was the alias of a Profintern official named Keetagnian.

Foster

New York

Ask Robert Dunn if he agree to head a formally independent economic research institute in Shanghai organized by RILU purpose not only research but also cover for Panpacific Trade Union Secretariat. Cable Shanghai our friends

Alexander Earl

I 928
11/7

---

yii, a Comintern operative who became one of the top leaders in the Chinese Communist party in 1931; he represented the Chinese party in Moscow from late 1931 until 1937 and was a member of the ECCI. We do not know Johnson's identity.

27. Browder to Secretariat and Wang-Ming, 21 January 1937, 495–184–9, 1937 file.

28. Secretariat to Browder, 24 January 1937, RTsKhIDNI 495–184–17, 1937 file. Comintern orders ending contact with Smedley are discussed in Klehr, Haynes, and Firsov, *Secret World of American Communism*, 64–70. Smedley was also forced out of the *Voice of China*.

Americans Stationed in Moscow

Comintern representatives came to America, and American Communists journeyed to Moscow. To American Communists, Moscow was the center of the world revolution and the source of all that sustained the socialist dream.[29] Every year throughout the 1920s and 1930s dozens of Americans traveled to the Soviet Union for Comintern consultations and training. It was a rare year when one or more of the top party leaders did not appear in Moscow to report on the activities of the American party and to receive guidance on its future plans. This Marxist-Leninist hajj began with the foundation of the American Communist movement.

In the early years, the representatives traveled to the Soviet Union to speak and lobby on behalf of their party or, after unification, their faction. Throughout the 1920s, the contending factions in the American party looked to Moscow for a mentor to keep them apprised of discussions about strategy and tactics and to defend their interests in Comintern committees and special commissions. There was no set term for these envoys, and the decision about who would go seems to have been left up to the Americans. This freedom led to discussions and sometimes dissension in the Central Executive Committee over whom to send.

John Reed, Louis Fraina, and Nicholas Hourwich

As noted earlier, in 1919 two competing American Communist parties were born, each proclaiming allegiance to the Communist International. Both parties immediately dispatched delegates to Russia in hopes of winning recognition as the official American Communist party. The delegates, John Reed of the Communist Labor Party and Louis Fraina of the Communist Party of America, were the first American representatives to the Comintern. Fraina's party was soon rent by yet more internal factionalism, and Nicholas I. Hourwich, a rival of Fraina's, next arrived in Moscow as second representative of the Communist Party of America.

29. Letters and telegrams from American Communists that might be intercepted by government authorities often employed the code name "Mecca" for Moscow. As a name intended to deceive it was poorly chosen, for its significance was all too obvious.

Ultimately, Moscow proved unlucky for these first American representatives. Reed's initial reception went well; the Soviets were delighted with the glorious portrait of the Bolshevik Revolution he had painted in his best-selling *Ten Days That Shook the World*.[30] The Comintern gave Reed an enormous sum in currency and jewels to subsidize the American movement, and in February 1920 he secretly crossed into Finland, carrying part of this fortune back to America. But the Finnish police arrested him as he was attempting to stow away on a ship leaving Finland. The jewels were confiscated, and he was imprisoned. He was soon exchanged for some Finns who were being held by Soviet authorities.

On his return to the Soviet Union, however, Reed fell into difficulties. At the Second Congress of the Communist International (July–August 1920), Reed opposed the Comintern decision concerning the appropriate Communist trade union strategy in the United States. Along with most American Communists, he wanted the Comintern to back the Industrial Workers of the World, the militant and radical union organization that openly sought to replace the American Federation of Labor. The Comintern, however, ordered American Communists to enter existing, moderate trade unions (the AFL) and radicalize them from within. When Reed objected, he was denounced by Grigory Zinoviev, at that time head of the Comintern, and other members of the Soviet Communist party delegation.

Reed resigned in protest from the Executive Committee of the Communist International. This brought down on him an even fiercer denunciation. The Soviets made it clear that in the Comintern individuals did not resign as an act of protest; submission to discipline was the only acceptable behavior.[31] As shown by **document 55**, Reed gave in, acknowledging that he had been "wrong" to resign and withdrawing his resignation. Soon afterward, Reed left Moscow to attend the Comintern's Congress of Oriental Nations in Baku, in Soviet Azerbaijan. He returned to Moscow in September, where he contracted typhus and died in October. Reed

30. Reed, a journalist, had been in St. Petersburg at the time of the revolution; there he was won over to the Bolshevik cause.

31. On this attitude of the Comintern's, see Granville Hicks, *John Reed: The Making of a Revolutionary* (New York: Macmillan, 1936), 395.

quickly entered the Communist pantheon as a revolutionary hero; in the 1930s the CPUSA named a group organized for intellectuals the John Reed Clubs in his honor.

Document 55 resolves a long-standing controversy concerning Reed's behavior in the last months of his life. There are several versions of the story. One account, by Max Eastman, onetime editor of *Masses* and a friend of Reed's, was based on information from Louise Bryant, Reed's wife. Eastman claimed that the feud with Zinoviev climaxed at the Baku congress, and Reed refused to back down, on principle. Granville Hicks, in a biography written when he was one of the leading CPUSA intellectuals, and Louis Fraina asserted that Reed resigned at the end of the second Comintern congress and that he was forced by the Comintern to withdraw the resignation and admit error. This document appears to confirm the Hicks-Fraina version.[32]

Fraina, too, found his stay in the Soviet Union a difficult one. In the fall of 1919, shortly after he helped to found the Communist Party of America, Fraina was falsely accused of being an agent provocateur for the U.S. government. A party trial in the United States cleared Fraina of the charge, yet when he reached the Soviet Union, some of his factional enemies revived the slander. Two separate Comintern commissions investigated the charges and once more found him innocent. Nevertheless, the Comintern decided that for the sake of unity, Fraina should stay out of the United States. He was ordered to Mexico as a Comintern agent.

Fraina, however, floundered in the role. Sometime in 1923 he dropped out of sight and left the Communist party. Rumors in left-wing circles had him absconding with an enormous sum of Comintern money. After he resurfaced, he admitted that he had kept some of the Comintern money. The FBI found an account he had sent to the CPUSA in 1922 that indicated that he had retained $4,200, a hefty sum in the early 1920s (roughly $35,000 in 1995 dollars), if far short of the sums later rumored in Communist circles.[33]

32. The many and complex versions of the final months of Reed's life are summarized in Theodore Draper, *The Roots of American Communism* (New York: Viking Press, 1957), 282–93.

33. Draper, *Roots of American Communism*, 296. Draper notes that Fraina's offer to repay the money was refused.

Documents 56 and 57 deal with Fraina's handling of Comintern funds. Document 56 is a Comintern letter to Fraina dated 18 April 1923. This document makes clear that two Comintern agents, Michael Borodin and one Thomas (unknown), had given Fraina $60,000 in 1921 (more than $500,000 in mid-1990s dollars). Fraina had transferred $26,000 of this to Charles Scott, a Latvian-American Communist and fellow Comintern agent. In the Comintern's view, of the remaining $34,000, Fraina had yet to account for how he had spent some $14,000—and at the beginning of 1922 had still had slightly more than $12,000 on hand that the Comintern wanted back. Fraina's reply (not located) did not satisfy the Comintern. In document 57 Osip Piatnitsky of the OMS expressed skepticism about Fraina's claim that $7,000 had been stolen and asked what he had spent another $3,000 on.

These documents illustrate what large sums Moscow entrusted in cash to individual Comintern agents, but they do not resolve the question of how much money Fraina took with him when he dropped out of the movement. They do suggest, however, that although he may not have been guilty of the colossal embezzlement some Communists later charged him with, Fraina did practice some sloppy accounting, and that the Comintern's doubts about him began before he left the party. The charge was not merely an after-the-fact smear.[34]

From Mexico, Fraina returned to New York, changed his name several times before settling on Lewis Corey, and found work as a printer. Several years later he surfaced as a Marxist economist and by the early 1930s had established a national reputation as the leading Marxist analyst of the American economy. He worked at the Brookings Institution in 1929–1930 and was an associate editor of the influential *Encyclopedia of the Social Sciences* from 1931 to 1934.

In addition to advocating Marxist economics, Corey/Fraina remained a political supporter of Soviet communism, and in 1932 he was a prominent member of the League of Professional Groups for Foster and Ford, an organization of American intellectuals, most of

34. For a different view, see Paul M. Buhle, *A Dreamer's Paradise Lost: Louis C. Fraina/Lewis Corey (1892–1953) and the Decline of Radicalism in the United States* (Atlantic Highlands, N.J.: Humanities Press International, 1995), 96–97.

whom were not Communists, that was created to support the CPUSA presidential ticket. Although Corey/Fraina's intellectual prestige added luster to the group, his position as an apostate made many of the Communists uncomfortable, and they tried to force him out.[35] Historian Theodore Draper concludes that the conflict over Corey/Fraina "was one of the principal reasons for the committee's dissolution" after the election.[36]

Document 58 gives Corey/Fraina's response to the CPUSA hostility. Writing to Earl Browder to complain that Harry Wicks, a prominent party figure, has denounced him as "an agent-provocateur and a thief," Corey/Fraina protests that he wants to work with the Communist party and that he still considers himself a loyal Communist, albeit one who must prove his commitment.[37] In fact, he is hoping to rejoin the party after he has earned forgiveness through his work. The CPUSA, however, continued to keep Corey/Fraina at arm's length. When his wife met with Browder in 1934 to discuss her husband's reestablishing a relationship with the CPUSA, Browder informed her that the Corey/Fraina affair was "closed" and "the Party has no desire to reopen the case."[38]

In spite of this rebuff, Corey/Fraina remained sympathetic to communism for much of the 1930s. But in 1939, disgusted by the Nazi-Soviet Pact, he denounced the Soviet Union and soon abandoned Marxism as well. In 1940 he helped found and became research director of the Union for Democratic Action, which rejected both Nazism and Communism as totalitarian movements. Unimpressed by his later views, the Immigration and Naturalization Service attempted to deport him to his native Italy in the early 1950s on the grounds that he had once been a Communist; the action was forestalled only by his death in 1953.

35. William Weinstone of the CPUSA told the Comintern that the CPUSA leadership had adopted a formal resolution demanding Corey's removal. Weinstone testimony, 4 April 1933, American Commission, RTsKhIDNI 495–72–225.

36. Draper, *Roots of American Communism*, 299.

37. Wicks was himself expelled from the CPUSA in 1937 on the grounds that he had at one time been and might still be a police informer. Based on the information in his FBI file, Wicks had been working as an undercover informant for the Chicago police and for a private company when he joined the Communist movement in 1918 (FBI file 100–29845; in authors' possession).

38. Browder Memo of 7 March 1934 Attached to Minutes of Polburo, CPUSA, 9 March 1934, RTsKhIDNI 515–1–3448.

Nicholas Hourwich, the third of the original American representatives to the Comintern, also ran into trouble in Moscow, when the Comintern concluded that he was likely to be obstructionist. At the third Comintern congress in 1921, Lenin himself met with the American delegation to impress on them the seriousness of the Comintern instruction that the American party concentrate on mass agitation and organizing, rather than maintain an underground party on the pre-1917 Bolshevik model. As Draper describes it, Hourwich "aroused Lenin's ire by interrupting him repeatedly and finally brought down on his head the rebuke that he was a Russian, not an American. Hourwich was never permitted to come back to the United States, which was one way of solving the problem."[39]

Document 55

James Flynn, Alexander Bilan, John Jurgis, John Reed, Louis Fraina, and A. Stocklitsky to ECCI, 9 August 1920, RTsKhIDNI 495–1–5. Original in English.

9/VIII.

To the Executive Committee of the Communist International.
Comrades:
While we recognize that Comrade John Reed was acting upon the spirit and letter of the considered decision of the Central Executive of the United Communist Party of America, we regret his action in leaving the Executive Committee of the Communist International which we consider ill-advised and hasty.

Comrade Reed, in reporting the matter to our delegation, has admitted that this action in leaving the Executive Committee of the Communist International was wrong.

Recognizing the necessity of Party discipline, we refuse to accept his resignation and have instructed him to continue as representative of America on the Executive Committee of the Communist International.

James Flynn.
Alexander Bilan.
John Jurgis.
John Reed.

---

39. Draper, *Roots of American Communism*, 280.

Document 55 *continued*

The delegation of the Communist Party of America, in accordance with the decision of the Executive Committee, subscribes to Comrade Reed, of the United Communist Party being on the Executive.

Louis Fraina.
A. Stocklitsky

Document 56

Zinoviev to Fraina, 18 April 1923, RTsKhIDNI 495–19–608. Original in Russian.

Comrade Fraina:

To follow up on and regarding [communication] to you of 15 August 1922, no. 1720, we inform you that upon our receipt of a report from Comrade Scott, your accounts with us are as follows.

Received by you in Berlin for the American Agency in 1921 from Borodin

	10,000	dollars
and from Thomas	50,000	"
	total 60,000	

Out of that amount you gave Scott U.S. dollars	20,204.70	
and 6,513.40 in Canadian dollars, which is about	5,795.30	

In all you gave Scott the equivalent of	26,000	U.S. dollars
which leaves you with "　　　"　　　"	34,000	"　　"

Regarding this amount we have received a report from you for the period 1 October through 31 December 1921 for 19,803 U.S. dollars, of which amount on 1 January 1922 you still had $12,228.50. We do not have a report for the period from 5 June 1921 (the day you arrived in America from Berlin) through 1 October of the same year for the amount of 14,196.50 U.S. dollars.

In view of the above we request that you:

1. provide us with a report for the period June–September 1921.
2. send us the remainder, which you had in hand as of 1 January 1922 in the amount of 12,228.50 U.S. dollars, since after 1 January the agency no longer

Document 56 *continued*

existed, and for that reason there could not have been any more expenses charged to the agency.

18/IV–23
No. 689

Translate into German
Zinoviev

Document 57

Piatnitsky to Fraina, 18 December 1923, RTsKhIDNI 495–19–608. Original in English. The "CEC of the WP" stands for the Central Executive Committee of the Workers Party of America (an early name for the CPUSA).

December,18,1923.

Louis C. Fraina.
Dear Comrade;—
Yours of Sept. 14 through the CEC of the WP has reached our hands. We note in your letter the intention expressed of getting into contact direct with the Comintern. Up to the present, however, we have received no communication from you and therefore must confine ourselves to the letter above-mentioned.

We wish to put several questions to you which we ask you to answer without any evasion:

1. When, where and how was the $7,000 stolen from you?

2. What did you expend the $3,000 on?

3. You admit having $12,228.50 as of January 1, 1922. What has become of the balance of $2,228.50?

4. What have been your activities since your departure from Mexico on Dec. 24, 1921?

5. You went from Mexico to Cuba and stated that you intended also to go to Argentina? Did you ever reach your destination?

6. What were you doing in Mexico in March, 1923, and why did you not get into touch with the Mexican Party?

7. Why have you sent no report to the Comintern in these two years?

Upon receipt of an <u>immediate</u> comprehensive reply from you through the CEC of the Workers Party, we shall make a decision and duly inform you.

With Communist greetings,
Piatnitsky

Document 58

Corey to Browder, 21 February 1934, RTsKhIDNI 515–1–3444. Original in English.

C O P Y (Letter from Lewis Corey (Fraina))

3986 47th St.
Sunnyside, L.I.,
New York, N.Y.   February 21, 1934.

Dear Comrade Browder:—

I am writing to you not only as general secretary of the Party; I am presuming on the fact that you and I met once in 1920 to give this letter a personal note.

It has been reported to me that one week ago today Harry Wicks, in a lecture in a hall located in the apartment house where I live, in a series of lectures arranged by the local party, made a vicious personal attack on me. He misrepresented my position in the left wing and the party of 1919–20; among other things, I am told, he said that I steered the party into IWW'ism. (In this he repeated the charge that the Michigan group, of which Wicks was then a member, made not only against me but against the whole party). In addition Wicks, who was introduced as a member of the Central Committee and who, I am told, said he spoke officially, declared that I am an agent-provocateur and a thief.

Does Wicks speak for the Central Committee?

There is a personal angle to this, but the political is more important. I am doing Marxist and communist writing; I don't want this to appear as work of an enemy of the Party, but as work done for the Party.

Only one issue is involved in my relations with the Party and the Comintern. I deserted the Party. Whatever the personal reasons may have been, the political act is clear. It is not an act to explain away in words, in pleas or in self-justification. That can be done only with work. And I want to work with the Party and the Comintern. But when a man has left the Party as I did, he does not come back with empty hands. He comes back with work, with concrete evidence that he has not abandoned his former ideas and that he can do work for the Party which the Party needs.

So my policy has been this, and I felt it all the more justified after I made two attempts to discuss matters with Ruthenberg, which he refused to do:

There is certain theoretical work that I want to do. One book, on which I have been working for some years, is "The Decline of American Capitalism", which

will be published shortly. I have also been working on two other books—
Fundamentals of Marxism and the American Labor Movement. My plan has
been, and I told this to Joe Freeman over a year ago, when I was asked to join,
and did, the League of Professional Groups, to write the books and then to
apply for readmission into the Party. And if the Party and the Comintern said
no, then I would continue my theoretical work and serve in that manner.

Some of my friends have told me this waiting policy is wrong, that struggles
and lines are tightening too rapidly. Perhaps they are right. I want to work for
the movement as effectively as I possibly can, to let work wipe out the mistake
of the past. If you have the inclination and the opportunity, I would like to
discuss the matter with you.

Fraternally yours,

Lewis Corey (signed)

Responsibilities of the CPUSA Representative

The chief duty of the CPUSA representative to the Comintern was
to keep Moscow informed of the American party's activities and to
transmit Comintern directives back to the United States. We have
already seen a sampling of the kinds of reports and policy directives
that passed through the American representative. But in addition to
this high-level communications role, American party representatives in Moscow performed a variety of other functions.[40]

Document 59, a 1930 report to the CPUSA from Randolph, the
American representative to the Comintern, illuminates some of
these responsibilities. ("Randolph" was an alias used by several of
the CPUSA representatives in the 1930s. In this case, it was William
Weinstone.) Here Randolph informs the CPUSA leaders that he has
briefed the Anglo-American Secretariat of the Comintern about
what has been going on in the American party and adds that William Foster and Harry Wicks, senior CPUSA officials who were
also in Moscow, as well as several American students at the Inter-

40. For a listing of all the American representatives to the Comintern and the
Comintern representatives to the United States, see the appendix.

national Lenin School, participated in the Comintern session. Foster also gave a separate report. Randolph notes that after discussions in the Political Commission of the Political Secretariat, the Comintern had cabled the Americans with "the directions in regard to" the CPUSA call for the formation of a Labor party.

Randolph also reports that he had participated in discussions on the "Negro question" and was preparing for discussions with Comintern leaders on party activities in the Trade Union Unity League (TUUL). Adopting the Comintern's perspective, he criticizes the coverage in the *Daily Worker* of the rapidly developing American economic depression, offers a few themes for May Day demonstrations, complains about comrades from the United States who went to the Soviet Union for a visit and then tried to stay permanently, requests help in finding a researcher, and alerts the CPUSA to the necessity of providing help to Latin American Communist parties. In another message, dated 18 December 1930 and signed with his own name, Weinstone warns his American comrades that some of their decisions at a recent party plenum have caused concern in Moscow: "I have forgotten to mention that Comrade K. spoke to me about changes in the Pol. Bureau made in the plenum. Comrade K. stated that it is not a good procedure to make changes without consultation with the Comintern."[41] "Comrade K." was Otto Kuusinen, the supervisor of the Anglo-American Secretariat.

The CPUSA's Comintern representative was also responsible for supervising the activities of the American students attending the various Comintern schools in the Soviet Union, where promising recruits were trained for revolutionary leadership. These students were usually subsidized by the Comintern. In 1924, for example, the Comintern sent the Americans $1,282 to pay the expenses of "ten Negro students to the Eastern University in Moscow."[42] The ten were slated to attend the Communist University of the Toilers of the East, which was a less prestigious institution than the Com-

41. Weinstone to Dear Comrades, 18 December 1930, RTsKhIDNI 515–1–1870.
42. Comintern Eastern Department to Central Committee, Workers Party of America, 26 September 1924, RTsKhIDNI 515–1–255.

intern's flagship school, the International Lenin School (ILS). The former served students of the Soviet Union's Asiatic regions as well as non-Soviet students from colonial countries; this distinction led many African-Americans to complain that they were being discriminated against.[43]

In document 59, Randolph discussed charges of discrimination and white chauvinism lodged against the CPUSA (despite the fact that the university assignments were made by the Comintern) by African-American students at the Communist University of the Toilers of the East. In addition to negotiating with the students about their complaints, Randolph also tried to help three late-arriving students to the ILS enroll in the course. In a February report to New York, he noted that "Comrade Lena and Childs may get through, but I am not certain about Mike."[44] Comrade Lena was probably Lena Chernenko, who later served as the CPUSA's district organizer in New Jersey; Childs was Morris Childs, who was discussed in chapter 2.

In addition to the official CPUSA representative to the ECCI, throughout the 1920s and 1930s other American Communists, ranging in numbers from two or three to a dozen or more, served in lesser posts throughout the Comintern. Several held the title of "referent" to a specific Comintern secretariat. The referent acted as a liaison officer and source of information about American conditions. The referent positions also functioned as internships for promising American Communists who were being groomed for more senior positions.

43. The Comintern's ideological analysis of the position of African-Americans in American society held that they were an oppressed nationality, and that what was termed the Black Belt in the American South needed to be freed from its colonial relationship to the United States; thus, African-Americans belonged in the institution for colonial peoples.

44. Randolph to Dear Comrades, 5 February 1930, RTsKhIDNI 515–1–1870.

Document 59

Randolph to CPUSA, 12 January 1930, RTsKhIDNI 515–1–1870. Original in English. A. J. Muste was the founder of a radical non-Communist party. Martin Tranmael was the leader of the Norwegian Communist party; he broke with the Comintern in 1923 and rejoined the Socialist Party in 1927. For the background of the La Follette movement, see chapter 1.

1—*To be returned.*

Copy

January 12, 1930.

Secretariat and Polbureau
CP USA

Report No. 3.

Dear Comrades:

REPORT.

As I wired you I reported on Dec. 31 concerning the present economic situation, the recent struggles of the workers, the political situation, the work and inner situation of the Party and the organizational and political tasks. In my report I recommended as the opinion of the Political Committee the dropping of the Labor Party slogan. In the discussion, all representatives and Lenin Students participated. Comrade Foster made a supplementary report. No one took issue with the general line of the Party. Comrade Wicks, however, was very critical in regard to our Plenum Theses maintaining that we did not see the development of the crisis and that we failed to underscore the social-fascist development of the Socialist Party. I must say that I replied very sharply to Comrade Wicks, first for developing a sixth sense since his departure from New York, namely, hind-sight and secondly, for misrepresenting the Theses. Also, I attacked Comrade Ballam's position on the question of self-determination agreeing, however, with the criticism that has been made that this slogan has not been taken up by the Party. Following the report, the question of the Labor Party was discussed in the Political Commission of the Political Secretariat. The opinions of the leading comrades on this question I shall note below. It was further agreed in the Political Commission that a letter would be drawn up to the Party on its tasks in view of the crisis. This letter will very likely be written in connection with the Party Congress.

LABOR PARTY QUESTION.

You have already received by telegram the directions in regard to this matter. For further clarification, I am here giving the outline of the remarks of

203

Comrade Manuilsky which served as the basis for the directions. These remarks were not taken down stenographically so that only the sense of them are given here—"The question of the Labor Party must be taken together with the prospects of the development of the Labor movement in the near future. What was the situation when we advanced the Labor Party slogan? Our Party was weak; capitalism was strong; the two party system was undergoing some change with the development of the LaFollette movement. We desired to break the old A. F. of L. system of supporting either of the capitalist parties. This method was appropriate for the given period. We desired to create a basis for mass movements. But there were no big struggles at that time.

What is the position now? Strong American capitalism has been shaken. We have big strikes as in Illinois and Gastonia. We are forming new unions. We have made progress in the Bolshevization of our Party. In this situation, the Labor Party slogan would be a false one. What are our perspectives? Great economic conflicts. A broad basis for the radicalization of the labor movement. The new unions also provide a broad basis for us. The important task of the movement is to strengthen the new unions by various methods, factory committees, etc. We must change our methods in according to the changes in the situation. If we take the Labor Party as the basis for uniting the masses, we may be out-manoeuvred by Muste.

We do not wish to liquidate the VI Congress resolution. We say that the present time is not appropriate for advancing the Labor Party slogan. We have our own Party. The reformists are coming out with the Labor Party slogan. If we could eliminate the SP and reformists we might adopt this slogan, but in the present situation we may, by adopting this slogan, leave the initiative in the hands of the reformists. Norway affords an example. We advanced the Labor Party slogan. The Social Democrats opposed it. But Tranmael adopted it and we were left "with the baby." There is no need to repeal the VI Congress resolution, but we say that the Labor Party slogan is not appropriate to the present period. The X Plenum desired us to reach out with other bodies, for example in Germany, the revolutionary factory representatives; the methods adopted in France, etc. All this is intended to create a broad basis for the Party. The Labor Party in America cannot be a substitute for this. There is mass unemployment, short-time, etc., in America. This gives us opportunity for creating such new bodies and other forms [as] can be devised. The question should not be raised as one of principle. Such a step would be harmful. We must expose the SP and the Muste group. The task today is to build the new unions and smash the A. F. of L. We must follow closely what the SP is doing. If it has success then we must penetrate the Labor Party in order to fight it. We must explain why we formerly supported the Labor Party slogan and what role the Labor Party slogan now plays.

Document 59 *continued*

In the personal talk which I had with Comrade Manuilsky on the occasion of the draft telegram, he stated that the question of the Labor Party may be raised again in the future depending upon the effects of the crisis and the strength of the Party in relation to the new unions. But the most important thing for us is now to expose the slogan of the Labor Party as put forward by the SP and reformists and to concentrate upon the building of the new unions and the TUUL.

NEGRO QUESTION.

At the time I arrived here there was a proposal for a special Negro conference. This matter is still before us. I have proposed that for the coming Congress of the Party the Negro question be made an important part of the agenda and pre-Congress discussion and that a special conference be held the day after the Congress to discuss more concretely the application of the resolution of the Congress to the immediate tasks, and that accordingly the date of the ANLC [American Negro Labor Conference] conference be fixed so that the discussions in the Party shall serve to clarify our line and mobilize for the ANLC. I shall, perhaps, within the next few days wire you the recommendations adopted on this matter.

ANGLO-AMERICAN SECRETARIAT.

The Anglo-American Secretariat is being reorganized and Comrade Gussev has been put in charge. At the coming meeting in the next few days, we shall discuss the question of the Party relations to the TUUL and to the new unions, and concrete proposals will be made for strengthening our work and building up the new unions and TUUL. Likewise the question of the Party Congress will be disposed of at this meeting.

THE CRISIS.

I wired you and received your reply in regard to the manner in which the Daily is treating the crisis. It was my impression that there was an underestimation of the significance of the crisis. From all signs the crisis will be a deep-going one and must be put into the foreground and serve as a basis for our work. The crisis will mark a turning point in class relations and therefore the entire Party must be orientated on the tasks arising from the crisis. Here the crisis is treated as one of the outstanding phases of the new stage in the Third Period. Consequently, the crisis is not only of importance for our Party but for the entire International. The vast unemployment, the gigantic conflicts which we should expect necessitates the most complete mobilization of our Party forces and the acceleration of the process of Bolshevization. The building of the TUUL, the throwing of the entire forces of the Party committees to build up the TUUL, the building of the new unions into mass unions, the rooting of the Party in the big factories, the politicalizing of the economic struggles, not only by regularly agitating and connecting up the economic slogans with the need for a revolutionary workers' government, but the question of the political strike, must become part of the orientation of the Party membership and must be intimately bound up with the strike struggles. The fighting tone of the Party and the militancy of its approach to the struggles of the workers is now a question which will determine how far it succeeds in the present situation. There is no doubt that there are still in the ranks of the Party many remnants of the theory of exceptionalism and the over-estimation of the strength of American imperialism, and this must be combatted energetically among the functionaries. Particularly must we raise the danger of social-fascism and the Muste group in particular. I await your material in regard to the programme which you stated in your telegram you had adopted in connection with the crisis.

LENIN STUDENTS.

All Lenin students that arrived recently came late for the Short Course of nine months which ends in June. The last one just arrived and I am not sure that he will get into the Course. In that case I shall make arrangements for him to work in the Profintern, Mining Section, and to prepare himself for the next Course. I shall try early enough to inform you of our quota of students for the Short and Long Course. I received your letter advising me to take up the matter of returning the Lenin Students who have completed their course. In regard to three of them already I have been unsuccessful, and they have been placed at the disposition of the International. I shall try to have the others return.

STUDENTS IN THE EASTERN UNIVERSITY.

I have had two sessions with them. They feel that they have been discriminated against in being segregated by themselves in the Eastern University and think that this is a manifestation of the white chauvinistic attitude which the Party has had in regard to the Negro question. The Administration of the Eastern University states that they will have room for 25 students from the United States and recommend that this not be composed only of Negro students, but shall be an American Section of Negro and White students with a majority of the former. I am in agreement with this proposal. If only Negro students are sent it will absolutely appear as segregation, since the only white students that come here go to the Lenin School. I will forward the qualifications for attendance at the Eastern University which has a lower political requirement than the Lenin School. I am of the opinion that one of the reasons for the Negro comrades believing that they have been discriminated against is because the requirements for the Lenin School have not been lived up to by the Party and this must be decisively changed. The practice of sending people into the Lenin School irrespective of the said requirements can only create many difficulties for us.

There are now five students at the Eastern University. Comrade Wilson has developed quite well. Young Comrade Bennett is likewise progressing well. Comrade Mise from Pittsburgh, who was only in the Party for a very short time before attending the school here has advanced much. But Comrade Rivers from Chicago and Vise have been no plus. Vise never entered the Russian Party and I doubt very much whether he will return to the American Party. Comrade Rivers has asked to return home, giving as the reasons for departure that the present economic crisis requires her work in the United States. In the Party cleaning, she and Vise made wild charges against Wilson that he was a spy, etc., which were completely disregarded by the Cleaning Commission because [unreadable] evidence. Nor has her conduct here been such as to in any way leave the impression that she will continue membership in our Party. The Administration of the School agrees to her departure and I see no reason for her staying on. Be prepared, therefore, for her return. I am herewith enclosing her statement requesting leave to return. We are paying the price of our neglect of Negro work in the past and our carelessness in selecting students. It is important that in the next delegation of students we send to the Eastern University, that we obtain a good proportion of proletarians.

MAY DAY.

May Day this year will be organized for real International Day of struggle and the lessons of last May Day as well as August 1st, will be drawn for the directions to be sent regarding this May Day. This May Day will have tremendous significance because it falls in this new stage of the upward swing of the masses. In giving consideration to the lessons of August 1st on which I will very likely report to the next Presidium meeting, it has occurred to me that our experiences of August 1st must be utilized for our May 1st demonstration. May 1st in the United States, even for our demonstrations, have had too much the character of a holiday, but August 1st showed that we can make a day of struggle out of May 1st as well. It would be necessary to issue the slogan of strike and to organize, particularly in the factories, to achieve much greater strike results than we did on August 1st. I would propose that the lessons of August 1st be discussed in the Party press in preparation for our May 1st demonstration and strikes. For us, May 1st this year will be the day of real mobilization and struggle against the burdens of the crisis being thrown upon the shoulders of the working class. I shall try to have the concrete directions forwarded to you in time for adequate preparation.

Document 59 *continued*

ABOUT COMRADES COMING HERE FOR VISIT AND WANTING TO STAY.

There are comrades coming here ostensibly to visit, secure work and then request transfer. In the case of engineers they receive support from administrators of factories, etc. I have adopted the policy not to make any requests to the Party for transfer in such cases unless the request comes from the Russian Party. Two such requests have come to my attention—Comrade Cohen, Williamsberg, District 2, and Golosman (member of the Technical Engineers). There are some comrades who leave with groups of engineers that are useful here, but only those who receive their transfers in advance from the Party will be given consideration by me. All others I must regard in the light of deserters from the struggle. In regard to Golosman I have a very urgent request from the Administration. You may enquire about him from Scherer of the technical men and if you are in agreement with my decision that he must return please wire accordingly.

REFERENT.

Comrade Smith is now working as reporter in the Inform Department and requests to be transferred to the Profintern who want him to work in the Transport IPC. It is my opinion that he should be allowed to go there. We want, therefore, a comrade who is worthy of training, but one who is acquainted with economic, political material and who can give good reports on the developments in the United States as seen from the press, journals and materials which you send. It is not useful to send an old functionary as he would not devote himself perseveringly to the tasks of an informational reporter. Can you find one like that? Wire.

LATIN-AMERICAN BUREAU.

The question of a Latin-American Bureau came up for discussion in a joint meeting of the Latin-American and Anglo-American Bureaus. There were two opinions: 1) which I supported, for the establishment of a bureau covering Canada, U.S., Mexico, Central America with headquarters in New York; 2) the other opinion that such a bureau to cover only S. America, Central America and Mexico with location in the S. American countries. Politically the latter proposition is the more advisable, but distance and connections suggest the first. The question will be decided and you will be advised further. Here, however, the utmost attention must be given in supporting the Mexican Party and Central American and S. American States, particularly in the North, as there is the greatest ferment and we should do everything to send people to assist the Parties. Criticism has already been made in regard to our not having anybody in Haiti at the time of the outbreak. I understand that you have sent somebody, but it is necessary to send another white comrade in addition.

Document 59 *continued*

<u>REGARDING FILM.</u>

The film which Nick Marr sent has not yet arrived. It is coming in by way of Murmansk. This is not the usual way of travelling. The trouble with the question of money is: 1) that Marr originally turned it over without requesting payment; 2) the matter of valuta. The latter is the most important, so when the film arrives I shall advise you further how far I have succeeded with the second.

Yours fraternally,

(Signed) Randolph.

The American representatives to the Comintern also exercised extraordinary powers over the lives of their compatriots. Letters from American Comintern representatives back to the United States often contained questions about the bona fides of Americans who had moved to the Soviet Union. Representative William Schneiderman wrote **document 60**, a typical example, in January 1935. After dealing with a variety of issues, including whether to accept the writer Anna Louise Strong's application for Communist Party membership (the Soviets were reluctant), Schneiderman asked his American comrades to check on a number of former CPUSA members who were then living in the USSR. He had learned, for example, that Bess Perel Braden, who had emigrated to the Soviet Union, had become a member of the Soviet Communist party and had given her CPUSA membership as a reference. Schneiderman remembered that she had been expelled from the CPUSA; he asked the party to check on the details. Similarly, in an addendum to the letter (not reprinted here), he noted that Sylvia Taylor claimed she had been given a leave of absence to come to the USSR; Comrade Olshansky needed verification of his charter membership in the CPUSA to become a member of the Society of Old Bolsheviks; a Finnish comrade claimed past Party membership, and so on. Once obtained, the CPUSA information was passed on to Soviet authorities.

While the CPUSA representative in Moscow was concerned with American Communists who came to the Soviet Union, the CPUSA asserted its right to control *any* foreign travel by party members. **Document 61** is a memo from the party's Organization Commission to all districts, announcing that the CPUSA Central Committee must approve all requests for transfer to a foreign Communist party or leaves of absence to go abroad. Party members were warned that "NO COMRADE IS TO MAKE PREPARATIONS TO LEAVE BEFORE FINAL PERMISSION IS GRANTED BY THE CENTRAL COMMITTEE." Members of the CPUSA were required to fill out a questionnaire detailing their plans, background, and party history and have it approved by the unit organizer, section organizer, district organizer, and central committee. We found scores of such forms in the RTsKhIDNI; we reprint one of them as **document 62**. In it, we can see that Margaret Orton had to obtain the permission of four party officials to visit a relative in England and take a round-the-world trip. And, like all party members, she was expected to purchase tickets through World Tourists, the party-operated travel agency.

Document 60

B. to Dear Friend, 8 January 1935, RTsKhIDNI 515–1–3750. Original in English, with some illegible annotations in the margins. "B." is William (Bill) Schneiderman.

January 8th, 1935.

0007 9 JAN 1935 [stamp]

Dear Friend,

The delegation to the SU to be organised for March 8th should be organised under the slogans "Struggle Against War", "Struggle Against Fascism", "Struggle Against High Cost of Living." The role of Clara Zetkin should be popularised, and also utilise the tradition that the American working women were for the first to take up the idea of International Women's Day in 1908–9. The delegation should consist mainly of the actives of the Womens Committee Against War and Fascism and the movement built around it: working women, firstly; second, wives of workers; third, petty-bourgeois women. It is suggested the delegation should include: a stockyard worker of Chicago; wives of Negro share-croppers; textile and needle workers; chemical plant. Every assistance should be given to the campaign for this delegation.

A review of the Daily Worker for the past 6 months shows that there is no systematic sustained attention paid to the events in Cuba and to the problem of mobilising the masses in the United States for struggle against American intervention in Cuba.

It would be well to assign a comrade from the D.W. staff to be held responsible for the handling of Cuban material in the Daily. It is also very urgent to establish immediately a regular correspondence from Cuba to the Daily. Such a correspondence dealing with the actual conditions and struggles of the Cuban masses and that of the Cuban C.P. would help tremendously in increasing the interest and sympathies for the struggle against American imperialism. The little news on Cuba which does appear in the paper lacks vitality and interests as it is mainly a reprint from the capitalist press.

What is most essential is for the Daily to act as the organiser in the struggle against American imperialism in Cuba. In this respect the Daily is very weak. For instance in the past few months the Daily published only one or two editorials on Cuba calling for struggle, explaining the role of American imperialism, etc. Hardly any articles appeared that would explain the daily role of American imperialism in Cuba and its responsibility for the reviving growing terror against the Cuban masses. To improve the role of the Daily in this respect it would be advisable to immediately begin a series of articles dealing with these problems as well as the publication of timely editorials dealing with current Cuban problems. The column on the "World Front" certainly could be more utilised for Cuban problems. In order to train the American workers in the spirit of internationalism, it is necessary to carry from time to time articles popularising the Leninist teachings on the role of the proletariat in an imperialist country in the struggle against its "own" imperialism for the liberation of the colonial peoples.

In reporting and dealing with the tasks of the League of struggle against war and fascism it is necessary to [be] systematically bringing forward the responsibility of the League against war and fascism in the struggle against American imperialism in Cuba.

The Carpatho-Russian question was discussed here. The line outlined some time ago in the proposals of F. Brown is correct. While developing the united front around economic issues which immediately affect the workers, we must at the same time utilise and popularise the Sov. national policy among these masses, organise the struggle against oppression of Ukrainian nationalities in Poland and Czecho-Slovakia, against the Russian White Guard and Ukrainian nationalist elements. We must also explain and popularise the policy of the CP of West Ukraine for self-determination and for unity with the Sov. Ukraine. The united front around popular issues should be utilised as an entering wedge to develop the political understanding of these workers, particularly on the national question and on the position of the USSR and the party in solving. It was suggested, by the way, that the attitude of the Ukrainian Buro might show the reflection of some remnants of Ukrainian nationalist tendencies which have not been completely eradicated as yet, and if there is any basis for this suspicion, it should be looked into.

An Armenian friend made some proposals for the work of the Armenian section which we are passing on to you. The propaganda of the Armenian Section is too much of a nationalist character, speaking about Sov. Armenia but not about Sov. Union as a whole. Our propaganda should be more of an international character. In order to improve the leading Armenian cadres, a school should be organised by the Armenian section. An instructor is available to take charge of the school as well as to improve the line of the paper. Our Armenian friends recommend Ado Adoian, a member of the Armenian CC, who is available for this work. Party literature in Armenian should be published; also organise the distribution of Sov. Armenian literature by the section.

Anna L. Strong's application for membership has been up for consideration here, and our friends want your opinion about it. They are not very anxious to accept her. [in margin: *P.B.*]

In the correspondence of Marx and Engels just published in the English edition, I notice the term "nigger" used (Marx' Letter No. 55, Aug. 7, 1862); this should be called to A.T.'s attention, so that if an American edition is being prepared, this should be changed.

Please send regularly small packages of "Party Organisers" (not more than 10 or 15) well covered and wrapped to the following addresses: Julian Geronemo, 1918 Katamanan Tondo, Manila, P.I.; Severino Parungao, 1212 Antonio Reven Tondo, Manila, P.I.; Francisco Marin, 50 Eleano Extension Tondo, Manila, P.I. Also send other literature that may be of help and interest to them.

Will you inquire in District No. 9 about my wife's leave of absence? The name is Leah Schneider (Party name Gene Nider). She left there in September, and turned in her Party book with the understanding leave would be granted through the centre. It has not come through yet, and they may have overlooked it there, so please find out.

Moorad Mooradian, (Valien Marxian) who was transferred to Armenia May 8, 1933, is being transferred back to USA.

If possible send additional material for the Congress exhibit on the work of the parties. The first batch of material was received.

Case of Bess Perel (Braden) Dr. Braden.

They were members of the Brownsville Branch of CP in 1924–25. Never active sometime in 1926 they were dropped as members for inactivity.

In 1927–29 they stayed in California near L.A. where her mother has a summer resort, and where a number of workers were exploited by her. They rejoined the party later on and were expelled. However, I do not recall the reason why.

Sometime in 1929 or 1930 she came to SU at first she worked in foreign

Document 60 continued

department of trade unions. Now she is working as editor in publishing house, issuing children's books. He was here as a tourist during the summer 1934.

She became a member of CPSU, presenting her activity in US as a basis. Further information on case is needed here. Possibly WWW knows something about case since he was representative at the time.

Please send information as soon as possible.

B.

Document 61

Org. [Organization] Commission C.C. to All Districts, "Regarding Leaves and Transfers to a Foreign Country," 7 July 1934, RTsKhIDNI 515–1–3458. Original in English.

CENTRAL COMMITTEE, C.P., U.S.A.
P.O. BOX 87, STATION # D
NEW YORK, N.Y.

July 7, 1934

To all Districts:

REGARDING LEAVES AND TRANSFERS TO A FOREIGN COUNTRY

Dear Comrades:

We are enclosing herewith new and more complete application blanks for leaves or transfers to leave this country, which must be used in all future cases. Each and every question must be answered completely by the comrade requesting leave or transfer.

NO COMRADE IS TO MAKE PREPARATIONS TO LEAVE BEFORE FINAL PERMISSION IS GRANTED BY THE CENTRAL COMMITTEE. In the event that any comrade does make such preparations before approval is granted by this office, permission to leave the country will be denied the comrade. In the event that the comrade leaves anyway, disciplinary action will be taken against the comrade.

Before a leave of absence will be granted, dues must be paid for the entire period of the leave at the regular weekly rate. No exceptions are to be made to this rule.

Every District is to notify every unit and section so that this information will be made known to each and every comrade requesting leave or transfer. The

Document 61 *continued*

Central Committee will not recognize ignorance of these instructions as a reason for granting leave or transfer if these conditions are not fulfilled.

Comradely yours,

B

ORG. COMMISSION C.C.

Document 62

CPUSA form: "Application for Permission to Leave the United States," filled in by Jean Markel, 4 January 1935, RTsKhIDNI 515–1–3875. Original in English. Mimeographed form with typed-in entries.

COMMUNIST PARTY of the U.S.A.

District ___13___   Leaving Jan/4, 1935

(DATE)

APPLICATION FOR PERMISSION TO LEAVE THE UNITED STATES

To the Central Committee
Communist Party of the U.S.A.

I, _Jean Markel_ Party Book No. _49284_ apply for a leave
(PRINT YOUR NAME)
of absence for _6 months_ months, to go to _around the world [handcircled]_
or a transfer to the Communist Party of _____
Give reasons for desiring to leave the United States: _Have been invited on trip with all expenses paid; desire to visit relatives in England; also desire first-hand info. on European situation and anti-war work in other countries._
If you have a job in another country, give details: _____

Age _29_ Occupation _housewife and mother_ Citizen _yes_
Married _yes_
How many dependents _____ Are you taking your family _no_
If not, can they support themselves _yes_
When did you join the Party _6/6/34_ Have you been a member continually _yes_
If not, when did you drop out _____ When readmitted_____
Were you a member of the Socialist Party before joining the Communist Party _no_
What Party offices do you now hold _none_
Are you a member of a trade union _no_ What union _____

214

Document 62 *continued*

Do you speak English _yes_ What other languages _French, German (slightly),_
Spanish (slightly)
Has disciplinary action been taken against you _no_ Give details on a separate
sheet.

Sign your (Party) name _Jean Markel_
Real name _Margaret Lee Orton_ Address _2380 South Court_
City and State _Palo Alto, California_
Party Unit _Palo Alto_ Section _San Mateo_

This application is approved by _John Markel_ Unit Organizer
This application is approved by _B.B. Nelson_ Section Organizer
This application is approved by _Sam Darcy_ District Organizer
This application is approved by _GM_ Central Committee

* *

WARNING

1. Get permission to leave from your unit, section and district first.

2. Make no preparations of any kind to leave before you receive notification
from the Central Office. Permission from the District Committee or from any
language Buro, is not enough. The Central Committee is not responsible for
sale of furniture or purchase of supplies for leaving, made without our permission.

3. In the event of a transfer, give a short outline of your history on a separate
sheet, telling where you were born, when and what industries you have
worked in and all other information about yourself.

4. Leave of Absence to the Soviet Union can only be granted for two months.
However, it must be understood that the Soviet Union visa is given for only thirty
(30) days. No comrade is to request further extension when they arrive there.

5. Do not turn in your membership book to the section or district. If your
application is approved, you will bring your book to the Central Office and
surrender it only when you get your leave of absence or transfer.

6. ALL TICKETS MUST BE PURCHASED THRU THE WORLD TOURISTS. 175–5TH
AVE. N.Y.C.

American Communists in the "Great Land of Socialism"

American party officials granted or withheld permission to travel
with an eye toward the applicants' political usefulness. Nonetheless, an American Communist living in the United States had the
option of ignoring the party if he or she were willing to risk expul-

sion and ostracism in left-wing circles, the only penalty the CPUSA could impose. For American Communists in the Soviet Union, however, the Communist party literally had the power of life or death. Usually Soviet authorities would not allow American party members to leave the country over Comintern objections.

In 1939 Nat Ross, a CPUSA referent working in the Comintern, sent a letter to Dimitrov (**document 63**) concerning Ben Thomas, a fifty-one-year-old American tool-and-die maker who had been in the Soviet Union for about eight years. His wife had returned to the United States, but his son was still with him in Moscow. A long-time Communist, Thomas had transferred into the Communist Party of the Soviet Union (CPSU). Pat Toohey, the CPUSA representative to the Comintern, and Ross both recommended that Thomas be allowed to go home, where he "could be extremely useful in explaining the truth about the Soviet Union to American workers," and asked that the Comintern supply him with funds. An annotation to the document indicates that Dimitrov agreed with the recommendation.

In Thomas's case, and for hundreds of other Americans who came to the Soviet Union, we do not merely see the Soviet government exercising its authority over the movements of foreigners on Soviet soil. Here *American* Communists are collaborating with the Comintern and the Soviet state in decisions about whether an American should be allowed to return to the United States. We shall look at more such cases, most of which did not end so happily.

Document 63

Ross to Dimitrov, RTsKhIDNI 495–14–132. Original in English. The document is un-dated, but the handwritten annotation is dated 17 December 1939.

TO COMRADE DIMITROFF: [illegible scribble]

Copy—Cadre Department:
Copy—File, Marty Secretariat:

RE: BEN THOMAS RETURNING TO THE U.S.A.

Comrade Ben Thomas, a native American, age 51, came to the Soviet Union with his wife and son about eight years ago. He came to work in Soviet industry at his trade as a skilled mechanic (tool and die maker). At present he is working as a mechanic at the SCIENTIFIC AUTO-TRACTOR INSTITUTE ("Natee") in Moscow. He is a foundation member of the CP USA and is now a member of the CPSU.

His wife returned to the USA about two years ago and due to some technical obstacles she has not returned. His twelve year old son is an excellent student here and is very happy. Thomas himself feels happy and useful here and as I understand has a good record here. But he feels that in the present situation he can be more useful to the cause of socialism in the USA and is therefore ready and anxious to go back.

Comrade Toohey was firmly of the opinion that Thomas should return and this is my own definite opinion. The Cadre Department is also of this opinion and has no objection whatsoever to his return to the USA. Comrade Thomas is an excellent type of working class agitator and in particular now could be extremely useful in explaining the truth about the Soviet Union to American workers. Thomas agrees and understands fully that the CP USA will have no financial responsibility for him when he returns. At the same time he will be fully at the disposition of the CP USA. He can be utilised to address unions and workers organizations on his experiences in the Soviet Union. This he can do remarkably well. Furthermore in view of the pick up in the war industries in the US it is very probable that he will find work at his skilled trade. He will also be able to rejoin his union in which he was formerly very active as a leader.

The total cost of passage and expenses for two to the USA will be about $500. If it is decided that Comrade Thomas should return the money will have to be provided since he has no personal means of getting valuta.

One further fact. Comrade Thomas as well as all American citizens who are REGISTERED at the American Embassy have received a FORM letter informing them that their passports have to be validated before Jan. 1, 1940 and that they must appear personally at the embassy before Jan. 1. The embassy will then generally validate the passport for immediate return passage to the USA or in exceptional cases will give a six months extension.

Comradely,
Ross
Referent CPUSA.

*I agree with the return
to U.S. of com.
Thomas
17.XII.39* [illegible initials]

The Death of Lovett Fort-Whiteman

The CPUSA and the Comintern agreed that Ben Thomas should be allowed to return to the United States. Lovett Fort-Whiteman was not so lucky. One of the early black activists in the American Communist movement and in 1924 the first African-American to attend a Comintern training school in Moscow, Fort-Whiteman became the first national organizer of the American Negro Labor Congress, the party agency to organize black Americans. A fellow Communist at the founding convention of the congress recalled the extraordinary impression he made:

> Fort-Whiteman was truly a fantastic figure. A brown-skinned man of medium height, Fort-Whiteman's high cheekbones gave him somewhat of an Oriental look. He had affected a Russian style of dress, sporting a *robochka* (a man's long belted shirt) which came almost to his knees, ornamental belt, high boots and a fur hat. Here was a veritable Black Cossack who could be seen sauntering along the streets of Southside Chicago. Fort-Whiteman was a graduate of Tuskegee and, as I understood, had had some training as an actor. He had been a drama critic for *The Messenger* and for *The Crusader*.[45]

During the years 1928–1930 the Comintern called on the CPUSA to support the right of African-Americans to self-determination in the Black Belt, the area of the American South that had a majority black population. Fort-Whiteman did not jump at the command, and he lost his leadership post.[46] The new black leaders did not enjoy having a defeated rival around, so to get him out of the way—and as consolation in view of his past service—the Comintern gave him work in Moscow.

Fort-Whiteman made the move with enthusiasm, telling an acquaintance, Homer Smith, that he was "coming home to Moscow." He married a Russian and, a friend noted, "adopted the practice of many Russian Communists of shaving his head, and with his sallow brown complexion and his finely-chiseled nose set into a V-shaped face he resembled a Buddhist monk." Smith, a

45. Harry Haywood, *Black Bolshevik: Autobiography of an Afro-American Communist* (Chicago: Liberator Press, 1978), 143–44.

46. See Harvey Klehr and William Tompson, "Self-Determination in the Black Belt: Origins of a Comintern Policy," *Labor History* 30, no. 3 (Summer 1989): 354–66.

young black American journalist who was in Moscow at the time, remembered that Fort-Whiteman "attempted to make himself into the ideological mentor of other black Americans living in Moscow" and invited groups of blacks to meet in his apartment to discuss Marxist theory. Smith also noted that Fort-Whiteman

> was often sent on speaking tours to Russian industrial and farming centers. On these tours he pleaded fervently for formal and material support for the Scottsboro Boys and Angelo Herndon, the Atlanta youth who had been sentenced to a Georgia chain gang for leading a thousand Negro and white families in a relief march on the capital in Atlanta. He expounded loud and long on lynchings, Jim Crow and oppression of his people in America and condemned with fiery emotions the enslavement of black people in the African colonies of European imperialist nations.[47]

But in 1933, after three years in Moscow, Fort-Whiteman decided that he would like to return to the United States (of which he was still a citizen) and applied for permission to do so from the CPUSA.[48] His request was not granted. Fort-Whiteman never returned, and three years after he made his application, he disappeared. Neither Soviet authorities nor the CPUSA ever explained what became of him. In his 1964 memoir Smith writes that in 1936 he called at Fort-Whiteman's apartment, where Fort-Whiteman's wife said that her husband wasn't home and asked him never to come back. Smith comments, "I had been living in Russia long enough to understand the implications" of these words, adding: "Bits of information reaching me from different sources afterwards indicated that he had died in a concentration camp about two years after his disappearance. I, of course, had no means of confirming this information, but I do know that he was never seen again."[49]

In his 1988 memoir, *Black on Red: A Black American's Forty-Four Years inside the Soviet Union*, Robert Robinson, an émigré to the Soviet Union in 1930 who had remained until 1974, was able to help explain what had caused Fort-Whiteman's downfall. Robin-

47. Homer Smith, *Black Man in Red Russia* (Chicago: Johnson Publishing, 1964), 78, 81. Smith is mentioned in document 64.
48. Lovett [Fort-]Whiteman to CPUSA, 21 September 1933, RTsKhIDNI 515–1–3102.
49. Smith, *Black Man in Red Russia*, 83.

son had known Fort-Whiteman casually, and he claimed that in
1936 Fort-Whiteman

> offered some criticism of a book by Langston Hughes, *The Ways of
> White Folks,* during a discussion at the Foreign Club. A black lawyer
> from the upper echelon of the Community [Communist] Party USA
> was in the audience, and he stated during the evening that Whiteman's
> criticism of the book was counter-revolutionary. About three weeks
> later, Whiteman was summoned to NKVD headquarters and told that
> he was a counter-revolutionary and was to be banished from Moscow.
> He was ordered to be in a certain town on a specific date, and imme-
> diately on arrival to report to the local police. None of us ever heard
> from Whiteman. However, in 1959, I heard news of Whiteman's fate.
> A Russian who had been banished to the same town as Whiteman was
> rehabilitated by Khrushchev and allowed to return to his family in
> Moscow. This man told a friend of mine that Whiteman was assigned
> to his group of laborers, and was severely beaten many times when he
> failed to meet the norm. He died of starvation, or malnutrition, a
> broken man, whose teeth had been knocked out.[50]

Smith's memoir was written nearly thirty years and Robinson's
more than fifty years after the events in question, and both were
based in part on second- or thirdhand information. Like many
accounts written by American leftists disillusioned with the Soviet
system, these books have been ignored by most scholars. Although
the position of African-Americans in the CPUSA has been a major
focus of late twentieth-century historians, most have avoided spec-
ulating about the disappearance and probable death of one of the
CPUSA's leading black figures of the 1920s. With the opening of
Soviet-era archives, however, we now know what happened to
Lovett Fort-Whiteman.[51]

50. Robert Robinson, with Jonathan Slevin, *Black on Red: A Black American's
Forty-Four Years inside the Soviet Union* (Washington: Acropolis Books, 1988),
361.

51. There is no mention of Fort-Whiteman's fate nor any commentary on his
disappearance from the American scene in Mark Naison, *Communists in Harlem
during the Depression* (Urbana: University of Illinois Press, 1983); Philip Foner and
James Allen, eds., *American Communism and Black Americans: A Documentary
History, 1919–1929* (Philadelphia: Temple University Press, 1987); or Philip Foner
and Herbert Shapiro, eds., *American Communism and Black Americans: A Documentary History, 1930–1934* (Philadelphia: Temple University Press, 1991). Earl
Ofari Hutchinson, *Blacks and Reds: Race and Class in Conflict, 1919–1990* (East

In 1935 Fort-Whiteman was the subject of a Comintern committee meeting concerning a number of matters related to the American party. The minutes of this meeting, **document 64,** show that three CPUSA leaders were present: Earl Browder, "Sherman" (the alias for the CPUSA representative to the Comintern; at this time, William Schneiderman), and Sam Darcy, who had recently arrived in Moscow and was slated to replace Schneiderman. Also in attendance were I. Mingulin, a senior Comintern official of the Anglo-American Secretariat, and "Gerhardt"—Gerhart Eisler, who had just returned from the United States after serving as the Comintern representative to the CPUSA.

The minutes record the following resolution: "In view of reported efforts of Lovett Whiteman to mislead some of the Negro comrades, decided that Comrades *Paterson* and Ford take the initiative in holding a meeting with all the Negro comrades to discuss the question before they leave."[52] The minutes do not say what Fort-Whiteman had done that had displeased the Comintern and the CPUSA. William L. Patterson and James Ford, the two comrades mentioned, were high-ranking black CPUSA leaders. Patterson was a lawyer, and he is one of the few people then in Moscow who might fit Robinson's description of the "black lawyer from the upper echelon" of the American party who publicly denounced Fort-Whiteman a few weeks before his arrest.[53]

Fort-Whiteman is also mentioned in an undated CPUSA report concerning support for Trotskyism within the party, which bluntly declares: "Lovett Fort-Whiteman, a Negro Comrade, showed him-

---

Lansing: Michigan State University Press, 1995), 54, reports rumors that Fort-Whiteman had become disillusioned and had lived in poverty in the Soviet Union until his death sometime before World War II. Gerald Horne, "The Red and the Black: The Communist Party and African-Americans in Historical Perspective," in *New Studies in the Politics and Culture of U.S. Communism,* ed. Michael Brown, Randy Martin, Frank Rosengarten, and George Snedeker (New York: Monthly Review Press, 1993), 199–237, never mentions Fort-Whiteman at all.

52. A large delegation of Americans was in Moscow at that time for the Seventh Congress of the Communist International, which was just ending.

53. The minutes instructing Patterson to act against Fort-Whiteman date from August 1935, however, while both Smith and Robinson put the arrest in 1936, so he may not have been the man. In his career in the CPUSA, Patterson served as a party organizer in Chicago and New York, an official of International Labor Defense, director of the party's Scottsboro Boys campaign, director of the Civil Rights Congress, and a member of the Political Bureau.

self for Trotsky."[54] And in document 94 (see chapter 4) Pat Toohey, the American representative to the Comintern, replies to an inquiry about Fort-Whiteman with the statement: "Whiteman is a Trotskyist." By 1938 anyone in the Soviet Union identified as a Trotskyist by a ranking official of the Comintern was either dead or in the Gulag.

Fort-Whiteman, in fact, was in the Gulag, and he was soon to die. In 1996, records about Fort-Whiteman compiled by the NKVD, the Soviet political police, in the late 1930s surfaced in the archive of the internal security service of the newly independent nation of Kazakhstan.[55] The documents show that on 1 July 1937 a "special session" of the NKVD held in Moscow sentenced Fort-Whiteman to five years of internal exile for "anti-Soviet agitation."[56]

The NKVD sent Fort-Whiteman to the city of Semipalatinsk in Soviet Kazakhstan. There he found work teaching at local schools. As the Great Terror continued, however, Soviet authorities administratively increased (that is, without a hearing) many of the punishments they had earlier imposed. On 8 May 1938 an NKVD board changed Fort-Whiteman's punishment to five years' hard labor (beginning from that date). From Kazakhstan, he was sent to the Sevostlag prison labor camp near Magadan, in northeastern Siberia.

The prison labor camps around Magadan, especially the Kolyma goldfields, were among the most lethal in the Gulag system. **Document 65** shows that Fort-Whiteman did not last long there. This document is Fort-Whiteman's official NKVD death certificate, stating that he died on 13 January 1939 at the Sevostlag labor camp

54. "Discussion Meetings on the Question . . . ," RTsKhIDNI 515–1–4109. From internal references, it appears that this undated document was written in the mid-1930s.

55. Alan Cullison, Associated Press correspondent in Moscow, located these documents, and the authors thank him for his willingness to share his research.

56. Special sessions of the NKVD were not trials in the Western sense. Rather, they were a method of imposing criminal penalties by administrative action. During the Great Terror, NKVD boards would meet in secret, following arrests and secret interrogations, to determine guilt and impose penalties on those accused of ideological crimes. "Anti-Soviet agitation" was a favorite charge. It derived from section 10 of article 58 of the Soviet Criminal Code of 1926, which declared that it was a crime punishable by imprisonment (with no upper limit on the term) to engage in "propaganda or agitation, containing an appeal for the overthrow, subverting, or weakening of the Soviet power . . . and, equally, the dissemination or preparation or possession of literary materials of similar content."

at the age of forty-four. For identification purposes the report included fingerprints taken from his corpse.

Document 64

Excerpt from "Minutes of Sub-Committee CPUSA Meeting on Organisational Questions," 25 August 1935, RTsKhIDNI 495–14–1. Original in English. There are a number of illegible scribbles in both English and Russian.

STRICTLY CONFIDENTIAL

MINUTES OF SUB-COMMITTEE CPUSA MEETING ON ORGANISATIONAL QUESTIONS - Aug. 25, 1935.

Present: Comrades Browder, Mingulin, Gerhardt, Darcy, Sherman.

QUESTIONS	DECISIONS
I. Disposition of Negro comrades. a) Homer Smith.	a) Homer Smith: To refer the entire case to Com. Chernin, with a recommendation that he be established as a sympathising correspondent in Moscow, to issue press services to all countries having Negro newspapers. Homer Smith is not a Party member.
b) Johnson (Ross). Not a Party member; question of our helping him to establish his American citizenship.	b) Johnson (Ross): To get further facts and to make decision only after facts are established.
c) Jones.	c) In view of reported efforts of Lovett Whiteman to mislead some of the Negro comrades, decided that Comrades Paterson[1] and Ford take the initiative in holding a meeting with all the Negro comrades to discuss the question before they leave.
d) International Negro Committee.	d) To postpone discussion until Com. Huiswood returns.

Document 64 continued

e) Return of Ford.

d) Comrade Ford to leave on the 5th of Sept. in order to catch the boat on the 11th.

Ford - Ercoly

He is to stop at Geneva to see the necessary people for improving the movement for Etheopian defence. There is to be no publicity attached to this trip at all. [illegible handwriting]

II. Party personel.

a) To recommend to Secretariat to replace Comrade Sherman No. 1 by Sherman No. 2 (Darcy) *(Randolf)* [illegible handwriting]

b) Sam Brown to return as soon as his unfinished business is settled, but not later than October, a new referent to be sent here by the American Party only when the C.C. received instructions from the C.I., the candidate to be decided at that time [illegible handwriting]

. . .

1. The name Browder is crossed out and the name Paterson written above it.

Document 65

First page of death certificate for Lovett Fort-Whiteman, 13 January 1939, Russian Ministry of Interior. Original in Russian with a few illegible annotations. Fort-Whiteman's place of birth is incorrectly identified, as is the date of his arrival "for training." He probably arrived in 1938. The second page of the certificate (reproduced in facsimile here) contains Fort-Whiteman's fingerprints. The authors thank Alan Cullison of the Associated Press for making this document available.

Death certificate blank   file sheet No. 204973
                            DEATH CERTIFICATE

13th day of *January* 1939
Undersigned: Physician in charge of medical sector *Kurenkova*
Representative of URCh [accounting and distributing unit] *Kucherenko*
Representative of NKVD *Samonen*
    Have drafted the present document certifying that the prisoner

Форма акта о смерти

АКТ О СМЕРТИ

л/д № 20-/973.

"____" дня Января м-ца 1937 г.

нижеподписавшиеся: Зав врачебным участком врач _Кукенко_

Составитель УРЧ _Кукенко_

Составитель НКВД _Самонин_

Составили настоящий акт в том, что з/к

Фамилия, имя и отчество _Форт Вайтмон Ловет_

Год и место рождения _1894. Американец._

Место жительства _г. Семипалатинск/ ул_
Первомайская 19

Национальность _Американец_

Соцположение _Служащий_

Кем и когда осужден _особ. сов. НКВД СССР._

ст. УК _АСА_ срок _5 пять_ лет

Прочие приметы _рост в/сред. телосложение норм._
волосы черные, нос обычн.
прибыл на поприще 12/XI-39.

Время и место смерти _13/1 39 в час ночи при следовании_
(Стационара в больницу в Усть-Таёжный

Диагноз _Декомпенсированный порок сердца_
с резковыраженными отеками

Причины смерти _Ослабление сердечной деятельности_

Примечание _Труп осмотрен, при осмотре_
насильственной смерти необнаружено, в/ч
может быть погребен в земле.

Зав. врач. участком врач _Кукенко_ (_Кукенко_

Составитель УРЧ ОЛП ЮГПУ _Русина_ (_Кукенко_

Представитель НКВД _Самонин_ (_Самонин_

Умерло. Начальнику
?озчик Лилушин

DOCUMENT 65. Death certificate for Lovett Fort-Whiteman, 13 January 1939.

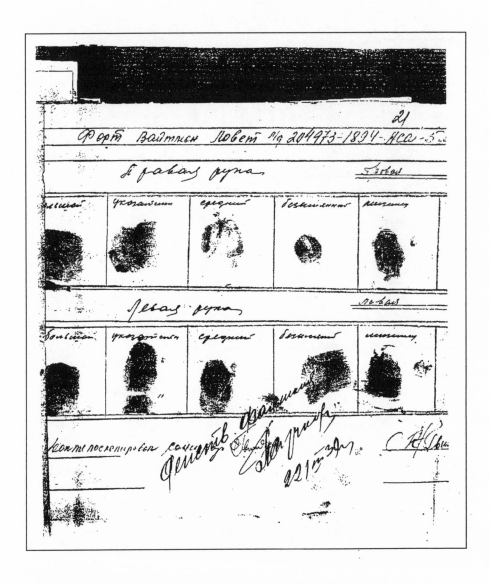

DOCUMENT 65. continued

Surname, name and patronymic _Fort-Whiteman, Lovett_
Year and place of birth _1894 American_
Permanent address _19 Peschannia St., Semipalatinsk_
Nationality _American_
Social position _White-collar worker_
By whom and when convicted _Special board of the NKVD of the USSR_
art. of criminal code _Anti-Soviet agitation_ sentenced to _5 years_
Other distinguishing features _Above-average height, normal build, black hair, normal nose. Arrived for training 12/11/39_
Time and place of death _13/1/39 at 1:00 at night en route [from] infirmary to the hospital at Ust-Taezhny_
Diagnosis _Decompensated heart defect with severe edema_
Cause of death _Weakening of cardiac activity_
Remarks _Corpse examined: examination did not indicate violent death. [Corpse] may be buried in [illegible]_
Physician in charge of medical sector _Kurenkova_
Representative of the URCh OLP YuGPU [Accounting and distributive unit of the Detached Camp Section of the Southern Mining Industry Administration] _Kucherenko_
Representative of the NKVD _Alexsandr Samonen_
[Illegible: the name of an additional administrative unit and the signature of its representative.]

Karelian Fever and the Purge of the North American Finns

During the 1920s and early 1930s more than 10,000 members of the American Communist party, most of them immigrants to the United States from the Russian Empire, returned to the Soviet Union along with their American-born children, in the hope of helping to build a socialist nation.

A large segment of this group consisted of leftist American and Canadian Finns, who settled in the Karelian region of the Soviet Union. (Karelia bordered on Finland, and many of its residents were of Finnish descent and spoke a Finnish dialect.) The migration of these North American Finns received support from both the Soviet government and the Canadian and American Communist parties. The Soviets were hoping to modernize Karelia's timber industry, and, as many of the North Americans were experienced lumberjacks, they offered a shortcut to the adoption of modern North American lumbering practices.

Document 66 is a 1931 request from Soviet authorities in Karelia that the Comintern urge the American and Canadian Communist parties to support the emigration. The authorities stress that: "We [for] our part assure [you] that Karelia is in position to receive and to take care of this number of men, to provide work for all of them as well as shelter, food, schools and to give cultural service to the maximum degree there are in general possibilities to give in the present situation existing in the Soviet Union."

The Finnish Workers Federation, an affiliate of the CPUSA, and the Finnish Organization of Canada, which was aligned with the Communist party of Canada, supported the Soviet Karelian Technical Aid Committee in raising funds and gathering supplies and in supervising the recruitment and transportation of North American emigrants to Karelia. Some federation officials in both parties feared that wholesale emigration would weaken their organizations. Fighting for control of Finnish cooperatives with defectors from the Communist movement, these officials feared that the campaign, by drawing away the most militant, pro-Communist Finns, would leave Finnish radical organizations in the United States and Canada in the hands of their enemies, the moderates. But most of the North American Finnish Communists eagerly embraced the Soviet agenda. As part of the campaign, *Työmies,* the chief Finnish-language newspaper of the CPUSA, published the following message from one of the emigrant groups:

A Battle Greeting of the Comrades Who Are Emigrating to Soviet Karelia to the Workers of America

Comrades: Emigrating to the country where a heroic giant of labor is standing, in the one hand a dreadful sword with which he has beaten numerous enemies and will beat enemies in the future; and in the other hand a trowel with which he is creating, unknown before in the history of mankind, heroism and energy, a new and happier society, a society in which each and everyone feels that he is a human being among people. Side by side with them we all promise that we will give our best to this glorious cause . . .[57]

57. "A Battle Greeting of the Comrades Who Are Emigrating to Soviet Karelia to the Workers of America," *Työmies,* 26 January 1931, quoted in Peter Kivisto, *Immigrant Socialists in the United States: The Case of Finns and the Left* (Rutherford, N.J.: Fairleigh Dickinson University Press, 1984), 173–74.

The campaign worked, and what came to be known as Karelian Fever was born.[58]

But by the mid-1930s, with the labor shortages over, Soviet authorities had stopped their recruitment drives and were discouraging further migrations. The immigrants themselves discovered that life under Soviet socialism was considerably more difficult than most had anticipated. The real tragedy of Karelian Fever, however, struck in 1936–1938, when hundreds of thousands of people with foreign ties, including many foreign Communist immigrants, were sent to the Gulag during a phase of Stalin's Great Terror. Soviet security police arrested several hundred—perhaps more than a thousand—North American Finnish immigrants (mostly adult males) and charged them with the ideological crime of "bourgeois nationalism," of having been spies for Finland or another foreign power, or of plotting to detach Karelia from the Soviet Union and unite it with Finland.

The charges leveled against these Finns were lies. They had been among the most devoted Communists in North America and had enthusiastically embraced the opportunity to help build a socialist state in Karelia. But despite their innocence, their loyalty, and their American connections, the CPUSA allowed them to go to imprisonment and death without a protest; in fact, American Communists took active measures to silence the voices of those Finns who were able to escape.

The story of the Karelian immigrants is little known. Scholars of Finnish-American ethnic history have written about Karelian Fever, but few other historians mention the episode. Yet two Finnish researchers have concluded from the Karelian records that between 1935 and 1939, "the majority of the Finnish American men disappeared without a trace," and judged that perhaps as many as three-quarters of the adult male immigrant Finns in Karelia were taken by Stalin's political police. And in a survey of 190 American and Canadian Finnish families conducted during the late 1980s and early

58. Estimates on the number of emigrants vary from 4,000 to 10,000. See David Ahola, "The Karelian Fever Episode of the 1930s," *Finnish Americana* 5 (1982–1983): 4–7; Reino Kero, "Emigration of Finns from North America to Soviet Karelia in the Early 1930s," in *The Finnish Experience in the Western Great Lakes Region: New Perspectives,* ed. Michael Karni, Matti Kaups, and Douglas Ollila, Jr. (Turku, Finland: Migration Institute, 1975): 212–13.

1990s, the daughter of one of the victims found that ninety of the fathers were taken away during the purges; in six of the families, both parents were taken.[59]

Among the victims was Oscar Corgan, an influential Finnish-American Communist who had led the Soviet Karelian Technical Aid Committee at the height of Karelian Fever. After arranging for thousands to go to Karelia, he emigrated himself, along with his wife and three American-born children. In 1934 Earl Browder personally endorsed the transfer of Corgan's membership from the American to the Soviet Communist party. Having once been the manager of the newspaper *Työmies,* Corgan went to work for a Karelian publishing house. He was arrested on 4 November 1937; his family was later told that he had been given a fifteen-year prison sentence. But he never returned from the labor camps. In 1956, after Khrushchev's de-Stalinization campaign began, the family received a death certificate stating that Corgan had died of stomach cancer in 1940. Finally, in 1991, under the Gorbachev reforms, they received a corrected certificate, which showed that he had been executed two months after his arrest, on 9 January 1938.[60]

Another who died was Robert Saastamoinen from Rock, Michigan. Saastamoinen had been born in Finland and came to the United States in 1909, at the age of twenty, to work in the forests and mines of northern Michigan. Like many Finnish-American Communists, he entered the CPUSA via the Industrial Workers of the World. As a local agent for the Soviet Karelian Technical Aid

59. Varpu Lindström and Börje Vähämäki, "Ethnicity Twice Removed: North American Finns in Soviet Karelia," *Finnish Americana* 9 (1992): 17–18; Mayme Sevander, *Red Exodus: Finnish-American Emigration to Russia* (Duluth, Minn.: Oscat, 1993), 18. Other accounts of Karelian Fever include Reino Kero, "The Canadian Finns in Soviet Karelia in the 1930s," in *Finnish Diaspora,* vol. 1, ed. Michael Karni (Toronto: Multicultural History Society of Ontario, 1981), 203–13; Reino Kero, "The Tragedy of Joonas Harju of Hiilisuo Commune, Soviet Karelia, 1933–1936," *Finnish Americana* 5 (1982–1983): 8–11; Mayme Sevander, *Of Soviet Bondage* (Duluth, Minn.: Oscat, 1996); and Lawrence Hokkanen and Sylvia Hokkanen, *Karelia: A Finnish-American Couple in Stalin's Russia, 1934–1941* (St. Cloud, Minn.: North Star Press of St. Cloud, 1991).

60. Mayme Sevander with Laure Hertzel, *They Took My Father: A Story of Idealism and Betrayal* (Duluth, Minn.: Pfeifer-Hamilton, 1992). Sevander was Corgan's American-born daughter. Corgan joined the CPUSA in 1920; for his transfer, see "Transfers of Finnish Comrades, Returned by CC CPSU," RTsKhIDNI 495–72–289. The document is undated, but it is after 1934.

Society, he arranged for eighty-five Michigan Finns to move to Karelia. In 1933 he emigrated himself, taking his wife and his American-born daughter and stepson. (Again, Browder endorsed his transfer from the CPUSA to the CPSU.) Kaarlo Tuomi, Saastamoinen's stepson, who was a teenager at the time, recalls that in November 1937 his stepfather was arrested: "Four men came at night, two led him away while the other two remained to make a search. They did not bother with such formalities as a warrant for arrest or search." Seventeen years later, Tuomi learned that Saastamoinen had been charged under Article 58 of the Soviet Criminal Code with conspiracy to overthrow the Soviet government, a capital offense, and had been executed in January 1938. Reflecting on Saastamoinen's devotion to the "teachings of Marx, Engels and Lenin," Tuomi writes: "I can only imagine the extent of my stepfather's disillusionment in those last seconds in front of a firing squad of Stalin's secret police."[61]

The Karelian Finns, having emigrated at the urging of the American and Canadian Communist parties, looked to their comrades for help. As Mayme Sevander, Oscar Corgan's American-born daughter, wrote many years later: "We, the family members of Stalin's victims, placed our faith in the Communist parties of the US and Canada to which our parents had devoted the best years of their lives. When the purges began and our parents began disappearing, we were sure those Communist parties would interfere and stand up for their comrades." They did not.[62]

Some Finns escaped, chiefly those with American or Canadian citizenship who had wisely retained their passports. (Many of the Finns had not become naturalized citizens in the United States or Canada before they moved to Karelia, and some of the naturalized citizens took Soviet citizenship after they arrived.) Those who came back to the United States usually found themselves isolated. The American Communist party waged a campaign to discredit their stories of political oppression. David Ahola notes that the public position of Finnish-American Communists was that "those ar-

61. Kaarlo Tuomi, "The Karelian Fever of the Early 1930s: A Personal Memoir," *Finnish Americana* 3 (1980): 71. Browder's endorsement is in "Transfers of Finnish Comrades."
62. Sevander, *Red Exodus*, 48.

rested were 'agents of the American Government' who were working against the Soviet State."[63]

Paul Hummasti writes that the CPUSA's Finnish affiliate, the Finnish Workers Federation, responded to returnees who spoke negatively of their experience by "challenging the character of those who made these charges. These men who were spreading discontent with the great workers experiment in Soviet Karelia were not true socialists dedicated to the good of the working man, but opportunists."[64] Sevander, who herself finally returned to the United States in the late 1980s, asked older Finnish-Americans about why the CPUSA had not intervened to help their former comrades; the response was usually "silence and ridicule." One person admitted that "the arrests in the Soviet Union were discussed in the leadership [of the CPUSA], in the context of combating whatever negative impact the arrests might have. There was no discussion as to the legitimacy of the arrests, nor any decisions to protest them." Sevander also searched through old copies of the Finnish-language newspapers *Työmies* (of which her father had once been editor) and *Eteenpäin;* instead of outrage over the purges, she found such headlines as "The Karelian Enemies of the People Must Be Done Away With Without Mercy" and "No Clemency to Enemies of the People." For Sevander: "Reading the Finnish-American communist newspapers of the 1930s, I seemed to be reading a Soviet paper of those days."[65]

The experience of Lawrence and Sylvia Hokkanen illustrates the pressures brought to bear on those who escaped from Karelia. Both grew up in Finnish Communist families in Sault Sainte Marie, Michigan. They were married in 1932; in 1934, they were given

63. David John Ahola, *Finnish-Americans and International Communism: A Study of Finnish-American Communism from Bolshevization to the Demise of the Third International* (Lanham, Md.: University Press of America, 1982), 178.

64. Paul Hummasti, *Finnish Radicals in Astoria, Oregon, 1904–1940* (New York: Arno Press, 1970), 263.

65. Sevander, *Red Exodus,* 49–52. Sevander spent most of her life as a schoolteacher and administrator in Petrozavodsk, the chief city of Karelia. In the late 1980s, after the glasnost reforms of Mikhail Gorbachev, she began to gather material on the American and Canadian Finns who emigrated to the Soviet Union ("My People," as she calls them), and she was able to visit the United States as well. She contacted hundreds of survivors, both in the Soviet Union and the United States, via letter, survey, or interview. Most, like her, had been children in the 1930s.

CPUSA permission to emigrate to Karelia: they were then in their early twenties. By 1938 Lawrence was working as the foreman of the machine-repair section of a large ski factory in Petrozavodsk, Karelia. In their 1991 memoir, *Karelia: A Finnish-American Couple in Stalin's Russia, 1934–1941,* the Hokkanens relate that one July night the NKVD swept through the town arresting scores of Finns, both native Karelians and immigrants from the United States and Canada. The next day Lawrence Hokkanen discovered that twenty-three of the workers in his factory section had been arrested. Over the next few weeks more of the Hokkanens' friends among the American and Canadian immigrants were arrested. The Hokkanens write that "most of the people who were taken were never seen or heard from again. None of our friends who were arrested ever returned. Either they perished in the concentration camps or else they received what the Finns called a 'viiden kopekaan tuomio' (five-kopeck sentence) which meant they were shot. Five kopecks was the price of a rifle bullet."[66]

The Hokkanens speculate that they were spared only because the NKVD overlooked them. After the wave of arrests had subsided, the couple applied for permission to return to America and were allowed to do so. When Lawrence Hokkanen told his family about the purges, his mother, a staunch Communist, asserted, " 'That couldn't have happened,' " and "she turned away." His sister also refused to believe him. At a welcome-home party, largely attended by relatives and friends committed to the CPUSA, a representative of the party gave a speech. He noted that in the Soviet Union "no innocent people had been arrested." Lawrence writes that between the pressure of the party and that of his family, "I remained silent." Only many years later did the Hokkanens speak publicly about what they had witnessed.[67]

Documents 67 and 68 illustrate how both American and Canadian Communists in Moscow worked to hide the purges in Karelia and to counteract stories that all was not well there. Document 67 is a 1939 memo from Pat Toohey, the CPUSA representative to the Comintern, concerning arrangements for a special Comintern radio broadcast to North America "answering some of the enemy

66. Hokkanen and Hokkanen, *Karelia,* 95–96.
67. Ibid., 1, 125.

slanders" about Soviet Karelia. Document 68 is a letter from the Comintern containing detailed instructions to North American Finnish Communists on how to handle the Karelian question. The comrades are urged to "sharpen our whole fight against the Trotskyist and fascist elements who have returned to Canada and the USA from Karelia and who are now carrying on an unprincipled campaign of slander" against the USSR. The letter justifies the large number of Finns arrested in the Soviet purges by claiming that the Soviet Karelian Technical Aid Committee had been run by traitors, out to "flood Soviet Karelia with all sorts of undesirable bourgeois-nationalist, fascist and Trotskyist agents; in short, under cover of a working class movement, these people became the advance agents of fascism aiming at the destruction of socialist economy in Soviet Karelia and its separation from the USSR."

The Comintern pointed out that Matti Tenhunen, a prominent Finnish-American Communist who had headed the Technical Aid Committee before Oscar Corgan, had been imprisoned in the Soviet Union for diversionist activities and for being an agent of the Finnish police and urged that Communists "begin a careful investigation of former contacts and present sympathisers of Tenhunen." After his arrest Tenhunen disappeared, and it is not known whether he, too, was executed quickly or whether he perished later in the Gulag.

The letter also urged Canadian Communists to expel a Canadian Finn, John Latva, as "an agent of the Finnish police" and to expose Edward Neoenin, another Canadian Finn, who had returned from Karelia in 1935, "as a member of the Finnish police," based on the confessions of Canadian Finns "arrested for wrecking and spying activities in 1937–38." But unlike the CPUSA, which accepted Moscow's purge of its former members without visible reservation, some Finnish-Canadian Communists were skeptical. The letter is signed by one "Tom," probably Tom McEwen, a Canadian Communist on the staff of the Anglo-American Secretariat, and he takes his Canadian Finnish comrades to task for failing to campaign strongly enough against the returned Karelians.[68] He criticizes

68. McEwen served a two-year term with the Anglo-American Secretariat starting in the late summer of 1938. Tom McEwen, *The Forge Glows Red* (Toronto: Progress Books, 1974), 201–3. The authors thank Gregory Kealey for his assistance in identifying "Tom."

Gust Sundquist, a leader of the Finnish Organization of Canada, for saying of those who returned that " 'they cannot all be spies.' " Tom protests: "We cannot and have not led a concerted offensive against these Trotskyist and fascist wreckers in the Finnish field, because some of our Finnish Party leaders, even those we consider the best at the moment, away down deep in their hearts seek to make exceptions of those elements whom the people of Soviet Karelia have proven to be spies, police agents, and wreckers." Speaking with the authority of the Comintern, Tom then announces that if Sundquist and others refuse to discredit the returned Finns, "it will be necessary to make some change in order to strengthen the Secretariat of the FOC [Finnish Organization of Canada]."[69]

Document 66

Autonomous Republic of Soviet Karelia to Political Secretariat, ECCI, 25 March 1931, RTsKhIDNI 495–72–141. Original in English. The signatures on the letter are in script and very difficult to read. They may be those of Edvard Gylling, a Finnish Communist leader in Karelia from 1923 to 1935, who was arrested in 1937 and died in 1944, and Gustaa Rovio, a high-ranking Finnish Communist leader in Karelia from 1929 to 1935. Rovio was arrested and shot in 1938.

To the Political Secretariat ECCI

Dear Comrades:

Plentiful national resources, so far utilized only to a very small extent, open for the economy of Soviet Karelia magnificent possibilities. With the small forces of our local population Soviet Karelia is, however, not in position to clear itself from the tasks placed upon it by the ever magnifying socialist construction of our Soviet Union. There is already an acute shortage of labor power. Last year there existed yet a possibility to bring in from territories outside of Karelia 48 thousand men in the lumber industry. This year it was impossible to carry out the recruiting plan, because everywhere in the Soviet Union there has been a shortage of labor power. In the years to come the labor power is bound to grow evermore acute. For these reasons the organs of the Soviet Union already have in the summer of 1930 passed a resolution, accord-

---

69. An official history published by the Finnish Organization of Canada contains nothing about Stalin's purge of Finnish Canadian emigrants to Karelia. William Eklund, *Builders of Canada: History of the Finnish Organization of Canada, 1911– 1971* (Toronto: Finnish Organization of Canada, 1987).

ing to which Karelia is allowed to bring 785 workers from the USA. Also the Comintern supported this decision, but due to the opposition attitude taken by the CC Finnish Bureau, CP USA, this decision is far from being carried out. After acquainting themselves with the problems of Soviet Karelia, the authoritative party and administrative organs of the Soviet Union decided in the beginning of this year in addition to the above mentioned number of men to allow Soviet Karelia to bring 2,000 more men primarily lumber workers from the United States and Canada.

An effective realization of these decisions require mutual understanding between the organs of our organizations here and in America. For achieving this aim we ask the Comintern to address a letter to the CC Finnish Bureau CPUSA, (a) re-endorsing its support pertaining to the import of 785 men, (b) supporting the decision made this year as regard to the importation of an additional 1,000 men from the USA.

Whereas, we have reason to believe that the American comrades continue to resist the taking away of men from the USA, we take upon ourselves to present some viewpoints showing that there cannot by any means exist any factual objections against transferring working power here when the matter is looked upon from the point of view of international class struggle.

We presume the American comrades will understand the importance of the matter if they take unto consideration the significance of the strengthening of the Autonomous Republic of Soviet Karelia, extending to the borders of fascist Finland. For coming into the position to carry out its task in the defense front of the Soviet Union, Karelia—the population of which to a large extent is composed of Finnish speaking Karelians, and the economic and cultural level of which is as yet very backward—must as an integral part of the Soviet Union raise its industries. In the present situation this can be done only with the assistance of the proletariat of old industrial countries.

Just now when the capitalist countries are systematically attacking our lumber products under their "forced labor" slogan it would be quite wrong to minimize the political significance of the emigration of 1,000 men from the USA in the lumber industry of our territory. Neither should the effect of the rapidly economically strengthening of Soviet Karelia among the working masses of Finland and of Scandinavian countries be minimized. Just now when the intervention propaganda of Finland's fascist generals based upon nationalism is at its height, it is up to us to produce a really demonstrative evidence of how the National Red Karelia is progressing.

Whereas the program of the administrative organs of the Soviet Union provides for getting into Karelia additional working power, it is also from the point of view of carrying out the national policy more advantageous to get from outside Finnish speaking labor power into Karelia than to bring in groups speaking many languages.

It is to be understood that the American organizations are anxious as to the question: Is it possible to take away from the USA such a large number of Finnish workers without endangering the movement of class struggle there. After consulting with many responsible American comrades we are convinced of the fact that especially during the present unemployment the class struggle in America would not suffer to any extent on account of transfering 1,000 men to another sector of the front, where this type of elements now would better serve the cause of the class struggle, providing the members of the Communist Party are being left intact.

In the United States there are thousands of Finnish workers schooled by the highly developed industries which in general have strong sympathy for the Soviet Union, but which due to many reasons (language difficulties, American chauvinism, isolated position in small saw-mill villages, in the countryside, and in the lumber camps) have not participated in the workers' organized activity, and which do not even now appear as active class fighters. For them there is a danger of landing into the reserve of the bourgeoisie. A part of these elements could now be brought behind the front of the working class to assist with their skill in their trade the strengthening of this front. We are being told about what a healthy effect the arrival of some small groups of men in the construction of the Soviet Union has mad[e] in the American Finns left behind, and how new strata of workers are in the mass organizations taking the places of those gone away.

Perhaps the Finnish Communist papers in America would for some time suffer to some extent from the emigration of people to the Soviet Union. But the papers should not be the main thing. Besides those workers which used to read these papers do by no means go outseide of our influence by being transferred on a more important sector of the class struggle.

To our understanding the recruiting of workers for us must take place in America through a representative sent there by the Soviet Karelia in cooperation with the Finnish Federation. We ask the Comintern to give corresponding directives to comrades in America.

We from our part assure that Karelia is in position to receive and to take care of this number of men, to provide work for all of them as well as shelter, food, schools and to give cultural service to the maximum degree there are in general possibilities to give in the present situation existing in the Soviet Union. The arrangements as to the working conditions, housing and schooling is already under way keeping in mind these prospective newcomers. Adequately serious attention will also be paid to the political and social work among these workers with the purpose of getting active functionaries from them for various fields in our socialist construction.

With Communist greetings.

In the behalf of the Autonomous
Republic of Soviet Karelia

Moscow 25th of March 1931

_____[illegible signatures]_____

_____

Document 67

Toohey to Kuusinen, 25 March 1939, RTsKhIDNI 495–14–131. Original in English with handwritten signature. The initials VKPB stand for the Russian name of the All-Union Communist Party (Bolshevik), which later became the CPSU.

Memo to Com. Kuusinen.

Dear Comrade Kuusinen: [illegible script]

1. We have arranged with the Inoradio Committee of the Comintern Radio Station the following: that the radio committee will connect with Soviet Karelia and have a complete radio broadcast prepared for transmission to the USA and Canada. This Karelian program will include a speech on the growth, advance and success of Soviet Karelia, and aim at answering some of the enemy slanders. I understand that the entire program will be arranged in Karelia and then transcribed on special records, which then will be used to rebroadcast it from Moscow on the regular English hour. The Radio committee will also do the same as regards Armenian, Ukranian and Slovak, which will be of excellent value for the United States.

2. For your information the CPUSA is now publishing the following amount of publications: Comrade Stalin report, 250,000; Molotov, Zdhanov Manuilsky reports, 100,000 copies; History of VKPB, 100,000 copies (all this in english only).

Comra[d]ely yours,
Pat Toohey
Rep, CC CP USA

Mar. 25
1939

Document 68

Tom to Dear Friends, 11 August 1939, RTsKhIDNI 495–18–1290. Original in English, with handwritten annotation in Russian. *Vapaus* was a Finnish-language journal aligned with the Communist party of Canada and the Finnish Organization of Canada. Yrjo Halonen was a leader of the Finnish-American Communist movement who broke with the party.

Dear Friends:—The so-called Karelian question and the many difficulties involved which have disturbed our Party and Finnish Organisation of Canada for some considerable time, has now reached a point where we can begin to draw some conclusions and to concretise a number of definite tasks for our party fraction within the Finnish Organisation, and most important, to sharpen our whole fight against the Trotskyist and fascist elements who have returned to Canada and the USA from Karelia and who are now carrying on an unprincipled campaign of slander against the su.

These tasks may be summarised as follows:—a) a cleaning out of all those elements within the ranks of our p. and the Finnish Org. of Canada who continue their anti-working class and Trotskyist activities under cover of these organisations; b) a wide campaign of exposure of all those elements in our press that will eliminate them from the ranks of the labour movement; c) the strengthening of our leading cadres in the Finnish Organisation of Canada and its press.

I need not recount to you the history of the "Technical Aid to Karelia" committee that was established in Canada in 1929 to facilitate the emigration of skilled Finnish lumber workers and also to supply badly-needed (at that time) logging equipment for Soviet Karelia. That is well-known to you. Moreover, I need not repeat here the claims advanced by John Latva, as representing the ["]Technical Aid" committee upon Intourist for the sum of $3,695, nor the grounds advanced by Latva as to why this money should be paid. These you are also well aware of.

Upon the advice of the CC of the CPSU, the CP of Soviet Karelia has investigated these claims and found them to be without moral or legal justification. These demands are regarded as a form of blackmail to cover the abuses of confidence and trust which characterised the leadership of the "Technical Aid" committee, and particularly in the case of Latva. Moreover, such demands serve to cover up the anti-Soviet activities of such elements, who through necessity, are compelled to adopt new tactics in their slanderous and wrecking activities. From unimpeachable sources it is known that documentary evidence is available showing Latva to be an agent of the Finnish Ochrana, and evidence from a number of reliable persons show that while he was recruiting emigrants, he recruited a number of known police agents to go to Karelia. Moreover, the records show that in addition to receiving $11.50 commission from Intourist for every adult that emigrated from Canada, Latva and Aronen received a large sum of money from the Swedish-American Lines.

Document 68 *continued*

Proof of this is shown by receipts held by Intourist, New York. A perusal of the documentary evidence from reliable sources shows that the main aims of Halonen, Aronen, Latva, Tenhunen and others who were associated with the work of the "Technical Aid to Karelia", was simply to enrich themselves and flood Soviet Karelia with all sorts of undesirable bourgeois-nationalist, fascist and Trotskyist agents; in short, under cover of a working class movement, these people became the advance agents of fascism aiming at the destruction of socialist economy in Soviet Karelia and its separation from the USSR. Fortunately, and thanks to the vigilance of the Soviet people, the objectives of these diversionists was never realized. Now they are operating on another front, in Finland and in our country, and utilising our organizations to carry on their anti-Soviet work.

To my knowledge, Latva is still a member of our Party and a member of the Finnish organisation of Canada. Matti Tenhunen was closely connected with the "immigration agency" and also with the "Technical Aid". Following 1935 he worked for a time on the paper "Keria". At his trial for diversionist activities, he was fully exposed as an agent of the Finnish police and sentenced to a term of imprisonment by the Soviet Courts. It is vitally important that our CCC begin a careful investigation of former contacts or present sympathisers of Tenhunen who may still be in the FOC or even in the ranks of the CP.

I think in view of the foregoing that our first concern should be, not what may happen if some of these counter-revolutionary elements throw Latva in jail for the non-payment of money they claim he owes them and which he in turn claim[s] cannot be paid unless Intourist meets his alleged claims as representing the "Technical Aid" committee, but how best we can carry through his expulsion from the Party and the Finnish Organisation of Canada, with the objective of greatly strengthening our whole struggle against all those Trotskyist and fascist elements, and incidentally, strengthen the Finnish Organisation of Canada itself, which these elements undoubtedly aim and hope to wreck.

If we begin an offensive against these elements by centering our attack, first of all upon Latva as an agent of the Finnish police, and all those closely associated with him, the question of "financial obligations" will fade into the background, and the Finnish Organisation of Canada will emerge with a stronger moral and political unity as a result of being freed from the influence of such people a[s] Latva.

It goes without saying that it will be necessary to proceed very carefully in the matter; first, by a series of meetings with our comrades in the National and local fractions of the Finnish organisation, and secondly, by a broader campaign of the popularisation of Soviet Karelia and its achievements in the mass organisation. Such a campaign will serve to create a new interest, not only in the socialist successes of Soviet Karelia, but in the activities and identities of its enemies, some of whom, like Latva, still pose in the role of "friends". The removal of Latva as a spy will undoubtedly bring forward others in our Party and the FOC who will bear close investigation.

It is important also, that our Party Control Commission should begin to determine to what extent Latva or others are in contact with the Halonite followers in the USA, as well as any associations or "friendships" that may exist between Latva and other of the deported Finns who are now carrying on an active campaign against Soviet Karelia and our organisations in Canada. Edward Neoenin came from Canada to Karelia in 1931 and returned in 1935. In the trials of a number of Canadian-Finns, arrested for wrecking and spying activities in 1937–38, Neoenin was exposed as a member of the Finnish police. It is vitally important to establish the contact, if any, between these individuals, as well as possible contacts they may have within the FOC and our Party. The main thing to keep in mind, and having regard for the utmost care, is that our Party must now go over to an active offensive against those elements. They have been thoroughly defeated in their aims upon Soviet Karelia. We must now begin to prepare their complete defeat in Canada and to free our Party and the progressive Finnish organisations from their evil influence.

Some materials on Karelia for press publication have already gone forward. These have been of a general popular character. Others of a more political and specific nature are in process of preparation and will be available in the immediate future. These, I hope, shall include a number of contributions from Canadian-Finns now resident in Karelia, whose names, by their labour, is hon[our]ed in the USSR.

The following information may be important to you now in case the press material has not yet arrived: During the period of 1931–35, as a result of the work of the "Technical Aid" and other auxiliary bodies in Karelia ("immigration agency"), 4,681 people were brought to Soviet Karelia from Canada and the USA. Reports available show that of this number, 3,580 have become Soviet citizens of USSR, while approximately 474 have returned to these countries. These figures are entirely separate from the large number of Finns that came from Finland and other countries, many of whom entered the territory of Soviet Karelia illegally.

Some time ago I wrote you regarding greater attention to our Finnish paper, "Vapaus". While I am not in a position to say what has been done, since we do not receive the paper very regularly, I think we can say that its content and political line generally, leaves much to be desired. I gave you one example, not an ordinary one it is true, but still sufficient to show that the agitational and propaganda materials carried on Soviet Karelia in the columns of our Finnish press and against these wreckers in Canada is almost negligible. One issue of the "Vapaus" containing 56 pages, with not a single word against those Trotskyist and fascist wreckers, and little or nothing of Soviet Karelia and the achievements of its people can hardly be called an oversight. It merely expresses the fact that within the FOC and its press there is developing a passivity and tolerance towards those enemies of the working class that in the long run will be disastrous for our organisations, unless it is checked. It is important that we indicate to our Finnish comrades on the "Vapaus" and within the shortest possible time, the need of overcoming this weakness and going over to a clear-cut offensive.

This brings us to the vital question of cadres in all the organs of the Finnish Organisation of Canada. Why have we not been able to reply decisively to those elements who slander Soviet Karelia and seek to [sm]ash the organisations of the progressive Finns in Canada? Because our leading cadres in the FOC are ideologically and politically weak. This weakness is expressed, first and foremost, in a hesitation to attack the enemy when he attacks us; to even allow him some moral justification for his slanders. I do not question the loyalty and integrity of Comrade Sundquist to the working class movement, but when Comrade Sundquist shakes his head and says of these enemies that "they cannot all be spies", he is unconsciously strengthening their position and their alleged right to slander the Soviet Union. Such an expression gives the answer to the question. We cannot and have not led a concerted offensive against these Trotskyist and fascist wreckers in the Finnish field, because some of our Finnish Party leaders, even those we consider the best at the moment, away down deep in their hearts seek to make exceptions of those elements whom the people of Soviet Karelia have proven to be spies, police agents, and wreckers.

If this deduction is correct, and I think it is, then it becomes a serious matter for our Party, and one in which we are not lacking in precedents, as the history of other national mass organisations prove. From this the next question immediately arises—has Comrade Sundquist or other of our leading Finnish Comrades any alliances with these elements, now or previously? Was he in any way connected with the work of the "Technical Aid" committee and with Latva in its early stages. Personally I do not know, but I am indicating to you a possibility that might explain the lack of any desire to carry on an aggressive struggle against these elements. The arguments that "we have no materials with which to reply to these elements" only hold good when dealing with specific cases and individuals. A great fund of factual and ideological material has been available during the last 10 months in the speeches and resolutions of the 18th Congress of the CPSU and in the "History of the CPSU (B)" which could have been utilised in an offensive against these slanderers of the Party and the Soviet Union, but I am afraid we have failed badly in this regard. The question before us now is to examine and remove all the obstacles that stand in the way of a sharp and consistent struggle against Trotskyist an[d] fascist activities affecting the FOC and the working class generally.

I am not here proposing that Comrade Sundquist be removed from his post as Secretary of the Finnish Organisation of Canada; but if upon careful examination of all the facts relating to his inability to conduct a sharp struggle against these slanderous activities of the Finnish trotskyists, it is found that he cannot lead in this struggle, then it will be necessary to make some change in order to strengthen the Secretariat of the FOC.

In addition to these three main questions which I have indicated should have your immediate attention, I will repeat in this letter a few remarks on the main question, so that there may be no misunderstanding on an issue that has dragged on for a number of years.

(1) That the financial claims put forward by Latva in the name of the "Technical" Aid" or the FOC against Intourist will not be honored, since it is found to be without moral or legal basis.

(2) That it is clear that while Latva and others already mentioned were at the head of the "Technical Aid", they used the organisation and large sums of money for their own personnel interest, in addition to betraying the cause of Socialism they were presumed to be aiding, by facilitating the work of the enemies of the USSR.

(3) Latva and others have been definitely established as spies and agents for the Finnish bourgeois-nationalists, working for the destruction of Karelian socialist economy, and for the separation of Soviet Karelia from the USSR and transforming it into a colony of a "greater" Finland.

(4) That with their complete defeat in Soviet Karelia these agents of fascism have transferred their activities to other fronts, Canada and Finland, where, under cover of working class organisations like the Finnish organisation of Canada, and under the pretext that Soviet institutions, like Intourist, have failed to respond to alleged obligations, these elements continue their slanders against the USSR.

(5) That while superficially there might appear to be a clear distinction between Latva and other elements who mix their slanders with threats of imprisoning him for non-payment of monies, basically there are no differences.

(6) The great achievements of the people of Soviet Karelia in socialist construction and progress, gives the lie direct to all the baseless claims and slanders of its enemies.

While it is impossible to comply with your request that all the books and financial transactions of the "Technical Aid", etc., be made available, this letter, plus the volume of materials which I forwarded in a press article on July 15th, should be sufficient to prove our case and begin an energetic campaign against these elements.

In view of the foregoing, I trust that upon receipt and discussion of this letter, you will consider the old chapter of this question, the chapter of baseless claims and misrepresentation closed, and a new chapter opened. One of an uncompromising struggle against the enemies of the USSR who have taken refuge in our country and who use our working class organisations to carry on their vile work on behalf of their Trotskyist and Fascist paymasters. Comradely yours, Tom.

Received and sent forward

11.VIII.39

Thomas Sgovio: An American in the Great Terror

The Finnish immigrants were not the only American Communist party members who moved to the USSR in the 1920s and 1930s and became caught up in the Great Terror. Estimates vary, but several thousand Americans were probably involved, to a greater or lesser degree.[70] In addition to the case of Lovett Fort-Whiteman, new evidence from the archives of the Soviet era has shed light on the fates of Joseph and Thomas Sgovio. Joseph Sgovio had been a founding member of the American Communist party and was briefly detained during the antiradical Palmer Raids of 1919. By the early 1930s he had become a full-time CPUSA functionary, organizing the unemployed for the Trade Union Unity League. On 28 December 1931 he was arrested for disrupting a city council meeting in North Tonawanda, New York. An Italian immigrant who had never acquired U.S. citizenship, Sgovio was deported in 1932 after serving a year in jail. Rather than returning to fascist Italy, Sgovio went to the Soviet Union, and his wife, daughter, and son, Thomas, followed in 1935. The twenty-year-old, American-born Thomas was a Young Communist League activist. He had been arrested three times as a teenager during YCL demonstrations and jailed once for five days.[71]

The Sgovios all took Soviet citizenship, but neither that nor their Communist credentials protected them against the Great Terror. In

70. See Adam Hochschild, "Never Coming Home: An Exclusive Look at the KGB's Secret Files on Americans in Stalin's Prisons," *Mother Jones*, September–October 1992, 51.

71. Thomas Sgovio, *Dear America! Why I Turned against Communism* (Kenmore, N.Y.: Partners' Press, 1979), 63–64, 69–84, 89–90. Joseph Sgovio's transfer from the CPUSA to the CPSU was endorsed by Randolph (probably William Weinstone); see "Numbered List of CPUSA to CPSU Transfers (Sgovio no. 101)," RTsKhIDNI 495-72-289. The document is undated, but it is after September 1935.

August 1937 the NKVD arrested Joseph. An NKVD report stated that under interrogation he had confessed that "he and other Italian political emigrants participated in hostile agitation and tried to wreck the Stakhanov movement in the state ball bearing plant" and that "the thought had come in his head to buy a knife and kill two employees of the Central Committee of the MOPR. He wanted to do it because he was angry at them." On 19 November 1937 an NKVD board sentenced Joseph to five years' imprisonment in the Gulag "for counter-revolutionary activities."[72]

Afterward, his sentence was administratively extended by the NKVD, and Joseph was not released until late 1946, having served more than nine years in the Gulag. He was then ordered into internal exile in Uzbekistan, and his Soviet citizenship was revoked. Utterly disillusioned, Joseph applied to the Italian consulate for an Italian passport. It was granted in late 1947, but he died before he could leave the Soviet Union. A medical certificate noted that he had suffered from malaria, pellagra, and dysentery but that the cause of death was probably pneumonia.[73]

Shortly after Joseph Sgovio's arrest, Thomas, then twenty-two, realized that despite his Soviet citizenship, his prospects in the USSR were not bright. Early in 1938 he went to the U.S. embassy, where he applied for a passport to return to the United States on the basis of his American citizenship. What happened next is told in **documents 69 and 70.**

Document 69 is an NKVD arrest record for Thomas Sgovio dated 22 March 1938, stating that he had been taken into custody immediately following his visit to the embassy because "Counter-revolutionary espionage activities are suspected." Document 70 shows that under interrogation Thomas refused to confess to espionage but did declare the following: "Before 1935 I lived in America, in Buffalo. I was accustomed to the American capitalist system, but

72. KGB Captain Boltnyov review of the case of Thomas Sgovio, 25 June 1954, State Archive of the Russian Federation 10035–1–p–26330, part 2. (This document also discusses Joseph Sgovio's case.) The "Stakhanovite movement" was a Soviet campaign to encourage workers to overfulfill their state-ordered work quotas. MOPR (Mezhdunarodnaia organizatsiia pomoshchi revoliutsioneram), often called the International Red Aid, provided legal aid and assistance to Communist-backed strikes or to Communists and the families of Communists jailed by authorities.

73. Thomas Sgovio, *Dear America!* 267–69.

here in the USSR everything seemed alien and hostile. Having such feelings toward Soviet power, I tried to return to America, which I regarded as my homeland." These words, in conjunction with his visit to the embassy, were enough to convince an NKVD board to sentence him to five years of corrective labor "as a socially dangerous element." As with his father, the NKVD extended Thomas's sentence, and he was not released from the Gulag until September 1946, more than eight years later.

As a prisoner, Thomas Sgovio saw the worst of the Gulag system. Like Lovett Fort-Whiteman, he was sent to the camps in the Kolyma gold fields of northeastern Siberia. He later attributed his survival to his skill as an artist; this ability earned him occasional prison jobs that allowed him both more food and a chance to escape the brutal physical labor in subzero temperatures that killed many of the other prisoners. His memoir of the deprivation, degradation, disease, misery, heartlessness, and death that was the lot of the millions sent to the Gulag is a horrifying tale of human cruelty.[74]

Even after his release Thomas Sgovio's ordeal was not over. The release order freed him from the labor camps but confined him to internal exile in Dalstroi, the Far Northern Construction Complex run by the NKVD that controlled the northern Siberian labor camps.[75] He was not allowed to leave Siberia until December 1947.

Sgovio was still forbidden to live in any of the major Soviet cities, however, so he took up residence in Alexandrov, a town about sixty miles from Moscow. Here he established contact with his sister and old friends in Moscow. This once more brought him to the attention of Soviet political police. Document 70, an MGB (a successor to the NKVD) report of 15 December 1948, continues Sgovio's saga: it notes that MGB agents had observed Sgovio visiting Moscow, where his sister was under investigation on suspicion

---

74. In document 65, above, Fort-Whiteman's death certificate, we saw Fort-Whiteman's fingerprints, which were taken posthumously. Thomas Sgovio describes how this was done. One winter he was assigned to assist the guard officer who fingerprinted the daily fatalities. The bodies, sometimes as many as twenty in a single day, were kept in an unheated shed, but they were usually frozen by the time the officer prepared the daily paperwork. Because it was impossible to fingerprint frozen flesh, the hands were chopped off and hung in a heated office until they were soft enough to be fingerprinted (Sgovio, *Dear America!* 245–46).

75. Sgovio, *Dear America!* 253.

of espionage because of her contact with British and American foreigners. The report added that Sgovio himself "spreads slander against Soviet reality." Sgovio was arrested that same day. In March 1949 he was charged with "suspicion of espionage" and "connections with Americans," and in May an MGB "special session" sentenced him to lifetime internal exile in the Krasnoyarsk region of western Siberia.[76] There he found work at various times as a painter, lumberjack, and commercial artist. After Stalin's death, an amnesty revoked his internal exile and allowed him to return to Moscow in 1954. In 1956 a further action rescinded his 1938 conviction. In 1960, with an Italian passport gained through his parents' Italian birth, Thomas Sgovio left the Soviet Union for Italy. From there he was able to reestablish his American citizenship. He returned to the United States in 1963.[77]

Document 69

Certificate of arrest for Thomas Sgovio, 22 March 1938, State Archive of the Russian Federation 10035–1–p–26330, part 1. Original in Russian. The authors thank Thomas Sgovio for making the documents of his suppression file available.

M.M.

"I APPROVE"
ASST. PEOPLES COMMISSAR OF INTERNAL AFFAIRS USSR
COMMISSAR OF STATE SECURITY RANK NO. 1
(ZAKOVSKY) *Zakovsky*

"22" MARCH 1938

CERTIFICATE
(OF ARREST)

THE 3RD DEPT. UGB UNKVD MO [Administration of state security and administration of NKVD, Moscow region] arrests SGOVIO, Thomas, born 1916 in Buffalo (America), Italian, citizen of USSR, before arrest worked as an artist

76. MGB Captain Kochurov, "Accusatory Finding" on Thomas Sgovio, 15 March 1949, with annotations of MGB Special Session of 5 May 1949, State Archive of the Russian Federation 10035–1–p–26330, part 1.
77. Thomas Sgovio resided in Arizona until his death in 1997. In his memoir, Sgovio names a number of other American Communists living in Moscow who, like him and his father, became victims of the Great Terror.

Document 69 *continued*

for the Periodical and Newspaper Association, res. 1st Ploshchadka VIEM, no. 10, apt. 5.

SGOVIO, Thomas, was detained by the 2nd Dept. of the GUGB [city division of the Administration of state security] after visiting the American Embassy on 21 March 1938.

During the preliminary investigation, SGOVIO indicated that he went to the American Embassy purportedly to find out if there was news about his application to regain his American citizenship and return to the U.S.A.

Counter-revolutionary espionage activities are suspected.

On the basis of orders from the NKVD USSR, SGOVIO, Thomas, is placed under arrest.

CHIEF OF THE 3RD DEPT. UGB UNKVD MO
CAPTAIN OF STATE SECURITY *Sorokin* (SOROKIN)
CHIEF OF THE 4TH BRANCH 3RD DEPT. UGB
LIEUTENANT OF STATE SECURITY *Remizov* (REMIZOV)

Document 70

Lieutenant Colonel Papurin of the MGB, "Report Regarding the Case of Sgovio, T.," 15 December 1948, State Archive of the Russian Federation 10035–1–p–26330, part 2. Original in Russian. "L.D." stands for "sheet of file" (page). The abbreviation "ITL" is used for a sentence to the "reformatory labor camps." Lucy Flaxman, mentioned in the document, was, like Sgovio, born in America and brought to the USSR by her Communist parents. She later confessed to Sgovio that she had become an informer for the Soviet political police and had reported on his words and activities. She herself was imprisoned in 1953 by the same agency that used her as an informer.

3–de

Top Secret

REPORT
REGARDING THE CASE OF SGOVIO, T.

SGOVIO, Thomas, born 1916 in Buffalo, USA, Italian, working-class background, citizen USSR, non-Party, high school education, sentenced in 1938 as a socially dangerous element to 5 years ITL, served his sentence. Before his arrest worked in Moscow as an artist for "Zhurgaz Association." At present lives in Alexandrov, Vladimir district, works as an artist for Gorkomkhoz.

SGOVIO, T., was arrested on 23 March 1938 by the UNKVD of the Moscow district and sentenced by the Special Session of the NKVD USSR on 14 May 1938 to 5 years ITL as a socially dangerous element. He was released in January 1948.

Document 70 *continued*

The investigative material of 1938 reveals that in 1935 Sgovio, his mother, and his sister left the USA and came to the USSR to join his father, Giuseppe Sgovio, who emigrated from America to the Soviet Union in 1932. (In 1937 he was convicted of attempting to kill employees of the Central Committee of the MOPR and of counter-revolutionary agitation.)

The investigation established that after arriving in the Soviet Union, T. Sgovio became a Soviet citizen, but because he harbored hostile feelings toward the existing Soviet political system, he did not wish to remain in the Soviet Union and planned to regain his American citizenship and leave the Soviet Union. For this purpose he visited the American embassy in Moscow three times. There he had conversations with an embassy employee.—MEKKI (L.D. 8, 10, 12–17)

During interrogation on 13 April 1938, T. Sgovio testified:

"I visited the American embassy three times in 1938. . . . My objective was to petition the consul for restoration of American citizenship.

"Before 1935 I lived in America, in Buffalo. I was accustomed to the American capitalist system, but here in the USSR everything seemed alien and hostile. Having such feelings toward Soviet power, I tried to return to America, which I regarded as my homeland." (L.D. 16)

During the course of the investigation it was also ascertained that in America [he] was arrested by American police three times, supposedly during Young Communist League disturbances. Twice he was released by the court, and the third time he spent 5 days in prison. While living in the Soviet Union, before his arrest he maintained a correspondence with relatives in America. (L.D. 14)

During interrogation T. Sgovio did not plead guilty to the charge of espionage activities. (L.D. 17)

In the period 1939–1940 T. Sgovio and his relatives lodged a series of complaints requesting reexamination of his case and release of T. Sgovio from custody.

In one complaint T. Sgovio's sister, G. Deitch-Boogay, pointed out that her brother, T. Sgovio, while living in Moscow as an artist, worked for the editorial offices of an English newspaper and the publishers "Foreign Literature." He also worked for the Foreign Workers Club. (L.D. 26)

In 1941 the archival-investigatory case of the accused T. Sgovio was reviewed by the procurator of the Moscow Military District. The conclusion, dated 27 May 1941, states that there is no basis for reconsidering the decision of the Special Session of the NKVD USSR in regard to T. Sgovio. The complaint was not satisfied. (L.D. 33)

Since serving out his sentence in 1948 and settling in Alexandrov, T. Sgovio, according to information given us by agents "Steen" and "Pool," systematically traveled to Moscow, where he established connections with foreigners, specifically with Lucy Flaxman, who was born in America and has

Document 70 *continued*

relatives living currently in the USA, as well as with persons who were sentenced for anti-Soviet activities, for example, A. L. Gurov (arrested).

Furthermore, T. Sgovio maintains a regular relationship with his sister, Grace Deitch-Boogay, a former American citizen who lives in Moscow and works as a secretary-translator in the library of the editorial offices of the English journal "British Unionist." The nature of her work puts her in the constant company of English employees of the "British Unionist" and press department of the British embassy. She also was in close contact with persons who had once been American citizens and now work for the American embassy in Moscow. G. Deitch-Boogay is being investigated on suspicion of espionage for England. (Main Administration of the MGB USSR)

According to information from our agents, T. Sgovio spreads slander against Soviet reality among those close to him. (Preliminary agent workup 8, 21, 24, 25)

This report has been compiled from archival-investigatory material of case no. 283818, located in storage at Special Department I MGV USSR and preliminary agent workup no. 1358 Alexandrovskii GO MGB. (SM. Memorandum)

CHIEF OF THE 2ND. DEPT. MGB ADMINISTRATION, VLADIMIR DISTRICT
LIEUT. COLONEL Papurin (PAPURIN)

"I AGREE": CHIEF OF THE MGB ADMINISTRATION, VLADIMIR DISTRICT
COLONEL Severukhin (SEVERUKHIN)

"15".XII.48
city Vladimir
exec. Sokolov

Negative evidence—documents not found—is by its nature never final. Something can always turn up. Nonetheless, we can state that although we have examined thousands of files in the Moscow archives, thus far we have not located a single document in which an official of the American Communist party attempted to save a party member or former member from Stalin's purges. There is no evidence, for example, that Earl Browder ever inquired about what happened to Oscar Corgan or Robert Saastamoinen after they emigrated to the Soviet Union. Even should such documents eventually turn up, it would appear that in most cases the CPUSA did nothing to save Americans from the Great Terror. Indeed, not only did the American Communist party abandon former associates to the Terror, but in several instances the CPUSA actively collaborated in the purges.

In *The Secret World of American Communism* we reprinted a 1933 document in which Charles Dirba, head of the Central Control Commission, the party's disciplinary arm, informed "Randolph" (the CPUSA representative) that Comrade Dourmashkin, an editor of *Novyi Mir,* was suspected of maintaining relations with an anti-Soviet relative. In consultation with Soviet officials in the United States, the decision was made that "Dourmashkin should be let go across [sent to the Soviet Union]" and that this should be done "(without arousing his suspicions), in order that he could not do any harm here and could be dealt with properly over there." We also reprinted documents indicating that American Communists participated in political purges within the International Brigades during the Spanish Civil War by identifying other Americans as suspected Trotskyists; in one case, American Communists were implicated in the arrest and probable murder of an American volunteer, Albert Wallach.[78]

The CPUSA rarely played an active role in sending Americans to imprisonment or deaths in the Gulag. No American Communist, for example, is known to have had any role in the ordeal of Thomas Sgovio. Nor, to our knowledge, did American Communists initiate charges or raise suspicions about Finnish-Americans in Karelia. But for more than a decade the CPUSA had depicted the Soviet Union as a workers' paradise, had assisted the emigration of Finnish-Americans to Karelia, and had encouraged exiles like the Sgovios to see it as a place of refuge. When the American emigrants were swept up in the Great Terror, the CPUSA either ignored the situation or actively supported the false characterization of these victims as spies and saboteurs and tried to cover up what was going on. Of the shameful episodes in the history of American communism recounted thus far, the CPUSA's abandonment of at least several hundred and probably more than a thousand of its own to Stalin's Terror is surely one of the worst.

78. Klehr, Haynes, and Firsov, *Secret World of American Communism,* 145–45, 153–63.

American Emissaries during World War II

During the 1920s and 1930s the CPUSA and the Comintern exchanged hundreds of messages each year. In addition, Comintern representatives came to the United States and American Communists journeyed to Moscow: Earl Browder traveled to Moscow annually in the 1930s. So efficient and comprehensive was the communication that any delay in the delivery of messages triggered complaints by Comintern officials. In 1932 a package of American reports took a month to travel by courier from Berlin to the Comintern's Anglo-American Secretariat. In **document 71** an irritated Comintern official asks: "How . . . can we engage in leadership of the parties, especially in more distant countries like the United States, if materials between Berlin and Moscow take a month to arrive? Could not some measures be taken to improve communications in this area, in order to keep the organs of the Comintern from changing from organs governing the work of the party into organs recording the history of the party?" Usually, however, directives and reports moved back and forth more quickly.

The start of World War II interfered with the Comintern's work: the war disrupted international mail service, governments began rigorous inspection of international letters and telegrams, and letters and packages were subject to loss en route because of the fighting. The CPUSA and the Comintern maintained a covert short-wave radio link, but the technology of the era restricted them to brief messages, and the connection was often unreliable. Passenger travel to Moscow across the Atlantic became increasingly difficult and hazardous; although the Pacific route remained relatively safe until 1942—and was still feasible even after that (the USSR and Japan were not at war)—it was time-consuming, expensive, and arduous. The stream of American and Soviet Cominternists traveling between Moscow and the United States dried up, a situation that greatly reduced the frequency and completeness of CPUSA-Comintern communications.

Pat Toohey, who had become the CPUSA representative in Moscow in 1938, returned to the United States at the end of 1939. Nat Ross, the referent, appears to have taken over the duties, if not the title, of American representative in 1940.[79] But Ross had been away from the United States for several years (he had arrived in Moscow in early 1939), and with communications crippled, he had no direct knowledge of what had been going on in the CPUSA since the beginning of the war.

In part to remedy this situation, the CPUSA sent Eugene Dennis to Moscow in the spring of 1941 to give Comintern officials a thorough briefing on American affairs. Dennis was then a key member of the party leadership, regarded as a possible successor to Browder. To protect him from arrest in an anticipated government crackdown during the Nazi-Soviet Pact period, the CPUSA had sent Dennis underground in 1940. His trip in March 1941, therefore, was a secret one: he traveled clandestinely by ship across the Pacific to Vladivostok and then took the Trans-Siberian railroad to Moscow. He did not return to the United States until after the Nazi invasion of the Soviet Union.

Document 72 is a cover letter from Dennis, under his Comintern alias Tim Ryan, to Dimitrov accompanying a package containing nine detailed reports for Comintern review. Dennis's lengthy reports (they come to more than eighty-five typed pages) covered every aspect of the CPUSA's organization and activities in early 1941, including membership and structural changes in the organization, the activities of the Young Communist League and the party-aligned American Students Union, the manipulation of the American Youth Congress, the creation of the American Peace Mobilization, the activities of the foreign-language immigrant affiliates, the party press, and the International Workers Order (a party-controlled fraternal insurance organization). In addition, Dennis reported on the party's left-wing rivals: Trotskyists, Lovestoneites, the Social Democratic Federation, and the Socialist Party. Dennis also devoted lengthy discussions to the party's position within the CIO and the AFL and the possibility of creating an antiwar farmer-labor party as a way to draw workers' votes away from President Roosevelt and the Democratic Party.

79. As was discussed in chapter 1, in 1940 the CPUSA officially ceased to be a member of the Communist International. Although the disaffiliation was purely nominal, it may have been the reason that Ross did not assume the title of representative.

According to Dennis, the party's activities in all these areas centered on its opposition to Roosevelt's policy of providing American assistance to Great Britain, then Nazi Germany's chief opponent. He assured the Comintern that young Communists were working within a variety of student organizations to bring about a "condemnation of the foreign and domestic policies of the government," while the "Left Wing in the CIO in which our Party is the decisive political factor" was "in the forefront of the struggle against the imperialist policies of the Roosevelt government."[80] Dennis specifically linked the CPUSA's activities within the labor movement to strikes in American war industries.

After the Germans attacked the Soviet Union, Dennis returned to the United States to help with the change in CPUSA policy to all-out support for U.S. entry into the war. His departure left the CPUSA without high-level representation in Moscow. The Comintern, therefore—not the CPUSA—appointed Maria Aerova to the position of American referent in the Marty Secretariat. Aerova, a Jewish-Russian immigrant to the United States in 1912, had been a young activist and founding member of the American Communist party. After a course at the International Lenin School in 1931 she worked for the Comintern's Eastern Secretariat and later went on missions to Germany and France. In the late 1930s she returned to the United States, where she worked for the propaganda department of the CPUSA and taught at one of the CPUSA schools for political cadre. She was back in Moscow by 1940.[81]

When she took up the position of referent, Aerova functioned more as a Cominternist with an American background than as a

80. Tim Ryan [Eugene Dennis], "On the Work of the YCL, USA," 2 April 1941, RTsKhIDNI 515-1-4091; Tim Ryan, "The Situation within the CIO," 29 March 1941, RTsKhIDNI 515-1-4091. Dennis reported that the CIO unions in which the party was the "decisive political factor" included the United Electrical Workers, the International Longshoremen's and Warehousemen's Union, the International Woodworkers Union, the Agricultural and Cannery Workers Union, the Packinghouse Workers Union, the Farm Equipment Workers, and "practically all the white collar and professional workers' unions." Dennis told the Comintern that the CPUSA had a "strong" but not decisive influence in the United Auto Workers and the Mine, Mill and Smelter Workers unions. He also claimed "dominant influence" in the CIO regional councils in New York City, Detroit, Cleveland, Chicago, Milwaukee, San Francisco, and Seattle.

81. Aerova biography, signed by Gulyaev and Neezov, 5 November 1940, RTsKhIDNI 495-74-483.

representative of the American Communist party. The war kept her from having much direct contact with the CPUSA. In 1944, for example, she based a lengthy Comintern report on the role of the CPUSA within the United Auto Workers union on a close reading and analysis of stories from the *Daily Worker* rather than on private information provided by the CPUSA.[82]

The final obstacle to the exchange of both personnel and information between the CPUSA and the Comintern was the 1943 dissolution of the Comintern. From 1943 to 1946, the Soviets avoided official contact with the Communist parties of the major Western powers, particularly that of the United States. When they had important instructions, they sent them by indirect means, such as the Duclos article.

Document 71

Williams to Piatnitsky, 16 August 1932, RTsKhIDNI 495–72–201. Original in Russian. "Williams" is Boris Mikhailov.

8640/2/copy
16.VIII.32   Secret
                    [illegible handwritten comment]

To Comrade PIATNITSKY

Today, 16 August, the Anglo-American Secretariat received some English materials (protocols of the Central Committee, Politburo, etc.). These materials were received in Berlin on 15 July, as indicated by the cancellation stamp on the envelope and arrived in Moscow yesterday, 15 August. How, one asks, can we engage in leadership of the parties, especially in more distant countries like the United States, if materials between Berlin and Moscow take a month to arrive?

Could not some measures be taken to improve communications in this area, in order to keep the organs of the Comintern from changing from organs governing the work of the party into organs recording the history of the party?

                                                          Williams

Enclosed: one envelope

82. M. Aerova, "Report about Situation in the United Auto Workers, CIO," 8 June 1944, RTsKhIDNI 515–1–4096.

Document 72

T. Ryan to Dimitrov, 1 April 1941, RTsKhIDNI 495–74–477. Original in English. Handwritten. This cover letter lists eight reports by title. A ninth report, entitled "The Political Situation in the U.S.A. and the Work and Tasks of the C.P. USA," is discussed in the letter but the title is not given. The reports themselves are in RTsKhIDNI 515–1–4091.

2 IV 1941 [partially illegible stamp]   April 1—

Dear Comrade Dimitrov—

I have prepared the following special reports and memoranda for the Secretariat which is now being translated:—

1. The organizational position of the CPUSA and the status of our press and publishing activities.

2. The mass work and organizational status of the YCL.

3. The program, activities and status of the American Peace Mobilization and some of the immediate tasks confronting our Party in the anti war movement.

4. The situation and re-alignments within the CIO.

5. Notes on the Farmer-Labor Party Question

6. The work of the Party among the national groups.

7. The activities and strength of the Socialists, Lovestone-ites and Trotsky-ites.

8. Developments within the American Federation of Labor.

I intend to include some of this material in my report to the Presidium, at least the main political points and conclusions. The other sections of my report to the Presidium will deal chiefly with the following questions: a) the extent of America's involvement in the war, and the imperialist aims of, as well as the differences among the bourgeoisie; b) the growth of political reaction and the drive to establish a more reactionary regime in the USA; c) the transition to a war economy and some of the effects of this on the masses; d) the demagogy and methods by which Administration and the bourgeoisie endeavor to deceive, influence and shackle the labor and progressive movements. The rest of the report will deal primarily with the growth of the economic struggle and the principles [? word unclear] anti war movement, and in this connection with the work and tasks of our Party (this section will be based on the special material already prepared for the Secretariat)

I wish you would inform me whether in addition to the special and supplementary reports which I have already prepared for the Secretariat you also want to have my report to the Presidium translated in advance.

Comradely,
T. Ryan

Morris Childs and the 1948 Presidential Election

After the war, the Soviets and the CPUSA resumed their exchange of delegates. In March 1947 Moscow hosted a conference of the foreign ministers of the Soviet Union, Great Britain, and the United States. The Soviets, who strictly limited the number of Western journalists in the USSR, admitted a Western press contingent for a short time to cover the conference. One of these was Morris Childs, chief editor of the *Daily Worker* and a member of the CPUSA national committee. Childs was present as more than a journalist, however.

While in Moscow, Childs held a series of meetings with officials of the Foreign Policy Department of the Central Committee of the CPSU during which he briefed Soviet officials on the CPUSA's activities and organization.[83] **Documents 73, 74, and 75 are three** of a series of memoranda prepared by the Foreign Policy Department regarding Childs's briefings. In document 73, whose cover letter shows that copies went to Stalin, Molotov, Andrei Zhdanov, Lavrenti Beria, and other senior Soviet government leaders, Childs reported on what the American diplomats and journalists were saying among themselves during the negotiations with the Soviets. Providing this kind of low-level diplomatic information was a routine task of Communist journalists.[84] Childs was, in effect, an informer; he did not deliver stolen documents, but as an American with access to "Americans only" gatherings of diplomats and journalists, he provided the Soviets with background, nuances of meaning, and confirmation of what they learned through formal, direct diplomatic exchanges.

83. The Foreign Policy Department, formerly the Department of International Information, assumed control of the remnants of the Comintern. It was later renamed the Foreign Relations Department and finally became the International Department of the CPSU.

84. During World War II, Janet Ross ("Janet Weaver"; the wife of Nat Ross), Moscow correspondent for the *Daily Worker,* provided the Comintern with lengthy reports on what was discussed in "Americans only" briefings and social gatherings to which she, as an American journalist, was invited. John Gibbons, a British Communist correspondent in Moscow, provided similar reports to the Comintern about the informal gatherings of British diplomats. See Klehr, Haynes, and Firsov, *Secret World of American Communism,* 286–91. Zhdanov headed both the CPSU's Foreign Affairs Department and its Agitation and Propaganda Department; Beria was the head of the KGB.

Document 74 concerns a briefing in which Childs reported to Soviet officials on the Communist role in the American labor movement, explaining the political dilemma American Communists faced as they approached the 1948 presidential election. As President Truman hardened his stance on the Soviet Union, opposing Stalin's foreign policy goals, American Communists could no longer support a Truman-led Democratic Party. In 1946 Eugene Dennis, who had replaced Browder as CPUSA general secretary, had devised a two-track policy, in which the CPUSA would work for a national left-of-center third party in 1948 while keeping open the option of supporting a left-liberal challenge to Truman within the Democratic Party.

Communists had therefore decided to support the candidacy of Henry Wallace, Roosevelt's former vice president and Truman's secretary of commerce. In September 1946 Wallace had advocated that the United States recognize a Soviet sphere of influence in Eastern Europe, for which Truman had fired him. Wallace then decided to run for president, claiming to be Roosevelt's true heir, but he and his backers were unsure of whether he should challenge Truman within the Democratic Party or run a third-party campaign.

The CPUSA thought it had a way out of the dilemma: Ask Moscow. As shown in document 74, Childs spoke with B. Vronsky, a section chief of the CPSU Foreign Policy Department, requesting the party's "opinion on the creation of a third party." Document 75 is a memo commenting on document 74 that is written by A. Paniushkin, deputy director of the Foreign Policy Department and Vronsky's superior. Paniushkin suggested answers to the questions Childs had raised in his meeting with Vronsky. With regard to the key matter of whether to form a third party, Paniushkin noted cautiously that a successful third-party effort would require united labor and "progressive" backing. The CPUSA ought, therefore, to "struggle for unity of action of all progressive forces. . . . Resolving the problem of creating a third party depends on that."

Paniushkin also suggested solutions to two other problems Childs had raised in document 74. In accordance with Soviet policy, during the period of the Nazi-Soviet Pact, the CPUSA had characterized the war as imperialist and had opposed U.S. aid to

Britain. Only after Germany attacked the Soviet Union did the CPUSA proclaim it a just war of defense. The CPUSA leadership was concerned because Stalin had recently referred to World War II as having been "from the very start . . . an anti-fascist war of liberation." Childs reported that although the American Communists agreed with Stalin's current view, they needed advice from Moscow on whether the CPUSA should publicly "acknowledge the party's error." Paniushkin suggested that the Americans make their own decision about when and how to admit their mistake.

The second problem concerned international disputes. The CPUSA, noted Childs, "adheres to a position of automatically following the policy of foreign Communist parties." But the Americans were uncertain about what they should do when two foreign Communist parties disagreed, as when the Italian and Yugoslav parties held conflicting attitudes about whether the city of Trieste should be Italian or Yugoslav. Paniushkin declared that the American party was not required to take sides in every dispute around the world.

In document 75 Paniushkin also asked Zhdanov and Aleksei Aleksandrovich Kuznetsov, his superiors in the CPSU Foreign Policy Department, for instructions "regarding Morris Childs's request to meet with comrades from the leadership of the CC of the AUCP(b) and likewise regarding a statement of our point of view on the issues he has raised." We have found no documents that refer to the resolution of these issues, but it is unlikely that Childs received much direction from Moscow. At that time Soviet policy was in a period of transition. We do know that in June 1947, shortly after Childs returned to the United States, the national committee of the CPUSA met to discuss party policy on the election. On the basis of the chief political reports, delivered by John Gates and Eugene Dennis, the CPUSA decided to continue with its two-track strategy.[85]

Philip Jaffe, in 1947 a close ally of the Communists who consulted frequently with party leadership, related what he had heard of Childs's trip in his book *The Rise and Fall of American Commu-*

85. John Gates, "The 80th Congress and Perspectives for 1948," and Eugene Dennis, "Concluding Remarks at the Plenum," *Political Affairs* 28 (August 1947): 716–29, 688–700.

nism (1975).[86] According to Jaffe, Childs reported that he had met with Solomon Lozovsky, former head of the Profintern and current director of the Soviet Information Bureau (a subsection of the Foreign Policy Department), as well as a member of the Central Committee of the CPSU. Lozovsky apparently urged caution in pursuing the third-party option and warned against precipitating a break with the leadership of the CIO. This accords with the tone of Paniushkin's memo. And the meeting with Lozovsky may have been the result of Childs's request for a meeting with a responsible CPSU official.

Childs also reported, according to Jaffe, that Lozovsky spoke approvingly of Yevgeny S. Varga's *Changes in the Economics of Capitalism as a Result of the Second World War* (1946). Varga was the head of Moscow's Institute of World Economy and World Politics and a leading Soviet authority on economics and ideology. In his book he argued that because of the destruction of European industry, the chief source of war—capitalist overproduction and competition for markets—was temporarily absent. True, the United States would face overproduction, but with Europe suffering from underproduction, the obvious remedy was for Americans to send capital to Europe to support the rebuilding of European industry. Varga also suggested that the economies of East European nations would remain capitalist in character and tied to West European markets for a long time.

Unfortunately for Childs, events in the Soviet Union had moved swiftly between his visit in March and the June meeting of the party leadership. Stalin was in the process of shifting his foreign policy, becoming more confrontational. Varga's book, which seemed to accept American economic domination of Europe, did not fit well with Stalin's new stance. In May, Soviet leaders launched an ideological attack on Varga for having failed to take a Stalinist position on the international situation. The CPSU ordered that Varga's institute merge with another Soviet agency, and Varga himself was sent to his native Hungary to take up a minor position in the new Communist regime there.

86. Philip J. Jaffe, *The Rise and Fall of American Communism* (New York: Horizon Press, 1975), 87–135. Jaffe relates that his own break with the party came toward the latter half of 1947.

Then, in September, Moscow organized the Communist Information Bureau (Cominform) at a conference of European Communist parties held at Szklarska, Poland. Zhdanov dominated the meeting, and his speech gave the organization its policy line. Zhdanov proclaimed that the time had come for "the division of the political forces operating in the international arena into two main camps—the imperialist and anti-democratic camp on the one hand and the anti-imperialist and democratic camp on the other. The main, leading force of the imperialist camp is the U.S.A. . . . The anti-imperialist and anti-fascist forces constitute the other camp. The U.S.S.R. and the countries of the new democracy [Eastern Europe] constitute the mainstay of that camp."[87]

Although it is sometimes treated as a resurrected Comintern, the Cominform had a narrower scope. While the Comintern supervised Communist movements throughout the world in order to achieve world revolution, the Cominform had a limited membership and its chief role was to be an anti–Marshall Plan agency, a mechanism for Soviet coordination of attacks by East and West European Communist parties on Truman's European economic recovery program.[88] Moscow did not invite the CPUSA to the Cominform's founding conference, and it never joined.

Varga's fall, along with the increasingly belligerent statements from Moscow, convinced CPUSA leaders that Childs had talked to the wrong people. He was fired from his job as editor of the *Daily Worker*. Once the news reached the United States of the formation of the Cominform and Zhdanov's attack on the Marshall Plan, the CPUSA leaders abandoned their two-track policy. In the fall of 1947 the CPUSA agitated for the establishment of a third party, even at the cost of a break with CIO leaders who opposed such a move.

We have located no documents that demonstrate that Moscow ordered the CPUSA directly to support the creation of a third party

87. A. A. Zhdanov, "On the International Situation," *Political Affairs* 28 (December 1947): 1095–96.

88. Present at the founding conference were delegates from the Communist parties of Czechoslovakia, Poland, Yugoslavia, Bulgaria, Hungary, Romania, France, Italy, and the USSR. It appears that the CPSU did not inform the other parties that they were there to create a new international Communist body. Nonetheless, all agreed to the Soviet agenda.

in the 1948 election. Documents 74 and 75 show only that the CPUSA asked for such direction, not that it was forthcoming. From all indications, the fluctuation in Soviet policy meant that Childs received only advice that left American strategy unresolved. The CPUSA finally shifted policy in response to its interpretation of Moscow's actions in the Varga controversy and the organization of the Cominform. In the absence of direct instructions, American Communist leaders nonetheless looked to Moscow. As Childs had reported, the CPUSA had a policy of "automatically following" the direction indicated by foreign Communist parties.[89]

After Childs's 1947 visit, person-to-person consultations between the CPUSA and the Soviets ceased until 1951, when the CPUSA sent an emissary to Moscow. Joseph Starobin, a senior party official who was supervising the CPUSA's "peace" activities, traveled to Moscow with a series of questions on issues that the CPUSA wanted guidance on; his purpose was also to answer whatever questions the Soviets might have.[90] Starobin's journey was the signal for resuming such trips to Moscow. One of those who became a regular liaison and courier was Morris Childs, but this time, as we have seen, Childs, along with his brother, Jack, was acting as an FBI informant. Over the course of nearly two decades Childs made fifty-two trips, carrying Soviet subsidies, consulting with Soviet leaders, transmitting information and instructions—and reporting to the FBI.

89. Joseph Starobin, at one time a senior CPUSA official and later a historian of the movement, commented that during the period when American Communists were cut off from direct contact with Moscow, they "maintained their allegiance to the international movement by a form of political telepathy" (Joseph R. Starobin, *American Communism in Crisis, 1943–1957* [Cambridge: Harvard University Press, 1972], 214).

90. Ibid., 214–19.

Document 73

Paniushkin to Stalin, Molotov, Zhdanov, Beria, Mikoyan, Malenkov, Vosnesensky, Kuznetsov, 2 April 1947, enclosing B. Vronsky, "Conversation with the Editor-in-Chief of the *Daily Worker* and Politburo Member Morris Childs," RTsKhIDNI 17–128–1128. Original in Russian. Childs was actually a member of the CPUSA National Committee, not the Politburo.

Top Secret

To Comrade I. V. STALIN
Comrade V. M. MOLOTOV
Comrade A. A. ZHDANOV
Comrade L. P. BERIA
Comrade A. I. MIKOYAN
Comrade G. M. MALENKOV
Comrade N. A. VOZNESENSKY
Comrade A. A. KUZNETSOV

The Foreign Policy Department of the CC of the AUCP(b) is sending you a record of the conversation between departmental sector head Comrade Vronsky and the editor-in-chief of the newspaper the "Daily Worker" and a member of the National Council (Politburo) of the CPUSA, Morris Childs.

Enclosure: the above-mentioned.

Deputy Head of the
CC of the AUCP(b)   (A. Paniushkin)

"2" April 1947
P–25–823

[enclosed document]

Top Secret

CONVERSATION WITH THE EDITOR-IN-CHIEF OF THE "DAILY WORKER" AND POLITBURO MEMBER MORRIS CHILDS

On 1 April of this year Morris Childs announced that since our last meeting on 26 March substantial changes have occurred in the attitudes of the American delegation at the session of the Council of Foreign Ministers. In their assessments of the results of the session's work, certain people sounded pessimistic notes. To bear out this opinion, Childs reported on the American and English reporters' initial preparations for departure from Moscow. The American reporters received special forms to fill out on their departure, with questions about their route back to the U.S., how much baggage they have, etc. The

263

English reporters received instructions to be ready to leave Moscow by 6 April, but sometime later another order came that they should be ready to leave on 12 April.

Childs reported further that there is not complete unanimity with the American delegation about how postwar Germany should be structured. Republican delegation member [John] Dulles is carrying out his party's policy, which, as is well known, is against the creation of a unified Germany. But Dulles's very frank position is encountering expected opposition from Marshall, who "as former chief of staff of the American army, is not accustomed to being dictated to." In addition, Marshall looks on Dulles with hostility because Dulles could replace him, Marshall, in the position of U.S. secretary of state, if the Republicans are victorious in the 1948 presidential election. Marshall cannot sign a single document without Dulles's authorization, however, since such a document would not be approved by the U.S. Congress, where the Republicans are in the majority. All of this, apparently, has caused tension between Marshall and Dulles. Not only do they not meet privately, but they avoid each other in public places as well—for example, at the end of last week, when Dulles was absent from a reception at the American Embassy. But Dulles emphasizes his friendly relations with General Mark Clark and often meets with him privately.

As to Harold Stassen's trip to the USSR, Childs reported that Americans in Moscow ascribed considerable significance to this visit. But talk among reporters for the most part centers on whether Stassen will be received by Comrade Stalin. They say that for the U.S. this issue is assuming particularly great importance. They believe that if Comrade Stalin receives Stassen while Secretary of State Marshall is in Moscow, regardless of the reasons motivating Comrade Stalin to do so (keeping in mind here Marshall's refusal to take the initiative to meet with Comrade Stalin), this would be seen in the U.S. as a challenge to official U.S. policy. The American people would not understand the motivation for such a step.

B. Vronsky (B. Vronsky)

"2" April 1947

Document 74

B. Vronsky, "Conversations with CPUSA Politburo Member Morris Childs," RTsKhIDNI 17–128–1128. This undated document was transmitted with document 75, which is dated 10 April 1947. Original in Russian. For the background of the "new CPUSA leadership" dispute and the revival of the Communist party, see chapter 1.

Top Secret

CONVERSATIONS WITH CPUSA POLITBURO MEMBER MORRIS CHILDS

In conversations taking place between 26 March and 1 April of this year, Childs noted the high cost of living buffeting a large part of the U.S. population. According to his figures, the cost of living has increased by 43 percent since 1939. He also reported on an increase in wealth among entrepreneurs. Since 1945, workers' wages have increased by 40 percent, while industrialists' profits have risen by 240 percent.

And nonetheless, he says, in recent months the strike movement has been waning. Childs cites the following reasons: 1) strong propaganda stating that workers receive sufficiently high wages, which, incidentally, workers believe; 2) the anti-worker legislative campaign, which workers perceive as a threat; 3) fear among trade union leaders that strikes could further intensify reaction against trade unions. For this reason trade unions are avoiding strikes and are negotiating with entrepreneurs. He says that the Communist party is waging an educational campaign in this regard, but without success.

According to Childs, establishing unity of action between the CIO and the AFL is the CPUSA's main concern. This position became clearly defined after the AFL leadership changed its views on the possibility of merging these two trade union centers. Previously, the AFL had wanted the CIO simply to return to the AFL without any sort of autonomy and with the industrial trade unions' being disbanded. At the present time these conditions are no longer being put forth, and for that reason "organic unity" between the two groups could be realized on an equal basis.

Our motto, said Childs, is Unity of Action in the workers' movement, and we are doing everything possible to achieve such unity. Specifically, without waiting for a resolution of that question at the higher levels of the CIO and the AFL, we are trying to realize it practically in the local organizations, creating unified committees of trade organizations as a part of the AFL and the CIO, in order to fight anti-worker legislation. We have managed to accomplish this in Chicago, Seattle, and other cities.

The main obstacle to achieving unity of action in the workers' movement is not at the lower levels but at the upper ones. Recently, there was a schism in the AFL leadership over this issue. [John L.] Lewis and [William] Hutcheson, members of the AFL executive committee, spoke in favor of unity of action with the CIO, and two other members of the executive committee, [Matthew] Woll and [David] Dubinsky, spoke out against this. As a result of the discus-

265

sion, most of the members of the executive committee ended up on the side of Lewis and Hutcheson. Another obstacle to achieving unification is the personal relationship between Lewis and [Philip] Murray (CIO representative) which has practically made them into irreconcilable enemies.

On the other hand, there is no unity in the CIO leadership itself. There is a left wing, a right wing, and a center headed by Murray. The right grouping is dominant in the CIO leadership and thereby exerts a strong influence on Murray. In addition, it is very closely linked with the AFL leadership, which in turn strengthens its position in the workers' movement. CPUSA policy on this issue is to provide for the unification of the left grouping with Murray's center and thus tear control of the CIO leadership from the hands of the right. "But," says Childs, "we are not yet strong enough to help Murray do this now."

The problem of uniting the independent progressive forces and creating a third, anti-monopolist party is extremely important. But the CPUSA leadership makes a distinction between the progressive movement and the creation of a third party. Childs says that the movement to create a third party is not as broad as the progressive movement. In addition, at the present time such prominent and influential people as Wallace, Pepper, Taylor, Murray, and others are speaking out against the creation of a third party. And without these people's participation, a third party would be extremely narrow. For this reason the leadership of the CPUSA is not setting itself the task of creating a third party at the present time if Wallace, Pepper, Murray, and others are not going to participate. Childs believes that promoting a third candidate for president in 1948 could be the beginning of the creation of a third party.

In answer to a question about what forces would promote a third candidate, Childs answered that the progressive forces could do this. The Communist party is carefully preparing for the upcoming elections, creating its own party machine and conducting work in this direction within progressive organizations, etc. To a subsequent question about whether the progressive movement's lack of a unified center, a unified plan of battle against reaction, carefully coordinated tactics, and the like would not reflect badly on the progressive movement, Childs answered that this was so, but that right now it was scarcely possible to achieve these things.

Childs began his account of the internal party situation with Jacques Duclos's article in "Cahiers du communisme," which, he declared, had shaken up all of them, mostly because they had thought that the policy they were following was the correct policy. At this time two French Communists were in Washington, one of whom was, as he remembered, [François] Billoux. Foster and Dennis went to see them in Washington in order to get additional information on this issue, since the criticism of the CPUSA was coming from the French Communist party leadership. But, naturally, the French Communists could give them no additional information.

Speaking of the new CPUSA leadership, Childs reported that with few exceptions, the leadership of the party consists of the same people as before, when Browder was heading it. Foster, Dennis, [John] Williamson, [Robert] Thompson, [Ben] Davis, [Elizabeth Gurley] Flynn, [Jack] Stachel, and others are members of the Politburo and occupy the same posts as under Browder. There are only a few people—[Irving] Potash, [Louis] Weinstock, [Bill] Lawrence, and others—who are new members of the CPUSA Politburo, but they do not play any noticeable role in the leadership and are often absent from the Politburo meetings.

Childs continued that when the Communist party was first being revived, there was clear mistrust and suspicion among members of the leadership. All of this passed with time. After the Communist party leadership became more stable, a decision was made to change its structure. With the revival of the Communist party, Foster was elected first secretary, Dennis became second secretary, etc. Recently, a decision was made to create the position of chairman of the National Committee of the Communist party and general secretary of the National Committee of the Communist party. Foster was elected chairman and Dennis was elected general secretary. The adoption of this structure was dictated by the fact that Foster considers himself too old and feeble to carry out the tremendous and complex tasks required of the first secretary. Childs added that at the present time Dennis is carrying out the main work of leading the party. He does political reports and briefings, develops major proposals, and handles all ongoing issues.

Childs reported further that between the ruling Politburo group (Foster, Dennis, Williamson, et al.) on the one hand and individual members of the Politburo (Stachel, Thompson, Davis) on the other, certain disagreements exist.[1] He emphasized several times that these disagreements do not have to do with the general party line. They have to do, for the most part, with issues of the strike movement, which certain members of the Politburo wanted to provoke artificially, or with the question of the attitude within the CIO toward Murray and his centrist grouping, or, finally, with the question of creating a third party. Still, Childs emphasized, even on these issues decisions have always been made unanimously.

Further, Childs gave a brief description of the party groupings, consisting of dissatisfied and hostile party elements. Childs named six such groups that are waging a struggle against the party from the left as well as the right (the Darcy group, Ruth [McKenney], [Lyle] Dowling, [Verne] Smith, the California and New York group and the sailors' group). All of these groups speak under their own name ("the Information Committee," etc.) and present their own programs. For example, Darcy's group has a program that requires the study of Marxism based only on the works of Marx and Engels but not on those of Lenin and Stalin. The California group's program is founded on the American Trotskyists' program, etc.

The membership of these groups is not large, from six people (the sailors) to fifty (the Californians). According to Dennis's information, which he passed on to Childs before the latter flew to Moscow, these groups comprise around two hundred people. This, of course, is not a large number, but the point is that all of them, or almost all of them, used to occupy important positions. Most of them have been excluded from the party; the others also, apparently, will be excluded in the near future.

The American Trotskyists, especially Cannon's group in California, the largest in the U.S., are appealing to these groups and attempting to establish contact with them and through them to infiltrate Communist organizations in order to rupture them from within.

In response to a question about Browder, Childs said that he and Dennis agreed not to raise that question here in Moscow, "but since you ask, I'll answer." Lecturing and giving reports at meetings and rallies, Browder is trying not to discuss issues having to do with the American party, but when that becomes impossible, he gets off the hook with one phrase: "I have been excluded from the party." The general opinion is that in acting this way, Browder is not helping the Communist party. Foster goes further in this regard, asserting that Browder is not only not helping, he is in fact harming the party. But no one shares this opinion.

Answering another question about the conditions for growth of the CPUSA and the strengthening of its position, Childs said that if the bill banning the party is not passed, the reactionaries may pass legislation strongly limiting the party's activity.

In a conversation on 1 April, Childs again returned to this issue and emphasized that the general threatening position of the CPUSA is being aggravated by Foster's prolonged absence (it seems that he is presently in Belgrade). Childs feels that Foster is needed in the U.S. now more than ever before. The thing is, Childs said, that the general secretary of the National Committee of the CPUSA, Eugene Dennis, is in a dangerous position for a number of reasons. He was born under a different name, Francis Waldron, which could serve as one reason for harassment. In addition, he could be charged with disloyalty to the U.S. in view of his past activity abroad. In any case, says Childs, he could be put in prison for a couple of years, if the commission investigating so-called American activity receives information which compromises Dennis.

In Childs's opinion, such a situation keeps Dennis from acting with full authority as party leader. Foster is the only one who can speak forcefully on behalf of the party and the working class. There is no other such person in the party. "I don't understand," Childs said, "why Foster is staying on in Europe. His place now is in the U.S." In addition Childs declared that if he were in contact with Foster, he would feel it necessary to remind him of this.

As regards growth in the party ranks, Childs reported that by 1 January 1947 we had 62,000 Communists through re-registration. In the past three months the party ranks have increased by approximately 5,000 and thus comprise about 67,000 people. Progress, Childs observed, is slow, but by September 1947, we count on having 100,000 people in our ranks.

Childs posed several questions to which he would like answers.

1. What is (our) opinion on the creation of a third party if Wallace, Pepper, Murray, and others refuse to participate in this at the present time?

2. What is the opinion on CPUSA policy regarding the unification of the left wing of the CIO with Murray and his supporters (the center)?

3. What is the best use to which the growing progressive movement can be put in the upcoming U.S. presidential campaign?

4. Comrade Stalin has explained that from the very start this war assumed the character of an antifascist war of liberation. This instruction has bearing on the CPUSA, which until Hitler's attack on the USSR regarded this as an imperialist war and acted accordingly. We have discussed this issue among ourselves and agree with Comrade Stalin's opinion. But while we agree with Comrade Stalin, we have not yet acknowledged publicly that we were previously in error. So we come off as if we are hushing up this mistake of the party. And insofar as in the eyes of public opinion the party has not taken a definite position on this important issue, enemies of the party are using this as a weapon against us. Does it make sense to speak out at the present time on this issue and acknowledge the party's error? (Childs is in favor of this, as he feels that this would tear the weapon from the hands of the party's enemies.)

5. In the area of international relations the CPUSA adheres to a position of automatically following the policy of foreign Communist parties. Childs elucidated this through the example of how the problem of Trieste was handled. Not only did Yugoslavia and Italy have divergent views on resolving this problem, but the Yugoslavian and Italian Communist parties did as well. The American Communist party found it necessary to speak out on this issue and supported the Yugoslavian Communist party. To what degree is this tendency to get involved in resolving controversial problems between various Communist parties helpful or detrimental, insofar as in many countries the latter embrace a national position?

* * * * * *

Childs said, as if in passing, that he would be immensely pleased and grateful if a meeting for him could be organized with the comrades in the leadership of the CC of the AUCP(b), meaning, in all likelihood, the Central Committee secretaries.

(B. Vronsky)

sent 3 cop.
lk, mp

Document 74 *continued*

1. [Footnote to original document]: Judging by the reluctance and reserve with which Childs spoke of disagreements in the Politburo, one could conclude that Dennis, with whom he discussed which issues he could bring up here, did not give him permission to mention them.

Document 75

Paniushkin to Zhdanov and Kuznetsov, 10 April 1947, RTsKhIDNI 17–128–1128. Original in Russian.

TO SECRETARY OF THE CC OF THE AUCP(B)
Comrade A. A. ZHDANOV

TO SECRETARY OF THE CC OF THE AUCP(B)
Comrade A. A. KUZNETSOV

I am sending you a record of conversations between sector head of the Foreign Policy Department of the CC of the AUCP(b) Comrade Vronsky and CPUSA National Council (Politburo) member Morris Childs.

Morris Childs posed several questions on which he would like to have the opinion of the CC of the AUCP(b). In particular, he would like to know our opinion on the question of creating a third independent progressive party. It seems to us that in the U.S. the conditions are not yet in place to create such a party at the present time. One of the main obstacles to this step is that unity of action is lacking in the workers' movement. As is well known, unity of action is lacking not only between the two main U.S. trade union centers—the Congress of Industrial Organizations (CIO) and the American Federation of Labor (AFL)—but inside these organizations as well.

The leaders of the AFL and the CIO are speaking out against the creation of a third party. Many influential liberal-progressive figures, including Wallace, Pepper, Taylor, and others, are also speaking out against the creation of such a party at the present time.

We must also take into account that the CPUSA has little influence in American society to resolve this problem on its own, without making use of these forces. It is perfectly obvious that if such a party were created, it would not receive broad support among workers' and progressive organizations and would not be successful in its struggle against the powerful political parties—Democratic and Republican. The apparent task of the CPUSA at the present time is to struggle for unity of action of all progressive forces and above all for unity of action in the workers' movement. And resolving the problem of creating a third party depends on that.

Document 75 *continued*

This may serve as an answer to Morris Childs's next two questions, regarding establishing unity of action in the CIO leadership and using the progressive forces in the upcoming electoral campaign.

Regarding the erroneous assessment of World War II as imperialist, it is perfectly obvious that the leaders of the CPUSA should be guided by the relevant instructions of Comrade Stalin. The leadership of the CPUSA itself ought to choose the form and the time to state its position on the question of assessing World War II, proceeding from an account of the current conditions in the country.

As to the CPUSA's position regarding international events, the party leadership should take into account the national character of its party, which is faced with its own enormous and complex tasks. We believe that it is absolutely not required that the CPUSA respond to all disputes and dissension that arise from time to time in various parts of the world.

Please provide instructions regarding Morris Childs's request to meet with comrades from the leadership of the CC of the AUCP(b) and likewise regarding a statement of our point of view on the issues he has raised.

Deputy Head
of Central Committee Division
of the AUCP(b)   (A. Paniushkin)

"10" April 1947
25–P–907

CHAPTER FOUR

Imported Hatred

COMMUNISTS WERE IDEALISTS, but idealists who combined their dream of a socialist tomorrow, in which perfect justice would reign, with a violent loathing of anything that threatened that future. Communists did not disagree with or disapprove of their opponents, they despised them. In 1929 the Communist poet Edwin Rolfe called on American Communists to develop a language with "the power to hate." Most did. The Communist historian Herbert Aptheker, for example, described the upper classes of American society as having "the morals of goats, the learning of gorillas and the ethics of—well, of what they are: racist, war-inciting enemies of humanity, rotten to the core, parasitic, merciless." The United States itself, Aptheker added, was "so putrid . . . that it no longer dares permit the people to live at all."[1]

Such expressions of loathing do not make American Communists unusual in American history. Many indigenous movements have demonized their opponents. The Communists differed, however, in the extent to which their hatred was imported. That they or other radicals hated capitalism or the established order is not sur-

1. Edwin Rolfe, *New Masses* 4 (April 1929): 21; Herbert Aptheker, "Hustlers for War," *Masses and Mainstream* 2 (May 1949): 27; Aptheker, *History and Reality* (New York: Cameron Associates, 1955), 112.

prising. The inequities of the capitalist system, the ruthlessness with which strikes were frequently put down, and the sense radicals had that the state had targeted them were reason enough for hatred: one need not look for a foreign source. But the fierce attacks made by American Communists on "Trotskyism" and "Bukharinist Right Opportunism" had little to do with social or political conditions in the United States and much to do with the ties between the American Communist movement and the Soviet Union. There is nothing in American history that explains why, when the Soviet Union executed thousands of Trotskyists, American Communists cheered them on, yet the following pronouncement from the *Young Worker* (the journal of the Young Communist League) is typical: "As for those who plotted the crippling of Soviet industry and Soviet farming and planned to have the only workers['] country ruled by the lords of money again—to them *DEATH! THIS SHOULD BE THE MESSAGE OF EVERY YOUNG WORKER TO OUR ENEMY CLASS, THE BOSSES OF THE WORLD.*"[2]

This murderous hatred toward the designated enemies of the Soviet Union can be explained by the conviction that stood at the core of American communism: that, as the Communist poet Tillie Olsen described it, Stalin's Soviet Union was "a heaven . . . brought to earth in 1917 in Russia."[3] American Communists wanted that heaven to include the United States and sought to destroy whatever threatened their goal.

The archives of the Comintern and the CPUSA in the RTsKhIDNI contain thousands of pages devoted to campaigns waged by American Communists against ideological enemies who barely existed on American soil. Neither Trotsky's followers in the United States nor those who adhered to the Bukharinist "right opposition" of Jay Lovestone seriously threatened the supremacy of the CPUSA within the American Left. At their peak, American Trotskyists made up only a few thousand and Lovestoneites only a

2. "Death Penalty Demanded!" *Young Worker,* 27 November 1930, 4, quoted in Aileen S. Kraditor, *Jimmy Higgins: The Mental World of the American Rank-and-File Communist, 1930–1958* (Westport, Conn.: Greenwood Press, 1988), 62–63. Kraditor has an extended discussion on the function of enmity in the American Communist mindset (59–77).

3. T. Lerner [Tillie Olsen], "I Want You Women Up North to Know," *Partisan* 1 (March 1934): 4.

few hundred members of the Left.[4] The membership of the CPUSA outnumbered these Communist dissidents by a ratio of at least twenty to one and often much more. Further, the CPUSA received generous Soviet subsidies, while the dissidents were self-support-ing—and the dues of their handful of members did not go far. Usually the CPUSA's paid cadre was larger than the entire member-ship of the Trotskyist organization. (It was *always* larger than the Lovestoneite organization.) Yet American Communists attacked these ideological opponents—products of an internal struggle for power within the Soviet Communist party—with a viciousness that mirrored Stalin's paranoia, rather than their own situation.

Early Training in Ideological Conformity

Document 76 shows an early instance of American Communists' acceptance of Moscow's ideological enemies. In 1925 the Com-intern denounced S. Bubnik of the Czechoslovak Communist party, Heinrich Brandler of the German Communist party, and Ludwig Lore of the American party for ideological heresies. In each case the denunciations were by-products of internal Soviet struggles, as Joseph Stalin, Grigory Zinoviev, and Nikolai Buk-harin sought to discredit Leon Trotsky.[5] The American party,

4. In brief, Trotsky argued that communism depended on worldwide prole-tarian revolution; the true Bolshevik did not compromise with capitalism. Trotsky-ists saw themselves as pure revolutionaries who embodied an uncompromised Marxism-Leninism. American Trotskyists were led by James Cannon, a founding member of the American Communist party who was expelled in 1928. Stalinists defined Trotskyism as a left deviation; they saw Bukharinism as a right deviation. Bukharin supported the New Economic Program, which allowed private business to play a restricted role in Soviet society, and opposed Stalin's plans for forced collec-tivization of agriculture and industrialization through the quasi-military mobiliza-tion of workers. Jay Lovestone was accused of supporting Bukharin's right devia-tion because he had been an admirer of Bukharin's. Lovestone was also accused of the ideological crime of "American exceptionalism": the view that the United States differed socially and politically from Europe and that Communist policies should accommodate those differences. Lovestone was expelled from the CPUSA in 1929.

5. Lore was not a Trotskyist, although his ultra-leftist stance resembled that of Trotsky. Brandler, however, had headed the wing of the German Communist party that was critical of Trotsky's ultra-revolutionary stance. Brandler was vulnerable because under his leadership the German party had failed at an armed insurrection in late 1923. The entire Comintern leadership had supported the insurrection, but after its failure, Trotsky's Soviet enemies decided to blame the failure on him. Bubnik was also opposed to an ultra-revolutionary position. He and a small group of his supporters later left the Communist movement and joined the Socialist Party.

whose leaders knew little of Brandler and less of Bubnik, endorsed the Comintern's position without reservations and expelled Lore and his followers. Document 76 is the report the Workers Party of America (American Communist party) sent to Zinoviev, endorsing the actions against Bubnik and Brandler and announcing Lore's removal from the party leadership. He was later expelled. The American Communist leaders explain why Lore's followers will go along: Lore "practically eliminated himself from serious consideration because he failed to go to Moscow and defend himself and his views before . . . the Comintern." This statement reflected the assumption—an accurate one—that rank-and-file American Communists accepted Moscow as the sole judge of Communist legitimacy.

Document 76

Excerpt from Workers Party of America to Zinoviev, 22 May 1925, RTsKhIDNI 515–1–423. Original in English, on Workers Party of America letterhead. The *Volkszeitung* was the German-language newspaper of the American Communist party. Carlson is probably Oliver Carlson, the head of the Young Workers League.

WORKERS PARTY OF AMERICA
NATIONAL OFFICE
1113 W. WASHINGTON BLVD., ROOM 301
CHICAGO, ILL.
PHONE MONROE 4714

NATIONAL CHAIRMAN
W. Z. FOSTER
NATIONAL EXECUTIVE SEC'Y-TREAS.
C. E. RUTHENBERG
DIRECTOR LITERATURE DEPARTMENT
N. DOZENBERG
RESEARCH DEPARTMENT
JAY LOVESTONE

"DAILY WORKER"
OFFICIAL DAILY ORGAN

IN CHICAGO BY MAIL $8.00 PER YEAR
OUTSIDE OF CHICAGO 6.00 "   "

May 22, 1925.

Dear Comrade Zinoviev:—

In accordance with your request, I am writing you on the situation in the American Party.

A few days ago we held our first Central Executive Committee meeting after the return of our delegates from Moscow. The C.E.C. heartily endorsed the actions of the Enlarged Executive Committee. The fight against Bubnik in Czecho-Slovakia, Brandler in Germany, Loreism in America, and Trotzkyism throughout the Comintern in general, was supported, together with the program of Bolshevising the various parties. Enclosed find the C.E.C. resolution on the proceedings of the Enlarged Executive Committee meeting.

The C.E.C. has fully accepted the decision on the Labor Party and is already putting it actively into effect. In Pennsylvania, where there is a skeleton labor party, we organized a left bloc and fought for a labor party policy in accordance with the decision of the C.I. We have also adopted an elaborate program for carrying out the Labor Party work throughout the United States. This quick acceptance of the Labor Party decision by the majority of the C.E.C. completely disposes of the unfounded charges that we are sectarian in this matter or opposed to the Labor Party in principle. We will utilize this campaign to the utmost in the building of our Party.

In the matter of Lore, the C.E.C. deemed it advisable to take immediate action. Hence, we adopted the enclosed resolution. This provides for the removal of Lore as editor of the Volkzeitung and his replacement by comrades Carlson and Bedacht, of the C.E.C. majority and minority respectively. It also recommends that Lore be not elected at the next Convention to the Central Executive Committee. In addition, it provides for the reorganization of the bureau of the German Federation on the basis of the latest C.I. decision. The Ruthenberg minority voted for all the resolution[s] regarding Lore excepting those sections removing him from the editorship. Lore himself has announced that he will accept the decision relative to his removal and will appeal it to the Comintern representatives in this country. This action against Lore has naturally provoked considerable opposition from his followers. But the feeling is that he practically eliminated himself from serious consideration because he failed to go to Moscow and defend himself and his views before the Enlarged Executive of the Comintern. It is unlikely that there will be any considerable defections from the Party because of his removal. It is quite possible, however, that we may lose control of the Volkzeitung, which is in the hands of an independent stock corporation.

. . .

After Trotsky was eliminated from the competition to succeed Lenin, the coalition that had defeated him split up. In 1926 Stalin deftly removed another rival by teaming up with Bukharin to oust Zinoviev, who had led the Comintern since its founding in 1919. Back in the United States, the leaders of the American party all owed their positions to Zinoviev's approval. Yet when he lost the factional struggle within the Soviet party, as **document 77** shows, they repudiated him without dissent.

In **document 78** American Communists further accommodate their worldview to that of the Soviet party leaders. Here the American delegation to a Comintern plenum declares its "whole-hearted solidarity" with the Soviet party; the Americans "unreservedly agree" with the condemnation of the "Opposition bloc" led by Zinoviev. Note that in both these documents the American party is not endorsing a *Communist International* position; rather, Americans are specifically adopting an internal factional position of the *Soviet* Communist party.

Document 77

Excerpt from seven-page "Minutes of Plenum of the Central Executive Committee of the Workers (Communist) Party of America," 10–12 November 1926, RTsKhIDNI 515–1–610. Original in English.

. . .

MINUTES OF
PLENUM CEC
11/10,11,12/26   #99   Pg 3

Session—Nov 12.

Discussion on Trade Union Work continued.

After discussion, report was accepted unanimously.

Russian C P

Comrade Bedacht reported on the situation in the C P S U and presented the following resolution for adoption:

The full meeting of the Central Committee of the Workers (Communist) Party notes with great satisfaction the organizational liquidation of the opposition in the C P S U by the last full meeting of the Central Committee and Central Control Committee, and by the 15th conference of that Party.

The Central Committee of the Workers (Communist) Party endorses the resolutions of its Political Committee passed unanimously by that Committee in July and again in October.

With the Political Committee, the Central Committee is of the opinion that on account of the deviation of Comrade Zinoviev from the path of Leninism, with his acceptance of Trotzkyism and his misuse of his official position as president of the ECCI for factional purposes, his further leadership of the ECCI had become impossible.

Document 77 continued

It also holds that our Party can and must help in the liquidation of the un-Leninist theories of the opposition which exist not only in the C P S U but in the whole International and therefore endorses the steps decided upon by the political committee for an ideological mobilization of our Party for the Leninist line of the Comintern and the C P S U.

After discussion, the following vote occurred:

The resolution was adopted unanimously.

. . .

Document 78

Excerpts from five-page "Minutes of Seventh Meeting of American Delegation to the Enlarged Plenum of the E.C.C.I.," 9 December 1926, RTsKhIDNI 515–1–584. Original in English. "CPSU(b)" stands for Communist Party of the Soviet Union (Bolshevik).

MINUTES OF SEVENTH MEETING OF AMERICAN DELEGATION
TO THE ENLARGED PLENUM OF THE E.C.C.I.
December 9, 1926.

Present: Pepper, Duncan, Bittelman, Browder.
Absent: Burch, Zam, Williamson.
Chairman: Pepper.

AGENDA: Continued on proposed statement of Delegation on Russian Party question.

. . .

The final text of the statement reads:
DECLARATION OF THE AMERICAN DELEGATION ON THE QUESTION OF THE
COMMUNIST PARTY OF THE SOVIET UNION.

The delegation of the Workers (Communist) Party of America to the VII Enlarged Plenum of the Executive Committee of the Communist International, declares on behalf of the Central Committee of the Party, as well as on behalf of the whole Party, its whole-hearted solidarity with the results of the XV Party Conference of the Communist Party of the Soviet Union. We unreservedly agree with and support the political line and Leninist leadership of the Central Committee of the CPSU(b), approved unanimously by the XV Party Conference, and are unalterably opposed to the ideology and policies of the Opposition bloc.

Document 78 continued

Our Party opposed from the beginning Trotskyism not only as an international phenomenon, but also in its American variation which was expressed in the gross Social-Democratic deviations of Lore. Our Party deemed it necessary to continue to fight against Trotskyism also when it received the support of the leaders of the new Opposition, Comrades Zinoviev and Kamenev whose platform is a deviation from Leninism and a surrender to Trotskyism. In July and in October and in its last November Plenum our Central Committee condemned severely the new Opposition and the new oppositional bloc as we were convinced that their policies were wrong, and that this Opposition not only imperiled the unity of the CPSU(b), and thereby the dictatorship of the proletariat in the Soviet Republic, but was also detrimental to the most vital and important interests of the proletariat of all countries as well as of our American Party.

The brilliant example of the Communist Party of the Soviet Union is one of the most important sources of inspiration and will to fight of our Party as well as for the class conscious section of the American working class. The Communist Party of America was founded in connection with the mighty wave of enthusiasm called forth by the outbreak of the Russian Revolution. In America (with its scarcity of other revolutionary factors), where capitalism is still on the upward grade, in the country of most powerful imperialism and most reactionary labour aristocracy where independent mass actions of the working class are so few, where the working class has yet no political mass party, the existence of the Soviet Union and the successful building of Socialism within it, play relatively a more important role as revolutionary stimulus to the working class than in other countries where capitalism is declining or which possess a revolutionary tradition. The American Party, therefore, condemned severely and fought against the Russian Opposition the attitude of which is tantamount to a relinquishment of the revolutionary perspective for the Soviet Union.

. . .

The Soviet Union and the Splintering of the American Left

The Comintern Proclaims "Social Fascism" to Be the New Enemy

In the 1920s and 1930s democratic aspirations in Western and Central Europe faced twin threats: fascism on the right and communism on the left. In many nations the social and economic crises that followed World War I put moderate political forces under severe strain; people increasingly feared that the center would not hold, that they would have to choose between competing extremes. Comintern strategies made the most of this developing sense of crisis. Joseph Stalin, in the final stages of establishing himself as Lenin's successor, initiated a sharp turn to the left in Soviet party policy. This 1928 shift, known in Communist parlance as the Third Period, was adopted by the Comintern, which ordered Communists worldwide to drop the united-front policies they had followed since 1921 and adopt a more explicitly radical stance to help usher in the revolutionary era that Stalin had predicted. Communists assumed that soon the only contenders left would be themselves and the fascists.

On the left, however, there were many who disputed the Communist view. The socialist, social democratic, and labor parties of Europe agreed that the West faced a crisis, but they believed that a third way existed, that of democratic socialism. In the United States, this view was most prominently represented by the Socialist Party. In the early 1930s, however, A. J. Muste, a radical Christian clergyman turned labor organizer, advocated yet another leftist path. Muste argued that Americans needed a revolutionary movement that was free from the CPUSA's dogmatism and its subordination to Moscow. He and a group of like-minded militants founded the American Workers Party. But although Muste briefly achieved some influence inside the burgeoning movement for industrial unionism that became the CIO, his political party remained small and soon disappeared.

In Stalin's Third Period there was no room for a third way; people chose either Soviet communism or fascism. To discredit the claim that the democratic left represented another choice, the Comintern developed the concept of "social fascism." Under this view, adherents of the British Labour Party or the Social Democratic Party of Germany were not socialists; they were "social fascists." Their socialist slogans were mere camouflage for programs that would deliver the working class into the hands of the fascists.

Throughout the early 1930s, Comintern directives lectured Americans on the need to combat social fascism. In early 1932 the Comintern sent the CPUSA a "Resolution on the Immediate Questions in the C.P.U.S.A." In it the Comintern exulted that the Depression was destroying America's "petty-bourgeois illusions." American Communists were warned, however, that

> the bourgeoisie resorts widely and systematically to demagogic and "democratic" maneuvers, using more and more the social-democrats, the "Musteites" and the various pseudo "Lefts" as a tool for confusing and disorganizing the workers. . . .
>
> In this situation American social fascism (A.F. of L., Socialist Party, particularly the Muste wing, with Lovestone, Cannon renegades) are greatly increasing their activity to carry out the imperialist policy of the bourgeoisie, trying, by establishing the most skillful, deceptive, division of work, to divert the radicalized workers from the class struggle against the offensive of the capitalists, to split the ranks of the workers and to bring about their defeat. This confronts the Communist Party with the task of increasing, sharpening and improving its fight against social-fascism, as the main enemy in the struggle for the successful mobilization of the masses in the fight against the bourgeois offensive and war danger.[6]

American Communists absorbed the lesson. In 1933 Earl Browder assured Moscow that the CPUSA had repudiated the effort by American progressives and radicals to form a broad center-left farmer-labor movement. Browder dismissed the movement as having been developed by "reformist and social-fascist misleaders"; it was, he claimed, and would "in the future become more so, a chief political instrument of the social-fascists in their struggle against the revolutionizing of the American Working class." He promised that the American Communist party would "overcome the left maneuvers and demagogy of the reformist organizations, of the social-fascist leadership" and would "combat the influence of the social-fascists . . . , to lead [progressives] away from the reformist organizations and to consolidate them in alliance with, and under the leadership of, the revolutionary working class."[7]

In line with Comintern doctrine, American Communists found social fascism everywhere. In its 1933 "Plan of Work for C.P. USA on the Agrarian Field," Communist farm organizers stated that

6. "Resolution on the Immediate Questions in the C.P.U.S.A.," 15 February 1932, RTsKhIDNI 495–3–308.

7. Browder transcript, Comintern Political Secretariat, 13 May 1933, RTsKhIDNI 495–3–375.

"the main political task of the Party in the recent period is to expose [President] Roosevelt's farm program and to prove concretely that its aim is to assist the bankers, insurance companies, marketing trusts and the rich farmers at the expense of the workers, poor, small and the ruined middle farmers." This task was part of "the fight against the Social fascist leadership and the danger of fascist development" and required Communists to "combat the growing farmer labor party tendencies." The CPUSA plan also denounced Milo Reno, the militant head of the Radical Farm Holiday Association in Iowa, and Walter Singler, leader of a dairymen's strike in Wisconsin, as "strike breaking leaders" who must be displaced, although both men were pioneering and successful leaders of farmers' strikes.[8]

The social fascism concept even worked its way into the personal vocabulary of Communists. In 1933 veteran Communist leader J. Louis Engdahl died. His wife, Pauline Engdahl, claimed his personal effects for herself and their children. Louis Engdahl, however, had abandoned his family and was living with Harriet Silverman, a fellow party militant, who also claimed Engdahl's personal property. In a letter to a party official appointed to hear Pauline Engdahl's complaint, Silverman denounced Pauline's claim as being based on "rotten capitalist ideology, hypocrisy and smug self-righteousness that we repudiate. More than that, it has the peculiar quality characteristic of a social-fascist."[9]

The Madison Square Garden Riot

The most dramatic confrontation between American Communists and the so-called social fascists came in 1934. Austria's fascistic Dollfuss regime had dissolved all political parties except its own Fatherland Front in February. In response, the Socialists had barricaded the working-class housing projects of Vienna. Dollfuss crushed the protest with a murderous artillery bombardment of the apartment complexes at which several hundred (Dollfuss's figures) or more than a thousand (Socialists' figures) people were killed.

8. "Plan of Work for C.P. USA on the Agrarian Field," 16 August 1933, RTsKhIDNI 515–1–3166. Singler's name is misspelled "Sinclair" in the document.

9. Harriet [Silverman] to Patterson, 4 February 1933, RTsKhIDNI 515–1–3363. The party decided to split the personal effects between the two women.

The American Socialist Party held a mass meeting in New York's Madison Square Garden to protest the massacre. Approximately 18,000 people went to the rally, at which such luminaries as Matthew Woll, a leading spokesman of the American Federation of Labor, and New York Mayor Fiorello La Guardia were scheduled to speak.

Several thousand CPUSA members attended the meeting, but they had not come to listen. A *Daily Worker* extra edition had appeared on the day of the meeting carrying a front-page editorial denouncing Woll and La Guardia as "agents of fascism" and urging: "Socialist Workers! for the honor of the heroic Austrian workers, do not permit Woll and LaGuardia to besmirch the heroic revolutionary struggles of our Austrian brothers. Woll must not speak at Madison Square Garden today. The wage-cutting, strike-breaking Mayor LaGuardia has no place at a protest meeting for the Austrian proletarian workers. . . . He must not be permitted to speak."[10]

A few of the Communists had come singly to the meeting and were scattered about the arena, but most were seated in organized groups. Many had marched to Madison Square Garden in formation, bearing banners and placards; even a Communist band showed up with its instruments. The ushers, who were Socialists, had let the Communists in but forced them to leave their banners, placards, and musical instruments outside. When the first speakers attempted to address the meeting, the Communists rioted: screaming abuse, they shouted that the Socialists were no better than fascists themselves, and they began fighting with the ushers, who tried to eject them. As the tumult increased, Clarence Hathaway, a member of the CPUSA Political Bureau, mounted the stage and advanced on the podium. Before he could speak, however, the Socialists forcibly removed him from the stage, and the meeting dissolved into chaos. Neither Woll nor La Guardia ever spoke. A mass meeting called by leftists to protest a fascist atrocity against leftists had been broken up not by fascists but by Communists.

Newspapers and journals condemned the Communists' actions, and a few prominent liberals resigned in protest from such Com-

10. *Daily Worker*, 16 February 1934, extra edition.

munist-aligned organizations as the American League against War and Fascism. The American Civil Liberties Union also issued a condemnation, although a mild one, of the Communists.[11] The Socialists were furious; they accused the CPUSA of deliberately disrupting their meeting and Hathaway of attempting to take it over. Hathaway denied the charge, although he admitted that he had been at the arena to oversee Communist activity. He explained that his instructions were to ensure order, and he had mounted the stage to try to calm down the Communists. The CPUSA expressed no regret for the riot, however, and blamed it on Socialist provocation.

Document 79 is a postmortem of the affair by the CPUSA Political Bureau, joined by Gerhart Eisler, the Comintern representative. A few Politburo members saw some positive results in the affair; but it was such a public relations disaster that most of the discussion revolved around what had gone wrong. Charles Krumbein and James Ford suggested (although other leaders disagreed) that having prominent party officials at the rally was a mistake because it made it easy for the press to depict the disruption as a planned Communist party action. Ford specifically noted that having Hathaway present and visibly coordinating Communist activities was probably ill-advised inasmuch as Hathaway was well known as the editor of the *Daily Worker*. (Hathaway was probably the author of the inflammatory editorial quoted above, which demanded that Woll and La Guardia be kept from speaking.) Eisler regarded the rally as a serious defeat for the party, taking satisfaction only in the injuries that Hathaway had suffered when the Socialists had tried to block his advance to the podium, for these made it possible for the Communists to present Hathaway as a martyr.

Robert Minor stated the obvious: "In reality by calling upon the workers not to let Woll and LaGuardia speak we called for a disruption of the meeting." In retrospect, he felt that "demand[ing] in

11. The condemnation was nonetheless too severe for several members of the ACLU board of directors who were close to the CPUSA. They issued an angry dissent. See "Report, Commission of Inquiry to the Board of Directors on Madison Square Garden Mass Meeting, February 16, 1934," American Civil Liberties Union (March 1934), reprinted in Bernard K. Johnpoll, ed., *A Documentary History of the Communist Party of the United States,* vol. 3: *Unite and Fight, 1934–1935* (Westport, Conn.: Greenwood Press, 1994).

the press that the meeting be broken up" was a mistake; such a move should have come "from the workers." Unlike the others, Earl Browder insisted that the riot had not been a setback for the party. But he did agree that tactical mistakes had been made and thought that it had been an error to demand that both La Guardia and Woll be kept from speaking, remarking that to most people, "LaGuardia is not exposed as a fascist." Like Minor, he believed, in hindsight, that " to raise the slogan: they shall not speak" had been a mistake. Instead, Browder thought that the Communists should have allowed Woll and La Guardia to start speaking, and then "to demonstrate against them when they sp[oke]."

These post hoc, private deliberations suggest that CPUSA leaders had had in mind a controlled disruption of the Socialist rally: they had planned for their members to prevent two of the rally's featured speakers from talking and to shout slogans but under the tight discipline of the party leaders. Krumbein, for example, noted that sections of Madison Square Garden had been assigned to no fewer than twenty-five party leaders; "we organized for this throughout the hall, so we would have these slogans cried only when a lull occurred, or when a speaker was introduced." Browder spoke of the assumption that Communist officials would have "moment by moment leadership and control of our masses."

What the leaders got, however, was an uncontrolled disruption that destroyed the rally. Rank-and-file Communists did not wait for Woll and La Guardia or for a signal from Hathaway or the other Communist officials placed throughout the hall; instead, they spontaneously rioted as soon as the Socialists attempted to start the meeting. As Browder put it: "We said, we do not want to break up the meeting, we don't want to take it over, yet we adopted a tactic which created that situation." Ordinary Communists, like their party leaders, had developed a worldview that mirrored that of Moscow. The Comintern had said that Socialists were not comrades on the left but a variety of fascists. At Madison Square Garden, several thousand rank-and-file American Communists acted accordingly.[12]

12. While the 1934 Madison Square Garden riot was the largest disruption of this type, there were a number of smaller incidents. In March 1930, for example, Communists infiltrated a Socialist Party rally in San Francisco at which Dan Hoan,

Document 79

Excerpts from thirteen-page "Discussion of Polburo on Madison Square Garden Meeting," Political Bureau minutes, 17 February 1934, RTsKhIDNI 515–1–3448. Original in English. "Edwards" was the alias of Gerhart Eisler. Green is William Green, the head of the AFL. Matthew Woll was his chief spokesman. During the Third Period the united front, sometimes called the "united front from below," was not seen as an equal alliance with Socialists and other leftists. Rather, it was a way for Communists to use calls for unity to gain influence over rank-and-file members of other radical organizations in order to pressure the leadership to accept Communist political guidance.

DISCUSSION OF POLBURO ON MADISON SQUARE GARDEN MEETING.

Report of Comrade Krumbein.

When the meeting was planned we did not [know] that Woll was to be a speaker, although it was announced that attempts were made to get Green. We decided to go in in organized bodies, to get out a call for a stoppage. Our Needle Trades Union got a statement to the Freiheit and the District also got out a statement. The comrades that were present at our meeting at the Coliseum will know that we also projected the same proposition there. Namely, that the workers should go inside by organizations with banners, etc., and raise the main cry of unity with Socialists, A. F. of L., and Communist workers in the struggle against fascism. The question arose the night before whether it was advisable for Minor to go int[o] there. Some of us thought not. We took it up in the District Sec. not only as far as Minor was concerned but any leader in the steering committee, and it was decided not. That we would try as much as possible to control the crowd, and we organized for this throughout the hall, so we would have these slogans cried only when a lull occurred, or when a speaker was introduced; that we would not interrupt speakers. We organized all this with that in mind. We had a section organizers meeting and we assigned each of them a section in the hall, and told them to get 25 people scattered around the hall, and to tell them to get others around them,—to fraternize with the workers inside, etc. From the reports we were fairly well scattered in there in this general formation, but things that happened showed that it was impossible to organize to any great degree to control.

It was my opinion that it was wrong for any of our leading comrades to be there.
. . .

We had an outside meeting of 5–6,000. So you have these two alternatives. They would have had a peaceful meeting with Woll and LaGuardia speaking,

the Socialist mayor of Milwaukee, was to speak. During the proceedings the Communists broke up the meeting in a melee that resulted in numerous injuries. They were protesting no particular issue; rather, they sought to discredit a perceived social fascist and disrupt a Socialist meeting.

if we had not been there. We decided to have a march to Union Square. It was spontaneously organized, and the result was 10–15,000 people gathering in the square. The parade was in length from 29th Street and 8th Avenue to 14th Street and 5th Avenue.

This is the report of the general situation, from the information that I got. I say it is a debatable question and I am inclined to think it was correct going in there, notwithstanding that it turned out the way it did, but I believe it was inadvisable for any of our leading comrades to be in there. Here the question must be raised how was it that Hathaway was inside and we did not know anything about it.

Edwards—Discussion on Madison Square Garden Meeting.

I was at this meeting and was sitting between Socialists and Communists. We have not yet got all reactions from the masses of this meeting, but I want to say that if somebody from the Social Fascists could have planned how to attempt to isolate us from the workers and to break the beginnings of the united front with the left wing in the Socialist Party, AFL, etc., he would have planned just what happened yesterday.

I estimate this meeting as a set-back in the united front with the workers, and the worst feature is that what happened was not around a political issue, for instance if Woll had attempted to speak, then we would have taken the biggest majority of the workers with us, and we could have discussed this with the workers, but what was the situation? Our people came in the hall and shouted, "Socialists and Communists Unite and Fight" and there was a good spirit in the hall. The socialists were singing and cheering and mixing with our workers, and I thought, well, it will go through, but what happened? After understanding all the provocation at the beginning before the people went in, taking away all leaflets, banners, etc., looking into brief cases. But what happened afterwards, well, then the chairman opened the meeting, and our people started to sing, to shout, etc. Well, the Socialists became angry because they wanted to listen, and this went on. The question of Woll and Laguardia did not come up here. It was not necessary to play them up because the Socialists had the meeting where they wanted it. Instead of a meeting of fraternization, where you brought our Party position to the workers, instead we destroyed the meeting. One of the workers said, "LaGuardia is a scoundrel, but why don't you let the others speak,["] and I saw the Socialist leaders get really wild, because we came in with the slogan "Unite and Fight," and then we did not let anybody speak.

The Second question. Comrade Krumbein complained that Hathaway was there. Before the meeting I advised very urgently that one or two leading comrades should go there for the PolBuro because I had the feeling what would happen if we sent our workers to listen to Dubinsky, and I can say more, although it was a spontaneous movement on the part of Hathaway, I saw him going, and Max went to him and asked him to go to the platform to quiet the meeting (Hathaway: Here it is necessary to point out that many comrades asked me to go and see what I could do.) That was the one chance to make one desperate effort. If Hathaway could have spoken to the crowd for one or two minutes just to tell them to be quiet, then the workers would have seen that at least our leaders wanted order. Should he have gone with a group? That would have meant taking over the meeting. Should he have spoken from the middle of the hall, there would have been even more confusion. There was nothing else to do. The steering committee had no authority. It was already clear that the meeting would have a bad political effect. The fights had already begun. If you had watched the transformation of the socialists from cheering our people to hate, then you would have known what is going on in this meeting. I say, if something good happened in this meeting, it was the attempt of Hathaway, and the fact that he was beaten up by the Socialist leaders. This is a political weapon in the hands of our comrades and we have to use it.

. . .

Discussion on Madison Square Garden Meeting—Stachel.

There is no need for panic. From the press I am surprised that on the whole it is not completely hostile to us. These people will use this as an excuse to withdraw. The origin of the mistake is two-fold. Confusion on the united front has produced the idea that just sending in the masses is a united front, and second, a little bit of adventurism in trying to correct the mistake, or rather a recklessness in trying to correct the opportunist mistake, and all of it arises from the fact that we were working under pressure and did not think out the questions. We all share in the responsibility. Our first reaction was one in which the Party can be commended, and especially the press. The Socialist Party seeing all this rushed also with a special edition and arranged this meeting, changing it from Town Hall to Madison Square Garden, because we were getting the sentiment of the masses.

. . .

<u>Minor</u>

I do not agree with Comrade Edwards that we should not have called our people to this meeting. We had to support the strike call, and we had to call for the workers to go to the demonstration. It was not possible for us to have diverted this demonstration from Madison Square Garden.

What should we have done? In reality by calling upon the workers not to let Woll and LaGuardia speak we called for a disruption of the meeting, We should have made our characterization of Woll and LaGuardia, but should have not demanded in the press that the meeting be broken up, that should have come from the workers.

Ford

A question on the tactics in the united front. Just what should have been done. Since the Anti War Conference we have been talking about the United Front, and up to this time we have achieved certain united front actions. Should we tell our comrades not to go to Madison Square Garden. Second, on the question of Hathaway appearing on the stand. Of all comrades Hathaway should not have been the one to go there. Comrade Krombein has already spoken about our steering committee. I don't know who was on it. But here is the Daily Worker coming out every day attacking Socialist leaders and so on, and Hathaway is editor of the Daily Worker. Under the circumstances, it would possibly have been better if Minor had gone there, but not Hathaway who is editor of the paper.

. . .

Discussion on Madison Square Garden Meeting—Comrade Browder.

I think it is necessary in estimating yesterday's action to be sure and keep the various questions in the proper plane and proportion. For that purpose I want to emphasize first that throughout the action and including yesterday's action, in every political issue we had a correct position and strengthened this position before the masses. This is important because this is the thing that is important in any view that extends beyond the moment. In the political sense the Socialists gained nothing, but on the contrary got themselves step by step into a worse political position, and considering the political strategy of the whole situation we have steadily moved forward and strengthened our position.

This is a fact. The questions that are to be clarified here have to do not with any of these larger political questions, but with the question of tactics. These are all tactical questions and must be considered on that plane.

. . .

The questions around which the most unclarity exists is first of all the question, should we have called the workers to go to Madison Square Garden. Unfortunately I am unable to solidarize myself with any of the views expresse[d]. These seems to be two general views. One says, yes, we should have gone because it is necessary if we are to be consistent. The other says, it was opportunistic to go. I do not agree with either. It was not necessary for consistency to go. We could have taken some other tactic and been entirely correct. On the other hand I cannot agree that it was opportunistic to go. Leaving aside for the moment whether it was advisable at this particular moment to do this, I want to say that in my opinion we will have many cases in the future

289

where it will be correct tactics for us to bring all the workers under our leadership into demonstrations called by our enemies and to bring them in there not for the purpose of breaking them up, but even to listen to these enemies, and in as well organized a way as possible express our disagreement with them and appeal directly by this expression to others who are listening. (Edwards: do you call this a united front?) It is not a united front with the leaders, but it is a direct approach to those workers to make the united front with us, and it is not in any particular different from calling upon Communist and Socialist workers to fraternize before the Austrian Consulate jointly and fuse their demonstration with Socialist and Communist banners in one demonstration.

I think we must examine this question to the bottom because it has tremendous lessons for our work, for our future work. After we called the workers to go there, which in my opinion was not in principle, wrong, but is still open to question as to whether it was advisable, after we called them, then it is clear that there were many weaknesses throughout. First, we did not ourselves sufficiently appreciate the dangers that were involved in such an action. We proceeded upon the assumption that we had moment by moment leadership and control of our masses, which we did not have. And because we proceeded on that assumption we did not place the necessary safeguards as to what would happen. The result is something happened that we did not intend, which is against our policy, and in every step of our policy the leading thought was closer fraternization with the rank and file, to break down the barriers. The result of the meeting was that some of these barriers have been strengthened, but some of them have been broken down. Let us not overestimate the outcome of this meeting. But in the most backward we have strengthened their prejudices, and this is a defeat, even if it had been only a minority, but I am sure that it is a majority, it was only a minority who came closer to us.

How could we have avoided this? We based our tactics in the first place with the understanding that we had before us the issue of the trade union and socialist leaders and not Woll and LaGuardia, but I hesitate to say that even this is a decisive question, because certainly as far as LaGuardia is concerned, it is not certain that the masses of the workers were roused against Laguardia, but were ready at the moment to demonstrate against Dubinsky, but on LaGuardia we do not have the clearest position. With Woll, yes, against Woll we could go to the limit, but not against LaGuardia. LaGuardia is not exposed as a fascist. When we went before the masses denouncing LaGuardia as a fascist we did not strengthen our position. Here is a tactical mistake, bringing forward LaGuardia as an equal issue with Woll. Of course we have to speak about LaGuardia's police clubbing the demonstrators on the same issue, but we should not have bracketed them together.

Document 79 continued

Second, in my opinion it was wrong to place the attack against these people as the central slogan in the extra edition of the Daily. This could not politically be our central slogan. Tactically it placed us at a disadvantage with the Socialists.

Third, I think we made a mistake in demanding speakers except as it was done first, through the union, and we should not have raised this demand in the extra edition. This places us in the position of breaking the meeting. A final and additional mistake, in my opinion was to raise the slogan: they shall not speak. It is absolutely correct to demonstrate against them when they speak, but not to raise the slogan, they shall not speak. This would be correct where we were in such an overwhelmingly predominant position politically and organizationally that we could break down the barriers and take over the meeting, but this we refused to set as our goal and we adopted a tactic which did not fit in with our fundamental strategy on the meeting. We said, we do not want to break up the meeting, we don't want to take it over, yet we adopted a tactic which created that situation.

The final question, whether we should have had the PolBuro there, and whether it should have been Hathaway. There is no question here. It is absolutely impossible for us to take the workers anywhere without having our leaders with them, and I think Hathaway was the correct representative, and I may say that we should recognize this, that Hathaway's prestige did not suffer because he was there, not even among those people that are turning against us.
. . .

The Moscow Trials and the Great Terror

The 1934 assassination of Sergei Kirov, head of the Communist party in Leningrad, initiated purge trials that decimated the Soviet population. Stalin presented Kirov's murder as part of a vast plot, and in a series of public trials Grigory Zinoviev, Nikolai Bukharin, Karl Radek, Mikhail Tomsky, Lev Kamenev, Aleksei Rykov, and other prominent veteran Bolshevik leaders confessed to fantastic plots against the Soviet state.[13] The defendants made abject confessions of having been in league with Leon Trotsky (then in exile) and of having spied for Japan, Germany, Poland, Great Britain, and

13. On the Kirov assassination, see Robert Conquest, *Stalin and the Kirov Murder* (New York: Oxford University Press, 1989). New documents on the Kirov assassination will be published in a subsequent volume of the Yale University Press Annals of Communism series.

other countries in complex conspiracies to overthrow the Soviet state. The trials were frauds and the confessions false, extorted by a combination of torture, threats of execution, and promises of clemency for the defendants and their families. These promises were not kept; almost everyone who confessed was executed, and in most cases their families were also executed or imprisoned in the labor camps of the Gulag.

The Moscow trials were the public aspect of a much vaster purge of Soviet society in which several million citizens were secretly arrested by Stalin's political police and sentenced to the Gulag on charges ranging from espionage and treason to ideological deviance. Many of the people sent to the Gulag died there of overwork and exposure. In addition to those who died in the camps, several hundred thousand, possibly more than a million, were executed by Stalin's internal security apparatus.[14] The Terror was wide-ranging, striking all sectors of Soviet society, including the leadership of the Soviet Communist party itself. Stalin apparently planned to wipe out all potential opposition to his complete control of the Bolshevik movement. Of the 139 members of the CPSU Central Committee who were chosen by the party's 1934 congress, 98 (70 percent) were arrested and shot by Stalin's political police.

Earl Browder Declares War on Trotskyists

How did American Communists respond to Stalin's annihilation of his enemies—most of them fellow Communists? One need not go to Moscow's archives to answer that question. Standard histories amply document the open and fierce defense of the Moscow trials offered by the American Communist press and CPUSA officials.[15]

14. The most comprehensive book on the Great Terror is Robert Conquest, *The Great Terror: A Reassessment* (New York: Oxford University Press, 1990). New documentation on the Great Terror will be presented in forthcoming volumes of the Yale University Press Annals of Communism series.

15. See Kraditor, *Jimmy Higgins*, 46–47, 60–66; Guenter Lewy, *The Cause That Failed: Communism in American Political Life* (New York: Oxford University Press, 1990), 47–53; Constance Ashton Myers, *The Prophet's Army: Trotskyists in America, 1928–1941* (Westport, Conn.: Greenwood Press, 1977), 133–137, 239; Harvey Klehr, *The Heyday of American Communism: The Depression Decade* (New York: Basic Books, 1984), 173, 358–362; Harvey Klehr and John Earl

The documents in the RTsKhIDNI archive not only confirm the CPUSA's public war on Trotskyists and Bukharinists; they describe the more sinister work being done privately by the American party. They also reveal the nature and extent of the Comintern instruction of the CPUSA in its attack on Stalin's political and ideological enemies.

In *The Secret World of American Communism,* we reprinted documents dealing with the CPUSA's covert activities against the "deviants." One of the documents discusses the burglary undertaken by the CPUSA of the apartment of Jay Lovestone, the leader of Bukharin's followers in America, in which party agents stole Lovestone's records and shipped them to Moscow, noting that these records contained material on "certain persons in the USSR who are mentioned in letters which discuss the trials of the Trotskyist-Bukharin spies"—this at the height of the Great Terror, when a Soviet citizen linked to any of the trial defendants faced imprisonment and/or execution. In another document, the CPUSA reports to the Comintern that the party has infiltrated the American Trotskyist headquarters in New York City. One of the people involved in this enterprise eventually helped Ramon Mercader, an NKVD officer, to gain access to Leon Trotsky's home in Mexico, where he lived in exile. Mercader murdered Trotsky in 1940.[16]

Document 80 is the transcript of a January 1935 speech Earl Browder made to the leadership of the CPUSA in which he explains how his colleagues should interpret the dramatic reports that have begun arriving from Moscow. Browder takes an unabashedly Stalinist position:

> What is the concrete relationship between the Trotzkyites and Zinovievites with the open white-guard [anti-Communist] elements, the police in the imperialist general staffs? Comrades, this relationship is becoming more and more direct and organic every day. From being the ideological vanguard of the counter-revolution, the Trotzkyites are becoming also the organizational vanguard of the counter-revolution. This was demonstrated above all by the Kirov assassination. This is one

---

Haynes, *The American Communist Movement: Storming Heaven Itself* (New York: Twayne, 1992), 90–92.

16. Harvey Klehr, John Earl Haynes, and Fridrikh Igorevich Firsov, *The Secret World of American Communism* (New Haven: Yale University Press, 1995), 128–32, 88, 142–43.

of the lessons that we must bring down to the Party, to every member of the Party, *to every worker, to all honest elements, to* make them acutely and keenly conscious of it and transmit this consciousness to the broad working masses in the United States.

Browder's speech included several of the fantasies that the Stalinist regime had concocted about internal enemies, such as the claim that "thirty or forty assassin groups" had been sent into the USSR to kill Stalin. He also echoed the Stalinist position that "continued opposition against the line of the Party inevitably leads directly over into . . . the camp of counter-revolution. This must teach us also the lesson to become much more irreconcilable in our struggle against *every* deviations in our movement." The CPUSA, said Browder, must show "sharp uncompromising, intolerant struggle . . . against Trotzkyism and everything that it stands for, to make Trotzkyism the hated word among the masses of the workers, to make it synonymous for what it is, . . . the murderer of the leaders of the revolution."

There are several noteworthy points about Browder's speech, one of which is surely his belief that "every worker" in the United States wished or even needed to know the details of the Kirov assassination. Clearest, however, is Browder's immediate and unquestioning adoption of the Soviet point of view for the American Communist party, and the strength with which he expressed his imported hatred.

Document 80

Excerpts from eight-page "Document 'E': Report of Comrade Heath on Kirov Assassination and Trotzky Counter Revolution," minutes of 15–19 January 1935 meeting of CPUSA Central Committee, RTsKhIDNI 515–1-3742. Original in English with handwritten corrections. "Heath" is a cover name for Earl Browder. Joseph Zack is Joseph Zack Kornfeder, a senior CPUSA organizer who renounced the party in the mid-1930s.

DOCUMENT "E"

REPORT OF COMRADE HEATH ON KIROV ASSASSINATION AND

TROTZKY COUNTER REVOLUTION

[?] FEB 1935 1163 [stamp]

Corrected

Document 80 *continued*

Comrades: I am not going to make a report, but a few remarks introducing the subjects of discussion at this meeting—the agitprop work of the Party in relation to the recent events in the Soviet Union, the assassination of Kirov and the disclosures that have followed the investigations of this murder.

It is very important that we should bring to the Party, and to the working class generally, *in the broadest possible manner* a serious and deep understanding of the significance of these events. We must say that the shock of these events did not in every case find our Party prepared to meet and answer unhesitatingly the questions that were raised, to meet and destroy the attacks of our enemies, for which the assassination of Kirov was a signal, internationally.

What was the greatest weakness, the outstanding weakness our Party showed in repelling these attacks. I think the chief feature of the inadequacy and weakness on our part was in the fact that we, to a certain degree, allowed the enemy to place the issues on the field that the enemy chose.

What was one of the main purposes in the assassination of Kirov and the campaign organized around it? One of the main objectives towards which the enemy was driving was precisely to try to cover up the tremendous achievements of the Soviet Union which had just been announced at the Plenum of the CC of the All Russian C.P. We must say that to a considerable degree the enemy succeeded in this. The enemy *with their press, radio and other propaganda agencies* succeeded in placing into the foreground, all over the world, the discussion, not of the tremendous successes of the Soviet Union, but the question: is not the Soviet Union very seriously shaken; or: is not the Soviet Union demonstrating its weakness by the execution of the terrorists, etc. And in our answers, we must see that we very seriously bring forward—sharply into the center of the whole picture, as the basis of our reply to all of the attacks and slanders—the actual achievements of the Soviet Union in the Construction of Socialism, the most recent victories of this construction; and to place the assassination of Kirov in its proper setting—as the desperate act of defeated and crushed counter-revolutionists.

. . .

We must say, comrades, that this skeptical and doubting attitude is one of the things that tends to weaken our struggle here and there against these counter-revolutionists. It is a remnant of a certain rotten liberalism, in essence quite closely related to the liberal outcries against the execution of the terrorists in the Soviet Union.

What is the concrete relationship between the Trotzkyites and Zinovievites with the open white-guard elements, the police in the imperialist general staffs? Comrades, this relationship is becoming more and more direct and organic every day. From being the ideological vanguard of the counter-revolution, the Trotzkyites are becoming also the organizational vanguard of the counter-revolution. This was demonstrated above all by the Kirov assassination. This is one of the lessons that we must bring down to the Party, to every member of the Party, *to every worker, to all honest elements, to* make them acutely and keenly conscious of it and transmit this consciousness to the broad working masses in the United States. Make them feel the significance of this thing and to organize the revolutionary offensive against all of the enemies of the revolution. *We cannot carry on our defense of the Soviet Union; we cannot carry forward* the struggle for the conquest of *power* unless we strengthen this offensive against the Trotzkyite counter-revolutionary ideology, which is the spear-head *of counter-revolution. Is it not clear that on the banner of every White Guardist, in their attack against the Soviet Union are written the slogans and quotations of Trotzky and the Trotzkyites.*

It is not an accident that in the period of the spring and summer and early fall of 1934 when there was thirty or forty assassin groups sent into the Soviet Union from the surrounding fascist countries with the specific objection [objective] to murder the members of the Political Buro of the Russian Party and first of all Comrade Stalin, that all of these terrorist groups within the border of the Soviet Union were successfully rounded up and none of them got close even to their objective. They *are* not such a menace. It was possible to meet and overcome quickly and very effectively this menace.

What enemy was it that reached the goal, struck down the comrade standing next to Comrade Stalin. It was precisely the remnants of the Trotzky-Zinoviev opposition in the Party . . . . They have become the armor makers, the weapon makers for all of the forces of counter-revolutionary imperialism and finally they became that arm of the imperialists which struck down one of the leaders of the Socialist Fatherland.

All of this has a most direct and immediate bearing on the subjects of this meeting, which is to consider agitational propaganda work of our Party, has a direct bearing significance upon every phase of this question. I only want to speak of one particular phase, the arming of our Party with the theories—Marx, Engels, Lenin, Stalin. What is the basis of the degeneration of those elements, formerly members and leaders of the Communist Party who became the very vanguard of the counter-revolutionary attack against our Party. It was in each and every case the starting point, the foundation for the whole development, the departure from the teachings of Marx, Engels, Lenin, Stalin. *These elements became the representatives of the hostile class forces against the proletarian dictatorship.*

What is the foundation for every similar development that we see in the United States, as for example, the open passing over into the counter-revolutionary camp—*the Cannons, the Schachtmans, and their newest recruit Muste—on the part of such a miserable renegade as* Joseph Zack at the moment when this camp had struck down Comrade Kirov? . . . It gives us our own excellent concrete example of the truth of what Lenin said when he pointed out that any sustained and continued opposition against the line of the Party inevitably leads directly over into the opposite camp, the camp of counter-revolution. This must teach us also the lesson to become much more irreconcilable in our struggle against *every* deviations in our movement. We can be very patient and long-suffering in dealing with the shortcomings and weaknesses of new, raw proletarian elements who are coming to us. But we have got to be more stern and decisive and unrelenting in dealing with the deviations of people who are not new raw people just clearing themselves of confusion and coming to us, but who represent certain fixed and stubborn deviations from our revolutionary theory and who are trying to implant these deviations into the center of our movement.

Our Party has got to be firmly founded upon the unchallenged leadership of the theory and practice of bolshevism and of the great leaders of bolshevism, and this must find its expression in the everyday reactions and activities of our Party into a sharp uncompromising, intolerant struggle, first of all, against Trotskyism and everything it stands for, to make Trotskyism the hated word among the masses of the workers, to make it synonymous for what it is, the struggle against Socialist construction, the struggle against the world party of revolution, the struggle against Bolshevism, the active collaboration with all the enemies of the revolution, the hand of imperialist reaction, the murderer of the leaders of the revolution.

These things are firmly, clearly established facts and these we must carry to the workers, to the broadest masses of the workers, establish these facts and all of the conclusions that must be drawn from them among the broadest masses of the workers as one of the central most essential part of the winning of the majority of the working class for the revolution, for the Bolshevization of our Party, for the rooting of our Party among the masses as capable Bolshevik leaders of the revolutionary class struggle in the United States.

The Trotsky-Zinoviev Trial of 1936

As Browder suggested in document 80, the Moscow trials engendered considerable skepticism in the West. Many people found it incredible that Trotsky, Zinoviev, Bukharin, and others who had been the leaders of the Bolshevik Revolution had been accomplices in foreign plots to overthrow the Communist state. The confessions themselves were difficult to believe because of their bizarre and often self-contradictory content, stilted language, and delivery by men who often looked psychologically broken.

The Comintern, realizing that only a sustained campaign could prevent the trials from becoming a liability to Soviet prestige, showered the CPUSA with directives to defend the trials, pointing out shortcomings in the American efforts to do so. In the Comintern archives there are hundreds of documents and messages—memos, reports, letters, cables—between American Communists and the Comintern laying out how the trials should be understood and how their verdicts should be presented to the American public. In this book we have space to quote only a few.

After Zinoviev's trial began in 1936, a coded Comintern cable sketched out the basic ideas that the CPUSA should try to convey:

> Trial gang Trotzky-Zinoviev unveils picture huge crime of those mean degenerates. Those abominable traitors of working class . . . made terror . . . chief method of their counter-revolutionary activity. Now it has been clearly established that criminal murder of Kirov has been prepared and carried through according to instructions of Trotzky and Zinoviev, that according to their immediate instructions have been prepared a series of other terroristic actions against leaders of CPSU and Soviet State, in first place against comrade Stalin. Now it has been ascertained documentarily that they have established direct connections with the fascist Gestapo in order to carry through their terroristic activity. . . . Trotzkyism is vanguard [of the] counter-revolutionary bourgeoisie, that he [Trotsky] maintains . . . secret connections with fascist Gestapo, that today he endeavors in Spain through criminal game with most extreme slogans to facilitate intervention of german and italian fascism. . . . Necessary now to secure full liquidation of Trotzkyism. With all forces carry on struggle against all those who during trial support terrorists of Trotzky.[17]

A further Comintern cable stated that the trials were proving "beyond doubt the identity of fascist and Trotskyist platforms, overthrow Soviet power, restoration [of] capitalism in USSR, coincidence [in] directives of Gestapo and Trotsky according to which Trotskyite-fascist bandits acted: organization of murder [of] leaders [of the] working class, sabotage most important industrial

17. Comintern Secretariat to Central Committee, 20 August 1936, RTsKhIDNI 495–184–73, 1936 file. The CPUSA acknowledged receipt in Kraft [Solomon Mikhelson-Manuilov], "Your directive . . . ," 29 August 1936, RTsKhIDNI 495–184–33, 1936 file.

centers, physical annihilation [of] workers."[18] Later a lengthy 1936 cable declared:

Secretariat ECCI points out necessity [of] systematic struggle against Trotskyites as counter-revolutionary terrorists agents, Gestapo. etc. Defeating their slander against Stalin, opposing their slander [of] Stalin by wide popularization his gigantic revolutionary activity, his role as leader [of] international proletariat and toilers [of the] world. We also call attention to danger of slanderous attacks of class enemy especially of Trotskyite nature being quoted in Communist press without reacting in convincing and principled manner. Necessary to refrain from quoting in detail counter-revolutionary slanders and propaganda [of] Trotskyites. . . . Necessary strict control [of] composition [of] editorial staffs in order to purge them of doubtful and double-dealing elements. Writing articles on Trotskyism should be entrusted only to most verified and politically qualified authors.[19]

In addition to general directives, the CPUSA received a number of specific instructions. When a delegation of American Communists visited Mexico, the Comintern reminded them to criticize the Mexican government for having allowed Trotsky to live there in exile.[20] A follow-up message directed the CPUSA to "demand in name of workers organizations, popular masses the expulsion of Trotsky from Mexico"; Trotsky should be handed over "to proletarian Soviet tribunal."[21] Just before the trial of Karl Radek and Yuri Piatakov, two former Bolshevik leaders who were subsequently executed, Moscow instructed Browder to ensure that the *Daily Worker* made space available for ample coverage.[22] A follow-up command noted that Moscow expected an "attempt to discredit trial" and instructed the CPUSA press to stress that Radek and the others were going to confess and that they were "a band of

18. Comintern Secretariat, "Historic Soviet Congress . . . ," 25 November 1936, RTsKhIDNI 495–184–73, 1936 file.
19. Comintern Secretariat to Communist Parties of USA, Czechoslovakia, Canada, Norway, Holland, Switzerland, Denmark, Belgium, Sweden, France, and England, 30 December 1936, RTsKhIDNI 495–184–73, 1936 file.
20. Comintern Secretariat to CPUSA-Browder, 14 January 1937, RTsKhIDNI 495–184–17, 1937 file.
21. Comintern Secretariat, "Basing on Results of Trial, Mobilize . . . ," 7 February 1937, RTsKhIDNI 495–184–19, 1937 file.
22. Comintern Secretariat to Browder, 17 January 1937, RTsKhIDNI 495–184–17, 1937 file.

wreckers, revisionists, spies, allies of German Gestapo."[23] Another cable informed Browder that Moscow was sending lengthy manuscripts to assist the CPUSA in preparing pamphlets defending the trials and that he himself should "organize large distribution of all trial editions."[24]

American Communists did their best to follow these orders, but they found themselves being criticized for insufficient vigor. In **document 81**, an evaluation of the coverage of the trials by the *Daily Worker,* the author, probably Sam Darcy, CPUSA representative to the Comintern, explains that because the Comintern press department cannot send official reports to the CPUSA newspaper until after Tass and *Pravda* have published their authorized versions, the *Daily Worker* was often forced to rely on other American newspapers for its accounts to add color to dry narratives. Yet he believes that in spite of this drawback, the *Daily Worker* has offered a good defense, giving extensive coverage to the evidence and the ancillary materials that proved the defendants' guilt. He quotes a number of headlines (such as, for 22 August, "Kamenev Admits Group Had No Mass Base; Terror Only Hope" and "Trotsky Spurned by Masses, Uses Nazi Aid Against USSR") to prove his point.

Journalists for the mainstream media were not the only ones who balked at the accusations. Soviet prosecutors had accused Trotsky of having plotted to break up the USSR by promising Belarus to Poland, Ukraine to Germany, and the Soviet Union's far-eastern provinces to Japan. He was also charged with plotting Kirov's murder and of having conspired to betray Lenin during the Bolshevik Revolution. Trotsky's reputation as a revolutionary leader, however, along with factual errors in the Soviet case against him and the absurdity of the alleged plots, led to skepticism among liberals and radicals. Some of the more prominent among them established the Committee for the Defense of Leon Trotsky, which then sponsored a commission, under the leadership of the respected philosopher John Dewey, to investigate the charges.

American Communists and their allies responded with sus-

23. Comintern Secretariat, "In a Few Days Trial against Radek . . . ," 18 January 1937, RTsKhIDNI 495–184–19, 1937 file.
24. Comintern Secretariat to Central Committee and Browder, 29 January 1937, RTsKhIDNI 495–184–19, 1937 file.

tained, vicious attacks on anyone who supported the Dewey commission. But in spite of the attacks, the Dewey commission held a series of hearings, which included direct testimony from Trotsky, in exile in Mexico. As a result, the commission issued a report claiming that Moscow's case against Trotsky was without foundation. In response, the CPUSA surreptitiously helped establish an opposing committee of liberals, who issued a statement supporting the Moscow trials. In **document 82**, Browder reports to the Comintern on the effectiveness of the CPUSA campaign. As Browder indicates, the party's effort to convince American liberals that "every enemy of the Soviet Union is at the same time an enemy of American democracy" had achieved considerable success. The counter-committee had defended the Moscow trials and the Soviet Union in general; it included many prestigious members of the American liberal Left and was much larger than the group of Trotsky's defenders. Such influential liberal journals as the *New Republic* and the *Nation* either endorsed the results of the trials or urged liberals to give Stalin the benefit of the doubt.[25]

Document 81

"The Daily Worker of CPUSA on the Trotsky-Zinovievist Terrorist Trial," 9 September 1936, RTsKhIDNI 495–14–51. Original in English, with handwritten corrections. The document is unsigned, but the style and corrections in the original suggest that it was prepared by Sam Darcy.

[illegible handwriting] <u>Not for publication</u>

9.9.36. - SS4.

~~CONFIDENTIAL~~

THE DAILY WORKER OF CPUSA ON THE TROTSKY-ZINOVIEVIST TERRORIST TRIAL.

The 'Daily Worker' printed complete reports of testimony of the trial cabled it by our Press Department. These were based upon the material issued by Tass and by 'Pravda'.

---

25. On the Dewey commission, see Alan B. Spitzer, "John Dewey, the Trial of Leon Trotsky and the Search for Historical Truth," *History and Theory* 29, no. 1 (1990): 16–37; Albert Glotzer, *Trotsky: Memoir and Critique* (Buffalo, N.Y.: Prometheus Books, 1989), 235–81; John Dewey et al., *Not Guilty: The Final Report of the Commission on Inquiry into Charges Made against Leon Trotsky and Leon Sedoff in the Moscow Trials* (New York: Harper, 1938); Sidney Hook, *Out of Step: An Unquiet Life in the Twentieth Century* (New York: Harper and Row, 1987), 218–74; and Lewy, *Cause That Failed*, 88–90.

In addition to these reports, the 'Daily Worker' was forced many times to utilise bourgeois news agencies for material. This is chiefly due to two facts:

a) Our Press Department did not send cabled material to the 'Daily Worker' until after it had been issued by Tass or 'Pravda'. This delayed the dispatches by one day. The bourgeois correspondents cabled their material immediately at the conclusion of the court sessions. If the 'Daily Worker' depended exclusively upon our press service, they would have been one day late in all matters. Even as it is, they were late on most days because much of the bourgeois correspondents' cables must have appeared of doubtful accuracy to our comrades.

b) Our dispatches lacked colour and had a tendency to be formal statements of the facts; and *what* limited them still more, *so far [as] American readers are concerned*, they were a repetition of the statement of facts which was drawn up for publication in the Soviet Union.

For that reason, the 'Daily Worker' many times took descriptive matter from the bourgeois press services in order to *give the* "colour" *of the trial.*

The front page display and headings on most of the stories were, despite some shortcomings, quite vigorous and adequate to the material. For example:

1) Aug. 15 - "Terrorist Plot by Trotskyists Bared in the USSR"; "Directed from Abroad by Trotsky to Kill Soviet Leaders".

2) Aug. 17th - "Trotskyist Tie with Nazis Revealed as Trials Near"; "USSR Masses Ask No Mercy for Plotters".

3) Aug. 20th - "14 Accused Trotskyists Admit Guilt in Soviet Trial; 2 Confess Contact with Foreign Centre in Counter-Revolution".

4) Aug. 21st - "Trotsky Gave Orders to Kill Stalin, Kirov, say Plotters".

5) Aug. 22nd - "Kamenev Admits Group Had No Mass Base; Terror Only Hope"; "Trotsky, Spurned by Masses, Uses Nazi Aid Against USSR".

6) Aug. 26th - "People Hail Sentence of Plotters".

In the first part of the trial, the 'Daily Worker' was obviously not alert to the opportunity to use the evidence given at the trial

a) against *the* American Trotskyi[tes? ink smudge];

b) against the left socialists' acceptance of the Trotskyites into their party;

c) against those elements who always fought to include Trotskyites in the united front movement in the United States.

In other words, the comrades *printed* all the material sent, but, in the first days of the trial, they did not grasp the significance of the material for the struggle within the United States. As a result, the initiative in the matter was left to the "left" socialist, Norman Thomas, who wrote an editorial in his paper, 'The Socialist Call', in which, in advance of the actual receipt of the transcript of evidence in the United States, he announced his belief that the defendants were innocent.

Only then did the 'Daily Worker' answer, in an editorial. Even in this edi-

Document 81 *continued*

torial, however, it takes a defensive attitude and criticises Thomas for having judged "before arrival of the evidence". It says *in part* on Aug. 22nd: "In the current issue of the 'Socialist Call', Norman Thomas has a column which should make every socialist blush with shame. Before any evidence has been presented, he already declares his belief in the innocence of the Trotskyist-Zinovievist gang, and raises the demand that the Soviet government should be placed on trial before the public opinion of the world"

It was not until the issue of August 25th that the 'Daily Worker' recovered the offensive and carried a leading editorial, the headline of which was "Socialists Should Repudiate Trotskyists in the Ranks". This editorial devotes itself chiefly to the telegram of the leaders of the Second International.

Together with the transcripts of evidence, the 'Daily Worker' also reprinted a substantial summary of the indictment and a number of articles, including the article of Rakovsky. This article by Rakovsky provided an excellent opportunity to make a big play about his former Trotskyite connections. The 'Daily Worker', however, printed the article in an *informal* manner. Thus, most of the readers who do not know who Rakovsky is or what the significance of his having written such an article is, missed the point, especially since, from reading the article itself, one does not get a very clear picture of what Rakovsky's position was, because, for the uninformed reader, he states it rather vaguely.[1]

One of the weakest points of the 'Daily Worker's' handling of the Trotskyist-Zinovievist trial was their inadequate answer to the published material in the capitalist press.

The more standard American capitalist press (not Hearst's) printed reports which were not viciously hostile to the trial, such as were printed in the British papers. *This was true* especially *of* the two leading papers, 'The New York Times' and the 'Herald-Tribune'. The two leading agencies, the Associated Press and the United Press printed reports which were as fair as a bourgeois writer could make them. In fact, Denny of the 'Times' actually defended the trial as being a legitimate and fair trial. However, both these papers published editorials which were vicious against the Soviet Union, declaring that this trial shows that democracy has not been established in the Soviet Union, and that the punishment meted out to the conspirators was far beyond what was necessary for the safety of the nation and its leaders.

Also, there were some insinuations in the press, in the course of the trial, that the confessions were given so freely by the defendants because they undoubtedly had a "deal" with the prosecution to give these confessions in return for having their lives spared. Other papers explained the confessions of the defendants as being those of "oriental" minds, and characterizing the whole trial as an "oriental manifestation".

The most vicious of the capitalist press was the Hearst papers and the right Socialist press, which spoke about the assassination of Lenin's co-workers by the present regime; about Bolshevism being born in and living by violence, and about the Bolsheviks killing one another.

All of these things were answered inadequately in the 'Daily Worker'. There was one 'Daily Worker' editorial in which a 'Times' editorial was criticised for belittling the charges.

Thus, the 'Daily Worker' can be said to have presented the evidence of the trial and all material in connection with the trial, including *supporting editorials,* original cartoons *against the renegades,* in an extensive manner. In an objective sense, this partly answered the slander from the American capitalist press, but it was also necessary to directly answer the insinuations and false statements and charges in the capitalist and Socialist press, and this, the Daily Worker did rather poorly.

This report is limited by the fact that the Daily Workers beginning with the returning of the verdicts are not yet here. Undoubtedly these will carry more material.

1. It is unclear whether this sentence (beginning "Thus, most of the readers . . . ") was marked for deletion.

Document 82

Excerpt from forty-two-page transcript, Earl Browder testimony to ECCI Secretariat meeting, 4 April 1937, RTsKhIDNI 495–20–521. Original in English, with handwritten corrections.

. . .

Opposing the January trial of the Trotskyites in Moscow, the attempt was made *by the Trotskyites* to organise a counter-offensive with the Committee for the Defense of Trotsky. This committee was in its majority composed of Trotskyites, and Socialists who were under the influence of the Trotskyites. But it also included about sixteen or eighteen non-Trotskyite liberals, people of standing before the country, whose names are important and give weight and credence to this Committee. Operating in the beginning with *only* liberal slogans of asylum, it rapidly passed over to open counter-revolutionary agitation, advocating insurrection against the Soviet power. The disclosures of the trial, however, brought the honest members of this committee to sharp awakening. They began to realise that their confidence had been abused, they had been duped. Led by a liberal editor named Mauri[tz] Hallgren, who issued a denunciation of Trotsky and Trotskyism, there was a movement to withdraw from this committee that took more than half of these non-Trotskyites out of it. The fact that this *little* group of liberals had identified itself with Trotsky had been of importance not because they represented a *general* tendency in these circles to move towards Trotskyism—there is no such *general* tendency—but it was important because the big newspapers, especially Hearst, uses their names in order to publicise every word spoken for Trotsky very loudly and energetically and to broadcast Trotsky's propaganda with the approval of these names. The newspapers made it appear that this little handful of people was an army. To counteract this newspaper campaign, a group of 88 outstanding public figures issued an open letter to American liberals condemning this Committee for the Defense of Trotsky. In their Open Letter they reaffirmed their faith in the Soviet Union, their confidence in the Soviet Government, and their friendship for the Soviet people. Among these 88 names (hundreds were added later, but the first publication was with 88 names,) among them were such outstanding figures as Heywood Broun, President of the American Newspaper Guild, several editors of the liberal weeklies, "The Nation" and "The [New] Republic", *Mary Van Kleek, outstanding economist*, Theodore Dreiser, the most prominent American novelist, Corlis Lamont, a very prominent liberal, Ring Lardner, one of the most popular writers in America, Dr. John Kingsbury, the greatest authority on public health, *Rockwell* Kent, one of the outstanding American artists, Robert Morse Lovett, leading intellectual and Socialist, Colonel Raymond Robbins, Democratic politician, known in Russia [in] 1917, as the head of the American Red Cross, Rev. William B. Spofford, leader of a big church movement, Lillian D. Wald, chief figure in American social work, Art Young, leading Socialist artist, etc. These names, these examples, will indicate the quality of *the* list, it was the cream of the American intellectual and artistic world. The most outstanding list *of names ever signed on one document in the U.S.* for the *defense of the* Soviet Union. It marked a deepening realisation among the American *middle* classes, especially, that every enemy of the Soviet Union is at the same time an enemy of American democracy.

The last defense of the Trotskyites in reference to the January trial was summed up in the exclamation that they wrote in all the newspapers: "Incredible, it cannot be believed"!! Norman Thomas and their other supporters took up this slogan. They protested that it is impossible to believe that any human being is capable of such depths of treachery. But we were able very quickly to organise a complete answer to that on the basis of American experience, they were refusing to believe *that which* American experience *presents* very close parallels.

We have been teaching the American masses American history in relation to Trotsky, teaching them about Aaron Burr, the Trotsky of the American Revolution. Aaron Burr was the Vice-President of the United States under Jefferson, who plotted with the British for the breaking up of the United States Government. He carried on this conspiracy in connection with a party that had degenerated to what has been described by American *historians* as "wreckers", *exactly the same word you use in the Soviet Union to describe the Trotskyites*. This American conspiracy also failed because it couldn't declare

Document 82 *continued*

its program to its followers without breaking up its organisation. As soon as their policy became known, their followers left them. For Americans to exclaim "incredible" to the revelations of the Moscow trial, is to disclaim American *experience*.

It would be a mistake to think that the Trotskyites are finished in the United States, that they are no more a problem. That is not true, for they are a serious problem. They are in a position *to be* more damaging than they could at any other time. This is due to their position inside the Socialist Party. This gives them a sort of respectability *passport*, etc., a membership card in the party of Eugene V. Debs, a tradition in America. Together with this, they have command of unlimited space in the news and editorial columns of numerous American newspapers. They are now being taken up as agents of the AF of L bureaucracy in the fight against the CIO. They are already appearing, as in Minneapolis, as open agents of the underworld *and* for the steel trust. Where there is needed readiness for any kind of criminal work, wrecking work, they came forward and became the agents of these reactionary forces that are preparing a big assault against the whole labor movement. Their continued exposure and final isolation to remedy [render] them harmless is one of the most important tasks.

. . .

The Lovestoneite Deviation

In the Moscow trials, Leon Trotsky and Trotskyism were the chief devils. But the danger from the right, in the form of Nikolai Bukharin and his allies, also received its share of denunciations. Bukharin himself was executed after a show trial; thousands of Soviets sympathetic with Bukharinism were arrested and either imprisoned or executed. In the eyes of American Communists, the American branch of the Bukharinist evil was represented by Jay Lovestone and his followers, who had been expelled from the CPUSA in 1929. Lovestone had formed a dissident Communist organization that, by the time it was dissolved in the early 1940s, had become social democratic in orientation. In **document 83** the CPUSA reports to the Comintern on the Lovestoneites.

The report, from 1938, begins with the Lovestoneite influence in the unions. Lovestoneites have begun to advise Homer Martin, president of the United Auto Workers union (part of the CIO), about the threat from the union's Communists. Charles Zimmerman, a long-time leading figure in one of the larger New York locals of the International Ladies Garment Workers Union (ILGWU), is also identified as a Lovestoneite.[26]

The report then moves on to Bertram Wolfe, a founder of the American Communist movement, its representative to the Comintern in the late 1920s, and a Lovestone ally. Wolfe had gone to Spain, which was in the midst of civil war, to meet with leaders of the POUM (Partido obrero de unificación Marxista), an independent Marxist party. Although POUM supported the Spanish Republic in its war against Franco's nationalists—as did the Communists—Spanish Communists regarded the party as a threat.[27] The CPUSA notified the Comintern of Wolfe's visit, urging that Moscow arrange for surveillance of his activities. (In response, the Comintern notified the International Brigades, its military arm in Spain, whose security police kept Wolfe under observation.)[28]

In several places, the report reflects Moscow's fable that the rightist Lovestoneites were in league with the leftist Trotskyists, as in the reference to "the Lovestoneite-Bukharinite-Rykov counter-revolutionary gang as travelling the same road as the other fascist agents, the Trotskyists."

Document 83

"Some Information on the Activities of the Lovestoneites in the U.S.A.," 7 January 1938, RTsKhIDNI 495–20–536. Original in English. The American League for Peace and Freedom is a misidentification of the American League for Peace and Democracy, a major Popular Front organization.

"8"   U. S. A.
172/6
rc copy.   CONFIDENTIAL.
7.1.38

26. In 1939 a coalition of opponents, including Communists, ousted Martin, who moved to the AFL, taking a small faction of the union with him. Yet in spite of sustained attacks, Communists were never able to destroy Zimmerman's influence in Local 22 of the ILGWU.

27. After the Communists had gained sufficient influence in the Spanish Republican government, they denounced the POUM as fascist. They suppressed the party and secretly executed its leaders.

28. Documents concerning the CPUSA's role in Wolfe's surveillance are reproduced in Klehr, Haynes, and Firsov, Secret World of American Communism, 153–55.

Document 83 *continued*

The Lovestoneites, some 200 to 300 in number, are growing closer both programmatically and in their activities to the Trotskyists and on practically every issue they attack the Party, the Soviet Union and the Comintern with similar methods and arguments as the Trotskyists. On the Soviet trials of the Trotskyist and Bukharinist wreckers, on the question of defence of the POUM, etc., the position of the Lovestoneites is almost identical with the Trotskyites. In the recent period they have also developed active disruptive work in several CIO unions. In the Automobile Workers' Union they influence Martin, the national president, and have been responsible for the organisation of periodic red-baiting campaigns against the Communists and progressives. In the Needle Trades unions, especially Local 22 of the International Ladies Garment Workers Union, through the Lovestoneite Zimmerman, they occupy several leading positions which they utilise for anti-Communist activity. To a lesser extent they are working also in the Textile and Shoe unions.

Though they have been isolated in the American League for Peace and Freedom, they still endeavour to carry on their hostile activities within that organisation. They also have some of their adherents in the Teachers' Union in New York and in some of the Public Relief organisations.

In connection with Spain, they have taken the same position as the Trotskyists. Bert Wolfe, one of the leading Lovestoneites, has been in Spain working with the POUM and other counter-revolutionary forces.

In regard to the struggle against the Lovestoneites, this has been conducted very inadequately up till recently, both ideologically and in everyday practical mass work. This has been due chiefly to a serious underestimation within the ranks of the Party of the changed role of the Lovestoneite-Bukharinite-Rykov counter-revolutionary gang as travelling the same road as the other fascist agents, the Trotskyists. The Party press has until lately carried on very little agitational and other ideological forms of exposure and struggle against the Lovestoneites, their program, role and activities.

In the Automobile Workers' Union, however, the Party was made sharply aware of the Lovestoneites' activities which came dangerously near wrecking the unity of the August National Auto Convention and which still is a serious disruptive element.

Since then, and particularly since the enlarged meeting of the Polburo, C.C., on Nov. 17th, the Party is seriously commencing to connect the struggle against Lovestoneism as an organic part of the fight against Trotskyism, and is beginning to develop this struggle in an effective manner.

Pressure for Even Greater Press Fervor

Documents 84, 85 and 86 illustrate the fervor with which American Communists embraced Stalin's version of the Moscow trials by showing that American Communists, in conjunction with the Comintern, continually examined the CPUSA's own press for signs of ideological weakness. In document 84 an American Communist, one H. Greenblatt, warns the CPUSA representative to the Comintern that two editors of the *Morning Freiheit*, the party's Yiddish-language newspaper, are soft on the Moscow trials. As evidence Greenblatt points to a column by Moissaye Olgin, a *Freiheit* editor. In the course of attacking Trotsky, Olgin described him as having acted contrary to Marxism-Leninism *since 1920*. In Greenblatt's eyes this suggests that Olgin believed that Trotsky had "followed the line of the Party up to 1920 and was correct until then." Apparently, Greenblatt had literally accepted Moscow's view that Trotsky had betrayed the movement earlier, even while he was leading the Red Army to victory over the Whites. Greenblatt's complaint against Moishe Katz is even more extravagant in its fanaticism. Katz had written approvingly that when Zinoviev and others made their confessions, they had begged to be executed. Katz agreed that they deserved death. But he also wrote that he wanted to believe that in asking for the death penalty, Zinoviev and the others were exhibiting a "spark of conscience." For Greenblatt, these formulations are unacceptably weak, and he indignantly concludes: "And these comrades, I believe, are teaching the History of the Party in the United States!"[29]

In document 85, A. Wechsler and J. Abelovsky, two Hungarian-American Communists working in Moscow, similarly sniff out shortcomings in an article by Peter Zvara, an editor of *Uj Elöre*, the CPUSA's Hungarian-language newspaper. Zvara's article fervently endorsed the executions of Zinoviev and his colleagues but noted that they had once been great men, who deserved some credit for having confessed their guilt and recanted. Wechsler and Abelovsky regard this attitude as "confused" "sentimentalism," and the two

29. Katz may have been too soft for Greenblatt, but he was pretty hard-line. In 1935 he wrote a CPUSA pamphlet applauding the announcement from Moscow that 103 members of the "Zinoviev-Trotskyist conspiracy" had been shot. See M. Katz, "The Assassination of Kirov" (New York: CPUSA, 1935).

charge that Zvara might give the impression that "the counter-revolutionary group ought not to be shot."

The American representative to the Comintern, Sam Darcy, endorsed the complaints contained in documents 84 and 85 and added his own. Darcy sent a letter (document 86) entitled "Concerning the Press" to the CPUSA leadership, informing them that they must "find time to consider the very bad state of our language press, and also such magazines as the 'New Masses'. Especially in connection with the handling of matters concerning the Soviet Union *and the recent trial,* some very bad things have come to light in the last period which require that we have some friend assigned to take up the question of checking up on the work of these editorial staffs more closely."

"Concerning the Press" quotes virtually the entire texts of documents 84 and 85 regarding *Freiheit* and *Uj Elöre* and comments: "Since the statement speaks for itself, we are simply reproducing it and leaving it to you to take such measures as are necessary to correct the situation."

Much of "Concerning the Press" was directed at *New Masses,* the CPUSA-linked literary-intellectual journal. Darcy writes: "In the last six months, it appears to us that the New Masses started with a correct intention to make a better appeal to the middle-class and professional elements, but, instead of presenting the Communist line in a form which would appeal to these people, they, instead, started writing on the same level as some of the most backward sections of the middle-class." Specifically, Darcy complained that in a series of articles about his visit to the Soviet Union, Joshua Kunitz, a veteran party journalist, had given attention to waiters demanding tips, incompetent baggage-handlers, and prostitution. Darcy condemned emphasis on this last as "biased reporting against a Socialist country." Darcy objected even more strongly to a manuscript Kunitz had submitted to the Comintern concerning the Zinoviev trial. Darcy complained that in a mistaken attempt to appear objective, Kunitz had presented "the defendants in a manner that can only arouse pity and sympathy in the hearts of people who are in any way humane." Fortunately, Darcy and the Comintern saw the manuscript before publication, and "we got him to write and wire a number of changes to the New Masses."

In document 86, Darcy is accusing some *American* Communists of being soft on Trotskyism. In **document 87,** another American representative finds that a *Soviet* Communist has fallen short. Document 87 is an "urgent and strictly confidential" letter dated 31 October 1937 from "T. Ryan" (Eugene Dennis) to Georgi Dimitrov. Ryan/Dennis complains that a manuscript for a book on Soviet trade unionism by Solomon Lozovsky, head of the Comintern's trade union arm, gives insufficient attention to Trotskyism. His evidence: in a summary chapter only a single page is devoted to "the struggle against Trotsky and the Trotskyites" in the period 1920–1921 and "not a single line is given to the subsequent counter-revolutionary role and history of Trotskyism and to exposing the Trotskyites and Trotskyism as agents of fascism." In contrast, Ryan notes that Lozovsky devotes six pages to the fight against the "Rights," that is, Bukharin and his followers. And even with that much space, notes Ryan/Dennis, the discussion is insufficiently comprehensive. Ryan/Dennis had probably hoped for greater condemnation.

Ryan/Dennis's ideological nit-picking illustrates how deeply American Communists had absorbed Moscow's paranoia. Eugene Dennis was not an insignificant fanatic. He had first made his name as a militant organizer of California agricultural workers in the late 1920s. In the early 1930s he worked for the Comintern as its agent in the Philippines, South Africa, and China. He returned to the United States in 1935 to become head of the Communist party in Wisconsin. His 1936 stint as CPUSA representative to Moscow was a reward for his success in gaining an influential role for Communists in both the Wisconsin CIO and Wisconsin liberal politics. A future general secretary of the CPUSA, Dennis had a big hand in shaping American Communist policy, and, as we see here, he had completely accepted the Soviet party line.

Document 84

Greenblatt to Randolph, 26 September 1936, RTsKhIDNI 495–14–54. Original in English. "Randolph" was the alias for the CPUSA's representative to the Comintern, at this time Sam Darcy. The "D.W." is the *Daily Worker*.

Sept. 26, 1936.

Comrade Randolph:

I wish to call your attention to the following extracts from articles which appeared in the "Morning Freiheit", written by the two editors, Comrades Olgin and M. Katz regarding the Trotsky-Zinoviev terrorist trial:

Comrade Olgin, in an article in the M.F. of Sept. 9th (This also appeared in the D.W. of the same date) states:

"Trotsky's bankruptcy began about 15 years ago, it was about 1920." The Daily Worker prints the statement as follows: "Trotsky was utilised when he followed the line of the Party," while in the M.F. the same is stated "When was Trotsky correct? Only when he followed the line of the Party." Therefore, according to this statement, Trotsky followed the line of the Party up to 1920 and was correct until then. And why the two different opinions in the two different papers?

The other editor, Comrade Katz, in the issue of Aug. 26, gives the following heading to his article: "The Death of the Trotskyist plotters is a Thing of Justice and Mercy". While giving a good analysis of the reasons which led to their becoming terrorists, he becomes humane and psychoanalystic, and says the following:
"

"If any [of] them had left a spark of conscience, they should have committed suicide before. They wished that death, the deliverer, should free them from the wormy swamp in which they were deteriorating while alive. And we want to believe that when they declared that the only thing which they deserve is death, that this was the last spark, which showed that somewhere in them sparks of human feelings were yet left."

Now we know why this band admitted their guilt! They wanted to die, therefore so, "while they were demoralized through and through before, they came to their last stage of which the Soviet court finally freed them".

And these comrades, I believe, are teaching the History of the Party in the United States!

H. Greenblatt.

Document 85

A. Wechsler and J. Abelovsky, "In the Case of 'Uj Elöre' Hungarian Daily," 21 September 1936, RTsKhIDNI 495–14–54. Original in English with handwritten annotations.

Statement
by A. Wechsler and J. Abelovsky
in the case of "Uj Elöre" Hungarian d
Daily.

Being long years members of the Hungarian Büro of the C.P in the States, we are still take an active interest in the revolutionary movement over there. Lately there are signs, that the dayly paper "Uj Elöre" is not following always the Party lines. In connection with the trial of the Zinoviev-Kamenev counter-revolutionary terrorist group, one of the editors—Peter Zvara—wrote an article on Aug. 27-th vol. XXXIV. No. 8269, which is so confused and mixed with sentimentalism, that the readers might think, the counter-revolutionary group ouht not to be shot, because "they were not so very vicious" that "they were great men" and so on.

In the paper of Aug. 31-st, the editor already answered two letters which apparently defended Trotzky and Zinovjev.

We are translating a few sentences in order to show the character of the said article which was entitled "Gondolatok" /T[h]oughts/.

". . . From my part I would not say anything about /the exesution/ if amongst them hade not been a Zinoviev and a Kamenev and if they had not made such speeches as they have made before the sentence was given."

".Zinoviev and Kamenev were great men, who long years played leading roles in preparing the revolution and afterwards in building the new society. Zinoviev for long years worked together with Lenin, before and after the revolution. The sentence depressed me. Depressed because I thouht of this Zinoviev and not of that miserable renegade, who conspired with Trotzky against Stalin and o[t]her leaders of the new society".

"But apparently Zinoviev did not fall so deep /morally/ but in the last hours of his life he would'nt try to stay as high as he stood once."

"This is the case [of] Kamenev also."

After giving a short outline of Zinoviev's and Kamenev's party lives he makes a remark, that "the first and only victim of their conspiracy were Sergei Mironovich Kirov."

The editor expressed the belief, that Zinoviev and Kamenev have now sincerely recanted their mistakes and finished his article thus:

"For their ugly deed they deserved to be executed."

"For their recant they deserve a praising word from their ex-comrades."

Such an article could be appear only because in the editorial staff there is not a tried bolshevik. The aut[h]or of this article a few years ago was an

313

Document 85 continued

employee of the Roman Catholic Church of Toledo and without getting a party training, he was taken into the editorial staff.

The chief editor, Somogyi, also not long ago became a member of the party and [is] ideologically not developed enough.

The third member of the staff is Zador Szabados, and old Soc. Dem, newspaper man, who in 1929–30 worked for the Hungarian fascist daily, the "Amerikai Magyar Népszava"

The Hungarian Büro was transfered from New York to Cleveland which means that the party control is loosening. There is a great danger that the "Uj Elöre" will be saturated with trotzkist and Soc. Dem ideology. Knowing well the peculiar situation in the Hungarian movement, the connection between the paper and the mass organisations, mainly the Sick Benefit Society / I.W. O./ we consider it our duty to call the attention of the American Section of the Comintern to these facts.

Sept. 21. 1936.

> A[illegible] *Wechsler member C.P.S.U. No 1218253*
> *working Inst. Marx Engels-Lenin*
> *Joe Abelovsky, member C.P. of S.U. N.2200917*
> working [illegible]

Address
[illegible] 109
[illegible] No 5 kb. 34.
[illegible]

Document 86

Excerpts from [Darcy] to Dear Friends, "Concerning the Press," 7 October 1936, RTsKhIDNI 515–1–3968. Original in English. Inscribed in Russian: "Translate into Russian." An incomplete copy of this letter, found in RTsKhIDNI 515–1–3969, is dated 5 November 1936. The document transcribed here has handwritten corrections that have been typed into the incomplete version, an indication that the October version is probably a draft of a letter sent in November.

2342—15OKT 1936 [stamp]   CONFIDENTIAL
7.10.36
SS/2.   translate into Russian

Dear Friends:

Concerning the Press:

It is necessary for you to find time to consider the very bad state of our language press, and also such magazines as the 'New Masses'. Especially in connection with the handling of matters concerning the Soviet Union *and the recent trial,* some very bad things have come to light in the last period which requires that we have some friend assigned to take up the question of checking up on the work of these editorial staffs more closely.

Here, we would like to call to your attention the work of *four* papers in connection with the Soviet Union, namely, the Freiheit, Uj Elore, *Finnish paper* and the New Masses.

1) Uj Elore: (The following is an excerpt from a long statement submitted by a group of Hungarian friends here concerning the Uj Elore. Since the statement speaks for itself, we are simply reproducing it and leaving it to you to take such measures as are necessary to correct the situation.)

. . . [Darcy here quotes most of document 84.]

2) Freiheit: (Because I am just as unable to read the Freiheit as I am the Uj Elore, I am here reprinting what has been checked by comrades here concerning what the Freiheit has written about the Trotsky-Zinovievist trial.)

. . . [Darcy here quotes most of document 85.]

3) New Masses:
In the last six months, it appears to us that the New Masses started with a correct intention to make a better appeal to the middle-class and professional elements, but, instead of presenting the Communist line in a form which would appeal to these people, they, instead, started writing on the same level as some of the most backward sections of the middle-class, Thus, instead of bringing Communism to the middle-class elements, what they really did was to bring middle-class ideology to our movement.

This is especially true of the handling of the reporting on the Soviet Union. In the June and July issues of the New Masses, for example, *Joshua Kunitz* writes a well-advertised series of articles, but, with all the tremendous events that are occurring here, his topics consist of the most ridiculously small isolated phenomena that one could possibly find in the USSR. He starts by saying that these phenomena are neither "typical nor permanent" and are "transitory and minor". Yet, despite this admission, he proceeds for the entire series to deal *only* with such facts as "a couple of doormen, who looked for tips", although his description is so exaggerated as to be an utter caricature of the situation. He quotes a fellow-passenger as saying:

> "The uniformed flunkies and waiters hovering all about you, scraping their feet, bowing, smiling ingratiatingly, and always looking at the palm of your hand—they're utterly disgusting".

He reports but he does not deny this idiotic exaggeration. The writer of this letter eats often at these hotels and is in every way a typical foreigner, includ-

Document 86 *continued*

ing lack of knowledge of the language, and has never seen anything even approaching this description here.

The other topics Kunitz deals with also are handled in a similar way. He describes "two barefoot youngsters"; "an incompetent baggage-handler"; "a beggar", etc.

In another article, he describes prostitution. (I especially ask you to note the topics he chooses as "objective reporting".) But, amongst the things he says concerning prostitution is, that he gives it as his opinion that a certain "liberal lady (his fellow passenger) is a little too sanguine in her assertion that the economic causes of prostitution have been completely eliminated". To make such a general statement because a handful of prostitutes exist somewhere around Intourist hotels, or maybe even in one or other isolated spot in the Soviet Union, is clearly biased reporting against a Socialist country, because he puts isolated cases of prostitution in the Soviet Union on the same plane with the mass phenomenon that exists in the capitalist countries.

It is true, in the same article he says some things in defence of the Soviet Union, but most of it in such an apologetic tone, as can only condemn the situation here.

He does all of this under the pretext of answering the "Romantic Lovers of Revolution", but what he really does is to take up the method of Will Durant who, after his stay in the Soviet Union, wrote a series of articles, the chief subjects of which were dirty tablecloths, tipping, and other such "shortcomings" of Socialism.

It is not a question of this or that detail in the series of articles; it is a question of the entire approach to the world historic problems of the construction of Socialism, an approach which does not aim to raise the middle-class to a higher level of understanding of the USSR, but *panders to the prejudices* of the most backward sections of middle-class people *in an effort to make his writings "popular."*

We do not have the last issues of the New Masses, but we have seen the manuscript of a series of articles which Kunitz submitted on the question of the Trotsky-Zinoviev trial.

In this series of articles, *written* in the name of 'objectivity', he paints the defendants with the following adjectives: "luminous", "sparkling", "typical of the Bolsheviks", "look like labor leaders", "handsomest", "sensitive young face", "mild", "innocuously idealistic", "good-natured", "famous revolutionist", "collaborator of Lenin", etc. He also characterises the prosecution and the judges in the following terms: "harshly", "close-cropped", "thin lips", "cold", "does not look up", "funereal". And this in the name of objectivity!

He also develops a theory in this series of articles that the reason why these elements became terrorists against the Soviet Union was because discipline in the C.P. is *so* severe, *that it* inevitably brings a reaction amongst people who are "defective".

Document 86 *continued*

In the closing part of his series, he describes the closing scenes of the trial, in which he presents the defendants in a manner that can only arouse pity and sympathy in the hearts of people who are in any way humane. By this, I do not mean that he writes the whole series in defence of the Zinoviev terrorists; on the contrary, it is his conception as to how to write against them, but to write in a way that is "acceptable" to the middle class. And, as a result, he wrote a series of articles which were very much against us.

We discovered the entire thing purely by accident, when he submitted his series to be published as a pamphlet here, and subsequently, we got him to write and wire a number of changes to the New Masses, although we do not know how far he went in making the changes, and we do not know if his changes arrived before publication.

. . . [A section on the Finnish press is omitted.]

I have gone to such great length to cite all of these instances in order to show that there is a dangerous loosening up of ideological control in [illegible] amongst these language groups, and amongst such groups as the New Masses, and I would urge that this entire matter be discussed in the CC and measures taken to correct the situation. *These remarks are only on the papers we checked—the others are probably no better.*

With warmest personal greetings.

Document 87

T. Ryan to Dimitrov, 31 October 1937, RTsKhIDNI 495–14–81. Original in English. Lozovsky is spelled "Losovsky" throughout.

2732 31 OCT 1937 [stamp]

October 31, 1937

Urgent and Strictly Confidential

Dear Comrade Dimitroff:

About a month ago I edited the English translation of Comrade Losovsky's new book: "A Handbook On the Soviet Trade Unions." At that time I sharply criticized the book, especially relating to its treatment of two questions: Trotskyism and the international labor movement. In addition to submitting my criticisms and proposals in writing to the Profintern (i.e., to Comrade C. Johnson), I informed Comrade Marty of my views.

I was told by Comrade Johnson that some of my criticisms were accepted by Comrade Losovsky. Yet I could not find out specifically which were accepted or rejected. Then upon my request it was agreed that I was to receive the final typewritten copy of the manuscript prior to its being sent to the publishers, so that I could ascertain which of my recommendations had been incorporated in the text. However, the next I heard of the manuscript was on October 29th when I learned that the Co-operative Publishers were already in the process of publishing the book which is now scheduled to be off the press and ready for circulation on November 3rd.

I have secured a typewritten copy of the final text from the Co-operative Publishers and have briefly examined Chapters I Brief Historical Review, XII The Trade Unions and the Communist Party, and XIV The Soviet Trade Unions and the International Labor Movement. The text is substantially the same as the original manuscript submitted to me. The question of Trotskyism is touched upon formally in a few passages, but, in the main, is either omitted or slurred over.

For instance, in Chapter I (Brief Historical Review) which sketchily covers the period from 1905 to 1937, Losovsky devotes about one page to the struggle against Trotsky and the Trotskyites, and this in a very inadequate manner. And what is of special significance is that this page deals solely with the period of 1920–21. Not a single line is given to the subsequent counter-revolutionary role and history of Trotskyism and to exposing the Trotskyites and Trotskyism as agents of fascism. Yet this same chapter devotes some six pages to the Rights, although here too, nothing is mentioned of the changed role of the Bukharinites and the recent developments.

In Chapter XII (Trade Unions and the Communist Party) not a single reference is made to the Trotskyites or Trotskyism and their counter-revolutionary role and activities in the Soviet trade union movement or in other spheres. Yet this chapter devotes three pages to Tomsky and the Rights.

And concerning Chapter XIV, the question of the Soviet trade unions and the International Labor movement is dealt with in a very schematic and unsatisfactory manner, especially is this true regarding the struggle for international trade union unity.

With-out raising at this time what seems to me to be other serious defects and weaknesses in the "Handbook on the Soviet Trade Unions" and certain political conclusions to be drawn from this I would like to propose for your consideration that Comrade Losovsky's book shall be withheld from publication, at least until such time as it is edited and approved by a commission of the ECCI or the CC,CPSU.

> Comradely,
> T. *Ryan*
> T. Ryan
> Rep., CPUSA

Comintern Education in Ideological Sensitivity

The hypersensitivity toward ideological deviation shown in these documents was not an aberration but the product of Comintern training. The files of "Sector D," the American section of the International Lenin School (ILS), yielded documents 88 and 89, which demonstrate the extent to which students were taught to worry about such issues. The ILS trained mid-level foreign Communists, along with Soviet Communists, in ideology, organizational techniques, and technical skills needed for Communist work around the world. From the mid-1920s until the mid-1930s several hundred promising American Communists were sent to Moscow for ILS schooling. Lenin school graduates were accorded great prestige in the party and regarded as models. By the end of the 1930s and 1940s, these graduates were employed as full-time staff by the CPUSA, the many front groups it influenced, and the unions under its leadership.

Document 88 relates to the accusation at a Sector D meeting by one student, Jenny Klevatan, that another, Pearl Orland, had claimed that she "had gotten better food in [an American] jail than in the Soviet Union." The ILS authorities did not dismiss the complaint as trivial; rather, they insisted that Orland explain this remark. She did so in a signed statement in which she stated that she had had a stomach disorder and that although the ILS fare consisted of "good food" made of "good products," it had not been prepared properly for her needs. She insisted that her remarks were "not made in a derogatory manner." As for her reference to jail food, Orland explained that she had really meant that when she was assigned to kitchen detail in a U.S. jail, the jail's food had been made of "poor products" but that she had personally "cooked them well." She also struck back at Klevatan by accusing her of complaining about the quality of Soviet tailors.[30]

The ILS authorities accepted Orland's rather convoluted explanation but admonished her to be more careful in expressing herself. In document 88 Klevatan angrily complains that Orland had been

---

30. Pearl Orland, "Comrade Kleaveitis stated . . . ," 21 May 1935, RTsKhIDNI 531–2–58. Jenny's last name is given here and in document 88 variously as "Klevatan," "Klevaite," and "Kleaveitis."

let off too lightly; her complaint about the food amounted to "counter-revolutionary slander against the Soviet Union." Klevatan may have thought that Orland had gotten off easily, but it is likely that American students at the Lenin school got the point that uttering even trivial criticism of things Soviet could bring one up before ILS authorities for examination.

Document 89 deals with a more serious lesson for Americans at the ILS on the danger of ideological crimes. In these notes of a summary speech at a Sector D meeting, the party committee recommends expelling an American student as an "alien element" and severely censuring two Russian teachers, Laroza and Urazov for, in Laroza's case, teaching Trotskyist concepts and in Urazov's case, tolerating Laroza's views. For good measure, the party committee also noted that it was a "serious shortcoming" on the part of Laroza's students not to have noticed these errors—although how the Americans would have known that the teacher who instructed them on correct ideology was ideologically incorrect is not clear. What is clear is that the Sector D committee's censure of Urazov had the backing of Soviet party officials. The documents refer to a "Trotskyist speech which he made in 1923." Only the CPSU would have had access to Soviet records of activities from more than a decade earlier. American Communists who wished to remain in the movement learned from these incidents to beware even the mildest deviation from the strict Soviet line.

Document 88

Jenny Klevatan to the Party Committee, RTsKhIDNI 531–2–58. Documents in the same file suggest that this was written circa 21 May 1935. Original in English. The author's last name is typed at the top of the document as "Klevatan," but the handwritten signature appears to be "Klevaite" (and the name appears in another document as "Kleaveitis"). The writer refers to one person as both "Bogan" and "Bogen."

To the Party Committee
From—Jenny Klevatan, Sector D

I live in Room 40—there are three comrades living in this room—Comrades Orland, Mead and myself.

I heard Comrade Orland complain many times about the food here.

To the Party Committee
From - Jenny Klevatan, Sector D

        I live in Room 40 - there are three comrades
living in this room - Comrades Orland, Mead and myself.
        I heard Comrade Orland complain many times
about the food here.
        One day when her meal was brought to her to
the room (she was ill) Orland made the statement "there
is better food in jail than here".
        A few days later she said to Stella Franks,
also student of sector D (Mead, Stella and I were in
the room) "I am starving - I am going to the Torgsin to
buy some food" Franks even made the remarks "are you
joking or serious"
        I raised this question at the Party meeting of
Sector D on May 16th. A meeting was called next day
to investigate my charges.
        Comrades XXXXXX Bogan, Vernon, the Party Or-
ganizer Helen and I were present.
        First Comrade Bogan questioned me as to how
I get along with the comrades - I answered well, but that
does not mean that I will tolerate any counter-revolutionary slander against the Soviet Union.
        Then i repeated Orland's statement. She did not
deny that she made this statement. Her explanation was the
following -
        1.   "Well, Jenny also complained when they spoiled
her coat (my note - well, I made no comparison with a jail)
        2.   that while in jail she cooked food for the pri-
soners and then the food became much better and the prisoners
liked her very much. She continued - the food is good here
but prepared very poorly,
        Comrade Bogen summed up the meeting with the
statementthat I as a member of the VKB(b) must know that the
Party will not tolerate such talk, and
        That Orland mustbe more tactful. All the comrades
agreed with Com Bogen's conclusions.
        The conclusion to be drawn (in my opinion) from
the decision of Bogen and the others supporting him, is that
if one hears counter-revolutionary talk one is to keep quiet
otherwise "the Party will not tolerate him"!!!
        I protest against such a decision and place this
question before the Party Committee,because in my opinion that
statement made by Orland can only be characterized as counter-
revolutionary.

J. Klevait

DOCUMENT 88. Jenny Klevatan to the Party Committee, circa 21 May 1935.

Document 88 *continued*

One day when her meal was brought to her to the room (she was ill) Orland made the statement "there is better food in jail than here".

A few days later she said to Stella Franks, also student of sector D (Mead, Stella and I were in the room) "I am starving—I am going to the Torgsin to buy some food" Franks even made the remarks "are you joking or serious"

I raised this question at the Party meeting of Sector D on May 16th. A meeting was called next day to investigate my charges.

Comrades Bogan, Vernon, the Party Organizer Helen and I were present.

First Comrade Bogan questioned me as to how I get along with the comrades—I answered well, but that does not mean that I will tolerate any counter-revolutionary slander against the Soviet Union.

Then I repeated Orland's statement. She did not deny that she made this statement. Her explanation was the following—

1. "Well, Jenny also complained when they spoiled her coat (my note—well, I made no comparison with a jail)

2. that while in jail she cooked food for the prisoners and then the food became much better and the prisoners liked her very much. She continued—the food is good here but prepared very poorly,

Comrade Bogen summed up the meeting with the statement that I as a member of the VKP(b) must know that the Party will not tolerate such talk, and

That Orland must be more tactful. All the comrades agreed with Com Bogen's conclusions.

The conclusions to be drawn (in my opinion) from the decision of Bogen and the others supporting him, is that if one hears counter-revolutionary talk one is to keep quiet otherwise "the Party will not tolerate him"!!!

I protest against such a decision and place this question before the Party Committee, because in my opinion that statement made by Orland can only be characterized as counter-revolutionary.

J. Klevaite

Document 89

C. Walters's Notes of Summary Speech, Sector D Party Meeting, 6 March 1935, RTsKhIDNI 531–2–58. Original in English with handwritten Russian annotation at the top of the page.

Resolution Sector "D" regarding Laroza, Urazov, Lieberman
APPROXIMATE notes of speech at Party meeting March 4, 1935 (outline)

Sector D this morning discussed the decisions of the Party Committee in the cases of Comrades Laroza, Urazov, and Lieberman and unanimously agreed with and endorsed these decisions. We particularly discussed the two different organizational conclusions mad[e] by the Party Committee and agreed that in the case of Lieberman we have to do with a non-proletarian element who from the first day of entering our Party aligned with its enemies and continued the struggle against it while hiding these facts from the Party, and therefore is an alien element in our ranks that should be expelled; in the cases of Comrades Laroza and Urazov their crimes deserve expulsion from the Party but their past record and the prospect of saving them for the Party justifies the decision to limit the organizational decision in their cases to severe censure and warning.

The mis-teaching of Comrade Laroza and the liberal attitude toward it by Comrade Urazov is of the most serious character when we consider that it was their task to help prepare cadres in an international Party school for the struggle against the enemy ideologies and slanders which fight against the Soviet Union and against the Communist Parties in the capitalist countries. Instead of preparing our comrades for this task on the basis of Leninism, they allowed the smuggling of Trotskyist contraband into the studies. Instead of arming the students for the struggle with our class enemies, they thus disarmed them.

Comrade Laroza, in the first discussions with him, tried to explain his mistakes by saying that he thought that Trotsky was finished, that he was no longer important, and that it was not necessary to pay too much attention to him in the studies. We know that Trotskyism still constitutes a considerable danger to our movement and leads the counterrevolution. In our country, the Trotskyites have only recently gathered around themselves a number of grouplets of social reformists, cloaked them with new revolutionary phrases, and together have formed a new "Workers' Party" in an effort to regenerate the struggle against communism. Our school must properly arm our students for the exposure and struggle against Trotskyism wherever it raises its head.

Comrade Laroza's teaching that the proletarian dictatorship is merely a state based on force coincides with the latest campaign being conducted in our country against the Communist Party by the most reactionary press. They are trying to drive a wedge between our Party and the masses by this distortion of our teachings. Our students must be prepared to answer these lies, to win to our side the poor peasantry and all oppressed by revealing clearly the Leninist meaning of proletarian dictatorship in all its sides as also the alliance of the proletariat with the toiling peasantry and the Negro masses for the building of socialism and a classless society. On this question as well as on others such as the fictitious ideological rearming of the Party in 1917, etc., Comrade Laroza taught not Leninism but Trotskyist distortions.

With regard to the roots of Comrade Laroza's mistakes, we must understand that which he was not able to understand at the Party Committee meeting. He states that he could not find the roots because he and his family were of proletarian origin, fought in the Civil War, etc. Th[is] does not change the fact that the source of his mistake remains the pressure of petty-bourge[o]is influences. These must be looked for not only in ourselves and our families, but in our whole social environment. They are present in the hostile capitalist world which surrounds the Soviet Union and in the remnants of capitalist and non-proletarian classes which remain in the Soviet Union.

Comrade Urazov's crime of liberalism is augmented by the additional fact that he displayed insincerity and efforts at deceiving the Party in connection with a Trotskyist speech which he made in 1923. We must demand honesty and open recognition of our mistakes in our dealings in the Party.

It was a serious shortcoming on the part of Comrade Laroza's students that they were not alert to his misteaching and allowed it to go on unchallenged. We must learn to be more vigilant against any distortion of the Leninist teaching. We cannot remain passive students. It is necessary to be critically alert especially under our conditions of w[o]rk wher[e] we often rely on translated, mimeographed material. More vigilance; fight all distorti[o]ns. That is our lesson.

March 6, 1935, CWalters

Tools of Discipline

Stalin could imprison or shoot Soviet citizens suspected of Trotskyism or Bukharinist deviation. The CPUSA did not have this option. But for those who wished to remain in the party, discipline was demanded and enforced. In 1937 James Ford, the party's ranking black leader, reported to the Comintern that although Trotskyism had little appeal for African-Americans, the leadership was taking no chances. As an example of how discipline was maintained, he described the case of Emmett Dorsey, a black professor at Howard University in Washington, D.C., who had chaired a Trotsky defense committee meeting. Noted Ford: "We have taken certain measures against this Dr. Dorsey. . . . We have at Howard University a group of about five Negro professors who are Communists. We have gone to that university and talked with our comrades. We have organized a special meeting and outlined a program of how to struggle against that professor on the campus. We have about 25 YCLers on the campus. We also have organized them to the extent that these two professors—there are two of them with Trotskyite tendencies—are completely isolated."[31] In 1939 the National Con-

31. James Ford transcript, ECCI Secretariat meeting, 4 April 1937, RTsKhIDNI

trol Commission (NCC), the party's disciplinary arm, approved the punishment of an individual identified in commission reports only as "W," described as a former leading member of the German Communist party who had escaped to the United States after spending time in a Nazi prison. Noting that W. "confesses 'earlier' doubts about the trials of the Trotskyist spies and wreckers in the S. Union," the report concluded: "Therefore, while we should work with him in anti-Nazi movement, he should not be placed in any responsible posts through our efforts and his further development should be watched."[32]

Expulsion

The loathing American Communists had conceived for Trotskyism and Lovestoneism was comprehensive and rigid. Indeed, the New York Communist party, the largest in the CPUSA, passed a resolution in 1938 "that anyone married to a Lovestoneite or Trotskyite [must] either separate or sever connections with Party."[33] In 1937 a local district of the CPUSA expelled Sue Adams, a Communist union organizer and member of the district political bureau in Colorado. The National Control Commission considered but rejected her appeal, citing as a major reason a report that she had recently had dinner with a Trotskyist. In many cases those expelled for ideological errors held the views ascribed to them. But when the CPUSA was on the hunt for deviationists, local party leaders who failed to identify and expel sufficient numbers of offenders faced chastisement from the party's national leadership. Under that pressure, local party units found it expedient to accuse members of Trotskyism or Lovestoneism who were guilty of no more than a slip of the tongue or doctrinal confusion. In such circumstances repentance and confession of error were insufficient to avoid expulsion.[34]

495–20–521.

32. Minutes of National Control Commission, 17 January 1939, RTsKhIDNI 515–1–4086.

33. Minutes of New York State Bureau, 25 April 1938, RTsKhIDNI 495–14–102. The enforcement of this ban is discussed in Klehr, Haynes, and Firsov, *Secret World of American Communism*, 139–41.

34. Minutes of National Control Commission, 3 January 1939, RTsKhIDNI

These expulsions, in turn, were expected to serve a double purpose: they not only removed a "deviant," they discouraged other
Communists from committing similar thought crimes. **Documents
90, 91, and 92** are reports from the NCC illustrating not only the
crimes for which members were expelled but the party's use of
expulsion as a disciplinary tool. Document 90 is a table that contains
a breakdown by district of expulsions in 1929–1930, the peak
period of Lovestoneite expulsions. Document 91 is a summary of
expulsions for the year 1938, taken from an NCC report. Here most
of the ideological expulsions were for Trotskyism, a crime that
belonged more typically to the 1930s. Document 92 illustrates the
procedure of the Central Control Commission, as the NCC was later
called. In this 1937 report confirming the expulsions of Philip Rahv,
F. W. Dupee, and Martin Garnier, the commission recommends that
the *Daily Worker* publish a report on the Trotskyist crimes of Rahv
and Dupee and that notices exposing Garnier, a seaman, as a drunkard should be sent to all districts with marine workers in the party.

Document 90

Excerpts from Charles Dirba, "List of Expulsions," RTsKhIDNI 515–1–2054. The document is undated, but internal references place it in 1930, following the seventh national
convention of the CPUSA in June. Original in English. Halonenists were the followers of
George Halonen, a Finnish-American Communist leader who was expelled when he
refused to obey CPUSA orders about policies relating to an association of consumer
cooperatives that he led. The cooperatives were dominated by Communists and gave a
share of their income to the CPUSA. Halonen balked when the party ordered them to
substantially increase the CPUSA share.

COMMUNIST PARTY OF THE U.S.A.

[ILLEGIBLE SCRIPT]

- LIST OF EXPULSIONS -

As approved by the Central Control Commission during the period between
the VI Party Convention (in March, 1929) and the VII Party Convention (in

---

515–1–4086. A 1938 National Control Commission report to the CPUSA's national convention criticizing certain local party units for not expelling enough deviationists is reproduced in Klehr, Haynes, and Firsov, *Secret World of American
Communism*, 132–39. One of the most irrational internal purges of the CPUSA
came in a 1949–1953 campaign against "White chauvinism"; it is described in
Joseph Starobin, *American Communism in Crisis, 1943–1957* (Cambridge: Harvard University Press, 1972), 198–205. Starobin also describes the postwar ideological hunts for party members who showed signs of Browderism or Titoism.

Document 90 *continued*

June, 1930), not including 18 members who were first expelled and then re-admitted during this same period.

———

ABBREVIATIONS USED:

Lov.—Lovestoneism, renegade right wing followers of Lovestone in opposition to the Comintern and to the Party.

Trotz.—Trotzkyism, renegade group of Cannon & Co., followers of Trotzky's opportunist line covered with left phrases.

Hal.—Halonenism, right-wing petty-bourgeois opposition to the Comintern and Party line and policies in the co-operative field.

Wh-Chauv.—White-Chauvinism, violations of the principle of "no race discrimination" and full economic and social equality to the Negro workers.

Ukr. Op.—Right-wing opportunist opposition to Party disapproval of a new Ukrainian hall in Detroit, Michigan.

Rt-Wing—General right-wing opportunism, especially in trade union work and in fraternal organizations.

Indisc.—Indiscipline, violations of Party discipline and instructions, refusal to appear before Party Committees, non-payment of dues, general inactivity.

District 1 - Boston

Bail, Alex - CC Cand. & DO.	- Lov.
Bixby, Chester CC Member	- "
Clayman, B.	- "
Dawson, Ellen - CC Memb. Needle Trades	- "
Duboff, S.	- "
Futrau, E.	- "
Glantz, S.	- "
Golden, Mary	- "
Lamoiras, -	- "
Lanovoy, M.	- "
Lanovoy, T.	- "
Marks, Lewis - Accountant	- "
Oikemus, John	- "
Oikemus, Olga	- "
Oliver, J.	- "
Pircs, R. - Editor	- "
Fulton/Elsie - D.W. Agt.- Needle Trades	- "
Shaines, Mary	- "
Stephens, Roy - D. O.	- "

Document 90 *continued*

Stone, Eva - Office Worker   -   "
Wallace, S.   -   "
Zukoff, S.   -   "

District 2 - New York

Abramowitz - Bootlegger - Unreliability
                    Indisc.
Aronoff - Leather Worker-   - Lo v
A[?]ler, J.   -   "
Bail, Sam   -   "
Bavash, Benjamin   -   "
Becker, Ethel - Housewife   -   "
Becker, L. - Printer   -   "
Benjamin, D. - Worker School
     Director   -   "
Bentell, J. O. - CCC Member   -   "

. . . [List continues, totaling 398 names.]

RECAPITULATION OF EXPULSIONS

	Love-stoneism	Trotzky-ism	Halon-enism	White Chauv.	Ukr. Hall opp.	Spies	Right Wing	Other Causes	Totals
D.1—Boston	22								22
D.2—New York	137	1		1		2	13	19	173
D.3—Philadelphia	13					1	1	14	29
S.D.3—Anthracite	11							1	12
D.4—Buffalo	2								2
D.5—Pittsburgh	4					1		2	7
D.6—Cleveland						1	3	10	14
D.7—Detroit	10		1	2	20	1	7	8	49
D.8—Chicago	6		1					1	8
D.9—Minneapolis		2	25						27
D.10—Kansas City	6							9	15
D.12—Seattle	2			11				3	16
D.13—San Fran-cisco	1							2	3
S.D.13 Los Angeles	1							3	4
D.15—New Haven	9						4	3	16
D.17—Atlanta								1	1
TOTALS	224	3	27	14	20	6	28	76	398

cd/nb-OWU-TUUL

Fraternally submitted,
Chas Dirba Sec'y, CCC.

COMMUNIST PARTY OF THE U.S.A.

- LIST OF EXPULSIONS -

As approved by the Central Control Commission during the period between the
VI Party Convention (in March, 1929) and the VII Party Convention (in June, 1930),
not including 16 members who were first expelled and then re-admitted during this
same period.

ABBREVIATIONS USED:

Lov. -------Lovestoneism, renegade right wing followers of Lovestone in opposition
            to the Comintern and to the Party.
Trotz.------Trotzkyism, renegade group of Cannon & Co., followers of Trotzky's op-
            portunist line covered with left phrases.
Hal. -------Halonenism, right-wing petty-bourgeois opposition to the Comintern and
            Party line and policies in the co-operative field.
Wh-Chauv.----White-Chauvinism, violations of the principle of "no race discrimin-
            ation" and full economic and social equality to the Negro workers.
Ukr. Op.----Right-wing opportunist opposition to Party disapproval of a new
            Ukrainian hall in Detroit, Michigan.
Rt-Wing-----General right-wing opportunism, especially in trade union work and in
            fraternal organizations.
Indisc.-----Indiscipline, volations of Party discipline and instructions, refusal
            to appear before Party Committees, non-payment of dues, general
            inactivity.

District 1 - Boston

Bail, Alex - CC Cand.&DO.	-	Lov.
Bixby, Chester CC Member	-	"
Clayman, B.	-	"
Dawson, Ellen - CC Memb. Needle Trades	-	"
Duboff, S.	-	"
Futrau, E.	-	"
Glantz, S.	-	"
Golden, Mary	-	"
Lameiras, -	-	"
Lanovoy, M.	-	"
Lanovoy, T.	-	"
Marks, Lewis - Accountant	-	"
Oikemus, John	-	"
Oikemus, Olga	-	"
Oliver, J.	-	"
Mires, R. - Editor	-	"
Sultan, Elsie- D.W. Agt.- Needle Trades	-	"
Saines, Mary	-	"
Stephens, Roy - D. O.	-	"
Stone, Eva - Office Worker	-	"
Wallace, S.	-	"
Sukoff, S.	-	"

District 2 - New York

Abramowitz - Bootlegger-Unreliability		
Agronoff - Leather worker-	-	Lov.
Adler, J.	-	"
Bail, Sam	-	"
Baruch, Benjamin	-	"
Becker, Ethel - Housewife	-	"
Becker, L. - Printer	-	"
Benjamin, D. -Worker School Director	-	"
Bentall, J. O.- CCC Member	-	"

District 2 - New York
(Cont'd)

Cohen, Rose- needle worker	-	Lov.
Cohen, S. C.-professional "cooperator"	-	"
Constas - food worker -		"
Cooper, F.-Indiscipline in trade union wk.		
Cork, Jim - teacher -		Lovestone.
Diamond, Lester - leather worker-		"
Disenhous, Jack -		
Dismont, Geraldine - Negro newspaper work - Violation of Party policy		
Dorf, Eva - teacher -		Lovestoneism
Dungee -Negro work functionary -	-	"
Duke, Marie, office worker -	-	"
Ehrlich, H.	-	"
Farber, Joe	-	"
Finkelstein, Nathan- Left for USSR without permission		
Fisher, Rose- office worker - Lovestone/		
Fishman, M.- insurance agt.		"
Forman, N. - needle worker-		"
Fox, Anna	"	"	"
Garcia - Indiscip. & refusal to appear before Sec. Com.		
Garshin, C. - needle worker -		Lov.
Gorson, D. - Professional "cooperator"- Lovestoneism		
Gerson, S.C.-needle worker-		"
Gilbert - Irresponsibility		
Gitlow, Benjamin-CC Folcom Memb. -		Lov.
Gitlow, Kate - Housewife -	-	"
Gitz - food worker -	-	"
Gladstone, Harry -Right Winger on Palestine-refusal to appear before Section Com.		
Goldman, J.- laundry owner- Lovestoneism		
Gordon, Fannie - teacher-		"

DOCUMENT 90. First and last pages of Charles Dirba, "List of Expulsions,"
1930.

	Love-stoneism	Trotzky-ism	Halon-enism	White Chauv.	Ukr. Hall Opp.	Spies	Right Wing	Other Causes	Totals
D.1-Boston	22								22
D.2-New York	137	1		1		2	13	19	173
D.3-Philadelphia	13					1	1	14	29
S.D.3-Anthracite	11							1	12
D.4-Buffalo	2								2
D.5-Pittsburgh	4					1		2	7
D.6-Cleveland						1	3	10	14
D.7-Detroit	10		1	2	20	1	7	8	49
D.8-Chicago	6		1					1	8
D.9-Minneapolis		2	25						27
D.10-Kansas City	6							9	15
D.12-Seattle	2			11				3	16
D.13-San Francisco	1							2	3
S.D.13 Los Angeles	1							3	4
D.15-New Haven	9						4	3	16
D.17-Atlanta								1	1
TOTALS	224	3	27	14	20	6	28	76	398

Fraternally submitted,

Chas. Dirba Sec'y, CCC.

cd/nb-OWU-TUUL

DOCUMENT 90 continued

Document 91

Excerpt from eight-page "Report of National Control Commission," 15 August 1939, RTsKhIDNI 495–14–127. Original in English. The category "spying and provocation" covers a wide range of offenders, including possible government informers, Communists suspected of providing information to private organizations, and rival Trotskyists or Lovestoneites.

"8"
6744/3
vt–copy
15.VIII.39

U.S.A.
CONFIDENTIAL

REPORT OF NATIONAL CONTROL COMMISSION

Comrades:

I am confident that every member of the National Control Commission is in enthusiastic agreement with me when I say that Comrade Browder's report is a splendid guiding light for our work in this period.

I do not detract from the great value of the central point of Comrade Browder's remarks, the situation in relation to war, if I say that we of the Control Commission feel especially gratified that Comrade Browder brought in so forcefully and clearly the question of that particular type of work to which comrades of the various national, state and district disciplinary committees have to give specialised attention. The high value of Comrade Browder's words in this respect arises from the broad and deep political importance that he shows these questions to possess. Seldom before, or we might almost say, never before in our Party Plenums, have these questions of work of the disciplinary organs been shown in their true proportions and their intimate, vital connection with the entire political life and growth of the Party and of the great mass movement of the working class and the American people.

The fact that the General Secretary of our Party, in the main political report, can give such serious attention to such questions, ou[gh]t to inspire every leader of our Party district and state and section organisations to feel that such matters are worthy of the attention of all leaders of our Party and that closest painstaking guidance can and must be given to the disciplinary work in its larger aspects, in every district.

Of course, the importance we must now give to this type of work is not independent of time and space, but is inseparably connected with the war situation and with the consequently increased role of hoards of spies, provocateurs and sabotage agents that are drawn to the rewards of fascist corruption as flies are drawn to garbage.

In reference to the statistical report for the year 1938, which is available in mimeographed form for those leading comrades who are more directly interested, the following brief analysis will suffice here:

Document 91 *continued*

The total number of expulsion cases during 1938 was 308, as compared with 243 during 1937, 132 during 1936 and 346 during 1935. The rate of expulsions in 1938 was 4.8 per 1,000 members, as compared with 4.5 in 1937 and a 12.6 average for the three preceding years (1933–34–35).

Among the seven largest States and Districts (over 2,000 members), the highest rate of expulsions in 1938 was in Ohio, 9.5 per 1,000; next came Eastern Pennsylvania with 6.6; then New England with 6.1; and then New York with 5.3. Among the lower was Minnesota—.5; then Illinois—1.5; and then Lower Michigan—2.6. But right here, it must be noted that these three States have been rather weak in sending in their reports on disciplinary cases, and also in their functioning of the disciplinary committees in general.

As to the causes for expulsion, 58 (or nearly 20% of the total of 308) were expelled for general disruption and factionalism; 48 (approximately 16%) for general unreliability; 47 for Trotskyism; 38 for financial dishonesty; 21 for spying and provocation—also 8 for White Chauvinism and 7 for Lovestone-ism. The Trotskyites, Lovestoneites and other spies and provocateurs account for about 25% of all expulsions, and this aspect of the statistical report for 1938 should serve very well to emphasise the need for special vigilance against these enemies and agents of fascist wrecking and espionage who do their nefarious work under a mask of one kind or another.

. . .

Document 92

Minutes of the CCC Meeting, 1 October 1937, RTsKhIDNI 515–1–4071. Original in English. By this time the National Control Commission had been retitled the Central Control Commission. "D2" in the text refers to CPUSA District 2 (New York); "D20" is Texas. Philip Rahv (joined the CPUSA 1933) and Fred W. Dupee (joined 1936) were literary radicals who had become disillusioned with the CPUSA's loyalty to Stalin and abandonment of cultural radicalism during its Popular Front period. Rahv and Dupee became leading figures in the influential literary journal *Partisan Review*.

MINUTES OF CCC MEETING of October 1, 1937.   No. D-35.

> 8 No 329
> 27 VIII 1938 [Russian stamp]

Present—Marsh (Chm.), Allen, Ball and Lapin.

Order of Business—1) Minutes; 2) Report of Secretary;
3) Cases—Philip Rahv-D2, Fred W.Dupee-D2,
Martin J. Garnier-D20.

Document 92 *continued*

Minutes of CCC meeting of September 10, were approved.

Report of Secretary. Draft of circular on accounting and auditing rules for national enterprises and offices was approved subject to editorial revision.

On reorganization of financial control work, the subcommittee is not yet ready to make definite proposals. Now, that Comrade Blake has just returned to the city, the subcommittee will be better able to tackle this problem, and will do it soon.

On the case of Max Sunshine (see minutes of 8/11/37),—in view of changed situation in the bakers' union, it is recommended that public exposure be withheld at least for the present. Approved.

Cases were taken up as follows:

Philip Rahv, D-2-, N.Y.City; writer; CP-1933; expelled by D.2 as a counter-revolutionary Trotzkyite (now collaborating with a group of Trotzkyites in efforts to revive the Partisan Review as a Trotzkyite periodical); D.2 does not say anything about public exposure, but it is proposed by Comrade [V. J.] Jerome, who represents the C.C. on the cultural field.

CCC Decision—To publish an exposure of P. Rahv in the Daily Worker.

Fred W. Dupee (Donald Day); D-2, N.Y.City; Writer; CP-1936; expelled by D.2 as a counter-revolutionary Trotzkyite (now collaborating with a group of Trotzkyites in an effort to revive the Partisan Review as a Trotzkyite periodical); D.2 does not say anything about public exposure, but it is proposed by Comrade Jerome.

CCC Decision—To publish an exposure of Dupee in the Daily Worker.

Martin J. Garnier; D-20, Port Arthur, Tex.; seaman; CP-old member, was Section Committee member; expelled and recommended for public exposure by D.20 as an irresponsible drunkard, who neglected his duties as a union official due to drunkeness.

CCC Decision—Instead of exposure in the Daily Worker, notices warning against Garnier are to be sent to all Districts that have marine workers among their membership, these notices to be transmitted to their marine fractions.

Then the meeting adjourned.

K.Lapin, Sec. CCC CPUSA

Dealing with Deviationists: Scott Nearing and Edgar Snow

As the case of Scott Nearing demonstrates, sometimes the CPUSA would continue to pursue a deviationist even after expulsion. Document 93 is a letter from Mary Reed, an American Communist working for a Soviet publishing agency, Gosizdat, to Pat Toohey, the CPUSA representative to the Comintern, requesting political information. Reed explains that she is reviewing American books for translation and publication. She wonders whether Toohey can vouch for the political acceptability of their authors: Pinchon's *Viva Villa!* Boyd's *In Time of Peace,* Lumpkin's *A Sign for Cain,* Nearing's *Free Born,* and Snow's *The Search.*[35]

Document 94 is Toohey's reply. He informs Gosizdat that he knows nothing about Pinchon, that Boyd (deceased) had been a "Communist and promising revolutionary writer," and that Lumpkin was "considered alright." With regard to Nearing, however, Toohey urged that "nothing should be published," particularly not *Free Born,* noting that Nearing had left the party because of ideological issues some years earlier. Toohey stated that "the CPUSA has cut Nearing off from all contact with its organizations and audiences."

Throughout the early decades of the century Scott Nearing had been a popular radical intellectual, publishing numerous books and articles and lecturing widely. He became close to the Communist movement in the mid-1920s and joined the party in 1927. Nearing, however, was highly individualistic and disliked the party's attempt to discipline his writing and control his public statements. By early 1929 he was feuding with the party over its attempt to stop him from lecturing under the auspices of groups the party disliked.[36] Later that year Moscow discovered unacceptable ideological formulations in his manuscript for what became *The Twilight*

35. Edgcumb Pinchon, *Viva Villa! A Recovery of the Real Pancho Villa, Peon, Bandit, Soldier, Patriot* (New York: Harcourt, Brace, 1933); Thomas Alexander Boyd, *In Time of Peace* (New York: Minton, Balch, 1935); Grace Lumpkin, *A Sign for Cain* (New York: Lee Furman, 1935); Scott Nearing, *Free Born: An Unpublishable Novel* (New York: Urquhart Press, 1932); and C. P. Snow, *The Search* (Indianapolis: Bobbs-Merrill, 1935).

36. For an example of this controversy, see Scott Nearing to CPUSA Political Committee, 12 January 1929, RTsKhIDNI 515–1–1640.

of Empire, and the CPUSA denied him permission to publish it.[37] Determined to publish the book, Nearing resigned from the party. Meanwhile, the CPUSA expelled him and published a report in the *Daily Worker* citing his unwillingness to submit to intellectual discipline. The party, the *Daily Worker* declared, "must demand subordination of the individual to the line and to the activities of the Party and the revolutionary working class."[38]

Nearing remained a Communist sympathizer, however, and for several years was accepted in the circle of intellectuals close to the party. His 1932 novel *Free Born,* the book discussed in these documents, presented Communists in a heroic light. In 1934, however, Nearing criticized the party's conduct in the Madison Square Garden riot and failed to adopt the Communist attitude toward Leon Trotsky.[39] In 1935, as Moscow increased the intensity of its campaign against Trotskyism, Nearing's attitude became intolerable. In particular, *Free Born* was no longer acceptable because of its favorable references to Lovett Fort-Whiteman, who by then had been secretly denounced as a Trotskyist.

The organizational department of the CPUSA sent a directive (**document 95**) to all units of the party, ordering: "Until such time as Scott Nearing finds it possible and necessary to clarify his position on this question in such a way as would remove all suspicions of his sympathy with Trotzkyism, we must at once discontinue the practice of enabling him to appear before working class and other audiences. We advise that you at once notify the whole Party organization, fractions of non-Party mass organizations, etc. to the effect that we are opposed to inviting Scott Nearing as lecturer or speaker or in any other capacity." Nearing earned much of his income from lecturing, and this directive, particularly the part ordering Communists who operated inside liberal and labor organizations ("non-party mass organizations") to blacklist him, significantly narrowed his market. As Toohey's letter shows, however, Nearing refused to go along.[40]

37. Scott Nearing, *The Twilight of Empire: An Economic Interpretation of Imperialist Cycles* (New York: Vanguard Press, 1930).
38. *Daily Worker,* 8 January 1930, 4.
39. Scott Nearing to Browder, 23 February 1934, RTsKhIDNI 515-1-3750.
40. Although Nearing refused to denounce Trotsky or comply with CPUSA directives, he never openly criticized communism or the Soviet Union. He strongly defended the Soviet Union's crushing of the Hungarian revolution in 1956.

Document 93's "Snow" was more easily brought into line. When Toohey recommended postponing publication of any book by Snow, he was referring to the journalist Edgar Snow. Reed, however, had been inquiring about the author of *The Search*, C. P. Snow, an English writer whose books contained commentaries on science and intellectual life.

But Toohey's comments do tell us something about the methods the Communist party used to influence sympathetic intellectuals, as well as illustrate the CPUSA's sensitivity to any criticism of Stalin and the Comintern. Although, during World War II and after, Edgar Snow was a well-known, highly influential commentator and writer, in 1938, when document 94 was written, Snow had just established himself as an important journalist with his book *Red Star over China*, based on his travels with the Communist partisan armies led by Mao Zedong. *Red Star over China* achieved a popular and critical success, went through numerous printings, and shaped informed opinion about China for decades.

Referring to the book, Toohey explained that two-thirds of it was "finely written, sympathetic" from the Communist point of view. But in the remaining part, "all of the woes of the Chinese people and the 'defeats' of the Chinese revolution he laid to 'Stalin' and to 'the Comintern.'" Consequently, said Toohey, the CPUSA had proclaimed Snow's book "Trotskyist poison." According to Toohey, after the CPUSA prohibited the book, Snow had contacted the party and "pleaded to have the 'ban lifted,'" explaining that he was not politically astute and attributing the offending material to his having been misled. Snow then "declared to the CPUSA that he would destroy the entire third part of the book and rewrite it to the satisfaction of the CPUSA for future editions."

Toohey concluded: "Whether Snow, *as* a young promising writer, was actually tricked and influenced by Trotskyism in this instance and his future works will be politically honest, or *whether* he is *actually* a Trotskyist,—insufficient time has elapsed since this incident for us to determine. Until *then* certainly none of his books should be published."

The document sheds new light on exactly how Snow came to revise the book the same year it appeared in the United States. Although the book treats communism sympathetically, it did contain some direct criticism of the Communist International and Stalin that was by definition unacceptable to American Communists. Also, although he by no means endorsed Trotsky's view of the Chinese revolution, Snow nonetheless gave serious consideration to Trotsky's critique of the Comintern's China policy. The CPUSA made its hostility to the original version of *Red Star over China* abundantly clear. *New Masses* refused to carry advertisements for the book; *The Communist,* the party's theoretical journal, gave it a scathing review; and *Pacific Affairs,* an influential American journal on Asian affairs edited by Owen Lattimore, carried two extremely hostile critiques written by "Asiaticus," the alias of a Communist commentator.[41] Communist party bookstores refused to stock copies. The Book Society, a popular left-leaning book club, initially ordered 1,500 copies of *Red Star Over China* but then canceled the order, Snow was told, on instructions from the Communist party.

Under this battering, Snow wrote to the head of the CPUSA. Snow protested to Browder that he "sincerely admired" Browder's activities but felt that the attack on his book was misplaced. Even though he had made some critical remarks about the Comintern, Snow argued, Browder ought to realize that *Red Star* was "calculated to win friends and real aid for the Chinese struggle." Snow also denied that his consideration of arguments made by the Trotskyists indicated sympathy with them, asserting that *Red Star* "flatly discredits their work in China, while a whole chapter is devoted to an appreciation of the guidance of the Comintern." He concluded, however, by throwing in the towel: "Some weeks ago I voluntarily wrote to my publisher, asking them to excise certain sentences from any new edition of my book—sentences which I thought might be offensive to the party."[42]

Snow's revised edition appeared in the United States a few months after the original edition, and in it, as promised, Snow had dropped or changed a number of passages referring to the Com-

41. V. J. Jerome and Li Chuan, "Edgar Snow's 'Red Star over China,'" *The Communist* 5 (May 1938): 447; "'Asiaticus' Criticizes 'Red Star over China,'" and "'Asiaticus' Holds His Ground," *Pacific Affairs* 11 (June 1938): 237–44 and 248–52. "Asiaticus" was the pen name of a German Cominternist operating from Shanghai known variously as Heinz or Hans Moeller and as M. G. Shippe.

42. Snow to Browder, 20 March 1938, University of Missouri, Kansas City, Archives, KC:19/1/4, F12.

intern and Joseph Stalin.[43] In the first edition, Snow described the relationship of the Chinese Communists to the Comintern—a relationship that paralleled that of the CPUSA:

> And finally, of course, the political ideology, tactical line, and theoretical leadership of the Chinese Communists have been under the close guidance, if not positive detailed direction, of the Communist International, which during the past decade has become virtually a bureau of the Russian Communist Party. In final analysis this means that, for better or worse, the policies of the Chinese Communists, like Communists in every other country, have had to fall in line with, and usually subordinate themselves to, the broad strategic requirement of Soviet Russia, under the dictatorship of Stalin. (374)

This passage was accurate in every particular, but three elements were anathema to American Communists. These were the references to the Comintern having become subordinate to the Soviet Communist party, the claim that this meant that the Chinese party, like all Communist parties, was subordinated to Soviet foreign policy, and that Stalin's regime was a dictatorship.

In the revised edition Snow dropped the objectionable references. As revised, the passage read simply:

> And finally, of course, the political ideology, tactical line, and theoretical leadership of the Chinese Communists have been under the close guidance, if not positive detailed direction, of the Communist International. (374)

Other references to the Comintern having become Soviet-controlled were also dropped. The first edition reads:

> The three periods of Sino-Russian relationship . . . accurately reflect also the changes that have taken place in the character of the Comintern during recent years, and its stages of transition from an organization of international incendiaries into an instrument of the national policy of the Soviet Union. (375–76)

43. Edgar Snow, *Red Star over China* (New York: Random House, rev. ed., 1938). Gollancz had published the original (first) edition in England in 1937, and Random House had published it in the United States early in 1938. Random House then published the revised edition late in 1938; a virtually identical revised edition was published in 1939 by Garden City Publishing. In-text references are to the original Random House edition and the revised Random House edition.

In the revised edition, this sentence became:

> The three periods of Sino-Russian relationship . . . accurately reflect also the changes that have taken place in the character of the Comintern during recent years, and its stages of transition. (375–76)

Snow's original also contained this pointed commentary:

> The important change that occurred in the Comintern after Stalin's victory, and the adoption of five-year plans and a passion for tractors, was that active schemes to promote immediate world revolution were temporarily set aside, while the revolutionary energies of the Soviet Union were concentrated in a mighty offensive of Socialist construction. The Comintern ceased being the dominant thing, and instead became a kind of bureau of the Soviet Union, gradually turning into a glorified advertising agency for the prosaic labours of the builders of Socialism in one country. Its main tasks altered from attempts to create revolution by force, or active intervention, to bringing about revolution by example. Because the Soviet Union, the "base of the world revolution," needed peace, the Comintern became a powerful organ of peace propaganda throughout the world. (378)

Snow's observation that under Stalin the Communist International had been converted from an engine of world revolution into an instrument of the Soviet state paralleled the complaints of Leon Trotsky. Snow deleted this passage in the revised edition.

Other changes reflect a similar urge to placate the CPUSA, which would brook no criticism of either the Comintern or the Soviet Union. In the original edition the Soviet Union is said to have "stupidly refused" to allow a prominent Chinese figure to visit Moscow (18). All reference to this incident was absent in the revised edition. One statement made in the original edition was so changed in the next one that its meaning was nearly reversed. "It appears that in 1927 the Comintern was not giving 'advice', but flat orders, to the Chinese Communist Party, which was apparently not even empowered to reject them" became "In 1927 the Comintern was sending its directives to Ch'en Tu-hsiu, who made his own interpretation of them, ignoring them sometimes when he disagreed, without consulting his comrades" (148). The original contained a reference to "the well-known contradiction between the immediate needs of the national policy of the Soviet Union and the immediate needs of the world revolution" (441). Snow deleted this in the revised edition.

Snow did not remove all criticism of Soviet or Comintern conduct in the revised edition. Some critical observations remained; those Snow dropped or revised were chiefly complaints that specifically named the Comintern or Stalin. Most of his consideration of Trotsky's criticism of Soviet policy and suggested alternative strategy stayed.[44] And the bulk of the text, which concerned the activities of the Chinese Communist movement in the 1920s and 1930s, remained unchanged.[45]

The second edition's more oblique references to Stalin and the Comintern did not go unremarked. Although they made up much less than the third of the book that Toohey claimed Snow had promised, the changes were sufficient to satisfy the CPUSA. The party may also have realized that given the book's popularity and its overall sympathetic treatment of communism, Communists could put up with its remaining ideological imperfections. The party lifted the ban on Red Star over China and encouraged intellectuals and all others who were sympathetic to the movement to treat the book as authoritative. The revised edition was carried by CPUSA-linked bookstores, and during World War II it was distributed by Communist-led CIO unions to military personnel.

In 1947 Freda Utley, a onetime operative for the Comintern who had become an ardent anti-Communist, brought up the issue of the changes Snow had made in Red Star over China.[46] Utley, however, did not realize that Snow had actually been in touch with the CPUSA about the changes; she was pointing them out in conjunc-

44. Snow did delete from the original edition a consideration of the Trotskyist charge that the Comintern aborted a Communist Chinese attack on Fukien because its success would have complicated Russian diplomatic relations (381–82). Also deleted from the original edition was Snow's comment echoing Trotskyist criticism concerning the need for the Soviet Union to "make the transition from a programme of Socialism in one country to Socialism in all countries, to world revolution" (449).

45. Not all of Snow's revisions were responses to Communist criticism. Snow also dropped a passage that referred to the "vast sums poured into China to support Christian propaganda, which is mostly capitalist propaganda" (1st ed., 379), which was offensive to the Chinese missionary movement that was strongly supported by American churches.

46. Freda Utley, "Red Star over Independence Square: The Strange Case of Edgar Snow and the Saturday Evening Post," Plain Talk 1, no. 12 (September 1947): 12–13.

tion with a broader attack on Snow's depiction of the Communist Chinese. Louis Budenz, a former editor of the *Daily Worker* who left the party in 1945 and also became strongly anti-Communist, referred to the revisions as well. He testified to a congressional committee that Snow "amended one edition of the book, as I recall, at the request of the Communist Party." Budenz, however, remembered few details.[47]

Snow's changes were also discussed in an unpublished autobiography by Philip J. Jaffe. Jaffe, a close friend of Earl Browder's, also edited the journals *China Today* and *Amerasia* and was a leading figure in the American Friends of the Chinese People, a CPUSA front group. In his autobiography Jaffe writes that "a revised American edition was published with much of the worst features of anti-Soviet material substantially modified, under Snow's direction and in part with my assistance."[48] Jaffe's papers also contain a detailed comparison of the original and revised editions of *Red Star over China*.[49]

Snow's susceptibility to Communist pressure to change his text in this instance is clear.[50] By the late 1930s, the American Communist movement had the power to pressure a leading American journalist into changing sections of a book the party found unacceptable.

47. Louis Budenz testimony, 23 August 1951, Senate Subcommittee to Investigate the Administration of the Internal Security Act, *Institute of Pacific Relations,* 82d Congress, 1st sess., 1951, pt. 2:680.

48. Philip J. Jaffe, unpublished autobiography, Philip Jaffe Papers, Robert Woodruff Library, Emory University, Atlanta, Georgia, box 1, folder 6, p. 74.

49. Philip J. Jaffe, "Critical Comparison of the Editions of Edgar Snow's *Red Star over China,*" Jaffe Papers, box 9, folder 12.

50. John Hamilton, however, disagrees. See Hamilton, *Edgar Snow: A Biography* (Bloomington: Indiana University Press, 1988), 85, 86, 89, 93, 96, 179, 180, 199.

Document 93

Mary Reed to American Representative to the Comintern [Pat Toohey], 6 September 1938, RTsKhIDNI 495–14–131. Original in handwritten English. Street name in hand-written Cyrillic.

<table>
<tr><td>8 Insert No. 151
4 " VI 19 39 [stamp]</td></tr>
</table>

Str. Tulmachev 11, cp. 22
Leningrad
Sept. 6, 1938

C.I.
American Rep. (C.P.U.S.A.)

Dear Comrade,

I am writing to you for information in connection with the work I am doing for Gosisdat as book-reviewer.

Two books are included in the Leningrad plan for the coming year, but nothing is known about the authors, and if you could obtain any information as to how they stand politically, it would be of assistance to the Foreign Sector here. The books are "Viva Villa" by Pinchon, and "The Search" (?)—in Russian "Iskanie" by Snow. The plan includes Also Boyd's "In Time of Peace."

Then there is the "Sign for Cain" by Lumkin and "Free Born" a novel by Nearing, with a reference to Howard Moore and Whiteman as outstanding figures of the Negro Congress which he describes. I don't know if he refers to real people or not, or if those two have changed politically enough to warrant their names being omitted in the translation. As to Nearing himself—; he was mentioned as speaker in a Daily Worker announcement a few months ago. If there has been any marked change since then it would be useful to know about it here.

If for any reason you cannot answer these questions I would very much appreciate your turning this letter over to some one who could, and in any case I beg you for an immediate reply.

Comradely yours,
Mary Reed

Document 94

American Representative to the Comintern to Gosizdat, RTsKhIDNI 495–14–132. Undated, but it is a reply to the letter of 6 September 1938 (document 93). Original in English.

Copy

[illegible stamp]   [illegible handwriting]
Gosizdat,
Moscow,

Dear Comrades:

We have received an inquiry from Comrade Mary Reed, book reviewer of the Leningrad Gosizdat, requesting information as to the political status of some American authors, whose books are included in the Leningrad plan for the present year. She states that nothing is known about these authors.

1. About Scott Nearing and his book "Free Born". It is our opinion that nothing should be published by Nearing, and especially this book. Nearing, himself, is a "socialist free-lancer" with very curious and dangerously demoralizing political ideas. He "resigned" from the CPUSA some years ago because the Party and the Marx-Engels-Lenin Institute rejected a "work on imperialism" which distorted everything Lenin ever said on the question. Nearing has no connection with the CPUSA or any of its sympathetic organizations and does not speak for any of these organizations. The CPUSA has cut Nearing off from all contact with its organizations and audiences.

His book "Free Born" refers to Lovett-Fort Whiteman as a leader of the Negro Congress. Whiteman is a Trotskyist.

2. If the "Boyd" which Mary Reed refers to is Thomas Boyd, he was a Communist and promising revolutionary writer who died in 1935.

3. Grace Lumpkin is generally considered alright. Her books and plays are utilized by the CPUSA.

4. About Pinchon and his book "Viva Villa". We know nothing about him.

5. About Snow. If this is Edgar Snow, we advise not to publish. Not enough time has elapsed to warrant any belief that Snow is definitely alright or no good. If you remember, Edgar Snow published last year an extensive book on the Chinese Revolution "Red Star Over China." He spent ma[n]y months with the 8th Route Army and two thirds of his book was finely written, sympathetic and excellent information. But the third part of the book, where Snow delved into politics, was *vicious* Trotskyist propaganda and anti-Communist. All of the woes of the Chinese people and the "defeats" of the Chinese revolution he laid to "Stalin" and to "the Comintern".

The CP attacked this book and declared it to be Trotskyist poison. Thereupon Snow connected with the Party and pleaded to have the "ban lifted". He stated that he was generally not "conscious of political matters" was "essen-

Document 94 *continued*

tially a descriptive writer" and "was mislead" into writing this part of the book, on the basis of materials gathered from "associates" in Shanghai. Since his wife is well known as a Trotskyist it is obvious that his Shanghai "associates" were Trotskyists. Snow declared to the CPUSA that he would destroy the entire third part of the book and rewrite it to the satisfaction of the CPUSA for future editions.

Whether Snow agreed to this because of conviction and honesty, or to assure a greater circulation for his book by making it acceptable to us, is yet not definitely known. But whether Snow, *as* a young promising writer, was actually tricked and influenced by Trotskyism in this instance and his future works will be politically honest, or *whether* he is *actually* a Trotskyist,— insufficient time has elapsed since this incident for us to determine. Until *then* certainly none of his books should be published.

Comradely yours,

Document 95

Org. [Organizational] Commission of the CC to All District Organizers; to Editors and Managers of the Party Press, 11 February 1935, RTsKhIDNI 515–1–3761. Original in English.

TO ALL DISTRICT ORGANIZERS; New York, N.Y.
TO EDITORS AND MANAGERS OF THE PARTY PRESS: February 11, 1935.

Dear Comrade:

This letter will deal with our attitude toward Scott Nearing.

You have undoubtedly noticed in one of the recent issues of the DAILY WORKER, in the "Change the World" column, reference to a news item that appeared in a Canadian Socialist paper in which it was stated that Scott Nearing expressed himself in a manner favorable to the Trotzkyist Workers' Party. Considering that Scott Nearing is being invited to deliver lectures by many organizations in which Communists are influential, it is of the utmost importance to clarify to what extent Scott Nearing really entertains sympathies for the counter-revolutionary Trotzkyites and their Workers' Party.

Efforts were made by comrades in some of the non-Party mass organizations to secure from Scott Nearing a declaration which would make it clear whether or not the information referred to in the Daily Worker was correct. These efforts have not been successful. On one occasion Scott Nearing did indicate his attitude to the information about him that appeared in the Daily Worker, but this indication failed to clarify the point in which we are most interested. Scott Nearing stated that he was not a member of the Workers' Party and that he didn't say or believed that the Workers' Party would replace the Communist Party. But this doesn't say that Scott Nearing has no sympathies for Trotzkyism. On the contrary, it clearly opens the way for a conciliatory attitude to Trotzkyism.

What does that mean? It means that Scott Nearing, in addressing audiences which Communists help to bring for him, will instill into the minds of his hearers an attitude to the Trotzky Workers' Party which Stalin has long ago described as "rotten liberalism". It is clear that we cannot, under any circumstances, help Scott Nearing spread conciliation to counter-revolutionary Trotzkyism which we consider as the worst enemy of the American workers. You will agree that conciliation to Trotzkyism is not one whit better than open support and also considerably more dangerous because it is hidden and covered.

We, therefore, propose that until such time as Scott Nearing finds it possible and necessary to clarify his position on this question in such a way as would remove all suspicions of his sympathy with Trotzkyism, we must at once discontinue the practice of enabling him to appear before working class and other audiences. We advise that you at once notify the whole Party organization, fractions of non-Party mass organizations, etc. to the effect that we are opposed to inviting Scott Nearing as lecturer or speaker or in any other capacity. It goes without saying that the Party press is not to publish any advertisements of Scott Nearing's lectures or other affairs.

Where lectures have already been organized and where it is inadvisable to cancel them, steps should be taken to have qualified comrades present to ask questions that will help clarify Nearing's attitude of sympathy for counter-revolutionary Trotzkyism.

No Party papers shall carry advertisements for Nearing's lectures.

Comradely yours,
ORG. COMMISSION CC

Both the CPUSA leaders and the rank and file absorbed Stalin's ideological hatreds as their own. This acceptance of the Soviet viewpoint was not a phenomenon that emerged suddenly when Stalin established his supremacy in the late 1920s. Rather, it developed out of a belief that was present at the foundation of American communism: the idea that Moscow was the sole judge of Communist legitimacy. As the belief was reinforced by Comintern training and discipline, American Communists came to see Soviet ideological struggles as their own and insisted on locating the same heroes and villains—even when they did not exist—inside the American movement.

CHAPTER FIVE

Fellowcountrymen

Fellowcountrymen: A standard term used in enciphered cables between Soviet intelligence officers operating in the United States and their headquarters in Moscow to refer to American Communists.

TO SAY that the American Communist party was "nothing but" an appendage of a Soviet-dominated Communist International would be an exaggeration. From the party's inception, several hundred thousand Americans have joined out of a deeply felt belief in the necessity of overturning America's economic and political order and establishing a new American society based on Marxism-Leninism. But the CPUSA has always also been a satellite, first of the Comintern and later of the Soviet Communist party. The ties between the two organizations, those of subordinate to superior, existed on every level. The Soviets established the ideology, provided the money, chose or approved the leaders, and monitored the tactics of the Americans. With only a few exceptions, American Communists did not question the Comintern's right to exercise that control: they freely subordinated themselves to Moscow. Any who felt that the CPUSA should enjoy autonomous authority—and especially any who attempted to exercise such authority—found themselves unwelcome in the party. There were periods when American Communists publicly advertised their loyalty to the Comintern and others when they spoke the language of American populism. Privately, however, there was never any difference. The professions of loyalty that American Communists delivered to the

Comintern at the height of their enthusiasm for world revolution during the Third Period and those they offered just a few years later, when they were loudly proclaiming Communism Is Twentieth-Century Americanism during the Popular Front period, were practically identical.

In this volume, we have documented the reflexive loyalty of American Communists to Moscow, but we do not thereby argue that all American Communists were merely responding to stimuli produced in Moscow. Individuals were constantly joining the CPUSA, only to leave. Turnover in membership was so rapid that Communists stayed in the party for an average of three or four years. But these short-term members, although numerous, did not determine the direction of the Communist party. The core of long-term members, paid cadres, and full-time leaders controlled the party's activities. Party turnover was high, in part, precisely because many individual Communists were not automata, and they were unable to tolerate the shifts in the party line. Long-term members, by contrast, took the changes of direction in stride. These loyalists could not avoid knowing that American Communist party policy needed to conform to Soviet desires. And no CPUSA leader who was uneasy with Soviet guidance could survive.

American Communists did not choose their own leaders. The Comintern vetted proposed slates of members for the CPUSA Political Bureau (the party's most powerful agency) and changed them at will. The deference that American Communists paid to Moscow on matters of leadership is best illustrated by the expulsion of Earl Browder. Recall that when Browder entered the top leadership of the CPUSA in 1930, the party was a shambles: Moscow had expelled Jay Lovestone and other leaders the year before, party membership stood at less than 10,000, mainly immigrants, few of whom spoke English fluently; Communist cadres were isolated in revolutionary unions far from the mainstream of organized labor; and the party's political and cultural influence was practically nonexistent. Under Browder's leadership, party membership grew by more than 600 percent, and most members were native-born; Communist labor cadres controlled the leadership of CIO unions that among them had more than 1.3 million members; the party had won both respect and influence among the nation's cultural and intellectual

elite; and Communists gained a measure of influence in the mainstream politics of New York, California, Minnesota, Wisconsin,
Washington, Oregon, and Michigan. But when Moscow sent its
indirect signal (the Duclos article) condemning Browder's policies,
the party stripped him of his authority and soon afterward expelled
him. The dismissal caused only a brief upset in the party's senior
leadership and an even lesser one among the rank and file.[1]

In February 1956 Premier Nikita Khrushchev denounced Joseph
Stalin as a dictator who had committed crimes on a massive scale
against the Soviet people. Belief in Stalin had been central to American Communists for so long that Khrushchev's speech devastated
them, and the party lost three-quarters of its members over the next
two years. Peggy Dennis, the wife of Eugene Dennis, remembered
that after reading Khrushchev's speech, "the last page crumpled in
my fist, I lay in the half darkness and I wept . . . for a thirty-year
life's commitment that lay shattered. I lay sobbing low, hiccough-
ing whimpers." The party's theoretical journal *Political Affairs*
carried a lead editorial that referred to "the impact of the
Khrushchev revelation," the devastation of "these revelations,"
and "the shocking disclosures." Leading Communists spoke similarly: William Z. Foster referred to "the sweeping revelations of
the Stalin cult of the individual"; Benjamin Davis, one of the party's
chief black leaders, spoke of the "Stalin revelation"; Dorothy
Healey, a party leader in California, called the news "Khrushchev's
revelations on Stalin"; Max Weiss, a long-time leading party figure, explained that "the disclosure of the mistakes made under
Stalin's leadership came as a stunning surprise to our Party leadership and membership"; and Eugene Dennis himself claimed that
"the facts disclosed about the errors of Stalin . . . are, of course,
new to us."[2]

1. For an example of local Communist activists' quickly embracing the Duclos
article's criticism of Browder, see Peter Meyer Filardo, "Town and Gown: Excerpts
from the Bloomington, Indiana Memoir of Kenneth Neill Cameron, Communist
Academic in the Working Class Movement," *Labor History* 36, no. 4 (Fall 1995):
622–24.

2. Peggy Dennis, *The Autobiography of an American Communist: A Personal
View of a Political Life, 1925–1975* (Westport, Conn.: Lawrence Hill, 1977), 225;
"The Communist Party Convention," *Political Affairs* 36 (April 1957): 3; William
Z. Foster, "Draper's 'Roots of American Communism,'" *Political Affairs* 36 (May
1957): 37; Benjamin Davis, "The Challenge of the New Era," *Political Affairs* 35

But the facts disclosed were not revelations; they were not even new. For more than twenty years, both the mainstream press and scholarly books had carried hundreds of stories, refugee accounts, and exposés of the nature and horrors of Stalin's regime. Yet although the insistence of American Communists that the news was a revelation was literally false, it was psychologically true. Since the beginning of the movement, American Communists had worn special glasses that allowed them to see only what Moscow saw and that rendered all else invisible. Stalin's victims were invisible to American Communists because Moscow did not see them. But when Moscow finally opened its own eyes, when Khrushchev, the new head of the Soviet Communist party, pointed to the bodies of Stalin's victims littering the Soviet landscape, American Communists saw those bodies as well. And this vision offered a shattering revelation.

Many party members could not stand the sight. For a few months after the speech, party journals, which rarely discussed or even acknowledged internal dissent, were filled with angry, tormented, and anguished letters from stunned party members. John Gates, editor of the *Daily Worker,* quickly emerged as the champion of a drastic reform of the American Communist party.[3] Under his leadership, the CPUSA national committee issued a resolution in September 1956 calling for an "American road to socialism." The resolution stressed the need to base American communism on "Marxist-Leninist principles as interpreted by the Communist party of our country" rather than on those "which reflect exclusively certain unique features of the Russian revolution or of Soviet society."[4]

(December 1956): 17; Dorothy R. Healey, "On the Status of the Party," *Political Affairs* 37 (March 1958): 48; Eugene Dennis, "Questions and Answers on the XXth Congress, CPSU," *Political Affairs* 35 (April 1956): 24. These quotations and others like them can be found in Aileen S. Kraditor, *Jimmy Higgins: The Mental World of the American Rank-and-File Communist, 1930–1958* (Westport, Conn.: Greenwood Press, 1988), 84–85. Weiss is quoted in Joseph Starobin, *American Communism in Crisis, 1943–1957* (Cambridge: Harvard University Press, 1972), 308n.

3. Gates had been one of the most effective political commissars in the International Brigades in the Spanish Civil War. He had risen quickly in the CPUSA after his return from Spain and became a member of its top leadership in the late 1940s. See John Gates, *The Story of an American Communist* (New York: Thomas Nelson and Sons, 1958).

4. "For Creative Marxism," *The Worker,* 23 September 1956, 7.

Although a large majority of the membership initially backed Gates's reform campaign, as the shock of the Khrushchev speech wore off, established habits reasserted themselves. William Foster became the spokesman for those who saw no need for fundamental change. Although he allowed that Stalin had made serious errors, he insisted that these mistakes paled beside the achievements of the Stalin era in building socialism. Foster publicly dissented from Gates's September resolution regarding an American road to socialism. Eugene Dennis, who had at first cautiously supported Gates's call for reform, moved toward Foster's camp, although he did not openly attack the resolution.

In August 1956, just before Gates's resolution was passed, John Williamson, a former leader of the CPUSA, had visited the Soviet Union. Imprisoned under the Smith Act in the United States in mid-1951 (along with Eugene Dennis), Williamson had been released in early 1955 and deported to his native Great Britain in May. There he became an active figure in the British Communist party, but for several years he maintained his ties to the CPUSA and acted as a liaison between the CPUSA and the CPSU. During his visit to Moscow, Williamson discussed the situation in the CPUSA with officials of the Department of Relations with Foreign Communist Parties of the Central Committee of the CPSU. His report was based on his correspondence with Dennis, Foster, and other CPUSA leaders, as well as on his knowledge of their personalities, a familiarity acquired during his long career in the CPUSA.[5]

Williamson described the disarray of the CPUSA in the wake of the Khrushchev speech and the success that Gates and his "right-wing faction," as he described it, had had in promoting a Communist party that would be independent of Soviet guidance. Williamson urged the Soviets to reinforce the position of Foster and Dennis by assuring them that their stance against reform was correct and that it had Moscow's support. Williamson also noted that "it

5. Williamson had joined the American Communist party in 1922 and headed its youth arm in 1924; after Comintern training in Moscow in 1928, he was assigned to help root Trotskyism out of the Canadian Young Communist League. In 1930 he became a member of the CPUSA Central Committee and later headed the party's Illinois and Pennsylvania organizations. He became part of the national leadership in 1941 and remained a leading party officer until his deportation. (He had never become a U.S. citizen.)

would be useful if the leading newspapers and journals of the CPSU published any kind of material in support of Comrades Foster and Dennis." Further, he suggested that Moscow repeat its strategy of 1945 and urged: "If all these efforts fail to improve the situation in the CPUSA, I believe we should ask Comrade Duclos to write a major article which would frankly discuss the situation in the CPUSA. Comrade Duclos is the best man for the job, because his article against Browder earned him great popularity in our party."[6]

These things were done. In September *Pravda*, the official newspaper of the CPSU, published a conspicuous review of a book by Foster in which the author was described as a "noted theoretician and Marxist historian"—a clear endorsement of Foster's hard line. This was followed by a letter from Duclos that was read to the CPUSA national convention in February 1957; in it, Duclos denounced the "dangerous" departures from Marxism-Leninism that were occurring in the CPUSA, an obvious reference to Gates's reform plans.[7]

In addition, in March 1957, the Soviet journal *International Affairs* carried an essay by one "T. Timofeyev" that interpreted one of the resolutions of the recently ended CPUSA convention as a defeat for the "revisionist and Right-opportunist elements" (Gates and his reform allies) and a victory for "the vital force of proletarian internationalism" (loyalty to Moscow).[8] Who was T. Timofeyev? When Eugene Dennis and his wife returned to the United States in 1935 after his service as representative to the Comintern, they left a young son in Moscow. Under the name Timur Timofeyev (Timofeev), this American-born child was raised in elite Comintern boarding schools and became a Soviet citizen. As an adult, he was

6. "Transcript of an Interview with Comrade Williamson," prepared by V. Korinov, attached to a document by B. Ponomarev, head of the Department of Relations with Foreign Communist Parties, to the Central Committee, CPSU, 20 August 1956, Tsentr khraneniia sovremennoi documentatsii (Center for the Storage of Contemporary Documentation) 5–28–438. This document is transcribed in Diane P. Koenker and Ronald D. Bachman, eds., *Revelations from the Russian Archives: Documents in English Translation* (Washington, D.C.: Library of Congress, 1997), 621–24.

7. Quoted in the *New York Times*, 28 September 1956, 8; Starobin, *American Communism in Crisis*, 309n and 311n.

8. T. Timofeyev, "American Communist Party Convention," *International Affairs* (USSR) 3 (March 1957): 103–4.

named director of Moscow's Institute of the World Labor Movement. From Moscow, he was able to send a clear message to his father, Dennis, who was already opposing Gates's reforms and who now moved squarely into the hard-line camp.

Meanwhile, John Gates found his majority melting away. As the implications of Khrushchev's speech sank in, and as the Soviet suppression of the Hungarian revolt further increased disillusionment, thousands of American Communists simply dropped out of the party. All during late 1956 and 1957, those who might have instituted a reform of the American Communist movement left. Dennis, Foster, and their hard-line supporters stayed. In January 1958, Gates gave up and announced his resignation from the party. In February, the CPUSA's national committee, led by Dennis, repudiated Gates's views as revisionist, the product of bourgeois ideology; it concluded that "there is no place in the Party for a Gates or his ideology."[9] In the winter of 1957–1958, the party undertook a reregistration of its members to determine how many were left. The total was 3,000; the CPUSA had lost more than three-quarters of its membership in the two years since the Khrushchev speech, and total membership stood at less than 5 percent of the peaks of 1939 and 1946–1947.

Gates's attempt to reform American communism was, as he himself came to see, fundamentally impossible. By trying to put aside the Soviet myth, he was robbing the movement of its core identity. Their belief in Soviet perfection gave American Communists strength: their vision of the Soviet Union convinced them that it was possible to construct a utopian society and that by modeling themselves on the Soviet party, they could create a Soviet America. The CPUSA confronted the task of overthrowing the most powerful nation in the world. It was a daunting challenge, but their belief in the Soviet system assured American Communists that they had as an ally a nation whose own power would eventually surpass that of the United States.

Although the Soviet myth was of great importance to other Communist parties, it was not as central to West Europeans as it was to

9. National Committee, CPUSA, "On the Resignation of John Gates," *Political Affairs* 38, no. 3 (March 1958): 7–9.

the CPUSA. The Communist parties of Italy, France, and other European nations were part of large working-class subcultures. In those more rigidly stratified societies, something resembling the paradigmatic Marxist class-consciousness existed, and communism was one of the means by which millions of workers voiced their resentments and aspirations. Although they never won majority backing, the Communist parties of Western Europe, both before and after World War II, were regularly supported by millions of voters in free elections. Thousands of Communists, running openly as Communist party candidates, were elected to public offices ranging from municipal to national government posts. In the postwar period in Italy and France, the Communist party had one of the largest representations in national parliaments, held cabinet positions in coalition governments, and headed the biggest labor union federations. These parties' ties to the Soviet Union and their Marxist-Leninist ideology shaped their policies, but the mass popular base that gave strength to West European communism was independent of Moscow.

In contrast, the American Communist movement never developed a popular constituency. Although its candidates ran in hundreds of elections, the highest office ever won by open party members was two seats on the New York City council, and that was only under a proportional representation system that allowed minority parties to maximize their support. When New York changed its electoral policy to a more typical plurality system, the Communist council members lost their seats. In the late 1930s and the 1940s the CPUSA did achieve a significant position in the left wing of New Deal coalitions in a few states and cities but never openly under its own banner, as did the West European parties. Similarly, even the CPUSA's activities in the labor movement of the 1930s and 1940s, probably the area of its greatest achievements, were largely covert. Communists dominated the leadership of unions that among them boasted at least a fifth of the CIO membership, yet almost every important CIO Communist concealed his party allegiance. (Ben Gold, head of the Furriers union, was one of the few exceptions.) Lacking a popular base among the masses, the CPUSA nearly disappeared when Khrushchev's denunciation of Stalin destroyed the

Soviet myth, whereas the West European Communists, whose parties did have such a base of support, though disturbed and embarrassed, were not devastated.

After Khrushchev's speech and the Soviet suppression of the Hungarian revolt, a few Western European Communist parties, most notably Italy's, fostered a concept that later became known as Eurocommunism: this communism was nationalized, democratized, and quasi-independent of Moscow. In the United States, however, the ties to Moscow and the reliance on the Soviet myth provided strength as well as guidance to the communist movement. American communism, lacking a working-class subculture whose ambitions and grievances it could articulate, could not develop a corresponding "Americommunism." Take away the Soviet myth, and American Communists would become simply another group of radicals, appealing to the egalitarian democratic beliefs that are integral to the American political tradition and are claimed by liberals and conservatives alike.

This volume does not offer a comprehensive portrait of American communism. It concerns only one aspect (although a central one) of the CPUSA—the party's relation with the Communist International and with Soviet communism. We make no effort to explore the activities of American Communists in such areas as the labor movement, race relations, politics, Hollywood, folk music, and a dozen other causes, except insofar as they concern this relation. Since the 1970s the other activities have been well documented. But a portrait of American communism must include its relation to Soviet communism and the central position that that connection held in American Communist life. So, too, it must include the American Communist party's underground operations and links to Soviet intelligence operations, which were discussed in *The Secret World of American Communism* and which will be documented further in a forthcoming volume dealing with the Venona decryptions of Soviet cable traffic concerning the CPUSA's participation in Soviet espionage against the United States during World War II.

Communism and anticommunism were central topics in domestic and foreign politics from 1945 to about 1960. After that time, although they remained important to American foreign policy, they all but disappeared from domestic politics—but the polarities created during that earlier period continued to influence American attitudes on such issues as the war in Vietnam and civil liberties. Any historical account of the domestic politics of the postwar period must reflect an accurate understanding of the nature of the American Communist party, including its relation to the Soviet Union. Only with such an understanding can we appreciate American anticommunism and the internal tensions generated by its conflict with communism.

American and Soviet Cominternists

This appendix has been compiled from Comintern documents, CPUSA documents, and the following secondary sources: Theodore Draper, *The Roots of American Communism* (New York: Viking Press, 1957); Vilém Kahan, "The Communist International, 1919–43: The Personnel of Its Highest Bodies," *International Review of Social History* 21, pt. 2 (1976); Vilém Kahan, "A Contribution to the Identification of the Pseudonyms Used in the Minutes and Reports of the Communist International," *International Review of Social History* 23, pt. 2 (1978); Branko Lazitch and Milorad Drachkovitch, *Biographical Dictionary of the Comintern* (Stanford: Hoover Institution Press, 1986). We would like to thank David Hornstein for his advice. Although this is the most complete listing of its kind published to date, it should not be regarded as comprehensive. Undoubtedly there were both Cominternists who came to the United States and American Communists who served the Comintern on foreign missions who are as yet unidentified but whose names may become known as more material is made available to scholars.

Comintern Representatives Serving in the United States

Alpi, Mario (birthname: F. Marini? alias: Fred Brown; Italian): Worked with Italian-American Communists, 1929–1940. CPUSA Organizational Secretary, early 1930s.

Bamatter, Sigi (Swiss): Young Communist International representative, 1920s.

Berti, Giuseppi (alias: Jacopo; Italian): On U.S. mission, 1939–1946.

Borodin, Michael (birthname: Michael Gruzenberg; Russian): Immigrant to the United States (1906–1917), returned to the Soviet Union at the time of the Bolshevik Revolution. Courier of funds to the United States, 1919.

"Comrade K.": Comintern instructor assigned to train CPUSA organizers, early 1930s.

"Comrade S.": Comintern instructor assigned to antiwar work, early 1930s.

Daneman, Boris (pseudonym: Max; Russian): Young Communist International representative, mid- and late 1930s.

Dengel, Philip (German): Member of plenipotentiary short-term Comintern delegation, 1929.

Eisler, Gerhart (pseudonym: Edwards; German): Resident plenipotentiary representative, 1933–1936.

Ewert, Arthur (pseudonym: Harry Berger; aliases: Grey and Braun; German): Worked in the United States and Canada during World War I. Plenipotentiary on short-term mission, 1927; short-term missions, 1929 and 1931.

Gibarti, Louis (Hungarian): short-term mission, 1934.

Gusev, Sergei I. (birthname: Jakov Drabkin; aliases: Kheriton, Lebedev, P. Green; Russian): Plenipotentiary on short-term mission, 1925.

Hynes, Harry (Australian): Profintern maritime organizer in the CPUSA's Marine Workers Industrial Union (TUUL).

Jenks, M. (pseudonym): Comintern instructor who trained CPUSA organizers, 1927.

Katayama, Sen (Japanese): Member of short-term plenipotentiary delegation, 1921.

Katz, Bob (pseudonym; Russian): Young Communist International representative, 1920s.

Katz, Otto (alias: Andre Simone; Czech): Made several short-term visits to the United States, 1930s.

Krebs, Richard (pseudonym: Jan Valtin; German): Profintern maritime organizer, Hawaii and California, mid-1920s.

Kuusinen, Aino (pseudonym: Morton; Finnish): Comintern supervisor of work among Finnish-American Communists, 1930–1933.

Loaf (pseudonym): Comintern Information Department agent, 1927.

Manner, Kullervo (Finnish): Comintern supervisor of work among Finnish-American Communists, 1930–1931 or –1932.

Mikhailov, Boris (first name sometimes given as Sergei; aliases: Williams, Carl Wall; Russian or Bulgarian): Resident plenipotentiary representative, 1929–1930.

Mikhelson-Manuilov, Solomon (aliases: Kraft, Spector, and Black; Russian): American station chief for the OMS, 1933–1938.

Münzenberg, Willi (German): On a short-term mission to the United States, 1934.

Nasanov, N. (Russian): Young Communist International representative, 1920s.

Nosaka, Sanzo (pseudonym: Okano; Japanese): Assigned to Pan-Pacific Trade Union Secretariat in California, 1930s.

Ostroff (Russian?): Young Communist International instructor, early 1930s.

Pepper, John (Hungarian): Member of plenipotentiary short-term Comintern delegation, 1922. Assumed the position of resident Comintern plenipotentiary, 1922–1925. Recalled to Moscow, 1925; sent back to the United States, 1928; recalled again, 1929.

Pollitt, Harry (British): Member of plenipotentiary short-term Comintern delegation, 1929.

Reinstein, Boris (Russian): Immigrant to America who had returned to the USSR during the Bolshevik Revolution. Member of plenipotentiary short-term Comintern delegation, 1922.

Rust, William (British): Young Communist International representative, 1920s.

Scott, Charles E. (Latvian): Immigrant to America who returned to the USSR during the Bolshevik Revolution. Member of plenipotentiary short-term Comintern delegation, 1921.

Shubin, Joel (Russian): On a short-term mission, 1932.

Sirola, Yrjö (pseudonym: Frank Miller; Finnish): Supervised work among Finnish-Americans but may also have functioned as resident plenipotentiary representative, 1925–1927.

Sormenti, Enea (birthname: Vittorio Vidali; alias: Carlos Contreras; Italian): Head of the American Communist party's Italian Bureau and editor of its newspaper, *Il Lavatore,* for part of the 1920s.

Virtanen, Niilo Karlovich (pseudonym: Allen; Finnish): Deputy bureau head of the ECCI Secretariat, undertook missions as an organizational instructor in the late 1920s and early 1930s to Canada and in 1932–1933 to the CPUSA.

Walecki, Henryk (also "Valetski"; birthname: Maksymilian Horwitz; pseudonyms: Brooks and Michelson; Polish): On a short-term mission, 1921; member of plenipotentiary short-term Comintern delegation, 1922.

Wallenius, Allan (Finnish): On a short-term mission, 1926.

Yuzefovich, Iosif Sigizmundovich (birthname: Shpinak? Polish): On a covert mission, 1931–1933. Long-time aide to Solomon Lozovsky, head of the Profintern.

American Communist Party Representatives to the Communist International Who Were Stationed in Moscow

1919–1920: John Reed (Communist Labor Party, later United Communist Party)

1919–1921: Louis Fraina (Communist Party of America)

1919–1921: Nicholas I. Hourwich (Communist Party of America)

1920–1921: Max Bedacht (United Communist Party)

1921: Charles E. Scott (United Communist Party)

1921: Robert Minor

1922: Ludwig Katterfeld

1923: Israel Amter

1924–1925: William Dunne

1926: Max Bedacht

1926: Robert Minor

1927–1928: Louis Engdahl

1929: Bertram Wolfe

1929–1930/1931?: William Weinstone[1]

1930?–1931: William Dunne

1931?–1932: Clarence Hathaway

1932: Joseph Peters

1932: Robert Minor

1933–1934: William Weinstone

1934–1935: William Schneiderman

1935–1937: Sam Darcy

1937–1938: Eugene Dennis

1938–1939: Pat Toohey

1940–1943: Nat Ross[2]

1941: Eugene Dennis[3]

---

1. Following the expulsion of Lovestone in 1929 there was rapid turnover in CPUSA representation; the exact dates of the services of Dunne, Peters, Weinstone, Hathaway, and Minor from 1930 to 1933 are unclear.

2. Officially designated referent, Ross appears to have been the de facto CPUSA representative after Toohey's departure. Formally, the CPUSA was no longer a member of the Communist International.

3. Dennis was on a special mission to Moscow in the spring and summer of 1941, but he functioned as resident CPUSA representative, and his authority superseded that of Nat Ross.

American Communists Serving in the Comintern in Minor Positions
or Sent on Comintern Missions to Other Countries

Aerova, Maria E. (pseudonyms: Reiss, Bosh, Goldberg, Perila, and Rock):
Worked for the Comintern Eastern Secretariat, 1932–1935, taking missions
to Germany and France; referent in the Marty Secretariat, 1941–1943;
continued in a similar capacity into 1944 with various departments of the
disbanded Comintern that were transferred to the CPSU.

Allen, James (birthname: Sol Auerbach): Went on a mission to the Philippines,
late 1930s.

Aronberg, Philip: Went on courier missions to the United States, China, the
Philippines, and Japan, 1920s and 1930s.

Baker, Rudy: Went on missions to Korea, England, Canada; served in the Pan-
Pacific Trade Union Secretariat office, San Francisco,[4] late 1920s and 1930s.

Barron, Victor Allen: Went on a mission to Brazil, 1935–1936.

Bittelman, Alexander: Went on a mission to India, 1930.

Bloomfield, Sidney: Referent in the Marty Secretariat, mid-1930s.

Brigadier, A. A.: On staff of the Anglo-American Secretariat and Cadre Department, 1930s.

Brooks, Alfred J. (pseudonym: A. G. Bosse): Referent in the Comintern Information Department, late 1920s.

Browder, Earl: Representative to the Profintern, 1926; general secretary of the
Pan-Pacific Trade Union Secretariat, 1927–1928; went on a mission to
China, late 1920s.

Burroughs, Wilhemina: Comintern/Soviet English-language short-wave radio
operations in Moscow, late 1930s and early 1940s.

Cohen, Maximilian: Went on a mission to Brazil, 1920, missions to Mexico
and Europe, early 1920s.

Cosgrove, Pascal B.: Went on a mission to China, 1929.

Darcy, Sam: Chairman of the International Children's Committee, Moscow,
1927–1928. Went on a mission to China and the Philippines, 1929.

Dennis, Eugene: Went on missions to China, South Africa, and the Philippines,
1931–1934.

Dolson, Jim: Went on a mission to China, 1920s.

Dunne, William: Comintern representative to Outer Mongolia, 1928.

4. The Pan-Pacific Trade Union Secretariat office in San Francisco was concerned chiefly with
foreign sailors working in west-coast ports, rather than with Americans; it reported to the Comintern, not to the CPUSA.

Emerson, Marion: Went on a mission to China as operative of the Pan-Pacific Trade Union Secretariat, 1929.

Feinstein, Elsa (Elsa Mack): Member of technical-clerical staff of Comintern from at least 1939 onward; on the staff of Institute 205, a post-Comintern CPSU agency, 1944.

Fraina, Louis C.: Member of a short-term plenipotentiary delegation to the U.S. in 1921; went on a mission to Mexico, 1921.

George, Harrison: Representative to the Profintern, 1927; went on missions to Latin America, 1920s, and the Philippines, late 1920s and early 1930s; headed the Pan-Pacific Trade Union Secretariat office in San Francisco, early 1930s.

Goldfarb, Max (birthname: Lipic or Lepic; pseudonyms: D. Petrovsky, Humbort, A. J. Bennet; Ukrainian immigrant): Went on missions to Great Britain and France; on staff of the Anglo-American Secretariat.

Granich, Grace: Went on a mission to China, 1930s.

Granich, Manny: Went on a mission to China, 1930s.

Harris, Katherine: Went on missions to China, late 1920s, and Mexico, early 1940s.

Harrison, Caleb: Went on a mission to Canada, 1921, as part of the founding convention of Communist Party of Canada.

Haskel, W. A.: Went on a mission to China, mid-1930s.

Haywood, Harry: Member of the Comintern Negro Bureau, 1930.

Huiswoud, Otto (Caribbean immigrant): Went on missions to Jamaica, Trinidad, British Guiana, 1929–1930; member of the Comintern International African Bureau in Berlin, 1929; chairman of the Profintern's International Trade Union Committee of Negro Workers, 1932.

Johnstone, Jack: Went on missions to Mexico, 1924–1925, and India, 1929.

Josephson, Leon: Went on missions to Europe and elsewhere, 1930s.

Krumbein, Charles: Went on a mission to China and did courier duty around the world, 1930s.

Kweit, Harry: worked on Comintern covert radio operations in Moscow, 1930s.

Minerich, Tony: Representative to Young Communist International, 1930.

Mink, George: Profintern maritime union assignments in Europe and South America, early 1930s.

Mins, Leonard: Served as Comintern staff translator, 1920s.

Miyagi, Yotoku (Japanese immigrant): Went on a mission to Japan, 1930s and early 1940s.

Nelson, Steve: Went on a mission to China, 1933.

Noral, Alex: Referent in the Red Peasants International, 1930.

Peters, Joseph (Hungarian immigrant): Served with the Anglo-American Secretariat, 1931–1932.

Reed, John: Comintern delegate to the Congress of Oriental Nations in Baku, 1920.

Schechter, Amy: Member of the Anglo-American Secretariat, 1931.

Scott, Charles E. (birthname: Karlis Jansons; pseudonym: Charles Johnson): Went on a mission to Canada, 1921, as part of the founding convention of Communist Party of Canada; representative to the Profintern, 1924–1925; on the staff of the Profintern, 1930s.

Shipman, Charles (birthname: Charles Francis Phillips; pseudonyms: Frank Seaman, Jesus Saremas, Jesus Ramirez, and Manuel Gomez): Went on a mission to Mexico, Spain, and Nicaragua, 1920s; secretary of the All-American Anti-Imperialist League.

Smedley, Agnes: Went on a mission to China, 1930s.

Toohey, Pat: Served as technical secretary, Anglo-American Secretariat, 1931.

Undjus, Margaret (Cowl): Went on a mission to China, 1930s.

Weiss, Max: Representative to the Young Communist International, mid-1930s.

Wicks, Harry: Representative to the Profintern, 1928–1929; went on a mission to Australia, 1930–1931.

Wilson, William: Member of the Comintern Negro Bureau, 1930.

Wolfe, Bertram: Went on a mission to Mexico, mid-1920s.

Zack, Joseph (full name: Joseph Zack Kornfeder): Missions to Colombia, 1930, and to Venezuela, 1931.

Americans Holding Positions in the Communist International's Highest Bodies

Bedacht, Max: Candidate member of presidium of the ECCI, 1926.

Browder, Earl: Member, International Control Commission, 1924. Candidate member of presidium of the ECCI, 1931–1933, 1935. Member of the ECCI, 1935.

Cannon, James: Member of the presidium of the ECCI, 1922.

Dunne, William F.: Candidate member of the ECCI, 1924. Member of the Orgburo, 1924–1925.

Engdahl, J. Louis: Member of the presidium of the ECCI, 1928.

Ford, James W.: Candidate member of the ECCI, 1935.

Foster, William Z.: Member of the ECCI, 1924, 1928, 1935. Member of the presidium of the ECCI, 1924, 1928, 1931, 1933, 1935. Candidate member of the ECCI, 1924. Candidate member of presidium of the ECCI, 1929.

Gitlow, Benjamin: Candidate member of the ECCI, 1928. Member of the presidium of the ECCI, 1928.

Green, Gilbert: Member of the ECCI, 1935.

Hourwich, Nicholas I.: Member of the ECCI, 1920.

Huiswoud, Otto: Candidate member of the ECCI, 1928.

Katterfeld, Ludwig: Member of the presidium of the ECCI, 1922. Member of the ECCI, 1922.

Lovestone, Jay: Member of the ECCI, 1928.

Minor, Robert: Member of the presidium of the ECCI, 1926–1927. Member of the International Control Commission, 1935.

Ruthenberg, Charles: Member of the ECCI, 1922, 1924. Candidate member of the plenum of the ECCI, 1924. Member of the presidium of ECCI, 1926.

Reed, John: Member of the ECCI, 1920.

Trachtenberg, Alexander: Member of the ECCI, 1923.

Tywerousky, Oscar: Member of the ECCI, 1921.

Weinstone, William: Member of the International Control Commission, 1928. Member of the presidium of the ECCI, 1929.

"American" Signers of the "Call for the Formation of the Communist International"

In January 1919 Lenin issued a formal call for the formation of the Communist International and for its first congress, to be held in Moscow. This call was signed by various Bolshevik and radical leaders. None of the signers was specifically authorized by an American political group, although several had standing as leaders or spokesmen of the radical Left; given the "internationalist" perspective of the Bolshevik movement, these signers were often identified by both the Comintern and the American Communist party as representatives of the United States who were present at the founding of the Communist International.

Boris Reinstein: Born in Russia and exiled for political agitation, Reinstein emigrated to the United States in 1901, where he became active in Daniel DeLeon's Socialist Labor Party. While in Sweden in 1917 on a party mission, he was converted to the Bolshevik cause and returned to Russia.

Fricis Rosin: A Latvian immigrant to the United States, Rosin edited the American Socialist Party's Latvian federation journal *Strahdneeks* (The worker) for several years and helped make Boston an early stronghold of the party's left wing. He returned to Latvia after the abdication of Tsar Nicholas II to head the short-lived Latvian Communist government. After the latter fell to anti-Communist nationalists, he escaped to the Soviet Union, where he won a high post in Lenin's government. He died in 1919.

Yrjö Sirola: A Finnish Socialist, Sirola had been in the United States from 1910 to 1913 as a political agitator and teacher at the radical Finnish Work People's College in Duluth, Minnesota.

The call specifically invited thirty-nine left-wing parties and political groups to send members to Moscow for the first congress. Four of these groups were American: the Socialist Labor Party, the Industrial Workers of the World, the Workers International Industrial Union (the trade union arm of the Socialist Labor Party), and the left wing of the American Socialist Party, which was defined in the call as the section of the party represented by the Socialist Propaganda League (a precursor of the American Communist party) and Eugene V. Debs.

None of these organizations sent delegates to the congress. Reinstein, who did attend, was given voting rights as the delegate of the Socialist Labor Party, but he did so without authorization from the party, and the Socialist Labor Party never joined the Comintern. (Rosin and Sirola did not formally claim to represent any American group.) Also present, however, was S. J. Rutgers, a leading Dutch left-wing Socialist. Rutgers attended the congress as a representative of the Dutch Social Democratic Party. But he had previously lived in New York City for several years, where he had been an influential figure in the left wing of the American Socialist Party and promoted the Socialist Propaganda League. At the congress, he was given official "voice" but not a vote as a representative of the Socialist Propaganda League.

Selected Readings

Biographies and Autobiographies of American Communist Party Leaders

James Ryan, *Earl Browder: The Failure of American Communism* (Tuscaloosa, Ala.: University of Alabama Press, 1997); Peggy Dennis, *The Autobiography of an American Communist: A Personal View of a Political Life, 1925–1975* (Westport, Conn.: Lawrence Hill, 1977); Edward P. Johanningsmeier, *Forging American Communism: The Life of William Z. Foster* (Princeton, N.J.: Princeton University Press, 1994); Benjamin Gitlow, *I Confess: The Truth about American Communism* (New York: Dutton, 1940); John Gates, *The Story of an American Communist* (New York: Thomas Nelson and Sons, 1958).

Comintern Representatives

Branko Lazitch and Milorad Drachkovitch, *Biographical Dictionary of the Comintern* (Stanford: Hoover Institution, 1986), contains brief biographies of a number of Comintern representatives to the United States. For biographies and autobiographies of Americans at the Comintern, see: Robert Rosenstone, *Romantic Revolutionary: A Biography of John Reed* (New York: Knopf, 1975); Peter Carlson, *Roughneck: The Life and Times of Big Bill Haywood* (New York: Norton, 1983); Charles Shipman, *It Had to Be Revolution: Memoirs of an American Radical* (Ithaca, N.Y.: Cornell University Press, 1993); Steve Nelson, James Barrett, and Rob Ruck, *Steve Nelson, American Radical* (Pittsburgh: University of Pittsburgh Press, 1981); Bertram Wolfe, *A Life in Two Centuries* (New York: Stein and Day, 1979); John Barron, *Operation "Solo": The FBI's Man in the Kremlin* (Washington: Regnery, 1996).

Communist International

Standard histories include Franz Borkenau, *World Communism: A History of the Communist International* (New York: Norton, 1939); Julius Braunthal, *History of the International, 1914–1943* (London: Nelson, 1967); Jane Degras, ed., *The Communist International, 1919–1943: Documents*, vol. 1: *1919–1922* and vol. 2: *1923–1943* (London: Oxford University Press, 1956 and 1960); Gunther Nollau,

International Communism and World Revolution (London: Hollis and Carter, 1961); and Milorad Drachkovitch and Branko Lazitch, eds., *The Comintern: Historical Highlights* (New York: Praeger, 1966). In the future these and other histories of the Communist International will be substantially supplemented or supplanted by works based on the newly opened Comintern archives. New publications and research based on those archives are announced in the *Cold War International History Project Bulletin* and the *International Newsletter of Historical Studies on Comintern, Communism and Stalinism* (Germany).

Communist Dissidents (Lovestoneites and Trotskyists)

Robert Alexander, *The Right Opposition: The Lovestoneites and the International Communist Opposition of the 1930s* (Westport, Conn.: Greenwood Press, 1981); James Cannon, *The History of American Trotskyism* (New York: Pathfinder Press, 1972); Constance Myers, *The Prophet's Army: Trotskyists in America, 1928–1941* (Westport, Conn.: Greenwood Press, 1977); George Breitman, Paul LeBlanc, and Alan Wald, *Trotskyism in the United States: Historical Essays and Reconsiderations* (Atlantic Highlands, N.J.: Humanities Press, 1996).

The Communist Party and the Labor Movement

Bert Cochran, *Labor and Communism: The Conflict that Shaped American Unions* (Princeton, N.J.: Princeton University Press, 1977); Max Kampelman, *The Communist Party versus the C.I.O.: A Study in Power Politics* (New York: Praeger, 1957); Harvey Levenstein, *Communism, Anti-Communism, and the CIO* (Westport, Conn.: Greenwood Press, 1981); Robert Zieger, *The CIO, 1935–1955* (Chapel Hill: University of North Carolina Press, 1995).

The Communist Party of the United States of America

Harvey Klehr, John Earl Haynes, and Fridrikh Igorevich Firsov, *The Secret World of American Communism* (New Haven: Yale University Press, 1995); Harvey Klehr and John Earl Haynes, *The American Communist Movement: Storming Heaven Itself* (New York: Twayne Publishers, 1992); Irving Howe and Lewis Coser, *The American Communist Party: A Critical History, 1919–1957* (Boston: Beacon Press, 1957); Theodore Draper, *The Roots of American Communism* (New York: Viking Press, 1957); Theodore Draper, *American Communism and Soviet Russia: The Formative Period* (New York: Viking Press, 1960); Harvey Klehr, *The Heyday of American Communism: The Depression Decade* (New York: Basic Books, 1984); Maurice Isserman, *Which Side Were You On? The American Communist Party during the Second World War* (Middletown, Conn.: Wesleyan University Press, 1982); Joseph R. Starobin, *American Communism in Crisis, 1943–1957* (Cambridge: Harvard University Press, 1972); Louis Budenz, *Men without Faces: The Communist Conspiracy in the USA* (New York: Harper and Brothers, 1948); John Earl Haynes, *Red Scare or Red Menace? American Communism and Anticommunism in the Cold War Era* (Chicago: Ivan R. Dee, 1996).

Memoirs by American Communists and Radicals Who Lived in the
Soviet Union during the Stalin Era

Thomas Sgovio, *Dear America! Why I Turned against Communism* (Kenmore, N.Y.:
Partners' Press, 1979); Lawrence Hokkanen and Sylvia Hokkanen, *Karelia: A Finn-
ish-American Couple in Stalin's Russia, 1934–1941* (St. Cloud, Minn.: North Star
Press, 1991); Mayme Sevander with Laure Hertzel, *They Took My Father: A Story of
Idealism and Betrayal* (Duluth: Pfeifer-Hamilton, 1992); Homer Smith, *Black Man
in Red Russia* (Chicago: Johnson Publishing, 1964); Robert Robinson with Jon-
athan Slevin, *Black on Red: A Black American's Forty-Four Years inside the Soviet
Union* (Washington, D.C.: Acropolis Books, 1988); John Scott, *Behind the Urals: An
American Worker in Russia's City of Steel* (1942; Bloomington: Indiana University
Press, 1989); Paula Garb, *They Came to Stay: North Americans in the USSR* (Mos-
cow: Progress Publishers, 1987).

Index

Page numbers in boldface refer to documents.